MAPPING
THE COLD WAR

MAPPING
THE COLD WAR

Cartography and the Framing of America's
International Power

TIMOTHY BARNEY

The University of North Carolina Press   Chapel Hill

Published with the assistance of the Authors Fund
of the University of North Carolina Press

The paper in this book meets the guidelines for permanence and durability of the Committee on Production Guidelines for Book Longevity of the Council on Library Resources. The University of North Carolina Press has been a member of the Green Press Initiative since 2003.

Cover illustration: Richard Erdoes, "How Strategic Material Circulates," *Life*, 1953 (Courtesy of Boatwright Library, University of Richmond, by permission of the Estate of Richard Erdoes)

Library of Congress Cataloging-in-Publication Data
Barney, Timothy.
Mapping the Cold War : cartography and the framing of
America's international power / Timothy Barney.
pages cm
Includes bibliographical references and index.
ISBN 978-1-4696-1854-8 (pbk : alk. paper) — ISBN 978-1-4696-1855-5 (ebook)
1. Geopolitics—History—20th century. 2. Political geography—History—
20th century. 3. Cartography—Political aspects—History—20th century.
4. United States—Foreign relations—1945-1989. 5. World politics—1945-1989.
6. Cold War. I. Title.
JC319.B385 2015
327.73009'045—dc23
2014039875

Portions of this manuscript were previously published in a different form and are used by permission: "Power Lines: The Rhetoric of Maps as Social Change in the Post-Cold War Landscape," *Quarterly Journal of Speech* 95, 4 (2009): 412–34; copyright © 2009 by National Communication Association. "Richard Edes Harrison and the Cartographic Perspective of Modern Internationalism," *Rhetoric & Public Affairs* 15, 3 (2012): 397–433; copyright © 2012 by Michigan State University. "'Gulag'—Slavery, Inc.: The Power of Place and the Rhetorical Life of a Cold War Map," *Rhetoric & Public Affairs* 16, 2 (2013): 317–53; copyright © 2013 by Michigan State University. "Diagnosing the Third World: The 'Map Doctor' and the Spatialized Discourses of Disease and Development in the Cold War," *Quarterly Journal of Speech* 100, 1 (2014): 1–30; copyright © 2014 by National Communication Association.

To Elinor

Contents

Illustrations

Acknowledgments

Knee-deep in maps for a number of years, I was fortunate to surround myself with colleagues, friends, mentors, and family who always seemed to have an impeccable sense of direction, especially at those times when I didn't. The road toward publication of this book began with an innocent email conversation about the geographer William Bunge with Joe Parsons at UNC Press; little did I know that this exchange about "Wild Bill" would turn into such an excellent collaboration. Joe's energy, good nature, and editorial smarts were bountiful, as was his patience with me. In addition, the steady and attentive stewardship of Joe's colleagues, especially Alison Shay, Dino Battista, Ellen Bush, Kim Bryant, Susan Garrett, and Sara Jo Cohen, has been outstanding. Paul Betz shepherded the manuscript quite well, and Brian A. McDonald served as a prudent and thorough copyeditor. Throughout my time working with UNC Press, I pinched myself more than a few times in hopes that this rewarding experience was, indeed, real.

I am also indebted to the careful readings and intellectual rigor of Matthew Farish at the University of Toronto and Ned O'Gorman at the University of Illinois, who both reviewed this manuscript multiple times and whom I came to see as valuable mentors. That they took time away from their own work to contribute to and support mine is much appreciated. Over the years working on this project, I also continually benefited from the smartest editors in the field of rhetorical studies whom I was lucky to have take a chance on maps—Martin Medhurst helped me become a better scholar and writer, Barbara Biesecker was generous in her support of this research, and John Louis Lucaites was instrumental in helping me get this work off the ground at an early stage. For portions of this book, all three of these scholars marshaled insightful anonymous reviewers from whose work I benefited. In addition, I owe thanks to the kind encouragement and ideas that I gained at various stages from Angela Ray, A. Susan Owen, James Kimble, Vanessa Beasley, Antonio de Velasco, Mary Stuckey, Shiv Ganesh, Rona Halualani, Nik Heynen, Susan Schulten, Cara Finnegan, Barbie Zelizer, Amber Davisson, Donovan Conley, Scott Stroud, Dave Tell, Julia Scatliff O'Grady, and Nathan D. Atkinson. I would also like to thank John Hessler and the Philip Lee Phillips Map Society of the Library of Congress for their support of this research and for providing a terrific audience for it in Washington, D.C.

The work on this book began at the University of Maryland, which provided strong support and a well of scholarly values that I continue to draw from. Julie Greene, Kristy Maddux, and James F. Klumpp sacrificed considerable time to read earlier versions of this manuscript, and their feedback was absolutely invaluable. Shawn Parry-Giles was also an incredible mentor, insightful reader, and the reason I took up the study of the Cold War in the first place. My friends and colleagues from UMD are of the "lifetime" variety, and I want to especially thank Belinda Stillion Southard, Bjørn Stillion Southard, Theresa Donofrio, Heather Brook Adams, Alyssa Samek, Stephen Underhill, Abbe Depretis, Ben Krueger, Tiffany Lewis, Elizabeth Gardner, Ioana Cionea, Lisa Corrigan, Adam McDaniel, and Martha Kelly Carr for their encouragement and commiseration.

My academic home at the University of Richmond provided just the right environment (and bricks, so many bricks) for developing this book. Dean Kathleen Skerrett and the Dean's Office of the School of Arts and Sciences offered terrific support. The chair of the Department of Rhetoric & Communication Studies, Mari Boor Tonn, has been a generous and thoughtful mentor, through both the example of her scholarship and her unflagging faith in this work; Mari Lee Mifsud, too, has been a kindred spirit during the writing process and a source of comfort in a time of transitions. Paul Achter has also been an insightful source of advice, while Nicole Maurantonio is the kind of friend and colleague you dream about having at your first job. And in no small part, Scott Johnson, Linda Hobgood, and Blake Abbott have all been models of collegiality. Robin Mundle was an unsung hero on various nuts and bolts of preparing the manuscript. Other great UR scholars such as Ed Ayers, David Brandenberger, David Salisbury, Uliana Gabara, Rania Sweis, Ernest McGowen, Eric Grollman, Scott Nesbit, and Rob Nelson all provided inspiration to this project. And of course my continually excellent students at UR have taught me more than a thing or two, and even if they were pretending to be interested in maps and rhetoric, it's a performance I applaud them for.

So many folks proved to be helpful and kind resources at the various archival sites and libraries consulted for this project, and they are too numerous to thank. But special gratitude must be given to Ed Redmond and his colleagues at the Library of Congress's Geography & Map Division, Jovanka Ristic at the American Geographical Society Library, and Sarah Springer and Lynda DeLoach at the George Meany Memorial Archives. At the University of Richmond, the great Laura Horne-Popp also provided immense help in tracking down sources and images, coordinating with her excellent colleagues at Boatwright Library (especially Crista LaPrade and Angela White), the University of Virginia, and other institutions. I am also grateful to the families of Richard Edes Harrison and Richard Erdoes for permitting the use of some beautiful maps for the pages of the book.

Most importantly, my own family has also offered much cheerleading (and, it must be said, patience) over the preceding years, and they have made valiant attempts at trying to get in touch with me through various channels: Mom and Dad (good call on getting me my first atlas); Sean, Sam and (scholar in training) Simon; Meghan and Paige; Bryan, Molly, Grace—it means a lot to be able to share this with all of you. The Frisa clan has also been hugely supportive: thanks to Ed and Jane Frisa, Carolyn Frisa and Garet McIntyre (with Rowan as important consultant), and, of course, Beth Frisa and Randy Rydell, who took such good care of us in Arlington. Eliza Brill's support has also been much appreciated over the past couple of years.

Finally, this work simply was not possible without Trevor Parry-Giles, who sets an impossibly high bar for scholarly generosity, editorial acumen, professional advocacy, and friendship, at which he especially excels. From the very beginning stages of the research through the long and daunting work of building a book, he was an enormously talented and reassuring adviser and collaborator at every stage. I didn't deserve all of his help but gladly took it nonetheless.

This book, at last, is for Elinor Frisa, who puts up with two academics in her house (Professor Bones received tenure on looks alone, which I will not) and, to paraphrase someone more eloquent than me, is the only person I would eat bees for.

MAPPING
THE COLD WAR

INTRODUCTION

The Rhetorical Lives of Cold War Maps

In the leading machine, the Head of the Air Force was sitting beside
the pilot. He had a world atlas on his knees and he kept staring first at
the atlas, then at the ground below, trying to figure out where they were
going. Frantically he turned the pages of the atlas. . . . In the seat behind
him sat the Head of the Army who was even more terrified.

"You don't mean to tell me we've gone right out of the atlas?" he
cried, leaning forward to look.

"That's exactly what I *am* telling you!" cried the Air Force man. "Look
for yourself. Here's the very last map in the whole flaming atlas! We
went off that over an hour ago!" He turned the page. As in all atlases,
there were two completely blank pages at the very end. "So now we must
be somewhere here," he said, putting a finger on one of the blank pages.

"Where's here?" cried the Head of the Army.

The young pilot was grinning broadly. He said to them, "That's why
they always put two blank pages at the back of the atlas. They're for new
countries. You're meant to fill them in yourself."

—Roald Dahl, *The BFG*

In his classic children's book *The BFG*, Roald Dahl expresses a fundamental cartographic conundrum that cuts deeply into the anxieties and
opportunities of charting political space.[1] On the one hand, the army and
air force experts are anxious that their trusted map no longer reflects the
land below—the uncharted space on the ground is empty white blankness
on the atlas. At the same time, the pilot smiles with the acknowledgment
that the space beneath them is something that is not a *given*, but has to be
actively *written*. In a sense, Dahl reveals the essential tensions around the
legibility of space through maps: the map is often taken for granted as a
representation of what *is*, but once its function as a constructed image is

1

acknowledged, a nervous loss of control is created—a feeling of "flying off the atlas."[2] Those with the power (and vision) to fill in the blank pages are presented with a momentous opportunity to write the world.

When the head of the army asks, "Where's here?" in *The BFG*, he may as well be speaking to the United States' struggle with its own cartographic conundrum throughout the second half of the twentieth century. By the dawn of the Cold War, world space had in many respects become closed— most of the nooks and crannies across the globe were accounted for, organized and classified with lines and borders.[3] Simultaneously, American power underwent massive spatial transformations, with U.S. elites and leaders enjoying an increasingly higher bird's-eye view of international space, while perceiving that they had the immense responsibility of being the writer of that space.[4] Moving from a worldview marked by traditional balances of power and hemispheric boundaries toward a more fluid, abstract, and above all modern internationalism, the United States faced a world that seemed both tantalizingly and alarmingly closer.[5] Cultural critic John Berger once wrote: "Our vision is continually active, continually moving, continually holding things in a circle around itself, constituting what is present to us as we are. . . . Every image embodies a way of seeing."[6] Like the pilot's view in Dahl's airplane crisscrossing over wide expanses of territory, the perspective of the cartographer often frames the world from a vantage point outside of the space itself, thus giving them (and their users and readers) a position of power—an encouragement to see terrain as abstract, able to be shaped, flattened, and simplified.[7] The very materials (like maps) through which Americans envisioned their nation helped constitute a sense of national identity and served as a visual guide for interpreting the scope of U.S. power in the world.

A fitting illustration of the stakes of cartography for Americans during the Cold War comes, perhaps ironically, as that very war was falling apart: on December 2 and 3, 1989, during an eventful season of protests across Eastern Europe, Presidents Mikhail Gorbachev and George H. W. Bush held a summit at Malta.[8] Alan K. Henrikson recounts a particularly tense exchange between the two leaders:

> Gorbachev handed President George Bush a blue-and-white map allegedly showing the Soviet Union's encirclement by US bases as well as American aircraft carriers and battleships. . . . President Bush was at a loss for words. President Gorbachev then said tartly: "I notice that you seem to have no response." Bush, in response, pointed out to Gorbachev that the Soviet landmass was shown on the map as a giant,

white, empty space, with no indication of the vast military complex that US forces were intended to deter. "Maybe you'd like me to fill in the blanks on this," he said. "I'll get the CIA to do a map of how things look to us. Then we'll compare and see whose is more accurate."[9]

This curt exchange between two superpowers encapsulates the contentious lines and boundaries of mapping.[10] Maps are ideological blueprints— they frame the language of politics in a melding of signs and symbols that both reflect and create colorful and charged worldviews. And as the two cold warriors knew well, maps communicate volumes not just in what they include but also in what geographer J. B. Harley called the "silences," or what maps choose to omit and obscure from view.[11] Bush and Gorbachev understood the map as a medium of control, but they also feared what the map did not tell them—a reminder of what they *cannot* know or control.[12] This power places cartography in a dynamic of revealing and concealing—a reductive, selective, and partial process where what is not mapped often becomes just as salient as what is lined and bounded on the page.[13]

The map scuffle at Malta, though, is not merely a tidy example of how cartography is used by powerful states; it represents well just how important historical context is in shaping our visions of the world. The Bush-Gorbachev exchange was, no doubt, borne out of the very particular spatial framework created and sustained by the Cold War. As late as December 1989, Bush and Gorbachev were still committed to the clearly bounded Cold War system, typified by bipolar intelligence maps that contained bases and battleships. As walls toppled, countries reunited, and borders ripped open, two influential world leaders still clung to the familiar cartographic shapes of their forty-five-year rivalry. Important questions then follow: How did such Cold War worldviews become so powerful and so entrenched through the flat, two-dimensional planes of maps? What about the map makes it uniquely suited to encapsulating the Cold War? In Dahl's terms, how were the blank pages of the atlas of the Cold War filled?

These questions form the basis of *Mapping the Cold War*. When the United States emerged from World War II as an undeniably global force, the country faced numerous decisions about where to direct its power across the world, and how to represent itself and its values in this new framework. The Cold War was an inescapably spatial conflict—from the post–World War II carving of the global landscape into spheres of influence right up until the Cold War vision of the world was challenged in the streets of Prague and Berlin. Maps, in many ways, are the archetypal artifacts of the Cold War. They, more than any other medium, represent the fundamental discursive and historical tensions that strategists, academics, and citizens negotiated throughout the whole of the conflict. As John Pickles writes, "If cartography is a form of discourse . . . then the cartographer and the map are at the centre of debates over technocracy and power in the modern world."[14] And there has never been, perhaps, a more contentious, rancorous, and epic debate around modern technocracy and power than the one in which the United States found itself during the Cold War. In the eventful second act of the so-called American Century, where and how America chose to place itself on the map, in reference to the rest of the world, was a powerful, political act—an attempt to obtain a sense of stability amid a complex and constantly changing globe.[15] Maps offered particular choices on how to depict missile silos and peace agreements; how small or large to portray the developing countries of the world; where to intervene; whom to fear; and whom to contain. They dramatized just how close our allies and adversaries were. These choices all had important consequences—they spoke to what kinds of values Americans possessed during the Cold War by mapping our place in the world vis-à-vis the international arena.

In *Mapping the Cold War*, I explore how cartography has powerfully positioned American identity in unique and particular ways. Specifically, I argue that maps articulated America's sense of its power in the Cold War by projecting crucial relationships between the tensions of art and science, space and place, and strategy and ideology. By acting as media of American power, maps offered important definitions of ownership, knowledge, containment, commitment, control, and even resistance that framed our perspectives of the Cold War. Maps *located* these central ideological tensions between American national interests and America's international aspirations. Their borders, scales, projections, and other conventions both prescribed and constrained the ways in which foreign policy elites, popular audiences, and social activists negotiated such tensions in a world of expanding alliances and explosive conflicts.[16] A distinctly modern internationalism had been taking root for decades leading up to the Cold War, the implications of which found their way into the very visualization of American power and global strategy.[17] Lester Olson, Cara Finnegan, and Diane Hope have defined visual culture as the "historically situated beliefs about vision and images that influence audiences' practices of looking."[18] Understanding the historical contingency of how maps were created and used in a conflict as wide and complex as the Cold War, I believe, is an important part of the modern history of the United States and provides an opportunity to accentuate its core spatial values.[19]

CARTOGRAPHY AND THE GEOPOLITICAL TENSIONS OF THE COLD WAR

Of course, the spatial "frames" of the Cold War did not suddenly appear in April 1945 when U.S. and Red Army troops met each other in Germany to sort out World War II's wreckage. The perspectives of Cold War maps have deep roots in American culture, embedded in a larger history of American discourses around national space.[20] As Isaiah Bowman, Franklin D. Roosevelt's principal geographer and a chief architect of the new American global space in the twentieth century, once said: "Empire builders must think in terms of space as well as time."[21] The conception of spaces in America, thus, has been accompanied by a geographic rhetoric that has a contentious relationship with history, often intervening to create tidy, sequential narratives of American destiny and progress.[22] And surely, maps' fraught and fascinating history as tools of nationalism and ideological education in the early Republic, as imperial justifications in the Spanish-American War, as boundary markers for the kind of ideal U.S.-led community of nations that President Wilson saw in the wake of World War I, and as strategic logics for security and intervention by the start of the Second World War could all be seen as fitting media in each of their times for the growth of American power.[23]

As I demonstrate, though, the Cold War represented its own set of unique spatial tensions, surely built on these historical ideologies of frontiers and hemispheres, but marked by an international scale and scope of data and accumulated scientific knowledge that had not been seen before. In the process, maps had to match, adapt to, and shape the values of the Cold War, as Americans themselves adapted to new fears and anxieties about this expanding scope of power. Such values were marked by a profound ambivalence about America's historical trajectory and its responsibility in (and to) the world. Robert Scott notes that this ambivalence was built into the very core of Cold War political culture, writing that "words and actions have thus far stopped short, and stopping short is essential to the meaning of cold war"; thus the conflict is fundamentally unstable.[24] The notion of tension is central since the Cold War can be defined not as any kind of static entity but more as a continually contracting and expanding force over the course of forty-plus years.[25] *Mapping the Cold War* traces maps over these contractions and expansions, in particular, through three major tensions that characterize both the cartography and the conflict itself and make maps such a fitting vehicle for the Cold War: the complex relationships between art and science, space and place, and strategy and ideology.

Art and Science

Like politics, maps bring together art *and* science. As Henrikson writes, "Cartography is a combination of science and art, of the objective and the subjective in human thought and activity. . . . Maps thus may be embedded in the discourse of politics and of art, just as political symbols can be embedded in the language of maps."[26] The lines, the shapes, and the colors that map historical and contemporary geopolitical struggles classify wide expanses of space, providing a perception of security that we can know the world.[27] But behind this rational, scientific "knowing," of course, lies the art and the artifice of mapmaking. Maps have always struggled between their expected abilities to present simply and precisely scientific information about the world "as it is" and their ability to dramatize perspectives artistically and to reflect ideological and political change.[28] Like Jorge Luis Borges's famous allegory about the map itself becoming the same size as the territory, we have come to almost replace our view of the material world with the image of a map.[29] From their uses as taxation systems for kingdoms to organizational frameworks for empires and onto their uses as surveillance techniques by modern superpowers, maps have historically helped naturalize state power as self-evident and "scientific" through their very strengths as artistically persuasive arguments.[30]

The Cold War was animated by this relationship between the artistic image and the scientific datum. For one, the Cold War saw the exponential growth of the academy's collaboration with the foreign policy and defense establishments, through both social science (and its implications on American perceptions of its global economic and political responsibility) and the hard sciences, particularly their role in the massive construction of the military-industrial complex.[31] The growth, in particular, of "spatial science" made geography and cartography much more than the field surveying of old. Such growth was based on the pursuit of inarguable spatial "facts"—or what Michael Heffernan has referred to as the "myth that the acquisition and control of 'pure' objective knowledge was the ultimate route to power."[32] The processes of mapping production were transforming, moving from craft to automation and standardization, and relying more on sophisticated photogrammetric and photomechanical methods.[33]

However, it was the simultaneous rise of air power and the escalation of America's involvement in the European and Pacific fronts in World War II that truly revolutionized cartography as a science. Airplanes provided a new synoptic view of American power, with a bird's-eye view of the ground below as classifiable and ordered according to one's own perspective unfolding; this was matched by cartographic technologies that capitalized on this new heightened vantage point. And with an increasingly global scope of American responsibility, there was an urgency for scientifically sound, "objective" knowledge production on a host of levels. Thematic mapping around an amazingly broad range of topics dramatically expanded. Public health, human rights, religious affiliation, the expanding entanglements of treaty obligations—all saw cartography advancing well beyond the topographic surveys typically associated with government mapping. The sheer amount of data needing classification and compression in spatialized grids was overwhelming—and cartographic specialists were increasingly hailed into public service.

In the process, cartography became much more of an overtly strategic practice. Maps served as vital sources of intelligence in World War II; and for geographer Jeremy Crampton, if maps had become "more scientific they did so as practices of 'government' during wartime and its aftermath. 'Peace' geographies are not divorced from war geographies. Furthermore the science that is produced was twisted together with geopolitical aims."[34] The Cold War would obliterate the artificial lines between a peacetime geography and a wartime one—the apparatus of World War II's cartographic militarization was in large part left standing, and that sense of collaboration across agencies, universities, and journalists remained. Large-scale academic and state collaborations on mapping programs came together in what John Cloud calls the "great Cold War geo-spatial convergence," involving universities, the State Department, and various defense institutions.[35] As the Cold War wore on, too, the digitization of maps dramatically changed the very ways in which cartographic data were synthesized and abstracted—converting spatial information into ones and zeroes and then reprojecting them for easy manipulation. In addition, digitization situated maps as a kind of screen or interface, doubling the sense of mediation but also technologizing the experience of using a map and instantiating its power of authenticity and accuracy.[36] Thus, the government's approach to map production accentuated the role of a map in providing an immediate ordering and seemingly transparent rendering of the space below.[37] This power allowed the U.S. government to also infiltrate the Soviet Union with sophisticated mapping technology and produce cartography that could place exactly what the enemy was doing and where. In short, mapping was redefined as not just a tool of national security but an *essential* one.[38]

At the same time, the burgeoning Cold War accentuated a development in the first half of the twentieth century, what historian Frank Ninkovich has referred to as kind of image-based internationalism, in which the very perception of power was continually at stake.[39] Commensurate in importance with actions taken by the U.S. government was the *image* of those actions in the world. In turn, U.S. foreign policy makers exhibited a more nuanced sensitivity to international public opinion. Fittingly, the expansion of the cartographic perspective into the air accompanied this modernist brand of internationalism with a powerful view from above: America could be the steward of the world and would help develop the globe in its own image, while still protecting its own national interests.[40] As Roderick P. Hart and Kathleen E. Kendall have written, modernist rhetoric acknowledges that "perception and reality are phenomenally interlocked in politics" and shows a "keen eye for the symbolic."[41] America's waging of the Cold War was a global performance that required an artistic and aesthetic facility with perception management; as a result, the symbolic importance of American maps grew proportionately.

In this sense, cartography's utility as a scientific discipline grew at the same time as did the need for an artistic visual interpretation of the U.S. role in the world. Many maps, for example, used unorthodox projections like a polar-centered view to show new proximities, or novel angles to position the perspective of the reader as hovering over a spherical earth. The relationship between a map's formal expectations as art and science continually frustrated and drove cartography throughout the Cold War. The need for objective scientific methods in mapping the world worked alongside the acknowledgment of the artistic craft needed for image development.[42] In chapters 1 and 2, for example, the early Cold War is exemplified by journalistic cartographers like Richard Edes Harrison and bureaucratic mappers like S. W. Boggs, the official geographer of the Department of State in the late 1940s and 1950s, constantly working through the balance between the advance of scientific innovation and the struggle to create a readable and convincing image of the rapidly changing world, complete with a nuanced understanding of audiences. In the Cold War, maps often served as powerful tools of propaganda precisely because of this tension: their scientific, reliable treatments of spatial relationships and their expectations to "reveal" the world to us often rendered them unquestionable.[43] The academic cartographers and public officials and journalists who circulated maps found that technical expertise rested right alongside the need for a coherent vision of American interests.[44]

<h2 style="text-align:center">Place and Space</h2>

This tension between art and science also relates directly to a second fundamental tension that made maps a particularly unique and essential medium for the Cold War: the difficulty in reconciling a map's inherent abstractions against the concrete areas and locations that were being mapped. A map's power is built on its ability to abstract and synthesize.[45] A map does not pretend to reproduce "real" landscapes or concrete areas—it reduces and simplifies, spatializes and plots, classifying a lived world into grids and positing relationships through its manipulation of distance and scale. Richard Edes Harrison once wrote that "when the attempt is made to show the entire surface of the globe on one sheet of paper, the cartographer's dilemma is completely revealed. It is like trying to wrap a grapefruit without wrinkling the paper, or like commissioning a portrait painter to do a head showing not only the face but the sides, back and top simultaneously."[46] As Harrison well understood, maps are abstract renderings of material spaces, and their processes of abstraction were crucial in Cold War conceptions of enemy capacities, potential alliances, scientific modernization projects, and weapons programs.

Scholars have often expressed this function of cartography in terms of the concepts of *space* and *place*. According to Greg Dickinson, Carole Blair, and Brian Ott, space and place have a "set of mutually constitutive relationships," in which space typically represents movement, openness, and abstraction, whereas place represents fixity, stability, and specific and located memories.[47] And in a passage that speaks almost eerily well to the American Cold War, Yi-Fu Tuan writes, "The ideas 'space' and 'place' require each other for definition. From the security and stability of place we are aware of the openness, freedom, and threat of space, and vice versa. Furthermore, if we think of space as that which allows movement, then place is pause; each pause in movement makes it possible for location to be transformed into place."[48] Maps offer the pauses in the Cold War's abstract definitions of space, positing placements for the viewer and, by extension, a placement for American values. The idea of placement often connotes stability, and the development of Cold War maps can be seen as a series of U.S. attempts at stabilizations, attempts to control and label that sense of meaning before others (e.g., the Soviet Union) could.[49]

Foreign policy strategists and technocrats have tended to reconcile the tensions of space and place by assuming a kind of *transcendence over geography* in the Cold War.[50] For example, geopolitical realists like Nicholas Spykman, writing before and during World War II, assumed geography was permanent—that certain principles were unchanging, thus giving way to a pervasive determinism that physical features and facts of the land prescribed the outcomes of foreign policy.[51] In the Cold War, many of these attitudes were adopted in practice; if geography was considered permanent, then it could be seen as a nonissue and could be reduced to simple locating and topography.[52] Maps could be seen simply as evidence rather than as shapers of national interests in the Cold War. But as Neil Smith has most forcefully argued, despite the belief by some that geography had somehow become obsolete, the Cold War was actually fought on intensely geographic terms.[53] The denial of geography in the Cold War, in many ways, allowed for the essentializing of space and place.[54]

Thus, *Mapping the Cold War* attends to how Cold War spaces become etched into binary images of us versus them and gives texture to the processes by which politically motivated spatial frameworks are solidified into what seem like natural divisions.[55] The Cold War was built on the paradox of abstraction—the ironies of a war with no traditional battles against very concrete (and violent) skirmishes, satellite wars, and "political-economic adventurism."[56] These abstractions included a "Three-World" spatial configuration where the superpowers competed for influence; a homogenization of the globe into blocs in which, according to John Agnew, "universal models of capitalism–liberal democracy and communism reigned free of geographical contingency"; and the naturalization of the war through spatial concepts such as containment, domino effects, and liberation.[57] Such abstract visions allowed American interests to be seen on a global scale and in more universal terms, in which interests were spread not just with weaponry but with information technology, capital, and ideas.[58] These big-picture approaches to space gave way to notions for foreign policy elites, military planners, and academics that space was a commodity that could be known and classified. Maps thus gave Cold War leaders a strong power of global surveillance, and encouraged the type of constant vigilance and fear of proximity that sustained policies of both containment and liberation. At the same time, this abstract and universal approach to space also required a significant investment in specific knowledge of particular places on the map. Matthew Farish has traced, for example, the immense interagency mobilization around regional experts in the Cold War and the rise of "area studies."[59] Certainly, the ambitious programs of modernization during the process of decolonization targeted particularly strategic areas that called for massive amounts of data on places and phenomena that the U.S. government had mere years ago considered off the radar.[60] This process often blurred the lines between what was space and what was place and could end up subsuming important local nuances for the large-scale universal waging of an often binary, seemingly fixed conflict.

For cartography, specifically, the clash of these concepts could have extreme and often tragic consequences—cartography's reduction of the world to these often-simplified constructions had material consequences on the ground and around the globe. The ways in which cartographers, for example, used the same base maps of village areas of Vietnam to both engage in humanitarian modernization and relocation projects while simultaneous targeting the same areas for military destruction speak starkly to the problem of the abstract and the concrete (see chapter 4).[61] The paradoxes of the Cold War become especially evident when civilians on real ground are killed over abstract ideas on a global level, and when space subsumes place. Cartography did matter in a very material sense in the Cold War, and the spatial constructions of maps made their way into the everyday practice of its waging.

Strategy and Ideology

This sense of paradox is also prevalent in a third tension that marks the unique relationship between maps and the Cold War: the use of maps as strategic instruments, produced and circulated for specific purposes, and their role as larger ideological forces in American culture. As Martin Medhurst writes, a strategic approach demonstrates the contingencies of realist assumptions in the goals of Cold War statecraft and assesses how national interests are framed by language and visual symbols.[62] On the other hand, Philip Wander finds the "grounding of meaning" to be a key concern of Cold War study, tracing how our definitions of Cold War audiences and arguments are "rooted in historical struggle and the ideological conflicts in which they appear."[63] *Mapping the Cold War* mines the intersection between these approaches to the Cold War and sees maps as necessarily embodying both.

My analysis of Cold War cartography relies and depends on the instrumentality of maps, assuming that maps are flexibly appropriated by actors for goals centered around national security. The choice to "display" is strategic and political and always caught between tensions of revelation and concealment—powerful Cold War actors proceeded carefully in what to show and what not to show in their displays of the spatial relationships driving the conflict's major antagonisms.[64] This notion of utility however, is directly bound up and complicated by the role of state power. The very idea that a map is an instrumental tool ready to be picked up and used is, for geographer Matthew Sparke, symptomatic of "modern, scopophilic, and masculinist power relations interconnecting the discourse of cartography with the imperial discourse of the modern European nation-state."[65] To situate maps only as instruments is to perpetuate the view of maps as mere means for strategy and ignore cartography's fraught and problematic imperial history as a practice in itself that perpetuates state power's significance. In *Mapping the Cold War*, maps are seen on a deeper level, as "technologies of spatial abstraction" that are "indeed *constitutive* of the state" and "enframe" state power.[66] In constructing a critical history of Cold War mapping, it is not enough to point out the new cartographic methods and techniques—there is a need to implicate these methods as ideological and to situate cartography as, in Sparke's terms, "a *recursive* social process in which maps shape a world that in turn shapes its maps."[67]

Understanding the instrumental and constitutive functions of Cold War maps together requires a sensitivity to the question of why maps were needed in the Cold War. What constitutes the impulse to map? In the 1950s and early 1960s, for example, State Department delegations for United Nations' cartographic conferences in Africa, India, and elsewhere sought programs to teach new mapping methods to native-born scientists and policy makers in decolonizing areas.[68] These efforts implicitly acknowledged that the ability to accurately map oneself was a marker of reaching the level of a truly modern (and, often from the U.S. perspective, Western) civilization. These representatives believed not only that such education could help nations align with the national security goals of the United States and influence Third World elites before the Soviets could but also that mapping would help shape the identities of these burgeoning nations toward true self-determination. For Cold War historians like Odd Arne Westad, for example, the goals of the U.S. government in the Cold War "were not exploitation or subjection, but control and improvement," thus representing a "genuine and deeply held ideological" social consciousness.[69] Mapping transcended mere instrumental strategy and rose to the level of ideology. Decades later, in the early 1980s, upon the rekindling of nuclear antagonisms with the USSR, Caspar Weinberger and his Department of Defense (see chapter 5) chose to justify their mobilization of new nuclear technologies by mapping the Soviet Union's own stockpile of new weapons and the speed and magnitude of their destructive powers across the earth and, importantly, to promote such maps in accessible public pamphlets.[70] The Department of Defense's spatialization of Soviet capabilities (as well as, Weinberger argued, Soviet intentions) on the flat page showed U.S. leaders' nuanced sense that maps could not only produce knowledge about the enemy but could also efficiently represent the values of what America holds to be important in the Cold War.

In both of these examples, mapping was embedded into America's very conception of the Cold War and its place in the world and not simply as a neutral technique or instrument that could be implemented for a specific purpose. Ned O'Gorman has written of how particular sets of languages in the Cold War form "congealed worldviews," or sets of simplified shorthand ideologies for viewing one's place in the world (e.g., stoicism, romantic dualism).[71] It is no stretch to see how the visual grammars of maps could also organize American perceptions of its place in the world. For Weinberger, maps located America as dangerously bombarded on the ground and in the skies by aggression and thus required dramatic displays of strength, while for the State Department, maps placed America as a benevolent teacher to a growing South (always *below* on the maps) that could be made safely in America's image. The fact that these two spatialized worldviews were so different yet could be reconciled and held simultaneously by important Cold War actors makes cartography the archetypal medium for such a multilayered conflict.[72] The ground of the Cold War was an *idea* as much as it was the very real landscapes that were targeted by nuclear missiles, and that essential tension continually drove the maps of the conflict.

At the same time, ensuring that the notions of strategy and ideology are held in suspension with one another helps to reveal significant challenges to the hardened lines of bipolar maps. An extraordinary tension was evident in the Cold War, for example, between the map's propensity to be a medium of state control and its capacity to draw the parameters of social change. In fact, the very cartographic technologies and instruments that helped produce these conduits for military power and other forms of surveillance were also appropriated in maps of protest against the perceived moral bankruptcy of how Cold War space was "produced." Cartographers like William Bunge (in chapter 5) were influential in advancing the kind of quantitative spatial science that revolutionized postwar cartography and led to the proliferation of the kinds of automation and digitization that would power military surveillance and mapping applications, like those of Weinberger and his Department of Defense.[73] And yet renegades like Bunge would use cartography as a medium of Cold War agitation, advocating for the reclamation of local "places" during a war of universals and abstractions, and drawing maps that indicted America's Cold War frame as constituted by lines of death and nuclear destruction. In this way, mappers like Bunge were exposing the maps of state power as ideological in nature and arguing that they were complicit in powerful modes of control.

THE RHETORICAL LIVES OF MAPS

Art and science, space and place, strategy and ideology—together, these three tensions situate cartography as a medium uniquely suited to the conflict's artificial, abstract, and especially spatial confines. Productive connections can be found in the intersections between a map's artistic displays and its scientific management, its concrete power of placement against the abstractions of space, and its strategic worth and ideational value. What ultimately unites these tensions together, though, is how they present the restless nature of Cold War cartography. In this era, maps were constantly appropriated, debated, revised, and reappropriated. Cold War maps *lived*; they were active and malleable documents, not merely displays or reflectors. Such a seemingly bipolar, universal, and fixed conflict as the Cold War required immense work to maintain an image of fixity.[74] Maps, thus, had to continually reproduce and maintain the essential artifice of the conflict. Bruno Latour has written of the concept of "immutable mobiles," in which a visual image of scientific data is frequently seen as a fixed and finished product, yet at the same time as an image that is constantly moving and reproducible for a multitude of contexts.[75] As an "immutable mobile," a map has an age-old power to appear as an unimpeachable representation of the world, while its easy usability makes for a remarkable flexibility in what it can offer its users.[76] The hardened lines between the United States and the Soviet Union (and by extension America's allies and satellite adversaries in so-called spheres of influence across the globe) may appear immovable and essential on Cold War maps; however, the hardening of these lines only comes from the maps' ability to draw and be drawn into the active construction of the Cold War.

In *Mapping the Cold War*, I trace these active constructions through a specific, critical approach to analyzing cartographic history. A map possesses what I would call a "rhetorical life." In other words, a map has a particular lifespan in which it exists as a communicative practice, as it works through the intersections of public and private spaces, institutional and popular contexts, and artistic and scientific modes of collection, synthesis, and expression.[77] By noting the concept of a rhetorical life, though, I am not concerned with some kind of defined origin point or "end of life" death moment for a map. Such points are always debatable and shifting depending upon context—and therein lies the point: a map is never a finished product.[78] Rather, the notion of a map's "rhetorical life" merely points to how a map reflects and shapes its multitude of contexts, as it *lives* and functions as a usable, material document.[79] Finding the connections, say, between the production techniques of a map and the ways in which that map is reused and recopied allows us to keep the business of cartography properly historicized and dynamic across wide expanses of time.[80] Finnegan has written of the "eventfulness" of visual images, specifically photographs, wherein the meaning-making of an image stems from the contexts of its production, the details of its composition, and the movement of that image through the complex contexts of its immediate reproduction, its circulation, and in the variety of responses from audiences.[81] For the lives of Cold War maps, we can similarly trace the residues of a map both as it moves through the culture and how it assumes a diversity of roles for its users.

The concept of a rhetorical life emphasizes the engagement of a map with its immediate context but also with other Cold War artifacts. Geographers Denis Wood and John Fels have argued that the map continually advertises itself to be taken authoritatively, and that advertisement takes the form of a *paramap*. The paramap is a construction that goes beyond the map itself and includes all of "the verbal and other productions that surround and extend" a map's presentation (dedications, inscriptions, epigraphs, prefaces, notes, illustrations).[82] In addition, the paramap includes all of the elements not just appended to the map but also circulating in the social space around the map (advertisements for the map, reviews, production information); for Wood and Fels, "ultimately, it is the *interaction* between map and paramap that propels the map into action."[83] What this approach seeks to prove is that a map is never just a map, but a confluence of social forces that constrains a culture's sense of its relationship to, and *in*, the world. Maps are central to a concept, prevalent among geographers and historians, of a "geographic imagination" where cultures obtain and circulate geographic knowledge.[84]

The idea of the paramap can extend to how mapping is described and accounted for by its practitioners and circulators. How powerful Cold War actors, often behind the scenes, actually talk about and conceive of their roles and their messages reveals the very fluidity and the constructed nature of the Cold War, as well as what kinds of collaborations and contestations brought certain ideologies forward while relegating others to the background.[85] In *Mapping the Cold War*, what cartography meant and what its practitioners believed its purposes, benefits, and drawbacks to be are brought into focus. Map producers and users wrote and spoke often about the role of space and how geopolitics positioned the United States in particular ways, and thus that "cartographic talk" is as important as the maps they accompanied. While the finished displays of Cold War maps often rested upon an aura of "truth" and objective detachment so common to scientific work of the era, the producers and users of maps showed a remarkable understanding of how maps could be molded to create very specific visions and advance complex arguments.[86]

This kind of movement of a map through Cold War culture, as well as the ways in which cartography is contested and debated by its users, is borne out through examples of some of the most influential maps of the era. In 1951 the American Federation of Labor (AFL) released a provocative map of the Soviet Union, plotting the location of secret Gulag prison camps (explored in chapter 3).[87] Across an enlarged Russian Caucasus was a rash of red dots indicting what Soviet officials were denying in international media. The AFL map is certainly important for how its visual codes and symbols politicize the space of the Soviet Union as a landscape of secrecy and oppression; yet, adding to the map's display on the page is its provenance and its remarkable life as an active, evidentiary weapon. The AFL Gulag map was actually produced out of collaboration between popular journalists, the State Department, and an AFL looking to strengthen its anticommunist credentials. The map arrived in a political culture rife with Holocaust memory and visuality as well as with the charged discourse of "slavery" against ideological foes. Lawmakers quickly adopted the map as an icon for hard-line anticommunism, American teachers used the map to teach current affairs in classrooms, overseas labor unions circulated the map to their "brothers" to protest working conditions, and official Soviet reaction to the map (in charged diplomatic exchanges and even in seizures of it on the streets of Eastern Europe) brought out the hostility against Western propaganda.

At the same time as the AFL charted the spread of political imprisonment behind the Iron Curtain, the American Geographical Society, through sponsorships from army and navy research grants as well as major pharmaceutical companies, embarked ambitiously on a project to map current knowledge of diseases and health epidemics such as polio, malaria, yellow fever, and even starvation. The resulting *Atlas of Disease* (discussed in chapter 4) produced an influential series of innovative, detailed maps between 1950 and 1955 that showed a world filled with parasitical invaders.[88] Particularly during a tumultuous period of decolonization, the *Atlas of Disease* demarcated the so-called three worlds that theorists and practitioners of development and modernization were using to "bring up" the "diseased" subequatorial nations. But, again, more than merely displaying knowledge of disease, the lives of the *Atlas of Disease* maps showed the active movement of cartography into Cold War spaces: used by corporations such as Pfizer to identify promising international markets, adopted by the army to study the spread of viral encephalitis among U.S. troops in Korea, redrawn in Congress to support funding and expansion of the Mutual Security Act, and employed by U.S. forces to study where "advisers" could safely tread in Vietnam.

Despite their different aims, the Gulag map and the *Atlas of Disease* maps are united in the ways they fuse institutional and popular discourses together and in the ways that their eventful rhetorical lives made them usable, material documents. Both also intersect with the immensity of Cold War state power in the United States as they reify the importance of spatial perception in defining American interests vis-à-vis the Soviet Union and the so-called rest of the world. The Gulag map was once referred to as "the most widely circulated piece of anti-Communist literature" and served to embolden the stark lines of the East-West dichotomies of the early post–World War II era, while the *Atlas of Disease* foreshadows the ways in which new North-South dichotomies would come to constrain the decolonizing Cold War landscape and America's increasingly intervening hand.[89] Such rhetorical lives even show the kind of important conversations that maps in a sense shared with other maps. At one point, for example, the producers of the *Atlas of Disease* consulted with the leaders of the American Federation of Labor and used their Gulag map data to pinpoint where the Soviet government was holding its prisoners, in order to plan their own map of human starvation.[90] Even small connections like these create a tangible sense of a wide cartographic scope that encompassed the Cold War and the compelling ways that American officials and other prominent institutions were dependent on particular cartographic perceptions of the world.

Cases like these from *Mapping the Cold War* affirm that cartography and, by extension, the production of Cold War space constituted, above all, a *practice*.[91] The "production of space" is often a term that is invoked vaguely—an idea easier to theorize about in the abstract than it is to see in everyday interaction. And yet the very ubiquity and usability of Cold War maps make this concept much more concrete, as they reveal what geographer Trevor Barnes (borrowing Andrew Pickering's concept) has called the "mangle" of collaborations and competitions between the foreign policy institutions of the executive branch of the U.S. government, the defense apparatuses of the armed forces, the spatial science establishments at universities, private and independent organizations such as the American Geographical Society and the AFL, the popular journalism at outlets such as *Time* and the Associated Press, and even supranational powers like the United Nations.[92] Common among these groups was the impulse to work out the spatial parameters of what exactly the Cold War was and how it should be fought. And while the rhetorical presidencies of central figures such as Truman and Eisenhower remain vital to Cold War study, as does the critique of its famed architects like George Kennan and Walt Rostow, one of the best ways to trace Cold War space is to follow its midlevel bureaucrats, practitioners, and policy makers who were actively writing world space and circulating geographic visions.[93]

To go too far, though, is to see maps as actually immutable; rather, the *perception* of maps as immutable is what powers cartography. Maps are fundamentally insecure. Rob Kitchin and Martin Dodge express that a map is "brought into the world and made to do work through practices such as recognizing, interpreting, translating, communicating, and so on. It does not re-present the world or make the world (by shaping how we think about the world); it is a co-constitutive production between inscription, individual and world; a production that is constantly in motion, always seeking to appear ontologically secure."[94] Maps, then are "always mapping," attempting to appear representative, and this process is what makes maps so dynamic in Cold War culture.[95]

Thus, from the origins of particular Cold War maps and their techniques of production and data management into their appropriated usages and diverse interpretations by sometimes competing and sometimes collaborating Cold War institutions and audiences, the story of how the United States mapped itself and the world in the second half of the twentieth century is a vital story about the synthesis, the framing, and the practice and the movement of America's international power. For Wood and Fels, to map is to claim that "this is *there*"—and America required images of strength and commitment in maps to legitimize its self-interest as commensurate with the interests of the rest of the world, and for those images to have productive (and inevitably contentious) lifespans across a wide array of contexts.[96]

THE LATITUDE AND LONGITUDE
OF *MAPPING THE COLD WAR*

Like the cartography it profiles, this book also required particular strategic choices around what to cover within its lines and boundaries. Since a fully comprehensive history of Cold War cartography is not the aim here (and not really possible), the chapters involve geopolitical tensions and themes that best represent the ways in which the rhetorical lives of maps in a host of contexts could be traced. In addition, since the intersections of popular, government, and academic cartography are a major focus of the study, the narrative revolves around maps that were publically distributed or at least available beyond one particular agency or institution. This choice also means an emphasis on cartographers who were engaging, at least to some degree, with public opinion. Such public contexts are important as I trace the artistic image component of Cold War cartography and how it constructed particular visions of American power to a diversity of audiences. John Cloud's influential work, for example, on the "black box" technologies, like CORONA's satellite photo mapping, of Cold War cartographers in classified contexts concerning the surveillance of enemy territories is discussed here only broadly.[97] Similarly, the fascinating growth of geographic information systems (GIS) technologies and the digitization of maps remained a largely classified phenomenon throughout the Cold War; some of this vital work is accessed in chapter 6 to discuss the development of nuclear map propaganda in the Department of Defense, but there is an emphasis in *Mapping the Cold War* on the map as it intersected with Cold War public aims and programs.

Similarly, because the focus of this study also revolves around the changing spatial perceptions in foreign policy and other political applications of cartography, the thematic map is chosen largely over the topographic map. As Susan Schulten has demonstrated, "thematic mapping" is a broad term invented in the twentieth century to name a practice that had started well before: the expansion of cartographers' ability to document a host of political and social phenomena (e.g., elections, health, taxation, immigration) in addition to the map's time-honored role as territorial manager had been happening for at least a century.[98] But it was the Cold War where the convergence of massive amounts of available data with increasingly sophisticated technologies took place on an international scale and made the thematic map an accessible and useful tool for policy makers in unprecedented ways. So in *Mapping the Cold War*, the historical and analytical focus is generally on maps that deal overtly with thematics of political, economic, and social issues and situate America's role in the world in specific ways. The immense and painstaking topographic work, and the great collaboration between cartographers and earth scientists, to survey the world is worth its own study and is only a small part of the story here, although many of the debates around surveillance and coverage in topographic work at key agencies overlap with the more overtly political concerns discussed in the pages ahead. The truly infinite possibilities in the massive storehouse of maps of a forty-year plus international conflict create new lines of important inquiry for Cold War historians and critical geographers; here we see a focused survey of some of these maps and the mappers who helped to prominently construct and maintain the geopolitical fault lines of the conflict.

Finally, the scope of this book is purposefully broad in order to trace the active, changing Cold War through maps over its long forty years of expansion and contraction. Certainly, in-depth treatments of particular mapping programs or eras during the Cold War (e.g., the cartography of economic development, the military development of GIS technologies, the role of the airplane in the growth of maps) could each merit book-length treatment. My goal, however, is to see how these cartographic initiatives and ideologies shape each other. For example, the air-age strategy maps of World War II that inspired early Cold War cartography, if taken to their logical extension, informed the ways in which the maps of the so-called Second Cold War in the early 1980s charted the role of nuclear technology; the collapse of distance that the airplane brought to maps was dramatically heightened by the appearance of the intercontinental missile. The book's roughly chronological structure allows a sense of the general trajectory of cartography's intersection with the major geopolitical developments, such as the postwar construction of Soviet relations, the growing importance of graphing North-South relations in the wake of decolonization, and the role of nuclear destruction in compressing space on maps. This longitudinal approach to maps can plot how particular conceptions of space are visualized and instantiated and then move and change through a multitude of contexts.

In general, each of the chapters revolves around particular geopolitical themes that incorporate and combine the broader tensions discussed here. In addition, extended examples and particular cases in each of these chapters draw out these themes and tensions more specifically. In chapter 1, for example, I situate *Mapping the Cold War* in terms of the "air-age globalism" that marked the popular journalistic cartography of World War II—a movement wherein maps showed new and partial bird's-eye-view perspectives of the world from above rather than the detached, omniscient perspectives of maps like the famous Mercator projection. Air-age maps displaced our sense of expected direction in viewing the world, and changed notions of distance and proximity: the world seemed more interdependent and closer but also more susceptible to one's vantage point and national interests. The opening discussion of air-age globalism culminates with an examination of the maps of Richard Edes Harrison, the quintessential air-age magazine cartographer in the 1940s and 1950s. The chapter considers not only his maps but also his cartographic strategies and theories of map audiences and his influence on the growth of a unique Cold War cartography. This chapter also documents how the spatial shifts of air-age globalism accompanied a new focus on uniting cartography with public opinion, thus emphasizing the role that maps played in mediating popular conceptions of the globe.

Chapter 2 follows the popular air-age assumptions emergent from World War II into the postwar realm of foreign policy and U.S. government cartography. Maps were constrained by the new flexibilities of air-age perspectives and complicated by the need to produce a vast amount of spatial facts about the world in order to protect American interests. As academic and popular cartographers built the architecture of a postwar spatial framework, maps were increasingly brought into the spaces of national security. The driving case of the chapter revolves around S. W. Boggs, the Department of State's official geographer from 1927 to 1954. Boggs oversaw the expansion of the State Department's geography division from humble origins as a map archive for the World War I Paris Peace Conference into a bustling center for geographic intelligence. Boggs was notable for bringing in artists like Harrison and others to make U.S. maps more accessible and dynamic, and he yet faced the very real institutional constraints of space as guarded knowledge. In the process, chapter 2 examines Boggs's academic work and public treatises on maps that circulated in the State Department as well as his interagency correspondence on maps and his behind-the-scenes conceptions of the State Department's function as a geopolitical leader. In general, this chapter works in the uneasy transition from the promise of air-age flexibility to the more complex public-institutional rapprochement that met government representatives involved in placing America on the map during an uncertain time.

Chapter 3 discusses how cartography participated in the creation of an East-West binary between the United States and the Soviet Union. A host of different popular and government institutions (sometimes in collaboration) used maps to display knowledge of Soviet spaces and as provocative arguments in actual diplomatic exchanges with the Soviet Union, where maps become evidentiary weapons used strategically to incite public opinion. At the same time, these uses show the ideological function of maps as "images of commitment" to a seemingly fixed world that needed to be contained. The chapter draws on a wide array of maps, bringing in journalistic constructions of America on the Cold War map from *Time*, *Life*, *Fortune*, and even the Associated Press but also showing how cartography functioned in congressional initiatives on "Mutual Security" and "Un-American Activities." The chapter's central case involves the origins, display, and use of the AFL's Gulag map. The map's popularity with American citizens, U.S. government representatives, and even international audiences showed how maps possess unique power in representing stark Cold War divisions and manufacturing authenticity as a central expectation for maps of the era. Altogether, chapter 3 shows how cartography was drawn directly into the informational propaganda of America's Cold War and illustrates how America attempted to stabilize its own identity in the Cold War by ordering and classifying cartographic knowledge of its ideological enemy.

Chapter 4 assesses the function of maps in advancing perspectives of the "Third World," a key part of the cartographic expansion of the Cold War. The tension between America as a benevolent developer of democratic ideals and economic modernization on the one hand and as an international enforcer of its own interests on the other is most poignantly displayed on these maps. This chapter broadly explores the Third World as a spatial concept and how the accompanying ideologies of development and modernization constrained the practice of cartography. The chapter draws particularly on the *Atlas of Disease* project that sought to track Third World disease as part of U.S. mutual security goals and initiatives for economic development, while also detailing America's leadership role in the United Nations cartography program, where U.S. leaders used mapping as a practice to teach other nations self-sufficiency and democratic ideals. Chapter 4 demonstrates how America was widening its commitments in a host of Third World fronts, while marked by a powerful uneasiness around America's vision of its place in a time when the nation's power was seen as vulnerable.

Chapter 5 arrives at the large-scale rekindling of the U.S.-Soviet arms race during the early 1980s. In this time, cartography was a contentious vehicle for quantifying and displaying the escalation of sophisticated nuclear armaments and digitized technologies, as it reflected how missiles almost completely dissolved traditional notions of distance on the globe. The chapter juxtaposes two central examples and puts them in conversation with one another, beginning with a focus on the propaganda volley of maps in "Battle of the Booklets" between Caspar Weinberger's Department of Defense and the Soviet Ministry of Defense and on how each projected nuclear capacity and vulnerability against its rival. This exploration is followed by a critical analysis of the maps of William Bunge, arguably the antithesis of the technologized defense cartography of Weinberger and company. His *Nuclear War Atlas* project cartographically represented the nuclear disarmament movement, with a crude but fiery set of maps that railed against the powerful weapons of the Cold War. While Weinberger's maps were a clinical look at the lack of parity between U.S. and Soviet arms, Bunge's maps were unapologetically radical—his skeletal, line-drawing maps covered the globe in swaths of blood red to indicate the human cost of cold war. Both cases show starkly different perspectives on the "nuclear geopolitics" that foretold the end of the Cold War in compelling ways—particularly in how maps negotiated between resistance and control in the projection of nuclear conflict.

Finally, a brief concluding reflection examines how geographers and cartographers began to envision the breakdown of the Cold War spatial system. The Cold War's brand of air-age globalism was giving way to globalization, and this shift in mapping discourse provides an opportunity to reflect on the ramifications of the Cold War's spatial power in defining America's geographic imagination even into the twenty-first century. By the time Gorbachev and Bush faced off over their own maps at Malta in 1989, even as the larger map of Eastern Europe was crumbling, they were engaging with a contentious, explosive cartographic history that made the lines, icons, and colors on their maps signify something larger and deeper about their own sense of national identity vis-à-vis the impossibly complex world around them. In that way, their very typical Cold War maps must have been both comforting and incredibly anxiety-provoking (not unlike Roald Dahl's pilot)—a fitting way to describe the function of maps for a range of audiences throughout the forty years leading up to Malta.

Ultimately, *Mapping the Cold War* operates under Susan Schulten's wise assumption: "We can never, of course, reach 'beyond geography,' for it is impossible to imagine the world outside of its interpretive conventions. But we can ask *how* geography has mediated the world for us, and how it has concretized the abstract."[99] It is also essential to keep in mind what Denis Wood and John Fels have written—that a map "transforms the world *into* ideology."[100] Above all, these transformations create a story of the growth of American power and the complex, beautiful, and often frightening ways it was displayed on a flat page and passed around a vibrant Cold War culture. The stakes for maps were high. As the following pages attest, Cold War maps lived rhetorical lives. They had significant material implications and flowed vitally through institutional, popular, and academic spaces; the choice to map and the choice to use maps were highly charged political ones in and between each of these contexts. For the purposes of this book, cartography is not a by-product of Cold War history, it *is* Cold War history, and I take the stance that study of the Cold War, and of America's historical position on the globe, is best approached by looking for the deeper discursive connections that underwrite the mapping of world space.

1

IRON ALBATROSS

Air-Age Globalism and the Bird's-Eye View of

American Internationalism

In April 1941, almost eight months before the Japanese attack on Pearl Harbor, the Saint Paul Institute's Science Museum in Minnesota premiered an exhibition entitled *Can America Be Bombed?* Using a series of massive spherical maps, the display visually explored the geography of North America and its relation to the Pacific and Europe in terms of bombing ranges and their strategic functions. As Louis H. Powell, the director of the exhibit, later wrote: "In those far-off days of 1940 and 1941 when America was being rudely forced into an awareness of its proximity to Europe and Asia, a new unit for measuring distance on the face of the earth was born—the distance to which a bomber could fly with a paying load of bombs and, with reasonable certainty, return to its base."[1]

Despite the exhibit's implications for America's burgeoning international relationships in the new World War context, most striking about the exhibit was the maps' dramatic form as well as the ways in which they circulated. The show traveled nationwide, to the Buhl Planetarium in Pittsburgh, the New York Museum of Science and Industry, and the art museums of Toledo, Minneapolis, and Albany. Powell was particularly proud that the exhibit "made museum history by surmounting the traditional barriers that separate art and science museums and appearing in leading museums of both kinds."[2] Reproductions of several of the units reached the office rotundas of House and Senate buildings in Washington, and some of the cartographic experiments used at the institute produced forty-inch blackboard-surfaced globes for tracing international routes in the navy's aerial navigator training program.[3]

Can America Be Bombed? was an example of the wide usage of new mapping forms during the World War II period. The exhibit illustrated the move from a flat-map conception of the world to a more flexible, active engagement with world space emerging at the time. A restlessness of vision marked this period in the 1940s—brought about by the concurrence of expanding world commitments with the military and commercial possibilities of air travel. Indeed, the emphasis on the entire globe as a field of strategy helped form the basis of a spatially conscious popular culture, imaginatively enhanced by the new cartographic technologies of what came to be known as "air-age globalism."

American isolationism was a dying ideology, but the planes that reached the stagnant ships in Pearl Harbor finally put the nails in its coffin for good, and maps would come to textualize the new global scope for a wide array of audiences.[4] Moreover, maps were employed as a lens of vision in the highest halls of leadership. In his fireside chat of February 23, 1942, President Franklin D. Roosevelt referenced the momentous political implications of this new perspective in geopolitics: "Those Americans who believed that we could live under the illusion of isolationism wanted the American eagle to imitate the tactics of the ostrich. Now, many of those same people, afraid that we may be sticking our necks out, want our national bird to be turned into a turtle. But we prefer to retain the eagle as it is—flying high and striking hard."[5] FDR's press secretary Stephen T. Early even dispatched statements to national newspapers a week prior to the chat. He requested that Americans bring their maps and globes with them as they sat and listened to the president's next war update "so that they might clearly and, in that way, much better understand him as he talks with them."[6] Appealing directly to armchair cartographers, FDR demanded, "Look at your map. . . . This war is a new kind of war. It is different from all other wars of the past, not only in its methods and weapons, but also in its geography."[7]

The new geopolitics dictated that the oceans no longer protected the United States from the world; the new cartographic measurement would become minutes, not miles. As head of the Library of Congress's Map Division, Walter Ristow, wrote in 1944, "All geography becomes *home* geography when the most distant point on earth is less than sixty hours from your local airport."[8] This discourse of the air was reflected both in the shift toward popular, journalistic cartography during World War II and in the rapid growth of the U.S. government's already sizable cartographic apparatus. Novel types of maps and globes covered the walls and desks of academics and defense bureaucrats but also found their way into American homes in new and compelling ways. World War II newsreels brought in maps as constant tropes to spatialize both American victories and desperation on the European and Pacific fronts, while commercial supporters of the war effort like Walt Disney saw cartography as a central medium for the new immediacy of America's expectations as world leader in such a devastatingly massive conflict.[9]

More important, though, for this discussion are the ways in which these new discursive formations, born of World War II strategy and anxieties, began to shape and support a larger liberal, modern internationalism that would come to characterize postwar conceptions of America's "place" in the global community. Alan Henrikson's crucial work on maps as "ideas" concludes that "this mental transformation and shrinkage of the earth during World War II was . . . a major cause of the 'Cold War,' a factor of no less significance than the well-known military, political, economic, and ideological causes."[10] While avoiding the causalism that marks Henrikson's conclusions, I suggest in this chapter how the novel air-age cartographic perspectives of this era helped shape the interpretive ground on which the Cold War could be waged. I argue that air-age mapping mediates a historic shift in American foreign policy and spatial worldview from classic principles of political realism (and its emphasis on geopolitically defined states and concrete balances of power) toward a more fluid, abstract, and image-based internationalism.[11] In this sense, the map served as both a mode of artistically envisioning a new internationalism and a powerful instrument of scientific precision in the protection of American interests. As Frank Ninkovich writes, "Interests, formerly 'hard,' material, and national, became by this new standard soft, symbolic, and international."[12] Thus, in Ninkovich's estimation, "interpretation" became the central focus, with both popular audiences and leaders coming to "'read' the international environment as if it was a text," and the global order imagined and argued into being, not simply achieved through a "mastery of objective details."[13]

The bird's-eye view from the airplane's vantage point was replicated in the formal conventions of maps, as cartographers attempted to encompass sweeping movement on the static page.[14] From journalists to academics to government technicians, there was a rising consensus that the hemispheric world of traditional boundaries and power relationships was no longer viable. The sheer amount of competing ways to project this shift, however, shows that there was little agreement about the forms this new internationalism would take. On the one hand, air-age maps are not unique to other maps, in that they present particular spatial problems that can be used to frame solutions—the map itself being used instrumentally for a strategic objective (i.e., "seeing" World War II correctly will help wage successful war), thus needing a sense of transparency and clarity. At the same time, the conventions of the map are now dramatically emphasized, with the novelty of perspective and projection itself a main subject of the map. The map now calls attention to itself in a way that converges artistic vision and scientific innovation. In short, the very rhetoricity of the map steps into the foreground. Every new perceptual angle and strange projection spatially revealed a new strategic relationship, setting a premium on being able to constantly shift one's visual perception through active adaptation and vigilance.

In the process, a tension emerged between the view of America's place on the globe as indicative of the promise of an idealistic global community and the frightening prospect of a world that was *too* close and that needed to be ordered and secured. This tension would encompass a struggle during World War II and into the early Cold War between the opportunity for a new openness on the international stage and a need for rigidity against challengers both militarily and ideologically—a struggle taking place at the highest echelons of American foreign policy. On one hand, practitioners like George Kennan in his original "Long Telegram" would argue for a return to a sober and stoic realist form of geopolitics where nations acted out of clear self-interests in classic balances of power.[15] Containment, of course, was built on this idea of admitting a tragic world where, for Kennan, "elements of weakness and virtue are too thoroughly and confusingly intermingled," and therefore Americans must accept, but constantly limit, the Soviet threat.[16] Peoples under this threat, wrote Kennan, were "less interested in abstract freedom than in security," and Soviet leadership acted like any government in that "it can be placed by tactless and threatening gestures in a position where it cannot afford to yield even though this might be dictated by its sense of realism."[17]

At the same time, more than a few of Kennan's colleagues were seeing a wider, universal trajectory for American power, the kind of moral exceptionalism that would eventually become the more all-encompassing view of the Cold War that emerged from the infamous NSC-68 articulation of national security goals. The NSC-68 committee expressed, for example, by 1950 that the limited realism of containment "tends to inhibit our initiative and deprives us of opportunities for maintaining a moral ascendancy in our struggle with the Soviet system."[18] In many ways, the very *construction* of the Cold War was founded on these kinds of tensions between the lonely steadiness of containment and the bold performance of liberation. And American maps were beginning to trace both that fearful sense of containment and the notion of a moral responsibility for the United States to set the tone for the world. Thus, the world was alarmingly smaller, but America's role was seen as larger and the stakes somehow higher.

While a wide range of cartographic discourses during World War II and the early Cold War evidenced such a struggle, this chapter highlights one compelling case to represent the complex and contested role of new cartographies in the visual displays of America's rise to internationalism. The popular geographies in newspapers and magazines galvanized air-age rhetoric in particularly profound ways, involving American audiences as consenting participants in global strategy. A close look at the work of *Fortune* magazine's longtime artist Richard Edes Harrison, the leading journalistic cartographer (and prolific map critic) during World War II, provides a particularly instructive example of this phenomenon. Harrison was responsible for the employment of provocative new projections that challenged conceptions of East-West and North-South, and he created maps that placed readers in the perspective of a pilot flying over strategic areas of international conflict.[19] His work was collected in best-selling wartime atlases such as *Look at the World: The Fortune Atlas for World Strategy,* and he wrote extensively in both popular and academic outlets about the need for flexibility in the use of maps.[20]

In Harrison's case, I consider his maps with specific attention to the visual and discursive characteristics of his mapping philosophy. At the same time, I also contextualize Harrison's contributions to air-age culture as part of a larger American development toward internationalism, while accounting for the constraints of the journalistic, popular medium in which he worked. Harrison's global worldviews implicitly accept cartography as a constructed, contingent, and contestable discourse, able to shape perception rather than simply reflect spatial relationships. At the same time, his cartographic contributions offer particular parameters for the ways in which the postwar landscape would be seen as a field of global strategy. It is in this nexus between the ideological and the strategic that this chapter unfolds. Air-age vision and cartographic perspectives from popular sources like Harrison helped draw the lines on which Cold War space was bounded and placed where American interests would find their geographic expression. By examining a case preliminary to the Cold War, I can explore how Cold War internationalism did not arrive fully formed following World War II but was born from preexisting systems and patterns of discourse, including cartography. Before discussing Harrison, however, I offer a contextual sketch of air-age ideologies and their relationship to the visual culture of the period in order to situate the potency of spatial discourse during World War II and its aftermath.

"Air-age globalism" was a complex phenomenon that constrained the geographic imagination of both American popular culture and government policy makers from the 1930s into the Cold War. Its roots obviously reach back to the famous flight at Kitty Hawk (and, some would argue, even further), and it gathered steam in the globalizing rhetoric of Wilsonianism.[21] But air-age globalism's primary expression revolved around the buildup and execution of America's involvement in World War II, and air-age theorists like Ristow continually invoked Pearl Harbor as its point of origin. The international implications of the newfound air flexibility were conflated with national interest and wartime security on multiple discursive levels. Pilot and aviation executive Alexander De Seversky, for instance, marketed his treatise *Victory through Air Power* (1942) into a best-selling sensation.[22] The Walt Disney–produced film adaptation of the book, complete with De Seversky's lectures arguing for the supremacy of American air technology in front of wall-sized interactive maps, interspersed with colorful animation sequences showing the influence of airplane power across the globe, displayed just how much the air visually conditioned 1940s discourse.[23] High school textbooks such as *Our Air-Age World* advanced the notion of a miniaturized globe that students could synthesize as one whole.[24] Elsewhere, military figures like General H. H. "Hap" Arnold, an early air force pioneer, became popular icons for symbolizing American ingenuity and superiority in the air. As Congresswoman Clare Boothe Luce said in a speech to Congress in 1943,

> It is a picture that has deeply entered the imagination of almost everyone in this country under 30 years of age. . . . Grammar school boys can tell you today that the best way to get to [Bombay and Singapore] is to fly north from Chicago, across the polar ice cap—in 40 flying hours. Incidentally, they never think in land miles, they think in flying hours. They know because they keep up on these things, that Lt. Gen. Hap Arnold flew from Australia to San Francisco in 7 minutes under 36 hours.[25]

Mass media profiles, as in a 1946 *National Geographic* spread on Hap Arnold's demand for a strong postwar air program and his dire warnings of an atomic Pearl Harbor, perpetuated such legends. The article even included photographs of test explosions alongside polar-centered maps showing the strategic avenues for American air technology.[26]

The fascination with new and transcendent polar air routes was also found in tracts such as *The Right to Fly* (1947) by John Cobb Cooper, which included twelve polar-azimuthal maps to supplement text arguing for the "indivisibility of air space" and indicting postwar complacency in strategic planning.[27] Cooper was especially influential because of his multiple roles as director of Pan Am Airways, as a member of President Harry Truman's Air Policy Commission, and later as a consultant drafted by President Dwight Eisenhower to lend legal opinion on the flyover of Sputnik. Another influential figure was G. Etzel Pearcy, who would helm Trans World Airlines, publish in the popular and academic literature about America's political responsibility as a steward of the air, and go on to serve as official geographer of the State Department.[28] As these examples indicate, the practitioners of air-age globalism tended to move fluidly from roles as corporate executives, government representatives, popular critics, researchers, and educators; at the same time, the functions of the air as an economic, military, and political vehicle blended in equally complex ways. Thus the geography of the age was highly fluid, with numerous overlapping discourses addressed to multiple audiences and incorporating various levels of power and expertise.

These air-age practitioners often shared similar assumptions. In 1944 Walter Ristow formulated such assumptions into eight basic principles that characterized the new geography. Most important is the first tenet that *air-age geography is global geography*.[29] With long-range aircraft and the multitude of state interests involved in the war, the traditional focus on regional geography had to be supplemented with world-minded surveys of the globe.[30] The second is that *geography is not a static science*, which reflects the view that perspectives and worldviews need to be changed and continually questioned.[31] Third, *air-age distance is measured by time rather than space*, where "there are no longer any far corners of the earth" and space is measured in minutes and hours rather than miles.[32] A fourth tenet is that *transport by air discounts geographic barriers* as borders become more irrelevant in terms of movement and occupation of space.[33] Many air-age maps, for example, eschew borders, as they stick to the topography of rolling mountains and basins, leaving out political boundaries and highlighting the fluidity of continental land.[34] Fifth is the idea that *the world is not divided into hemispheres*.[35] Air-age geography makes hemispheres obsolete: America was now seen as closer in proximity to the "Eastern Hemisphere" of Eurasia than to Latin America, which called into question conceptions central to U.S. foreign policy since the Monroe Doctrine. Relatedly, the sixth tenet is that *world transportation routes are no longer restricted to east-west lines*. The seafaring mind of the Mercator projection accentuated geographic imaginaries of east and west, but in the air, travel from a given place was possible in all directions on a spherical earth.[36] Finally, Ristow's seventh and eighth tenets are also interrelated, positing that *ocean basin geography is out of date* and that there is a *new significance of weather and climate in the air age*.[37] The centrality of ocean basins like the Mediterranean or the Caribbean was thus challenged here, while the barriers of desert and ice no longer sealed off access to important parts of the world.[38]

Cartography provided an essential projection for this new air-powered globalism, as it altered the visualization of American political space in profound ways. Fundamentally, the sheer accessibility of maps as a popular form dramatically expanded. Sociologist (and later propagandist for the State Department) Hans Speier wrote of maps' ubiquity around the outbreak of America's involvement in World War II in the journal *Social Research*: "Today, maps are distributed on posters and slides, in books as propaganda atlases, on post cards, in magazines, newspapers and leaflets, in moving pictures and on postage stamps. . . . They may give information, but they may also plead."[39] John K. Wright, the American Geographical Society's president throughout the 1940s, not only noted the wide array of map outlets but also reminded readers of how diverse and contingent they were in how they were made. As Wright noted, many maps "are not drawn from nature but are compiled from such documentary sources as other maps, surveyors' notes and sketches, photographs, travelers' reports, statistics and the like. As these sources are themselves man-made, the subjective elements they contain are carried over into the maps based on them."[40] This characteristic of cartography, Wright believed, allowed maps to "form public opinion and build public morale."[41] In accounts like Speier's and Wright's, the notion of cartography as a contingent discourse is fully emergent. While theories of map subjectivity were by no means new, the extent to which the map was slowly seen as a cultural dialogue between cartographer and audience was a novel contribution. This necessarily involved popular map users as much as it did the elite, making strategy a more inclusive national directive, dependent on public opinion. As De Seversky put it, in the air age "tactics are the province of specialists, while strategy is the province of the people."[42] While De Seversky was engaging in characteristic hyperbole, as strategy would largely remain in the realm of experts and policy makers, the notion that maps contributed to a sense of public *image* for America grew during this time.

An increased focus on the quality of perception marked this new inclusive strategy as a central theme. A new global outlook, which supplanted a focus on fixed borders and lines with fluidity and a synthetic gaze that captured the world as one, held important implications for American power and values. For example, air-age authors like Heinz Soffner, writing in a 1942 issue of the *American Scholar*, were advancing World War II as one inclusive visual text that could be *read*, dependent on a kind of totality of perception. Referencing maps, for example, Soffner noted that "pictures of this kind reduce the mental process of reading words one after another and of transforming their content into images and ideas, to a simple matter of perceiving, directly and as a whole, one more or less complex message."[43] It was notable, for example, that FDR's large, specially fashioned office globe during World War II did not even have axes; it simply sat in a giant glass bowl to facilitate easy gazing from any direction, without limits.[44]

FDR sought to translate his own ease of gaze at the globe to the American public, placing an emphasis on "looking" at a globe as a form of popular participation and seeking to make maps a potential emblem of citizenship. His new emphasis on mapping and maps as part of popular citizen action validates Susan Schulten's thesis that the era of air-age globalism was especially marked by the common acceptance that geography itself could be equated with power; in a way, FDR's solicitation for radio listeners to follow along with him on maps was less about increasing participation in the government strategies around war and more about social assent for the ways he was waging it.[45] Maps' new challenge was to help keep citizens up-to-date with simplified, digestible arguments in a world where time (in war) was dramatically speeding up.[46] It was no coincidence that one of Richard Edes Harrison's most popular set of maps was collected under the title of "Atlas for the U.S. Citizen"; the lay audience became a participant (or at least a consenting witness) in the cartographic process to a greater extent than had been seen before.

Constantly updating the "state of the world" for American audiences meant that air-age globalism (and its maps) also connoted a sense of constant movement and a reconfiguration of the relationship between time and space. Geographer Louis Quam's 1943 critique of cartographic propaganda in Germany offered that "maps designed to illustrate the lightning speed of modern war must suggest movement."[47] In commenting on the increased use of "maps as weapons," Hans Weigert wrote in 1941 for the famed early social research journal *Survey Graphic* that "the static map reflects a fixed state and conditions, while the dynamic map shows action, intentions, influences, developments, the growth and downfall of civilizations and their ideologies" and that "only the dynamic map can do justice to the vital fact that the world of today is constantly shrinking and can stress the power lines on which deadly or peaceful messages are conveyed from air base to air base."[48] During the final days of World War II, influential geographers such as Derwent Whittlesey, president of the Association of American Geographers (AAG), were wary of the map's heritage as a static rendering of political borders. In 1945 Whittlesey theorized in his presidential address to the AAG that there was a "new horizon" in geography that required an acceptance of a new vertical dimension: "Every advance in the vertical plane alters the potential capacity of the earth. . . . Extension of man's range thus multiplies his power, rather than adding to it. The simultaneous closure of the era of surface expansion and opening of unmeasured potentialities latent in a three-dimensional world are setting new values upon every part of the earth."[49] The flat map now confronted a third dimension, thus altering the angle and perspective by which maps were used, and dramatically changed the way surfaces could be read by both elite and popular audiences.

These changes emphasized a new kind of mobility in maps that was not just about the transport of military might but about the transmission of commercial goods and communication as well. As historian James C. Malin wrote in 1944, "The air age is a new world opening to man through the medium of air communications—radio, television, and aircraft. . . . The air age must be thought of as more than the age of flight, however, because flight, like discovery, is only one form of mobility. The air-age trilogy is sound, sight, and flight."[50] Thus, air-age globalism could not simply be reduced to maps of military strategy; it was marked by a new premium on speed that employed the air as a conduit for ideas and money.

In the process, the traditional realist dichotomy between domestic life and international relations was breaking down; the values of everyday life at home were becoming more synonymous with the values of the international community.[51] Henry Luce is an exemplar of this complex movement to liberal internationalism.[52] In his famous articulation of the American Century in 1941, for example, Luce articulated globalism as a pursuit of both economic interests and "world opinion," which publications like *Time* and *Fortune* would cultivate. With pronouncements like "our world . . . is for the first time in history one world, fundamentally indivisible," Luce saw America as the responsible steward for maintaining such a rolling, unified space.[53] The isolationism of American cant was still seen as having a hold on the culture, even if it had been eroding at least since the turn of the century, and Luce and his cartographers-for-hire like Richard Edes Harrison were making clear attempts to break through its ideological hold on U.S. geopolitics. Air transportation itself became the new dividing border, pitting those who would use the new power for its supposed beneficial potential (e.g., for free trade, free movement, and free government) against those who would use it for "evil" (the empire-mad armies of Germany, Italy, etc.). In the introduction to the classic 1943 geopolitics text *The Compass of the World* (featuring maps by Harrison), Archibald MacLeish, the poet and former *Fortune* editor, wrote of both the awe and responsibility of the new air-age globalism:

> Neither master of the air nor power in the air nor the airmen's global image of the earth can make, alone, the world we hope to live in. . . . Nevertheless we know, all of us, the power of images in our lives and in the lives of nations. We know that those who think their world a free place of free movement, of free commerce both in men and words, are already free men, whatever limitations are put upon their freedom by brutality or force. . . . Men have mastered the air. And the question now, on which this terrible war is fought—is whether . . . the air will be an instrument of freedom such as men have never dared to dream of or an . . . instrument of slavery by which a single nation can enslave the earth . . . without the hope or possibility of rebellion and revolt.[54]

The air age's image-based values marked moral choices between a path of good and a path of evil, with air power now "considered essential not only to the security of the United States but to world peace."[55] As De Seversky bluntly put it during the heart of the Cold War: "The manifest destiny of the United States is in the skies."[56]

In this way, the unfolding international space of the air age was a site of both idealist liberal hopes for modern progress and immense anxiety at the new proximities suggested by the power of mediated images from a plane.[57] For example, on the one hand, air-age discourse could embody the hopeful, humanistic internationalism of a Wendell Willkie, the 1940 Republican nominee for president who gained acclaim for his book *One World*. Willkie's book used his crisscrossing experience around the globe in his own plane as evidence that the world was ready to transcend "narrow nationalism" and work toward global peace, inspired by maps that used the new global projections popularized by cartographers like Harrison.[58] The discourse of the early United Nations also was built on this kind of transcendent internationalism—its famous logo, in fact, features a polar-centered globe (a projection made famous by Harrison) surrounded by branches symbolizing peace.[59] On the other hand, the air age also encompassed a sense of the air as a frightening constraint on global security. The opening minutes, for example, of Leni Riefenstahl's *Triumph of the Will* offer the viewer a Fuhrer's-eye view from a plane descending through the clouds over Germany.[60] In large part, America's air-age cartographic techniques were a conscious contextual response to what was perceived as Axis propaganda through the "message maps" of Hitler's geographic consultant Karl Haushofer and his theories of German *Geopolitik*.[61] Isaiah Bowman, in particular, excoriated geopolitics as a sham science borne out of fascist academic journals and instead upheld "political geography" as a more acceptable (and accurate) American standard.[62]

Altogether, the new discourse of air-age globalism housed a complex rhetoric of tense, spatial contradictions that spoke to the truly global. And maps would come to chart these contradictions in latitude and longitude. Thus, the relationships between the map's function as a strategic argument and a symbol of scientific presentation are bound up in a diversity of usages and assumptions during the shift to a more globally minded perspective. Air-age cartography's hailing of academic, popular, and institutional discourses encompasses the work of one of the leading popular, journalistic purveyors of fresh, international perspectives, Richard Edes Harrison, who sketched his maps amid the uncertain spaces of this interpretive internationalism and laid down the kinds of cartographic lines that would harden in the Cold War.

RICHARD EDES HARRISON AND THE BIRD'S-EYE VIEW OF MODERN INTERNATIONALISM

The society page of the July 9, 1960, issue of the *New Yorker* published a vivid account of a recent bird-watching expedition by the Linnaean Society of New York—a group of amateur ornithologists. The trip was notable for a rare sighting of a particularly special bird. As one of the participants recounted,

> The bird took off, and as it dipped its head I caught the bright orange yellow on top of its bill. It spreads its wings—seven feet—and we saw what it was: *Diomedea chlororynchos*, the yellow-nosed albatross, the last bird you would expect to find in the North Atlantic! . . . The albatross was wonderfully cooperative; he'd fly a short distance, sometimes

within fifty feet of our boat, then land and let the gulls dive-bomb him for a while, all within a very short compass. . . . An adult bird in full plumage—a picture-book exposition. You couldn't ask for anything better.[63]

The witness to this ornithological wonder happened to be an esteemed resident of East 51st Street in New York City, one Richard Edes Harrison. Mr. Harrison was a minor New York celebrity, as president of the Linnaeans.[64] But this albatross chaser and well-to-do New Yorker had another key item on his résumé, not discussed in this interview: that of a professional cartographer. His 1994 obituary in the *New York Times*, begins with the headline, "Richard Harrison, Avid Bird-Watcher and Map Maker, 92," with the "and Map Maker" reading like an afterthought.[65]

Harrison's two life pursuits were not necessarily mutually exclusive, however. As fighter planes traversed the earth and spread their wing-spans and weaponry, mapmakers were devising a bird's-eye view of the world, actively changing our view of the globe and our placement in it. Like FDR's "striking eagle" in his 1942 fireside chat, Americans became enamored with a new air-age global perspective. From this vantage point, the world was now closer—an exciting and frightening prospect. As house cartographer for *Fortune* and consultant for *Life* magazine, for almost two decades, Richard Edes Harrison certainly permeated the "geographic imagination" of World War II and postwar culture.[66] His most famous maps revived long-forgotten modes of projection that anchored maps around the Arctic instead of establishing Europe as the center of the world, changing the entire spatial perception of proximity.[67] Other maps dispensed with the "North on top, South on bottom" viewpoint, placing his readers instead, like his albatross, "from a vantage point high above the earth so that the distances draw together in perspective, as they might to an incredibly farsighted man poised at an altitude of many thousand miles."[68]

Recent scholarly interest in Harrison has put the "mapmaker" before the "birdwatcher." In particular, Schulten's work positions Harrison as a central player in the debates during the second half of the twentieth century that discuss geography and cartography as discursive phenomena, and Matthew Farish has suggested the links between Harrison's viewpoints and the strategic spatialization of the Cold War.[69] In defining cartography as "the difficult art of trying to represent the impossible," Harrison seemed acutely aware of this discursive function of his trade, chiding his field for being rigid and precise and calling for an acceptance of "art as a full partner of technology in the design and drafting of maps."[70] Harrison's dogged amateurism evidenced his realization that maps were part of a cultural dialogue, rather than simply a top-down presentation of elite, scientist objectives.

In the process, Harrison's air-age aesthetic became an important part of a new interpretive paradigm that eschewed the "truths" of the classical power politics and balance of interests and posed new relationships and proximities.[71] Not only do his maps reflect global changes in this period, but he also called attention to the discursive nature of space itself at a historical moment that foregrounded the world's textuality during global war. Harrison's arguments for cartographic flexibility contributed to the powerful ideology that the world can be molded through the symbolic image. In this way, Harrison encouraged the type of visual abstraction necessary for American national interests to be cast as universal—a vital piece of how the Cold War would come to be constructed.

Perspective and Projection in Harrison's Maps

Harrison's unique approach figures especially into two particular themes that would come to influence Cold War cartography: the foregrounding of the very idea of vision and perception in the map; and the way the maps both uphold and challenge notions of what strategy means in a new air-age context, reenvisioning borders and proximities, and reflect-ing an uneasy globalism where goods, information, and peoples are continually in flux. Through both of these themes, Richard Edes Harri-son's cartography evidences how air-age perspectives housed the kind of new abstractions that supported emerging, midcentury internationalist values.

Harrison hailed from turn-of-the century Baltimore. Traveling often with his family, and led by his prominent Yale biologist father, he had a talent for field sketching and was a quick study in architecture, for which he would attend Yale in 1926. During the Depression, he found work in the art department for a products company, designing an assortment of oddities such as matchbook covers, record jackets, liquor labels, ashtrays, and lighting fixtures.[72] Schulten remarks of Harrison that "his style owes more to the persuasive look of contemporary advertising than to cartog-raphy," and certainly his time toiling away at ephemeral design contrib-uted in some part to his sleek, streamlined, and, above all, marketable cartographic style.[73]

Mark Monmonier dedicated his 1989 book *Maps with the News* to Harrison "whose unplanned career in journalistic cartography enhanced public awareness of the potential of news maps."[74] Indeed, Harrison was an accidental mapmaker—essentially a substitute cartographer, called by a friend at *Time* in 1932 to etch out a quick map when the regular draftsman could not be found. His fill-in job became a fairly regular assignment until, by 1935, he joined the full-time staff of *Fortune*.[75] In that year, Harrison made his mark by introducing the international perspective map for the first time in what he termed the "Vulture's View" of the Italian-Ethiopian conflict, oriented with the southwest at the top of the page.[76] As the European war escalated, Harrison became a *Fortune* fixture and remained affiliated for the next decade.

The ubiquity of news maps today is taken largely for granted; during Harrison's ascent to popular prominence, news maps were just starting to circulate, and without a significant history of news cartography in American culture, cartographers like Harrison had a wide range of freedom in their design and iconography.[77] Harrison and other up-and-coming news cartographers sought to unburden spatial information from the yoke of academic and elite control.[78] Such work brought home a sense of the globe so that "Americans imagine and comprehend a world that most [did] not experience firsthand."[79] Harrison himself reflected, "It is among the weekly and monthly magazines . . . that the greatest assault on tradition has been made. . . . [T]hey have borne the burden of making the public conscious of global geography."[80] Despite his success, though, he did find that his "assaults" were not always welcome. Harrison himself noted how he was fired as an official staff member from *Fortune* because his editor found his innovative 1938 map of Czechoslovakia "confusing." Of course, he would continue to be associated with *Fortune*, to great acclaim, but not as permanent staff. Harrison was thus constantly navigating between his philosophy of flexible, strategic mapping and what he thought his editors (and the general public) would be able to accept.[81]

Harrison's meticulous production techniques subverted the mapmaking tradition of the omniscient, North-South (typically Mercator) viewpoint through his twin innovations of perspective and projection.[82] *Life*'s profile of the *Fortune* atlas provides a fascinating account of Harrison's process behind the "perspective map," which plays with dimension to make the globe appear as if it is coming off the page.[83] He begins with a small freehand sketch of the portion of the globe to be included and then photographs the globe from a distance of six feet (placing the mapmaker at a theoretical altitude of almost forty thousand miles over the Atlantic Ocean).[84] Harrison then chooses a greatly enlarged close-up of the area produced from the photograph, which provides the basis of his vividly detailed sketches, out of which he produces his trademark three-dimensional sense of the reader flying over mountainous terrain.[85] These techniques in and of themselves were not innovative—yet it was the sense of movement and extreme angles that evidenced Harrison's particular ability to help "redevelop a native freshness of perception."[86] Projection refers simply to the choice of focus or center of the map; according to Monmonier, projections "transform the curved, three-dimensional surface of the planet into a flat, two-dimensional plane" and anchor the focus of the reader's eye.[87] In choosing polar centers, or by showing a round globe on the flat page, these projections become a salient rhetorical choice—the selection of a particular center on a map has political ramifications in the message disseminated to readers; all other points and lines on the map flow from that origin point.[88]

A representative map by Harrison from his *Look at the World* atlas evidences these themes of projection and perspective. "Europe from the East" (fig. 1.1) is one of Harrison's most striking and simple maps in the atlas and covers a full two-page spread, unadorned by any legends or captions save its title. The image is typical of Harrison's "perspective maps," showing the reader a rolling, rounded sliver of the globe, with three-dimensional accents to connote flying over the topography of Europe. What is remarkable about this perspective, though, is that it centers on Eastern Europe from the viewpoint of an imposing Soviet Union.[89] The very center of the map rests in Poland; Moscow is dotted at the bottom center of the map, and the entire European continent appears to flow out of it. At the top of the map is Spain, with the Atlantic Ocean on the horizon, and in the northeast is a glimpse of North Africa. Harrison's framing foreshadows some important spatial frames of the Cold War: it is easy to assume a Soviet-eye view of an Eastern Europe for the taking, unfolding almost naturally before a great expanding power all the way to the Atlantic. In the corner above the perspective map, in the margins of the white space, is an inset projecting the whole globe, highlighting in red the slice of Europe and North Africa that is the subject of the larger map.

A cartographic reorientation such as this one suggests how contentious the perceptions of World War II alliances with the Soviet Union were, and how a simple change in spatial perspective could reveal new relationships. Harrison's map resonates with these conceptions of an uneasy partnership between the two emerging superpowers. During the early days of America's involvement in World War II, for example, Sir Halford Mackinder's theories that the Soviet control of the "Heartland" (namely, Eastern Europe) was a potentially explosive strategic problem reached notoriety

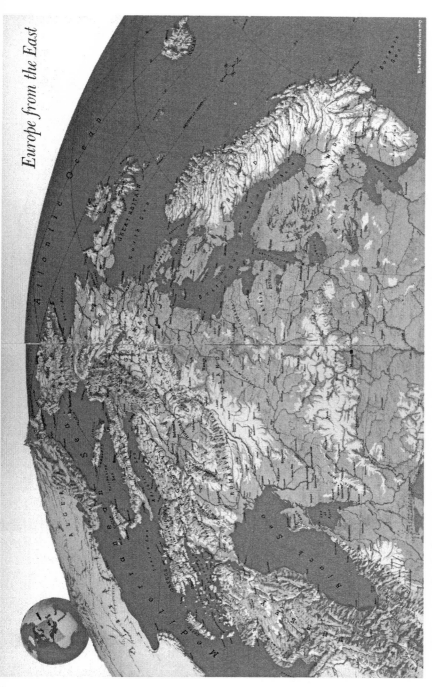

Europe from the East

Figure 1.1. Richard Edes Harrison, "Europe from the East," Look at the World: The Fortune Atlas for World Strategy, 1944. (Courtesy of the Geography & Map Division of the Library of Congress, by permission of the Estate of Richard Edes Harrison)

in academic, popular, and foreign policy circles; in a piece for *Foreign Affairs* in 1943, he concluded that "if the Soviet Union emerges from this war as conqueror of Germany, she must rank as the greatest land Power on the globe. . . . The Heartland is the greatest natural fortress on earth. For the first time in history it is manned by a garrison sufficient both in number and quality."[90]

In addition, Walter Lippmann's influential best seller *U.S. Foreign Policy: Shield of the Republic* from 1943 was passed around and praised by key members of the Joint Chiefs of Staff as important reading for both wartime foreign policy and postwar planning, with Lippmann warning that once America and the Soviet Union lose their common enemies in Germany and Japan, "Russian-American relations will no longer be controlled by the historic fact that each is for the other a potential friend in the rear of its enemies. Russia will, on the contrary, be the greatest power in the rear of our indispensable friends."[91] Harrison's rendering of "Europe from the East," then, entered a discursive air-age culture in America that was sensitive to the relationship between nation-space and perception. Typically, maps of the Heartland, including Mackinder's own famous maps, would be indicated on conventional projections and with a standard, almost omniscient perspective. Harrison's map, however, is selective in offering the Soviet vantage point, thus leaving American viewers potentially vulnerable. That elimination of a so-called objective and detached view of the world suggests a potential anxiety for U.S. foreign policy: with perspectives like these, a Soviet stronghold in Eastern Europe is made to look easy.

At the same time, the very power of maps as strategic tools becomes part of the map's subject. The lack of captions or any linguistic description (aside from place names) challenges the viewer to see the inevitability of this novel perspective, as a seemingly transparent geographic depiction that requires no explanation for the discerning viewer.[92] Harrison's flexible amateurism, in this way, engaged with the classic American tenet of commonsense philosophy, a self-consciously unpretentious construct where truths are made self-evident.[93] "Geographic sense" meant, for Harrison, that all maps distort and that mapmakers are human and that each kind of unique distortion could *actually* be useful.[94] In addition, having the global inset in the corner reminds the viewer of the connection of the region to the larger globe—that what takes place in one sliver of the world is just a piece of bigger, broader strategic spatial relationships and proximities that Americans face in the new air-age era. Harrison's map represents the turn to the symbolic and interpretive in world affairs that globalized security and charted national interests on an international scale.

Situating Vision in Harrisonian Maps

The very title of Harrison's most famous and best-selling collection indicates the air-age era's new premium on the value of vision and visibility. *Look at the World* is an imperative for clearheaded perception of new supposed realities. This plea to readers is not insignificant to how his maps work inside the covers of the atlas: as noted, maps are bound up in complex tensions of art and science. The choices on how to navigate the line between artistic interpretation and scientific "truth" reify the producer's power over the user's perception—and those choices are political. Lawrence Prelli notes that "the dynamic between revealing and concealings . . . exhibits partial perspectives—an orientation, a point of view, a way of seeing—that both open and restrict possibilities for meaning for those who become audience to them."[95] Thus, the act of spectatorship itself is problematized; the *method of seeing* transfers a set of values and images that are "always situated in complex circumstances of viewing, interpreting, and consuming."[96]

In this foregrounding of "vision," Harrison contends with the historic role of maps as unmediated frames for reality. The map "Eight Views of the World" puts these dimensions on visual display.[97] Harrison often uses the orthographic projection throughout *Look at the World*. The air age appeared truly global on the orthographic maps, as this type of map represented in two dimensions the benefits of the average desk globe.[98] Unlike the perspective maps, which tried to represent the sphericity of the earth in regional fragments, orthographic views portrayed the totality of a freely rotating globe. Yet the novelty of "Eight Views" is that there are indeed eight different projections over the two-page spread; the reader contends with eight globes, all centering and highlighting different areas of the world. The first globe features a centered United States, with the tagline, "The U.S.: its geographical isolation is more seeming than real," as Harrison's view is situated so that all continents can be seen on the globe in relation to America.[99] The United States is highlighted in bright red on each of the eight maps, amplifying its connection to the other continents of the world. Another one of the eight maps shows Antarctica at the north of the globe, with a sharp, orange Argentina protruding toward it (complete with a caption reading, "Argentina: a dagger pointed at the heart of Antarctica").[100] Europe's orthographic projection shows the tiny peninsula dwarfed and sandwiched by Asia to its left and Africa to its right, with a caption stating the visually obvious, "Europe: more close neighbors than any other continent."[101]

In "Eight Views," the total arrangement of these eight maps connotes an active, rotating, and often vulnerable earth, as if the relative worth of all parts of the world simply depends on the perspective (and interests) of the map user. Harrison could have provided the reader with one world map highlighting all of these relationships, but by choosing to place eight different views in succession, the user can flip around and choose a focus in "Eight Views," like a desk globe at home. Visually, this choice connotes that no matter which way you look at it, the "one world" is entangled with relationships in all directions.[102] Harrison's choice to use the globe itself inside the conventions of a flat map is key: as Denis Cosgrove writes on the complex genealogy of the globe in the Western imagination: "On a flat map the known can be extended to the very edges of representational space, leaving implicit the question of what lies beyond the frame; on the globe the 'ends of the earth' cannot be ignored."[103] Thus, what were former peripheries become potential centers, shifting the very idea of vision in the Harrisonian approach.

This notion of visual arrangement, of course, recalls Harrison's particular focus on audience. His emphasis on flexibility puts the audience in charge of, and implicated in, the reading, placing the user right into the pilot's seat. But the reader also can assume a variety of personas in these perspectives. In a 1942 issue of *Fortune*, for example, Harrison contributed a map entitled, "Southeast to Armageddon," in which the viewer is given a "Hitler's-eye view" of the Middle East and beyond from a point high above Berchtesgaden.[104] The map offers a sense of the geographic difficulty facing the Nazis in an attack on Asia Minor; but in also highlighting the novel perspective, the map invites the user to inhabit the "enemy's" spatial worldview through the function of the map itself.

Similarly, a 1943 *Fortune* map entitled "The Not-So-Soft Underside" places the viewer in perspective from a point over North Africa looking at the "underbelly" of Europe from the Mediterranean.[105] Harrison included a note with an early draft of the map: "The view was selected to undermine Churchill's insistence that Europe had to be attacked in its 'soft underbelly.' My working title for this map was 'How soft is the Belly?' The weasel-worded printed title was the selection of the editors."[106] So, in taking on Churchill's claims of strength in attacking Germany from North Africa and accusing the Allies of misunderstanding basic geography, Harrison makes the case that the angle of vision given to the user can be used to dispute the truths of powerful strategists; cartographic perspective becomes a kind of evidence itself for strategic argument.

Both "Southeast to Armageddon" and "The Not-So-Soft Underside" position their audience in the roles of enemy and ally from the air. In the process, each map pointedly argues about wartime strategy, while evidencing the malleability of cartographic conventions in a notably rigid medium. In this way, the very timely subjects of the map may seem limited to World War II, but the manipulation of perception is what would make its way into later Cold War cartography. As Harrison admits in *Look at the World*, most maps are seen as architects' blueprints and give the reader an infinite viewpoint where "one is not over a particular point on the map"; rather, "one is over all points simultaneously."[107] Harrison's perspective maps, however, foreground selectivity and partiality; in the same introduction, he mentions talking with pilots of the Eighth Air Force in Europe about their experiences: "A conventional map, they complained, only looks right when you are directly above the objective, i.e., some time *after* release of the bombs. The problem was solved by making maps with a *finite* viewpoint that shows the objective from the normal angle and height of approach. The new maps coincided with a true view of the target."[108] Harrison immersed popular audiences within partial worldviews, and his fixation on audience engagement reflects the new internationalism's focus on world opinion and flexible, global communication that opinion shapers like Luce were boldly calling for, and that Cold War cartographers would grapple with. His perspectives place the audience into dialogue with the cartographer and manifest an awareness of space's social constitution.

Of course, Harrison's quotation about the "true view of the target" speaks to his complex engagement with truth and transparency in maps. This complexity stems in part from Harrison's contextual framework. Harrison was immersed in a journalistic visual culture that designed maps to order, illustrating war problems that were unfolding by the day. Such maps were thus judged by their ability to provide a window into a particular strategic issue, rather than their illumination of fact. For example, an editor instructed Harrison, writing directly on one of the tracing sheets for his July 1941 *Fortune* map of the Soviet Union: "Don't be too mathematical about centering it."[109] At the same time this journalistic paradigm was firmly in place, many of Harrison's colleagues in the disciplines of geography and cartography were drafted by the Office of Strategic Services (OSS) to produce a monumental amount of spatial data in what would eventually become a quantitative revolution in geography.[110] The leaders of this revolution sought to produce clear, reliable spatial facts for America's strategy, and in many ways were reacting to the perceived distortion of geography by the Third Reich.[111]

Harrison's use of distortion in his maps represents these tensions between cartography as an argument and cartography as transparent mirror of the world. For example, one of *Look at the World*'s several polar-centered maps, "Arctic Arena," uses the full, global orthographic projection, distorting the familiar shapes of continents and placing the Soviet Union and Europe north of the United States in order to illustrate the new proximities that air routes over the North Pole bring to life.[112] Such novelty maps are certainly not the types of sketches that would be found in the halls of the State Department during the war. But Harrison's distortions challenge the "commonsense" viewpoint of the Eurocentric and East-West-minded Mercator map—maps that Harrison believed were a misleading "truth" about the way the world was *supposed* to be viewed.[113] In Harrison's introduction to the atlas, for example, he attacks Nazi Germany's leading geographer, Karl Haushofer, for his almost exclusive reliance on Mercator.[114] Harrison was not attacking German maps for their lack of accuracy or for promoting a propagandistic viewpoint but for their lack of *flexibility*, and this is a key distinction. For Richard Edes Harrison, Germany's cartographic crime was not the manipulation of geographic truths but a failure of vision itself.

Harrison was concerned about what S. W. Boggs, the State Department geographer of the 1940s and early 1950s, called "cartohypnosis," where the audience "exhibits a high degree of suggestibility in respect to stimuli aroused by the map."[115] Harrison's answer was simply to give users a bevy of tools at their eyes and fingers, with each of his own novel perspectives just one in a series of possible views. As he wrote in the *Saturday Review*, "American geography and cartography are exhibiting growing pains. They are emerging not from infancy but from a static condition bordering on senility."[116] And later in *Surveying & Mapping*, Harrison wrote, "In the military agencies, I keep hearing the words 'user requirements' over and over again. There is only one over-riding user requirement and that is: can the poor fellow understand the map?"[117]

Harrison's conceptions of vision and perspective are innovative, but also very much products of their time. Certainly, Harrison's notions of a fluid, relational space elevated the power of both the mapmaker and the user and thus implicitly questioned the natural equilibriums of the balances of power that maps traditionally highlight. In accentuating flexibility of perspective, the map itself loses some of its power as a control mechanism, yet the audience is still constrained by the limited choice of perspectives provided to them by the cartographers.[118] Relational space depends on the act of how one looks at the world and the search for a better perception of world space. Hence Harrison reminds us through his approach that maps do not necessarily show the world as it is but more as it could be—a very liberal notion of modern progress at work.

Situating Strategy in Harrisonian Maps

Richard Edes Harrison's promotion of flexible internationalism on the cartographic page shifted the focus from whose maps were more accurate in a war to whose maps were the more dynamic communicators. Highlighting the techniques by which audiences gained new perspectives becomes a key part of the display. In these new globalist perspectives, strategy itself became a lens by which to view the entire world. As Ninkovich concluded, "The perception of the globe's unity in space and time was crucial, for it obliterated the geographical, cultural, and temporal distinctions that gave life to the historical myth of old and new worlds," and thus there came a need to conceptualize national interest from the standpoint of unity of global processes rather than from the particularist frame of traditional statecraft.[119] American liberal strategists during World War II and into the early Cold War found space pliable and more universal, but that new flexibility of perspective ushered in a reductive worldview.

One of Harrison's most celebrated maps provides a sense of how conceptions of strategy were changing in this time. For his opening world map in *Look at the World*, entitled "One World, One War," Harrison chose to use the polar azimuthal equidistant projection, which he referred to as "the darling of the proponents of the 'air-age.'"[120] The use of the polar center places North America in close quarters with North Asia and the Soviet Union, with the world shown in one unbroken piece. In the description next to the map, Harrison entertains the idea that "[i]f the continents were equidistantly separated . . . almost all areas of the globe would have equal strategic value."[121] Though a great distortion (Australia on the edges of the map is stretched beyond recognition), the visual of the polar center has important ideological connotations. World power is equalized, and the globe is brought into a tightly wound collection of landmasses. As Harrison notes, it maps "the problems and the opportunities of fighting all over the world all at once."[122] Thus, strategy itself becomes an ideology of managing complicated interdependences and being flexible in response to aggression in a much closer world.

A similar map from *Fortune* 1941, using a polar azimuthal projection, illustrates the new continuities of space and proximities in even bolder relief: the fascinating "World Divided" looks almost the same as "One World, One War."[123] Here, however, the large expanse of the Soviet Union is actually colored in pitch black as an Axis country, uniting it with Germany, Japan, and Italy. Over the blacked-in country is a small caption, noting for the reader to "count this black if Nazis win a quick and complete victory."[124] The projection not only connotes a sense of dangerous closeness that changes perceptions of strategy, but Harrison also uses color as a bold tool that realizes the situation's immediacy to the reader.[125] Coloring in one of the largest Allies as a potential Axis conquest suggests that maps could go outside their conventions of showing world space "as is" and connote future projections and strategic relationships that play with both space and temporality. Without the contextualizing of the caption, though, the reader simply sees the landmass of the Soviet Union as a black mass, a threatening pall to be cast on a multicolored world. Captions can certainly constrain the reading of any map, as Denis Wood and John Fels have pointed out, but they often cannot compete with the totalizing power of color and shape in the map, and here the very real possibility that the Nazis might conquer the Soviet Union becomes a character in the presentation.[126] That essential tension between word and image is a constantly mitigating factor in Harrison's maps, and in popular cartography in general. Perhaps more importantly, though, the map suggests that an entire world can be divided into two camps through the use of color. In fact, Harrison revived this very same map for his "U.S Commitment" spread (fig. 1.2) for *Fortune* in 1952, fully realizing the Cold War architecture that his earlier maps had foreshadowed.[127]

America's shift to an image-based internationalism, though, is best seen in maps that specifically frame America's interests in terms of the rest of the world. Harrison's works capture this shift by simultaneously highlighting the anxieties and opportunities inherent in the perspectives. An air-age world created interdependences that could mean both strengths and vulnerabilities for American power. In terms of the dangers, a map like "Three Approaches to the U.S." in Harrison's "Atlas for the U.S. Citizen" shows three perspectives of the United States from Berlin, Tokyo, and Caracas.[128] These maps attempt to show drastically how vulnerable the United States is from all three locations. While the Berlin and Tokyo maps have obvious strategic implications for World War II, the inclusion of Caracas highlights that we are vulnerable even in our own hemisphere. Once again, the totality of the presentation is key—rather than show each of these perspectives in their own separate maps, Harrison puts each perspective from Berlin, Tokyo, and Caracas on the same page, on top of one another as if to lay out an argument. Geography is reduced to strategy, and vulnerability becomes an integral part of such a strategy—trust no one from any geographic perspective. While many other Harrison maps offer a more proactive vision of America, putting the American reader inside the map and at the helm of the action, the "Three Approaches" map looks *at* America, and the sense of juxtaposition offers the American audience feelings of vulnerability, left at the mercy of potential enemies from all directions.

Such a perspective recalls the realist's fear of international anarchy that necessitates a balance-of-power perspective. For example, Harrison's maps adorn the pages of realist geographer Nicholas Spykman's famous treatise, *America's Strategy in World Politics*, which offers a power-politics plea for world strategy.[129] Spykman, with his air-age principles, indicted American isolationism and disseminated the idea that even in peace the United States is unsafe and vulnerable. "A balance of power," Spykman wrote, "is an absolute prerequisite for the independence of the New World and the preservation of the power position of the United States. There is no safe defensive position on this side of the oceans. Hemisphere defense is no defense at all."[130] Arguably, the choice of the polar center in many of Harrison's maps highlights this kind of realism and prefigures how the Arctic would become a key piece of "cold war psychosis."[131] Through the influence of polar maps that connected the fortunes of the United States and the Soviet Union, the icy wasteland skyrocketed to political significance—and the potential for international cooperation in the polar world's new proximities was stifled by the culture of Cold War national security.[132] In the rush to defend American interests, this newly realized geographic proximity helped to create the conditions for an ever-widening ideological distance.

Despite these possible readings and appropriations of his maps, Harrison's work cannot be simply reduced to the ideologies of realism. His approach involves a much more global appreciation of how American interests could be synonymous with world interests. Perspective maps such as "Great Lakes to Greenland," for example, visualize the air-age perspective of the Great Lakes and the Northeast United States.[133] Just over the horizon, over what looks like a truncated Atlantic Ocean, Harrison has drawn in the coasts of Norway, Scotland, Ireland, France, and Spain, bringing Europe into the normally Western Hemispheric point of view. Also contributing to this change is that Harrison downplays the rigidity of borders. While there is a line separating Canada from the United States on the "Great Lakes to Greenland" map, the eye focuses more on the continuity of the three-dimensional style landscape, and thus the two countries appear as one mass. Air route lines on the map track the trajectory

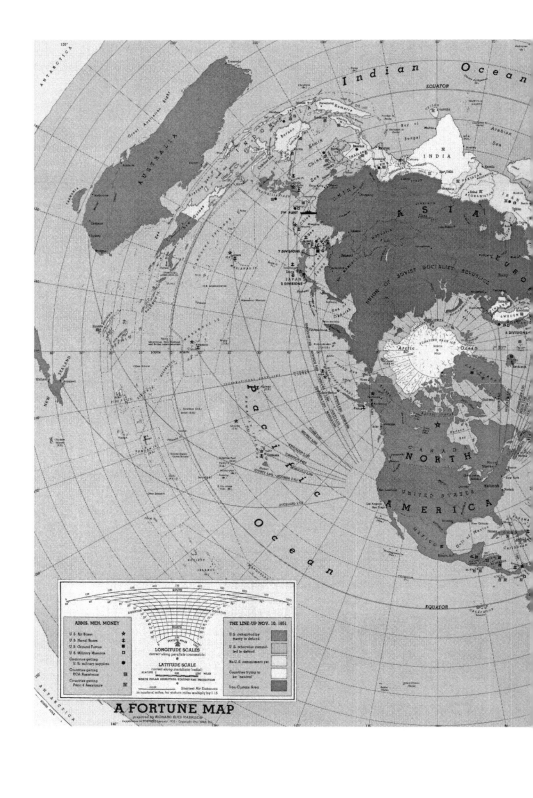

ANTARCTICA

Indian Ocean

EQUATOR

AUSTRALIA

INDIA

ASIA

EUROPE

CHINA

JAPAN
3 DIVISIONS

7 DIVISIONS

7TH FLEET

UNION OF SOVIET SOCIALIST REPUBLICS

SWEDEN

4 DIVISIONS

Arctic Ocean

FLOATING PACK ICE

NORTH POLE

NEW ZEALAND

Pacific Ocean

CANADA

NORTH

UNITED STATES

AMERICA

MEXICO

Gulf of Mexico

EQUATOR

ANTARCTICA

SOUTH

LONGITUDE SCALES
correct along parallels (concentric)

LATITUDE SCALE
correct along meridians (radial)
STATUTE 0   500   1000 MILES

NORTH POLAR AZIMUTHAL EQUIDISTANT PROJECTION

Shortest Air Distances
in nautical miles; for statute miles multiply by 1.15

ARMS, MEN, MONEY

U. S. Air Bases   ★
U. S. Naval Bases   ⚓
U. S. Ground Forces   ▢
U. S. Military Missions ◻
Countries getting
U. S. military supplies ●
Countries getting
ECA Assistance   ▣
Countries getting
Point 4 Assistance   ▥

THE LINE-UP NOV. 10, 1951

U. S. committed by
treaty to defend

U. S. otherwise commit-
ted to defend

No U. S. commitment yet

Countries trying to
be "neutral"

Iron Curtain Area

A FORTUNE MAP

prepared by RICHARD EDES HARRISON
Reproduction in FORTUNE January 1952 · Copyright 1951 TIME, Inc.

The U.S. Commitment

This map is not a fantasy of Soviet propaganda or a tax-payer's nightmare. It is a bald reality. Here is measured "The Cost of Being an American" (see page 55). Here the sweep, and the specifics (so far as security and space allow), of America's worldwide commitment. Here is the geography of an American citizenship, A.D. 1952.

The map is actually an understatement of the U.S. involvement. By mid-1952, for example, the U.S. will have 131 overseas air bases, of which some two dozen have never been publicly identified. On the map a single star designates each country (or U.S. overseas possession) in which the U.S.A.F. has one or more announced air bases. All the military information is a matter of public record.

FORTUNE has distinguished between areas the U.S. is by treaty obligated to defend; "otherwise" committed to defend (presence of U.S. troops, or statements of U.S. officials); and not yet committed to defend. Among the last are many places, e.g. the Belgian Congo, which we would defend. Alongside all this, of course, is our general U.N. commitment to prevent "aggression."

The map details only three major types of material aid to other nations—military supplies, ECA, Point Four. Since the end of the war, by statute or other official definition, the U.S. has in fact given away dollars under about thirty different programs. Foreign loans falling under more than twenty formal categories have been made—expectations of repayment ranging from good to nil.

NATO

The North Atlantic Treaty Organization (1949), extended last year to Greece and Turkey, now covers fourteen nations. "An armed attack against one . . . shall be considered an attack against them all."

RIO

The Treaty of Rio de Janeiro (1948) converts the oldest U.S. commitment, the Monroe Doctrine (1823), into a multilateral defense pact. Twenty countries have ratified it.

PACIFIC PACTS

Unlike Rio and NATO, our Pacific defense arrangements are written into separate treaties (1951). So far the U.S. has signed up with Japan, the Philippines, and (jointly) Australia and New Zealand. The Senate has not yet ratified.

Figure 1.2. Richard Edes Harrison, "U.S. Commitment," Fortune, 1952 (Courtesy of the Geography & Map Division of the Library of Congress, by permission of the Estate of Richard Edes Harrison)

from New York through Nova Scotia, Newfoundland, and onto Ireland, connecting the continents' interests and lessening the impact of the wide Atlantic expanse. In terms of strategy and ideology, such perspectives place Canada in the forefront of American interests, as a kind of gateway to other parts of the world, and hence the conception of manifest destiny becomes much more global in scope on the page.

The introduction to Harrison's "Atlas for the U.S. Citizen," entitled "The U.S. and the World" and written by the *Fortune* editors, is a telling description of how air-age perspectives framed a multifaceted internationalism. Predating America's entry into World War II, the article equates the new perspective of a shrinking world as a kind of call to arms and reveals the way in which Harrison's perspectives were situated:

> At last, however, the great awakening may be upon us, and we may be prepared to demand that the realism we love so well in lesser spheres now rules our thought in the larger spheres where our fate will be determined. Such realism may show us that we are as unique in the world and as alone as we were in 1840. But realism cannot end there. For realism does not fulfill itself in mere recognition of facts. After recognition, realism leads to action, to a true change; and when the change has occurred, then the realistic view is different from what it was before. If, for instance, recognizing our weakness, we proceed to make ourselves strong, then a realistic view of the world may lead us to foreign policies that we cannot now consider. . . . And so, facing our loneliness, we may also recapture our old aggressive spirit. . . . For the atlas, which these maps make up, is so designed that the citizen of the U.S. may here, with the whole world before him, begin to make manifest to himself the outlines of his nation's destiny.[134]

Thus, while the word *realism* is used here, its implications are much broader than only maintaining a balance of power: the modern internationalism brings forth a new manifest destiny that prizes a relational, interpretive vision of world space. The strategist can remake the world. The classic realist operated out of an acceptance of weakness and aloneness as natural condition; here this loneliness is seen as a construct that can be disputed by use of the right perspective.

In much of Harrison's work, this new internationalism visually projects interdependence and cooperation as a possible goal. The aerial view of Europe in the "Atlas for the U.S. Citizen" makes this call for internationalism most poignantly. The map uses Newfoundland as its vantage point at the center bottom of the map, with England serving as a center point (the equator becoming a vertical arc, rather than its traditional horizontal position).[135] Hovering right above England is an imposing Germany with the gigantic expanse of the USSR immediately to the left, its girth stretched all the way off the map's frame. Turkey, Syria, and Palestine sit at the top of the sphere, making the Middle East a strategic location on the horizon. At the bottom, Harrison also lists strategically specific American cities such as Botwood (New Hampshire), New York, Philadelphia, Washington, D.C., Atlanta, and Mobile next to an arrow pointing off the map, again bringing the affairs of the Old World into American sights. The inclusion of Botwood and Mobile indicates that Harrison was interested in bringing the universal into the American home. Small cities and towns were just as strategic in disseminating the new air-age geographic information as were conventional points like New York and Washington, D.C., suggesting that Americans share cultural geographic similarities and an inherent unity with other places in the world. As the caption points out, "Since the Farewell Address of President Washington the U.S. has been trying to avoid entangling alliances with these foreign countries, and to live in isolation behind the Atlantic. Yet Europe has been somehow involved in every major war of the U.S., and 30,000 Americans lie buried in Flanders."[136] The caption supplements the immediacy drawn into the lines of the map and adds an emotional element to the calls for abandoning isolationism. These ideas reiterate the internationalist view that Europe is a central American concern and that our influence in the European arena must be a function of a commonsense perspective.

Finally, Harrison revisualizes global transformation by highlighting how strategy now involves the spread of communication, economics, and culture, and not simply political and military assets. For example, the gnomonic style of projection exhibits some of the greatest distortions of any type of cartographic projection. But Harrison praises it as "probably the most accurate map . . . of the communication lines of the modern world, for its weird stretchings of familiar shore lines are present to achieve one objective, true great-circle direction. Any straight line on the map is a great circle and therefore the shortest route between any two points."[137] In his "Great Circle Airways" map, Harrison's gnomonic projection with a north polar center encompassed and visually displayed all of the world's "great" powers and represented a large proportion of the world's strategic routes of communication.[138] The north polar gnomonic captures the interconnectedness (and interdependence) of nation-states in a wartime context, giving the feeling of mutuality and prizing communication as a new fulcrum of strategy.[139]

Other maps in Harrison's archive illustrate the importance of both industrial and commercial air interests in this new era, evidencing that the new internationalism was not simply a function of traditional state power. For example, the striking, elaborate "World According to Standard (N.J.)," from *Fortune* in 1940, argues about the complex embroilment of the Standard Oil Company of New Jersey in World War II.[140] A tangled flow of thick, colored lines and directional arrows connect an icon of Standard's oil fields in Texas to factories in New Jersey and Illinois and then to strategic points all over the earth, from Canada to Venezuela, Great Britain, Romania, and then far East to Indonesia. The more important the region is to oil production and the company's potential profit, the larger it is projected on the map, thus making for a distorted world as seen through the eyes of an oil company executive. An accompanying chart shows a collection of national flags made proportional to the size of that country's Standard tanker fleet tonnage, with the United States dwarfing the others. It is also telling that Harrison was hired to create a world map for Pan Am in 1946 (fig. 1.3): a Harrison-style globe is rendered in blue-gray with crisscrossing deep-red spiderlike lines all over the map showing the airline's routes across the entire globe.[141] In a postwar map such as this one, the American global transport of air weaponry is replaced by the transport of American capital. Such a point is a poignant demonstration of the complexities of the burgeoning air-age internationalism, as visualized in cartography: the spread of soft power, carried by technologies like oil tankers, airplanes, and later satellites, is infused into conceptions of global space. Increasingly in the early Cold War, the power of U.S. private corporations to frame world spaces greatly expanded, particularly in the moves toward development ideologies of so-called Third World nations in the wake of decolonization. The maps' aerial perspectives and choices of projection connote a sense of rolling, inevitable movement above space, and visually mediate the new movement of capital, technologies, and "ideas" that came out of the shift to liberal American globalism at midcentury.

Harrison's Legacy

The entire corpus of Harrison's World War II maps acknowledges that a world of new proximities could certainly bring empire-thirsty armies closer to the United States but answers that it is the transcendent power of American perspective that can transform world space. There is a certain irony in the fact that Harrison bemoaned the "too-long-forgotten realities of world geography," even as his novel cartographic perspectives were

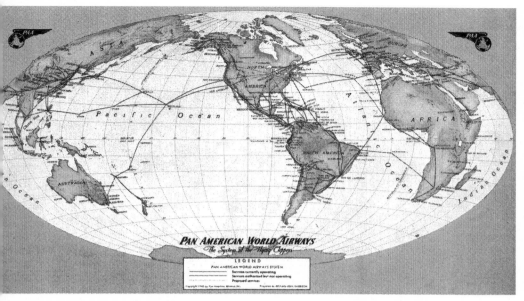

*Figure 1.3. Richard Edes Harrison, "Pan American World Airways," 1946
(Courtesy of the Geography & Map Division of the Library of Congress, by permission
of the Estate of Richard Edes Harrison)*

part of the kind of abstraction that modern internationalism needed—the air-age detachment of seeing the earth unfold in front of you, from the standpoint of one's own particular interests.[142] The realities of world geography were shapable, according to the sheer variety of perspectives that Harrison offered.

Despite Harrison's pursuit of a realistic picture of the world, he was more than aware of the ironic conundrums cartographers face in making necessary distortions. For example, his archive contains a diary with sketches and notes for an unfinished book he was writing in the early 1940s called "The World is Round-O!," and it speaks to his recognition of the discursive nature of cartography. Harrison writes: "This book is subtitled a treatise on maps, but it is really about the skin of a spherical object and man's painful efforts to take the hide off the sphere and spread it flat so that the pattern of it still remains recognizable."[143] By reminding viewers of the discursivity of maps through his dramatic emphasis on perception, Harrison takes the map out of its traditional role as an impartial display of states and geographic information, in a sense challenging the old classic metaphor that the "map is the territory."[144] In the process, however, Harrison reifies the power of the new map in the sense that *all* is now strategic, with his cartographic perspectives and projections displaying new vulnerabilities, strengths, and proximities. Harrison is caught in the tension between textualizing the world and revealing its artifice, caught between concealing the map's construction and making it a naturalized instrument of liberal foreign policy and strategy.

These tensions were borne out by some of Harrison's own work in the years following the end of World War II. The State Department would continue to consult with Harrison after World War II ended, and the fact that he was drafted to produce maps for General George Marshall's report to the secretary of war on the victory in 1945 does indicate that his perspectives were being appropriated at high levels of policy making crucial to early Cold War strategy.[145] But it was still within the popular realm where Harrison would adapt his work to a new uncertain international context. His map of the USSR's first atom bomb for *Life* in 1949, for example, took the global orthographic projection and showed a series of concentric circles around a small mushroom cloud radiating destruction across the globe.[146] "The Communist Fastness" (fig. 1.4), from *Fortune* in 1950, repurposed the polar perspective of World War II to show the menacing proximity of the new world force. Harrison also refashioned his "Europe from the East" to present it as "Satellites in Arms," in Leland Stowe's 1951 *Life* article of the same name, which details the extent of Soviet influence through railroads and waterways for transporting weapons and mobilizing forces throughout Eastern Europe.[147] Veinlike red lines wind their way all over the continent, using the Soviet-eye perspective to show the anxiety of the Soviet Union's vantage point of power. His "Fatherland Is Again Divided" map for *Life* in 1954 revived his classic perspective approach in a large-scale rendering of a split Germany as seen from an imagined height over the Mediterranean.[148] The ease with which Harrison's World War II–era productions were adapted to the strategic environment of the Cold War is important—his maps' sense of projection and perspective transcended their specific origins and his cartographic style ably spatialized a new set of international values.

A poignant example of the values, and ideological contradictions, of Harrison's brand of air-age globalism comes out of his works' contentious relationship with the principle of manifest destiny. In 1947, in the same year that President Harry S. Truman spoke doctrinally of a new manifest destiny in the fight against communism, the second edition of the *New Compass of the World* appeared, with Richard Edes Harrison listed as a coeditor. The introduction to the classic geopolitics text, credited to Harrison, Weigert, and Vilhjalmur Stefansson, reads as follows:

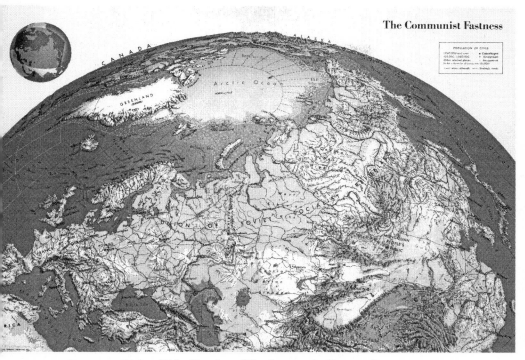

*Figure 1.4. Richard Edes Harrison, "The Communist Fastness," Fortune, 1950
(Courtesy of the Geography & Map Division of the Library of Congress, by permission
of the Estate of Richard Edes Harrison)*

We are aware of the "dangerous beginnings of an American geopolitics, with blueprints for American imperialism riding the waves of the future." In 1943, we described its aims as "disillusioned balance-of-power solution on the basis of regional groupings, in preparation for what the sponsors of such 'realistic' plans consider inevitable: the Third World War." We feel the same way today, four years after. In fact, we realize more strongly than before the challenge to a geography which may have to teach both some science and some history, to raise its calm voice and to warn against the false values of a new Manifest Destiny based on geographical truths.[149]

America's ideological expansion during the 1940s, as seen in these differing conceptions of modern manifest destiny, saw Richard Edes Harrison caught in an air-age ambivalence around America's global power. In Harrison's wake, the politicization of air space continued. The very contestability of the air's supposed potential for international transcendence is best evidenced by the Soviet Union's famous downing of Francis Gary Powers's U2 spy plane in May 1960; the "perspectives" from air space developed into highly charged Cold War struggles for power and far from the simply abstract. John Cloud's historical work on Cold War geography, for example, has noted the increasing sophistication of air technologies to provide maps for the highest levels of Cold War classification; the pilot's human eye (and thus the cartographer's as well) was replaced by the mechanical eye of the satellite in determining the spaces for national interest.[150] In addition, as geographer William Bunge's radical appropriations of Harrison-style perspectives during the 1980s Cold War resurgence made clear, the airplane's small world was made infinitely smaller by the programmable nuclear missile.[151] Thus, the art of the amateur journalist-cartographer in World War II sketched the beginnings of a dramatic transformation of speed and distance that would come to frame the Cold War.

It is no wonder that Richard Edes Harrison's captivating yarn about his pursuit of an elusive albatross in the society pages of the *New Yorker* appeared almost exactly one year before Khrushchev erected the symbolic manifestation of the iron curtain through the center of Berlin. Now, in a post–Cold War landscape, a world where globalism has transformed into globalization, and money and information technology change the very definition of transportation, Harrison's compelling calls for fresh perspectives remain important (and still eye-catching). By 1961, his beloved albatross had in an important sense become an iron one.

THE CARTOGRAPHIC TRANSITION TO COLD WAR

Recalling Harrison's role in articulating a new cartographic perspective demonstrates how cartography during World War II and the immediate postwar period highlighted the perspective of vision, the means of the map, as being just as important as the content of the map itself. In the process, Harrison revealed that perception and interpretation are key influences on, in Olson, Finnegan, and Hope's terms, "audiences' practices of looking."[152]

Examining the rhetoric of cartography during the air-age period offers an opportunity to reflect on how visuality was intertwined with American values. From an American perspective, the world was (re)imagined from a host of different academic, popular, and government perspectives, and each of these perspectives informed and constrained the others. Such perspectives support Klaus Dodds's theory that the intertwining of practical, formal, and popular geopolitical reasoning in the Cold War created inter-pretive dispositions in how the world was read and how the globe was rendered as a platform for action.[153] The development of postwar foreign policy reflects the complex solidification of the new air-age globalism's spatial tenets. As John Lewis Gaddis has hinted, any serious student of policy could hardly see every point on the earth as equally strategic; yet the new ideology of requiring a constantly shifting perspective would dra-matically enlarge the field of what would be considered part of strategy. Postwar administrations had all accepted in some form a world of diver-sity, and a future in which America remakes the world in its image was not considered realistic or even ideal.[154]

The problem, though, was that another view prevailed during this period—the view that America was the only power to enforce such diver-sity; thus all threats became more threatening, and all interests became even more vital. As the draftees of NSC-68 wrote, "In a shrinking world, which now faces the threat of atomic warfare, it is not an adequate objec-tive merely to seek to check the Kremlin design, for the absence of order among nations is becoming less and less tolerable. This fact imposes on us, in our own interests, the responsibility of world leadership. It demands that we make the attempts, and accept the risks inherent in it, to bring about order and justice by means consistent with the principles of free-dom and democracy."[155] NSC-68 envisioned Cold War America in a future position of declining strength—and saw that position as unacceptable. The document sought to amplify the sense of moral stakes as well as to situate America's Cold War as an active, ongoing display of strength—an accentuation of "means" and image, and a move away from classic real-ism. Gaddis writes of this emergent attitude that the "the effect had been to push the United States into universalism by the back door: the defense of diversity in what seemed to be a dangerous world had produced most of the costs, strains, and self-defeating consequences of indiscriminate glo-balism."[156] Thus, perception equaled reality, and the entire traditional idea of strategy being a "calculated relationship of ends and means" was trans-formed into a paradigm where means and process were of greater impor-tance than ends and objectives.[157] Threats against America, however large or small, began to determine interests, and this certainly worried a realist like George Kennan, who speculated wishfully in a 1954 Princeton lec-ture that "international life would be quieter and more comfortable . . . if there were less of sentimentality, less eagerness to be morally impres-sive."[158] Post–World War II internationalism, however, moved on from his realist acceptance of conflict and disharmony; the perspective from the "iron albatross" attempted to transcend such conflict with better vantage points. And with threats and opportunities present from any angle on the globe, a cycle of American overextension was set in place—the kind that encouraged a theater like Vietnam to become, for liberal policy makers, a symbol of American power and credibility.

The flexibility of air-age visual rhetoric thus mediated a move toward a fairly fixed worldview that would come to mark at least the early days of the Cold War conflict. And the ways in which these worldviews came to frame the visions of foreign policy makers and institutions of national security become especially important to the story of the Cold War. Maps would come to absorb the air-age global values of popular cartographers like Harrison; in turn, agencies like the Department of State, especially, would draw on cartography to synthesize, compress, and articulate the opportunities and vulnerabilities of American power in the face of an emerging "superpower" enemy. These maps would project how the very tensions of realism and idealism, truth and value, art and science, means and ends were also bound up in the way American foreign policy makers "fixed" these new worldviews in a time of transition.

2

ONE WORLD OR TWO?

Mapping a New Foreign Policy in the
Transition to Cold War

In April 1945 the war on the western front was at its end, and Floyd Hough was sent looking for maps. Postwar planning was in full effect; Allied forces were scrounging all over Europe for highly sensitive intelligence that would facilitate such planning. Hough was a U.S. Army geodesist, leading a special unit for the Military Intelligence Division of the Office of Chief Engineers. Geodesy, an earth science concerning the accurate measurement of the shape and roundness of the earth, had fascinated scientists for centuries, but the air-age military context made the accurate shape of the earth (particularly for bomber routes and the delivery of missiles) a more urgent concern. Hough's team was moving through Germany in "cloak and dagger fashion," according to *Life*, directed to steal maps and geodetic survey information from a host of abandoned German university archives and institutes, when Hough received intelligence about a massive cache of military maps captured from the Russians by Germany.[1] His team located the stash in an old warehouse in the village of Saalfeld and found a rich trove of military data that was well beyond expectations. But Saalfeld was scheduled for transfer to the Russian zone; the legend is that Hough quickly commandeered a group of U.S. artillery trucks and filled them with the contents of the archives, with the last truck just loaded on one side of the village as Soviet tanks rolled in on the other side.

The Hough team's findings "would change the course of the Cold War."[2] Hough's infiltration of contested space to capture classified Soviet knowledge became a kind of heroic, geographic "explorer" narrative for the increasingly technologized and abstract charting of Soviet territory. Hough's story was often featured in public coverage of Cold War cartography: a *Life* article from 1956, on "the missile-era race to chart the earth," lionizes Hough for using clandestine knowledge of the earth to advance Cold War objectives. *Life* reported a later incident at a conference in Russia where Hough was speaking: "One Russian delegate eyed the American with cold politeness. 'We have heard a lot about you, Mr. Hough,' he said."[3] America's ability to penetrate Soviet and Eastern bloc space, with reliable accuracy, was Hough's enduring Cold War legacy, and the U.S. government would come to use this knowledge itself as a weapon. The findings produced foundational data for geodesy, photogrammetry, and cartography for the next twenty-five years. Over the course of the Cold War, military cartographers and earth scientists converted the information into a standardized set of coordinates for points all over the heart of the Eurasian landmass, which aided the development of satellite reconnaissance technologies sponsored by the army, navy, and air force and was used for intelligence by the Central Intelligence Agency and the Department of State.[4] This work also led to a coordinated effort by the U.S. government to standardize international cartographic policies so that Cold War strategic allies could benefit from the same spatial information about the Soviet Union.[5] On the one hand, Hough represented the last vestiges of the traditional geographic explorer, the pioneer who risks his safety in order to triumphantly chart new spaces. On the other hand, his mission posed a new role for cartography that would increase during the postwar era—the "hailing" of geography as a basis for state intelligence in international conflicts and a site for crucial integrations between the U.S. government, the military, and the academy.[6]

My concern, though, is not about Hough or his findings, but rather about the kinds of transitional spaces in which government cartographic policies were conceived and executed—the kind of context in which an actor like Hough could achieve notoriety. The strategic use of maps had dramatically increased during World War II, and the world was fast becoming a field of strategy that could be read as a whole text. These popular air-age perspectives were filtered through the U.S. government's institutional lens, with profound implications for the ways particular agencies converged geospatial data to situate American power around the globe. John Cloud writes of these essential shifts for mapping in the Cold War, noting the immense "expansion in the scope and activities of federal cartographic and intelligence agencies," driven especially by new technologies that could closely monitor the threat of nuclear war.[7] World regions became "part of geopolitical Cold War imperatives," and thus cartographic science was forged by interactions through scientists, military, industry, and the state in order to meet common strategic goals.[8] Fighting the Soviet Union required the power to construct spatial knowledge of the entire earth with the utmost precision.

Maps are not simply images—they are abstractions, refiguring material spaces into bounded symbols of colors and lines and creating a unique world apart from the space they supposedly depict. Between those lines is, of course, an array of power relations between mapmaker and map interpreter.[9] As Henri Lefebvre remarks, spaces are not natural givens that we inhabit but are produced by cultural forces in a continuous process of creation.[10] Often, it is the elites or experts of a society that produce what Lefebvre called "representations of spaces," or the politicized practices that construct and abstract spatial relations.[11] Thus maps are continually bound up in these processes of representation, as visualizations made by powerful forces that argue space into being.[12] The development of modern internationalism in American culture is one such "representation of space." The case of Richard Edes Harrison manifests the premium placed on the value of new perception. This development in perception had substantial foreign policy repercussions on the character of America's new internationalism during World War II and into the Cold War. John Lewis Gaddis noted that it was often the perception of power and credibility that determined strategy, thus creating a tension between the need for clear and scientific spatial information about the world and the acknowledgment that a particular image of America needed constant reinforcement.[13] In this chapter, the ways in which certain institutional elites in power navigated these expectations of art and science, between "truth" and vision, are brought to the foreground. Maps constrained the form of perception by which the Cold War would be waged, and so, not only the finished maps but the ways in which the collaborators in government agencies, military institutions, and the academy conceived of cartography's opportunities and limitations are important. These actors saw and sketched the Cold War in certain ways and also circulated those constructions into a host of contexts; their representations of space form the basis of this chapter.

After discussing how the new mapping culture of the new air-age globalism framed the development of government cartography and its technologies, I consider specifically the Department of State's use of cartography in postwar policy design through the wartime and postwar work of S. W. Boggs, the department's Official Geographer from 1923 to 1954. Like Harrison, Boggs often idealistically absorbed his time's geographic imagination as manifested in new flexibilities of global mapping. But as a representative of the U.S. government, Boggs's cartography was also beholden to the shifting institutional necessities of a foreign policy apparatus that sought a blueprint for a postwar world. While Boggs, like Harrison, promoted the new air-age flexibilities, he was also constrained by his role as a government technician and the new institutional necessities of a foreign policy culture that sought a blueprint for a postwar world. Government cartographers were especially caught between the idealism of the one world and the chance for international scientific cooperation to map the earth and the reality of the U.S. government's need for maps to help strategically "contain" hostile spaces. Boggs's cartographic output navigates these essential tensions, and sheds a revealing light on the spatial transition of the U.S. government during the postwar and Cold War eras.

U.S. FOREIGN POLICY AND THE IMPLICATIONS OF AIR-AGE GEOGRAPHY IN THE EARLY COLD WAR

The air-age approach in the development of America's spatial values, operating as it did in such a charged context as world war, hinted at a kind of idealism, as if with the new premium on fluidity and "atmosphere" Americans could somehow fly away from borders, nationalism, and war machines. In practice, however, the shift to globalism was less about transcending such concerns and more about reenvisioning them. Geographer Neil Smith points to a crucial reconception of space, concurrent with the new perspectives from the air, where absolute geography (seeing spaces as a preexisting identity—that space "is") shifted to a relational geography where distance is relative and space is constituted socially.[14] The act itself of *seeing* global space was critical here, opening up the world to new interdependences that required constant, vigilant management.[15] For example, Paul Smith, writing for the American Congress on Surveying & Mapping in 1954, championed legibility as the defining need of aviation-related maps, with the dramatic expansion of scale controlling "the amount of legible material that can be shown."[16] During that same congress, Albert Lieber recounted a popular maxim of the air-age era that "an Army without maps is an Army without eyes," thus noting the importance of a map's ocular function in the exercise of U.S. power.[17]

New, interdependent spatial relationships meant that transportation fluidly connected capital and communication networks, and the realist power politics that bounded the nation-state as the key political unit was challenged.[18] In geopolitical terms, realism posited that "it was the natural environment and the geographical setting of a state which exercised the greatest influence on its destiny."[19] But air-age perspectives signaled a key change: geographers no longer had to travel the land in order to describe its contours; the power of the airplane challenged such expertise, privileging the technological means by which the perspective was obtained. The Hough narrative, for example, was largely about the act of amassing forbidden data and using that information in the service of sophisticated (and increasingly classified) technologies. Thus, the perspective of those with access to such technologies was also privileged, giving a new power to liberal government strategists' reading of the world. FDR's principal geographic consultant (and adviser to Woodrow Wilson at Versailles) Isaiah Bowman was a clear representative of the appropriation of relational power politics into a modern, liberal framework.[20] Bowman upheld a kind of "interpretive turn" in understanding world space: "It is often said that geography does not change. In truth geography changes as rapidly as ideas and technologies change; that is, the *meaning* of geographical conditions changes."[21]

For Bowman, and many air-age political geographers, there was no natural balance of power in the world but rather a contestable field of space constituted by ideas. "Geography, like history and politics," Bowman noted, "is a discipline by which we can better understand 'power'" and "if we are wise we shall focus our attention on the unending process of readjustment among the many, rather than on a temporary condition of balance among the few."[22] To Bowman, that process revolved around the idea of "liberty," which he argued was America's ultimate object. As a geographer, liberty meant a restless condition of national spaces across the world always striving toward improvement and openness; the old "balance of power" approach to geopolitics, he thought, rendered these spaces as static areas for control. Liberty, in other words, was an ideational force that, for Bowman, was irresistible once regions all over the world had a taste for it. In this way, Bowman was making geography part of an ideological and moral strategy, transcending the pure power politics of the balance-of-power approach.[23] In terms of cartography, this power of liberty came from the ability to *get a better perspective* and hinted that the way to spread such a force was to see that world clearly (and, in Bowman's terms, "freely"—the ability to have one's own unfiltered perspective was what elevated America, for him, above its Soviet counterpart). Maps could then become the vehicle of visualization for these ideas. Because of the institutional and academic reach of figures like Bowman, geography was advancing beyond the thorough regional description prized by titans of the field such as Richard Hartshorne and became much more globally politicized, and idea-centered, in the halls of the Departments of State and Defense.[24]

As Frank Ninkovich has noted, during this shift to an interpretive kind of internationalism, American policy makers suffered from a condition that was "the opposite of dyslexia: incoherence inhered in the text rather than in the minds of the readers."[25] The rhetorical world of air-age globalism fit this condition. It did not mean changing the liberal modernist approach to progress; it meant finding new ways to perceive where that incoherence was, in this case from a vantage point high above the earth. If the globe was seen textually rather than as some fixed entity, it could be molded and approached from different angles. Neglecting the balance of ends and means in the old geopolitical realism for a sharper focus on "credibility" meant that there would be constant attempts to get a more credible perception of world events.[26] As Alan Henrikson puts it, "How reliable are the mental maps by which American diplomatic and military officials navigate the world? For them, the problem of faithful representation of the world has always been an acute one."[27]

Realism was not abandoned by any means, as the development of high-level Cold War strategy and military science showed. Balancing power politics against raw, rational calculation still was integral to reading the landscape; as Richard Ashley has pointed out, realist power politics does not have to be antithetical to the liberal modern narrative and can even serve as a supplement to it.[28] But realism was indeed transformed and made much more nuanced: in George Kennan's terms, a new universalism of American interests vied against the particularism of past foreign policy, forming an essential tension of post–World War II strategy.[29] Kennan saw particularism as a sound, "geographic" approach that is "based upon real community of interest and outlook, which is to be found only among limited groups of governments, and not upon the abstract formalism of universal international law."[30] While Kennan especially found such universalism untenable because of its tendency to overstate American interests as commensurate with the rest of the non-Soviet world, his colleagues, particularly in the Department of State, saw more room for experimentation.[31] The sense of America's influence to all parts of the world hastened a rhetoric of universalism—a kind of idealized belief that U.S. security interests were in the best interests of all; and with initiatives, for example, like NSC-68, early Cold War bureaucrats and policy makers began framing the Soviet conflict as a more total war that transcended the particular regional centers of interest that consultants like Kennan still clung to.[32] One thing, though, that both the particularists and the universalists agreed on was the greater need for America to influence international public opinion—"other" means to wage war. It is no wonder that maps were an important part of these means for mediating public opinion; political maps anchoring America and its expanding commitments into a global network made international entanglement seem commonsense and necessary.

With this new focus on flexibility, and the power of strategic perception in reading the earth, came the inevitable anxieties about having the right expertise and technologies to make such judgments. For example, Leonard Wilson reflected on his experiences in the Map Division of the Office of Strategic Services during the war and was haunted by what he saw as inadequate cartographic training and methods, especially against the sophistication of European geographers.[33] Certainly, air-age global theorists frequently critiqued German "message maps" and often prescribed map literacy for government officials and "discerning" publics. A 1944 State Department report memorandum called "An Evaluation of German Geopolitics," for example, by research analyst Herbert Block, excoriated the "geo-mania" of Hitler's influential geographer Karl Haushofer and declared that "German geopolitics is not a science; it is a slimy cluster of wishful thinking, political scheming and mendacious propaganda, interspersed with scientific facts."[34] A map was included with the report that sketches Haushofer's theory that the United States and the Soviet Union were imperialists looking to expand to South America and Southeast Asia.[35] While, of course, this theory foreshadows the bipolarities of the coming Cold War, Block dismisses such a prediction as distorted geography and "wishful as well as dreadful thinking." The research and analysis for postwar planning at institutions like the State Department were constructed in conscious response to the use of German geopolitics and were constrained by anxieties that America would reproduce Germany's pernicious use of geography. Such government discourse often ran on an implicit fear of what could emerge from mistaken interpretation and misappropriation.

As popular forums appropriated maps more than ever before, academic and government discourse around maps debated the matter of expertise in these interpretations. The director of the American Geographical Society, George Kimble, reported to the American Congress on Surveying and Mapping in 1951: "I am far from saying that all we need to give us better times and more stable economies is better maps or more surveys. What we need even more, I submit, is better map users—better men in fact. The best maps in the world and the most ambitious surveys may help us to diagnose the troubles of humanity, but it will take all the sympathy, understanding, and unselfishness of all the good men in all the parties to solve them."[36] Kimble's example of internationalism encompasses both an idealistic faith in the abilities of "good men" to interpret the world in ways that will benefit the world and a fear that maps themselves are not up to the task of presenting the globe clearly enough, especially if they end up in the wrong hands. Government geographers like S. W. Boggs would come to embody both of these inclusive and exclusive strains of the new internationalism, serving as a reminder of the complexity of America's perspective during the Cold War's formative stages.

From at least a government standpoint, maps in many ways became emblems of knowledge production, used to compress and arrange strategic information about global spaces in legible forms; but, by extension, maps also represented the power of "knowledge workers" (i.e., "good men") and the premium on cartographic expertise. To perform this knowledge-producing function, maps required more flexibility in their capacities to converge technologies (and accompanying experts) across a host of government institutions. At the American Congress on Surveying and Mapping in 1950, for example, a defense expert pointed out, "Electronic navigation, strategic bombing, amphibious operations, anti-marine warfare; and the use of radar, radio-ranging devices, and supersonic aircraft inject complex requirements for maps and charts that scarcely a decade ago would have been considered for a 'Buck Rogers' character."[37] The U.S. government would have to adapt to these new requirements in order to construct a consistent, strategic vision of the Soviet Union that could be managed and contained. They thus required cross-collaboration between U.S. groups like the Army Map Service, the Air Force, and the State Department and international institutions like the United Nations Economic and Social Council.[38] To make these collaborations effective, the business of mapping required redefinition as central to broad values of national security. As Herbert Loper, a special weapons expert and brigadier general pointed out, "Mapping . . . as an instrument of national defense cannot be circumscribed by definitions which would place it in a distinct or isolated category related only to movements and operations on a battlefield. On the contrary, its role is as broad and all inclusive as is our total capacity to maintain our national integrity."[39]

While the prospect of international and interagency collaborations was hopeful, the high stakes of national security complicated the U.S. government's ability to truly share cartographic information. In particular, continuing advancements in the theoretical world of mapping, built on the Hough findings, redefined the very notion of distance and made it much more of a contestable, guarded concept.[40] In 1956, for example, the

Army Map Service reported an astonishing finding that the world was actually smaller than what was previously thought. Using new high-precision techniques, army geodesists amassed enough information about a strategic line of points from Finland to South Africa affirming that the world was about 128 meters shorter than previously thought.[41] *Scientific American* pointed out that this development "should theoretically increase the accuracy of maps fourfold"; more importantly, as *Time* offered, "improved knowledge of the earth's size and shape will also be useful to dispatchers of long-range guided missiles."[42] Maps could no longer simply tell us the *where*; they now had to specify with certainty relationships between targets. In *National Geographic's* terms, "the *exact* distance from, say, Tallahassee to Timbuktu may suddenly become crucially important."[43] *Almost exact* was not good enough. The introduction to an air force manual on geodesy expressed this starkly: "Somewhere in an Air Force control center, alert for a warning of aggression, a man is prepared to 'push the button' which will launch powerful retaliatory weapons to the far reaches of the earth. . . . Thus, in addition to the need to develop capable and reliable weapon systems, we must answer the questions: Where? How far? In which direction?"[44]

Producing knowledge of the earth's surface and its curvature could mean the potential difference between triumph and defeat in a nuclear conflict. The "shrinking world" of Richard Edes Harrison and others in World War II had taken on new dramatic meaning. The entire historical function of cartography and geography was changing because of such developments. Now we could know the important strategic points in the Soviet Union without having to actually invade its borders. That kind of abstract spatial management continued to mark the duration of the conflict.[45] As *Life* put it, "The most surprising solution which the geodesists have found to the problem of mapping the earth is simply to ignore the earth as it is. They have learned to distrust its outward physical look and to devise a theoretical world of their own devoid of all natural wonders."[46] In a sense, the world could more easily be flattened to a series of "inanimate platforms" for strategy.[47]

To properly place America in relationship to the Soviet Union required continuing advances in reconnaissance and surveillance from far above the earth. Aerial photography for cartography and the increasing use of satellites to do such work provides an important example here. Stephen Bocking argued that shifts in observational technology from the air defined the Cold War in the late 1940s and 1950s: when the processing of aerial data was taken out of the field and the realm of subjectivity and into the laboratory, mapping became less about local knowledge and more about interpretation of data.[48] In addition, a premium on secrecy and controls on access to the air began to constrain these developments. President Dwight Eisenhower's public "Open Skies" proposal of 1955 suggested that NATO and Warsaw Pact nations should be able to conduct mutual, bilateral aerial reconnaissance of each other to protect from surprise attack and prepare defenses against the other's weapon systems.[49] Once Soviet premier Nikita Khrushchev rejected this proposal, efforts to develop undetectable satellite technologies for mapping and reconnaissance accelerated. These efforts resulted in initiatives like the highly classified CORONA project in 1958, which provided the first photographs of Soviet nuclear bases from an unmanned satellite orbiting the earth. Dino Brugioni has noted the redefinition of the traditional military concept of the "high ground" through such technology: "Each increase in altitude has given an ever-widening view, until humans can now envision the ultimate prospect of achieving an unlimited perspective of the universe."[50] But this expansiveness and abstraction of vision had its consequences: as General W. Y. Smith, a member of President John F. Kennedy's National Security Staff pointed out: "Sometimes we relied on CORONA's data too much. . . . We mistakenly believed that if we could see enemy targets and count them, we understood their strength and our objective. Nevertheless, we found out that wasn't the case at all."[51] Or, to put it in Cloud's terms, "once the Figure of the Earth is ubiquitous, it becomes invisible."[52]

Cartography was a central mode of knowledge production during the early Cold War, but it also framed the world for the conflict's powerful architects and ordered and clarified America's new responsibilities. This impressive campaign to expand the map was part of an ideological impulse to advance a set of values that separated America from the Soviet Union and affirmed the nation's need to bring such values to the rest of the world. The world had to be seen clearly and self-evidently to carry American interests across the globe, and maps helped to set such parameters. In the process, the pollination across government agencies, popular outlets, and academic institutions evidenced just how much maps were being militarized (even for a supposed "Cold War") as a medium for American power. The rhetorical lives of maps thus took on greater circulation and involved a much deeper sense of cross-collaboration. But these new functions for America's maps also left some potentially problematic consequences: "self-evidence" and the power of quantification could inflict a myopia around America's ability to make the world in its image.

The U.S. State Department felt these tensions acutely as it marshaled an immense amount of spatial intelligence through increasingly sophisticated technologies and played an integral role in designing international space for the volatile postwar landscape. The department's conception of geography especially represented the opportunities and constraints of the air age as maps evolved into complex managers of American interests and national security.

AMERICAN PROJECTOR: S. W. BOGGS'S CARTOGRAPHIC VISION FOR THE STATE DEPARTMENT IN THE EARLY COLD WAR

On January 21, 1947, the Department of State's official geographer, Samuel Whittemore Boggs, sent over a state-of-the-art air route globe and his own patented geometric plastic hemisphere to his new boss's office. Secretary of State George Marshall (who started his tenure on that very day), received the globe with a memo attached that read, "I hope that you will find them very useful in studying 'global relations,' some of which cannot be perceived from maps." He even offered to "replace the large Mercator map" currently in Marshall's office with either a Miller cylindrical projection world map ("with much less exaggeration in polar regions than the Mercator") or two hemisphere maps centered on France and the Pacific Ocean.[53] To Boggs, this was not merely a diplomatic welcome gesture of geographic wall and desk art: the perception of a full, accurate earth was a matter of necessity for the responsible conduct of international relations.[54] The following was his oft-used maxim:

> He who would solve world problems must understand them;
> He who would understand world problems must visualize them; and
> He who would visualize world problems should study them on the
>   spherical surface of a globe.[55]

S. W. Boggs was indeed a product of the air-age generation, where conceptions of distance and perspective were revolutionized by planes spreading bombs, money, and ideas across the earth; thus he acutely appreciated how maps do not simply reflect relationships but can sustain, shape, and challenge them.[56] Boggs's tireless proselytizing for policy makers and academics to absorb a truly round and worldwide view suggests the postwar premium on the quality of global perception.

Boggs was also animated by a central cartographic conundrum of the era, which manifested itself in his work, his publications, and even his private correspondence. While he promoted the map's possibility of expressing flexible and novel connections in a better world, he was haunted at the same time by what he called "cartohypnosis" and maps' suggestibility in a dangerous, explosive postwar landscape, informed by the pseudo-science of World War II geopolitics.[57] For example, as Boggs writes in a 1946 State Department memo, "Peace requires orderly development, which in turn necessitates a vast knowledge of the earth, its peoples, and its resources; and maps are essential in recording and presenting facts."[58] He thus prized the culture of the geographic, scientific expert in being able to teach and disseminate the "best" ways to read this changing world, and how to aptly map a sense of ordered and (often) classified knowledge.

Boggs also seemed to understand the importance of artistic license in ordering that knowledge. For example, in a letter to Richard Edes Harrison about consulting work for an animated film about maps, Boggs wrote: "I very much desire that, while the whole presentation shall be completely factual, those facts which are of extraordinary significance and striking quality will hit the audience with their full significance. We want no Hollywood stuff for good effects, unless the facts themselves call for such effects in order to be truthful."[59] In other words, cartographic realities sometimes needed extra emphasis to connect with an audience. Unlike Harrison and other commercial cartographers who might wish to make a pointed argument about war strategy, Boggs faced the added representational problem of producing maps and marshaling geographic facts for official diplomacy, and thus he confronted a heightened emphasis on accuracy and authenticity of the picture of the globe and its expanding relationships. As John Wright wrote during the heart of World War II, "The trim, precise and clean-cut appearance that a well drawn map presents lends it an air of scientific authenticity that may or may not be deserved."[60]

S. W. Boggs thus functions as a compelling bridge between the amateur, artistic, and flexible perspectives exemplified by Harrison, and the worldview of the disciplinary expert who helped the science of geographic facts become an indispensable tool of the military-government-academic complex during the Cold War. Focusing on his shifting role in the emerging Cold War through his postwar mapping projects (until his death in 1954) and their inventional processes can provide a snapshot of the strategic functions and priorities and the ideological commitments of the State Department's geographic practice, as well as Boggs's unique place within these often competing forces. This snapshot serves to represent the larger relationships of artistic vision, scientific authority, and the powers of abstraction in state-powered mapping and to draw out the rhetorical life of cartography as it circulated through the institutions that were active in building the spaces of the Cold War that would sustain it for forty more years. Boggs, in many ways, exemplifies the kinds of anxieties that faced the postwar's spatial architects and foreign policy makers, and shows that these kinds of anxieties plagued not just the leaders at the top but those involved in the everyday practices of charting and classifying the world.

The Office of the Geographer of the United States, Department of State

The Office of the Geographer at the State Department was commissioned in 1921, a direct result of the Paris Peace conferences. In the heady days of post–World War I global reorganization and its new geographic partitions and boundaries, numerous maps were produced. The Department of State established an office responsible for cataloging and providing access to these maps for foreign policy makers and their staffers. Colonel Lawrence Martin, an integral part of the Military Intelligence Division during World War I, was chosen as a member of President Wilson's retinue in Paris. Because of his central role in drafting treaty maps, he was assigned to lead the new division at State, not only to classify and log the maps but also to provide technical advice on boundary disputes.[61] As geographer Lewis Alexander has noted, "From its inception the Office served as a central point . . . for the handling of material relating to political control of territory throughout the world."[62] When Martin transferred to the Map Division at the Library of Congress, Boggs was chosen for the job at the State Department. He was influenced by Martin's idealism and the wave of geographic leaders that were part of the Paris generation—men like Isaiah Bowman and Columbia University's Douglas Johnson.[63] Boggs would become most renowned as one of the government's foremost boundary experts—an early pioneer in the academic discipline of political geography.[64]

At the height of the division's influence toward the end of World War II, the staff was close to ninety strong. This group, though, did not include the increased number of people working under contract on State Department geographic projects through the American Geographical Society in New York, the Office of Population Research at Princeton University, and the Office of Foreign Agricultural Relations in the Department of Agriculture.[65] The division housed a research branch containing sections in population, agriculture, minerals, power/industry, and transportation and a cartographic branch with sections in planning/editing, program maps, and special maps.[66] Part of Boggs's responsibility was to establish constant rapport with the various other cartographic branches of the government, particularly in the War Department. Specifically, one of Boggs's main functions was in "future geography," anticipating the world of states after

World War II ended and conceiving of America's place in a new world.[67] Thus, clarity of vision was central to his leadership of the division. As he wrote in a 1943 memorandum, "In order to see world problems in global relationships, the emphasis, throughout, is on seeing things *whole*, in perspective. The distribution of peoples and resources is being considered . . . impartially . . . formulated to achieve optimum development of every portion of the earth, for the benefit of all people everywhere. Any qualifying assumptions would add confusion by introducing artificial and temporary factors into the picture."[68] The importance of vision seemed in direct relation to Boggs's emphasis on the usability of maps produced under his direction; if his job was, as he put it, "intended to be of maximum practical assistance to the principal policy-making officers of the Department of State," then his mapping program needed to constantly adapt to the rhetorical needs and values of his audience.[69]

Boggs was aware of the challenges he faced in leading such an office during an era of great geographic upheaval. In a 1943 progress report from his division, Boggs spoke of the problems of trying to meet requests for "spot research" while still executing long-term research and analysis of geographic data, writing that "it should be recognized that many individual maps and research studies can not be executed in less time than several months."[70] In a time when boundaries and partitions were in constant flux, this became a constraint (and frustration) on Boggs's ethic of thorough, well-researched mapping. As seen in Harrison's case, World War II and the ensuing postwar years were marked by a new journalistic paradigm where maps were continually drafted to make arguments about world problems, and Boggs was certainly influenced by (and contributed to) this new rapid-fire style of "keeping up" with world problems through maps. At the same time, Boggs was part of an older guard, a culture of the "gentleman geographer" where the expectation was that smart, reasonable men looking at the facts of a round earth had the capability of making the best possible decisions. He emerged from a tradition of geography as a kind of semihard science related to geology, a discipline that Terry Eagleton once referred to as "maps and chaps."[71] Boggs was part of the new geographic vanguard to expand the visualization of the world through new patterns and relationships but also part of an attempt by state "experts" to amass immense amounts of geographic facts about the world.

After World War II, there was a significant restructuring of Boggs's division at the Department of State. Staff was cut, and the division's function morphed into a more advisory capacity as it was moved to the intelligence sections of the State Department (from its original place in the

Division of Public Affairs).[72] Government cartography was spread across an array of institutions, some open, some closed, and State Department cartographers and geographers became primarily researchers and intelligence gatherers. At the same time, academic geography was on the wane, as pioneering departments of geography, like Harvard University's, were closing.[73] As Neil Smith has persuasively pointed out, this was a time when geographic thinking was at its most influential, yet also paradoxically at its most denied. In other words, the more important geography became and the more access to its maps became widespread, the more people thought they could somehow transcend geography.[74] Boggs's worldview and his position symbolized the architecture of postwar American spatial perspectives in the tumultuous transitional period from World War II to the Cold War.

The Form of Roundness: New Projections and Perspectives in Boggs's Cartographic Discourse

"Projection" itself was a highly charged term during this period, as it obviously carried geographic connotations of the need for technical accuracy in devising a vision of the world. Projection also spoke to the translation of new power relationships on a global scale—that, in a sense, the right projection was of paramount importance because it predicted what future geographic problems and solutions might need solving. The map needed to contain these relationships and manage them, and the choice of projection set such parameters. Boggs was part of a movement, in which cartographic style was widely accepted as a conscious rhetorical choice, and audience played a more important role.

Boggs believed that his job required emphasizing the weight of such choices; in fact, he was no latecomer to the air-age interest in devising ways to project new relationships.[75] Early on in his tenure as State Department geographer, in 1929, Boggs presented a paper to Britain's Royal Geographical Society in which he advanced his own new formal projection for maps. Called the equal-area "eumorphic" projection, Boggs's innovation makes for a rounder earth on the flat page and is an explicit corrective on how the shape of the Northern Hemisphere is enlarged by the Mercator.[76] As he points out, "With man's growing desire to 'see the world whole,' the use of maps of the entire globe is increasing. The properties most desired in world maps . . . are the representation of the shape of large areas as accurately as possible, and areas in their true proportions."[77] Boggs's new map shows the full earth in one sphere with an elongated equator. Its plainest difference from traditional maps is the enlarged size of Africa, centered and prominent, and a sprawling Southeast Asia that is stretched in unfamiliar ways. As he says in the notes to the map,

> It will be noticed that the more densely populated regions of the northern half of the eastern hemisphere (Eurasia and Northern Africa) have a peculiar relationship to latitude. The fact is that greater human importance attaches to the parts of Eastern Asia which lie *below* 40° north latitude, whereas in the west, practically all of Europe lies *above* 40°. Approximately half of the world's population lives in Asia between latitudes 10° and 40°, and it would therefore appear highly desirable to preserve the shape of the land areas of China, Japan, and India as accurately as possible.[78]

Thus, through his restructuring of the relationships between land and population, Boggs hints that we ignore the importance of the so-called developing areas at our peril.

Boggs's attempt to strike a balance between area and shape distortion represents an increasingly idealist expectation of maps to be both scientifically accurate and socially responsible. In a subtle way, the intertwined notions of proportionality, shape, and power are put on display—notions that came to mark the global geopolitics of World War II and its aftermath in the development of the Cold War.[79] For example, his later work at the State Department in postwar planning, during World War II, bore this out: he was consulted by the Division of Cultural Relations at the State Department to advise on a high-level postwar planning program called "The Permanent Cultural Relations Program as a Basic Instrumentality of American Foreign Policy."[80] Boggs then initiated a cultural mapping program in his department, commenting to the head of Cultural Relations that "the emphasis of non-western viewpoints seems to me very fortunate. We shall expect the half of the world's population that lives in eastern and southern Asia to take a much more important place in world affairs in the near future."[81] Projects such as these acknowledged the role of maps in shaping new cultural relationships for strategic ends, a characteristic that grew in importance during the Cold War.

His eumorphic projection itself appeared periodically in State Department maps in the early Cold War, perhaps most notably in maps for Boggs's 1951 treatise on national claims in adjacent seas (fig. 2.1).[82] Each continent is outlined in various lines of red, designed to show the width of zones for waters over which sovereignty is claimed by the coastal state. In a Cold War world, the global projection was used to show the complexity of boundaries and sovereignties accompanied by text warning about "international friction" in both the jurisdiction of seabeds and air space and worrying about the "chaos from which to create a viable world of order."[83] In addition, the focus of the map becomes control over oceans rather than the land, making the point once again that it is the entirety of the earth that was moldable and shapable in the air age. This, of course, represents the increasing Cold War abstraction where natural features such as ocean and land blend together into items that evidence how "the entire Earth became a generalized space of American military strategy," according to geographers Trevor Barnes and Matthew Farish.[84]

Boggs's eumorphic projection was never widely used (although it was distributed commercially by the A. J. Nystrom Company for use in classrooms), but it clearly represents an important transitional bridge between other more popular projections such as the Miller cylindrical projection.[85] Geographer Edward J. Baar, writing in 1947, noted Boggs's direct influence in inspiring O. M. Miller of the American Geographical Society to fashion a cylinder-based world map for popular usage.[86] As Miller wrote in 1942, he attempted to find an acceptable balance that "to the uncritical eye does not obviously depart from the familiar shapes of the land areas depicted by the Mercator projection but which reduces areal distortion as far as possible."[87] The Miller projection finds its way into many different Cold War–era media, such as the United Nations' 1953 "Student Map of the United Nations," the 1965 map of the world produced by Civic Education Inc. (publishers of such educational periodicals as the *Young Citizen*), and *Scholastic Magazine*'s "Economic Map of the World" from 1966.[88] These are political maps depicting simple Cold War–era alliances, so that students in schools could locate America's commitments in a global world. They provided texture to the way many saw the postwar landscape on classroom walls and in popular magazines, and their circulation highlights the wide popular impact of the new projections.

Boggs also circulated messages around the State Department about the evils of the old-school Mercator to anyone who would listen, attempting to change the vision expressed by what was in the hands and on the walls of policy makers and military strategists.[89] For example, he was in frequent contact with the House Foreign Affairs Committee in 1947 to furnish its committee rooms with new air-route globes and Miller maps and was also continually attempting to supply various branches of the military with Mercator replacements.[90] In an almost humorous exchange between Boggs and Lieutenant Colonel Desloge Brown with the Army Corps of Engineers, the colonel responds by agreeing with Boggs's suggestion

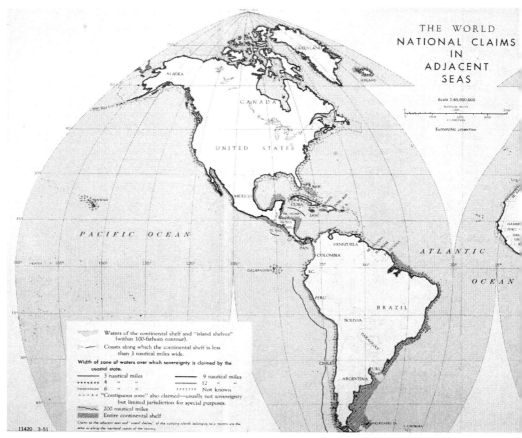

Figure 2.1. S. W. Boggs, Department of State, "The World National Claims in Adjacent Seas," Geographical Review, 1952 (Courtesy of Boatwright Library, University of Richmond)

that the Miller cylindrical map is a better one to use, but he cannot do it because they had already spent too much money printing copies of the Mercator.[91] Thus, there were economic constraints to the circulation and usage of government maps in this period, and the Mercator often prevailed because of its ubiquity and ease of access.

Boggs's mission to expand U.S. global perceptions can also be found in his project to challenge hemispheric perspectives, specifically in relation to how they constrained American strategic thinking in a postwar environment—an idea that was endemic to the air-age movement.[92] Hemispheres, of course, are a staple of American spatial thought, pervading the discourses of politics and foreign policy since at least the Monroe

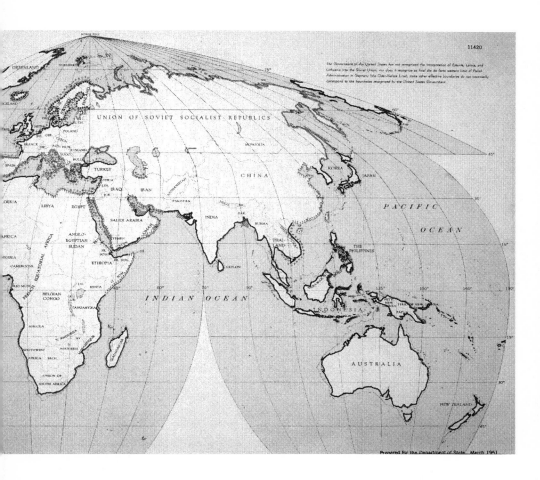

Doctrine, and later by the Roosevelt Corollary appearing after the Spanish-American War and America's occupation of the Philippines. Like other
air-age geographers, he was stepping away from the notion that placement
on a globe had some sort of natural division to it; to him, hemispheres were
constructs, slices of perspectives that made for political shorthand. In an
April 1944 memorandum sent to Secretary of State Cordell Hull, Boggs
suggests a "de-europeanization" of the government's geographic nomencla-
ture, proposing to get rid of terms such as "western hemisphere" altogether,
as well as other terminologies that use names on the basis of the direction
and distance of regions from Europe, such as "Far East." Boggs goes on to
attribute these potential symbols of insensitive diplomacy to "misconcep-
tions derived from uncritical use of maps."[93]

In an influential piece, distributed to the State Department and
appearing in the *Journal of Geography* in 1945, Boggs asked the

provocative question, "When a person speaks of 'this hemisphere' as the one in which the United States of America is located, one may well inquire, 'Which hemisphere?' "[94] Boggs also included a series of diagram maps that accompanied the text's arguments about hemispheres as often arbitrary political choices. In his maps of the "so-called Western hemisphere," he uses the rounded globe to show that the Americas are located in a hemisphere that is mostly constituted by ocean. By placing this map alongside maps of "the northern hemisphere" centered on the North Pole, Boggs plays with traditional notions of distance, as he shows U.S. proximity to Europe with a focus on the North Atlantic. Boggs notes in the text below the maps that "Dakar, Moscow, and Northern Manchuria are nearer to the center of the United States than is Buenos Aires," thus foreshadowing some of the postwar architecture of international relations.[95]

In 1954, as the Cold War was well underway, Boggs wrote in an update of his hemisphere article for the State Department: "Thus there is no human being anywhere on earth who does not live in some hemisphere that includes *all* of the United States." [96] In an emerging Cold War that was purportedly a battle between East and West, Boggs's placement of America into multidirectional relationships was a reminder of the full global reach of American responsibility; the early Cold War was marked by the division of blocs, pacts, treaties, and security alliances that were no longer partitioned according to traditional hemispheres and deterministic geopolitics, but by more fluid strategic "interests." The necessary abstraction from round earth to flat page creates a cartographic anxiety over how best to show a fuller world within limitations that are always revealing themselves. Boggs's interplay of perspective, projection, and hemisphere complicated the spatial frames of the early Cold War by which policy makers would see the world.

Boggs and the Role of Geographic Imagination in State Department Cartography

In March 1947, in response to the crisis in Greece, President Harry Truman articulated the framework of the early Cold War with his doctrine of fighting communism wherever it expands. It is fitting that, in the same month, John K. Wright published his presidential address to the American Geographical Society with the title "Terrae Incognitae: The Place of the Imagination in Geography."[97] At a time when the familiar alliances of World War II had collapsed, and colonial empires were nearing exhaustion, the new postwar globe had to be rethought and restrategized;

as Lippmann wrote, "The world that we have to deal with politically is out of reach, out of sight, out of mind. It has to be explored, reported, and imagined."[98]

Wright's provocative response to these developments proposed that geography and its visualization in maps must embrace at least a degree of subjectivity and an appreciation of what he called "aesthetic imagining," notably during an era of extraordinary distrust of any overlap between art and politics.[99] Because "geography deals in large measure with human beings, and the study of human affairs and motives has not yet reached a stage in which more than a small part of it can be developed as a precise science," Wright coined the term, "geosophy," or "the study of geographical knowledge from any or all points of view," thus widening the importance of a humanistic perspective.[100]

Boggs's work and writings embodied the humanistic-scientific tensions of a "geosophic" outlook. While geographer Denis Cosgrove referenced Boggs as a representation of "the postwar move to recapture the map for professional cartography," this simplifies too much Boggs's nuanced appreciation of map audiences and the role of subjective imagination in cartographic presentation.[101] Recall Luce's famous 1940 reimagining of the globe in air-age discourse through the "American Century" that posited globalism as a pursuit of American economic interests and a cultivation of world opinion.[102] Interestingly enough, two of the Luce empire's most prominent artistic articulators of these notions, Harrison at *Fortune* and Boris Artzybasheff, the *Time* cover portraitist and graphic artist, corresponded extensively with Boggs and the State Department during World War II and its aftermath. Artzybasheff was a Ukrainian-born illustrator who drew 215 covers (among countless other designs) for *Time* from the mid-1930s up to his death in 1965. His art was marked by a realist style of portraiture but also influenced by surrealism's grotesquery, as seen in his anthropomorphic drawings of planes with human faces.[103] Boggs was responsible for initiating partnerships between artists such as Artzybasheff and the State Department for technical cartographic advice and map production, but in the process he absorbed an appreciation of these artists' global visualization and their sense of the larger American public.

Boggs's interaction with Harrison reveals his proactive role advancing a new flexibility in the government's appreciation of spatial problems. Boggs recruited Harrison on wartime projects such as map construction for the OSS and the State Department's contribution to the Army Training Atlas. Boggs developed new techniques based on Harrison's innovation of using the nomograph in drafting maps, a device that eliminated time-consuming mathematical work and allowed the mapper to easily draw great-circle routes.[104] Harrison's skilled amateur background and his unorthodox methods were noteworthy to technicians like Boggs because of their efficiency in creating maps faster.[105] Harrison's approach energized Boggs; in their correspondence about various cartographic projects, the notion of "audience" stands out. Working together on a new system of shading and iconography for a Boggs map, for example, the two explored how novel contrasts in cartographic symbols can reveal new realities, with Boggs commenting to Harrison, "In making maps which really get across to the man on the street, and to the busy statesman or executive, perhaps these radically different shadings would result in making maps so characteristic that they would attract attention and be easily distinguishable from the run-of-the-mill products of the present."[106]

Both Harrison and Boggs also shared distaste for what Harrison termed "the air-age prophets," such as George Renner at Columbia, who sparked a fiery controversy when he drew a map for a 1942 *Collier's* article that predicted a postwar world divided into cultural zones that would replace traditional national boundaries.[107] Renner's critics were incensed that he would use the new internationalism to advance a crude cultural determinism.[108] Harrison and Boggs certainly accepted the air-age changes to cartographic practice, but they saw such changes as creating open-minded flexibility based around strategic purposes rather than as a political pseudo-science. Thus, Harrison and Boggs saw cartographers like Renner as "spreading geographic misinformation accelerando."[109]

At the same time, Boggs's acceptance of Harrison's flexibility was constrained by his notions of technical expertise. For example, when Harrison asked Boggs for expert advice on his forthcoming *Look at the World* atlas, Boggs replied:

> I believe it would be well if you were to tone down your criticisms of the geographers with reference to maps a bit. I believe the geographers have understood the world more as one does by using a globe better than you give them credit for. Their sin has been largely that they fail to see to it that the non-professional had available to him the kinds of maps that the uninitiated need in order to grasp some of the concepts that many of us want to get across. . . . You are fortunate in being associated with publishers who are not content unless they do something rather new and different.[110]

The relationship between Boggs and Harrison thus represents an implicit conception of cartography as a contingent discourse, needing experts to translate for the uninitiated but also requiring an engagement with constructive imagination to connect with multiple audiences.

Relatedly, Boggs's friendship with Boris Artzybasheff was responsible for putting a *literal* human face on the new cartographic perspectives of the air age.[111] In a 1942 letter to Artzybasheff, Boggs asks if the artist could potentially draw the head of a man on a white billiard ball, in hopes of designing a model that could show how projecting global features creates significant distortions on a flat map—in other words, flattening the nations and populations of the world is much like flattening a person's face beyond all recognition. As he points out to Artzybasheff, "What I would like to get across to the 'flat-mappers' is that when we are looking at a flat map which includes the whole world, we are looking at a caricature which is analogous to representing the face, both sides of the head, back and top of the head, and beneath the chin all on one flat surface."[112] Artzybasheff's bizarre creation makes its way into Boggs's 1954 report (fig. 2.2) to the State Department on global foreign relations as a diagram where the globe with the human head is shown split into seven different popular map projections, such as the Mercator, the Miller, and the azimuthal hemispheric projections. In each case, a distorted face shows the limits of choosing particular world projections—none of the seven projections look like a real human face.[113] There is a humanistic strain in Boggs's calls for flexibility: by taking maps out of staid, academic partitions and meridians and using human features, he was interrogating, by way of Artzybasheff's artistic outlook, the very process of vision by which we see a whole earth.[114]

Another example of Boggs's reaching beyond traditional conceptions of geography was in his work on an animated educational film, for which he served as consultant and for which he also recruited Artzybasheff.[115] The 1947 film, entitled *Expanding World Relationships*, was produced through Springer Pictures and was later distributed internationally through the United States Information Agency.[116] The picture is a fascinating midcentury artifact designed to grapple with the new global relations of the United States in a changed postwar landscape, and it emphasizes the role of perspective itself through heavy use of maps. In one production memorandum (for a scene eventually cut) to Artzybasheff, Boggs expresses his thought process in designing an appropriate air-age global perspective for educational objectives. Boggs proposes that Artzybasheff design for the film a series of scenes where aliens approach the earth from a rocket ship, gaining a "bird's-eye

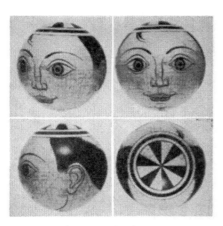

Figure 2.2. Boris Artzybasheff, Department of State, "Human Head on Geographical Globe," and "Human Head on Seven Well-Known Map Projections," Department of State Bulletin, *1954 (Courtesy of Boatwright Library, University of Richmond)*

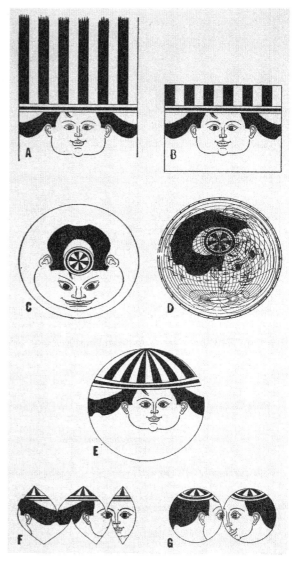

view" of the earth as they descend toward it. What the aliens find when they explore earth is a "strong indication that man may not have sense enough to organize his affairs" and "they end up with a very factual, realistic picture of the world as it is, especially as the relations between peoples in different parts of the world . . . have changed very unequally." Boggs goes on to discuss how humans must gain a better bird's-eye view and knowledge of the earth before they commit "racial suicide."[117] Here we see the brand of idealism behind

Boggs's approach—that better spatial knowledge can somehow "save" us. Boggs was also, importantly, investing in a lay audience's ability to conceive of what he saw as both the opportunity and the danger of the internationalism that constituted the postwar world. This work on what was essentially a propaganda film for advancing U.S. interest in world affairs is, of course, in tension with his own anxieties during that same time, expressed in his writing, of a "cartohypnosis" that was lulling the populace into submission.

Finally, this new focus on artistic imagination was directly related to Boggs's idea of new data that maps should incorporate. Even in the beginning stages of American involvement in World War II, one of Boggs's roles at the State Department was to anticipate U.S. mapping needs in a peacetime international environment. An early example can be found in Boggs's 1941 piece for the Association of American Geographers, produced after consultation with Richard Edes Harrison. In this piece, he proposes a new mapping program that depicts the economic and social effects of increases in the speed of travel and communication, which are matched by a decrease in transport costs. As he noted, "It is as if a quiet game of croquet had been transformed into a stirring contest of polo, with its mounted players covering a greatly enlarged field at high speed, while the game was yet in progress."[118] Four years later, Boggs produced a diagram for the State Department that extended this argument through use of a "cartogram," which, instead of making territory on a map proportional to its area, represents territory as proportional to some other chosen trait.[119] Boggs's cartogram has five world maps—one for steamship, motor truck, railroad, airplane, and primitive transport, and each map is proportioned in size so that the same linear interval spans approximately equal transport-cost on all of the maps.[120] In maps like these, Boggs substitutes the traditional ways of showing travel speeds and communication changes (like arrows and directional icons emanating from given centers or as a series of maps showing the changes over a period of time) and uses a single world map of comparisons and degrees of development that can be synthesized by the reader in one gaze. Like Wright's notion of "geosophy," Boggs understood that the air age's ever-shrinking globe brought maps into an inescapably social realm.

Artists such as Harrison and Artzybasheff were purveyors of flexibility and "fresh perception," as Harrison would call it, and their recruitment by Boggs for collaboration on State Department projects reveals the interest of the government in classifying and controlling the shape of a turbulent postwar world. Boggs was advancing a distinctly American geographic imaginary, a new kind of manifest destiny of capital and communications that could be spread throughout the earth. His air-age arguments, for example, that mapped the new speeds of transportation and the world economy found their way into the development theories and Cold War social science of liberation advanced later by Walt Rostow during the Kennedy and Johnson administrations.[121] Boggs recognized not only that was there was an artistic element in designing the postwar American world through intertextual relationships between government and journalistic mapping but that the audience, as bearer of public opinion, became central to the production of space.

Boggs's Cartographic Dualities of Idealism and Vigilance in the Early Cold War

Boggs's brand of peacetime cartographic planning took him in two different, complex directions: a pursuit of global scientific cooperation for the benefit of humanity and the vigilant guarding of geographic intelligence to advance national interests. Boggs managed both simultaneously. Throughout his work, Boggs clung to a heroically idealized vision of science. In an impassioned essay written for the American Political Science Association in 1948, he says: "To scientists, a majority vote would mean nothing. . . . They shun confusion over words. Those vague agglomerations of tradition and rationalized folkways known as 'ideologies' have no place in their deliberations. Scientists do not withhold from one another their knowledge, techniques, and equipment. . . . Why should they, when there is only one universe, one earth-world, one human race, to study?"[122] To Boggs, science could transcend the partitions (and inherent ideologies) of political boundaries; this belief found its way into his key cartographic projects of the period.

For one, Boggs was a central advocate for U.S. participation in the International Map of the World (IMW) project. The IMW was a transnational initiative that began in 1891 at the Fifth Geographical Congress in Germany. It proposed one series of maps on a uniform scale and standardized projections to cover the entire world.[123] A U.S. proposal was finally accepted, after a series of summits in 1909, that the scale of 1:1,000,000 be adopted.[124] Each participating nation would marshal its geographic resources to produce sheets of its territories to the particular specification, willingly cataloging its entire geographic mass of information into standardized units that would be shared among each other with an unprecedented level of detail. As historical geographer Michael Heffernan has pointed out, this project was meant to challenge the imperial and national foundations of cartography and use geographic fact as a basis for connecting humanity, rather than merely marking divisions.[125]

The IMW project was hampered by constant difficulties due to World War antagonisms, the lack of consensus over specifications, and the slow responses of individual cartographic agencies in each of the participating nations. Their efforts were inconsistent and intermittent; the United States essentially abandoned the project temporarily before World War I so that it could produce a 1:1,000,000 map of South America unencumbered by international agreements. For many years, the U.S. government did not even pay its dues to the IMW organization; the funding was raised by private organizations like the American Geographical Society, and only four sheets out of a needed forty were produced of America by the 1920s.[126] In short, there was an American reluctance to fully embrace the internationalism of a project that could affect its power in its own hemisphere.[127]

In the mid-1930s, Boggs embraced the project for the State Department, and he fought a losing battle to produce the IMW maps until his death in 1954. In 1936 he requested that the Bureau of the Budget secure an appropriation of $250,000 from Congress, a sum that was never granted. His rhetoric regarding the IMW was often sharp. In one memorandum that synopsized the project, Boggs noted, "The U.S. has lagged lamentably in making the map of the United States and its territories. It will require approximately 42 sheets to cover the U.S. proper. . . . It is a matter of embarrassment that the United States has done only one sheet in the last 20 years, and that it is making no progress now. . . . International comity calls for active participation by the United States in this project."[128] Accompanying these rebukes were "update" maps of IMW progress in the United States. In a 1936 world map, for example, Boggs indexed where the IMW sheets had been produced across the globe: black squares with red shading were used to indicate what parts of each continent had been mapped according to the international specifications. Hundreds of black squares cover Asia and Europe, but only four squares mark the United States. Projecting the United States as mostly a blank space on the map, Boggs indicts his own nation's disengagement with the world.[129]

Yet, despite Boggs's critique of the U.S. lack of involvement, "international comity" could not triumph over other national objectives. World War II stalled the international cooperation needed to sustain the IMW initiatives; the increasing postwar specialization of government geographers and the primacy of intelligence and security magnified the sheer administrative difficulty of both getting funding and having maps produced. Eventually, by 1951, the formerly independent IMW was transferred to a new division on cartography at the United Nations; Boggs would continue to be the U.S. adviser on the project, but aside from occasional updates, the project fell apart.[130] There would be notable attempts right up to the late 1960s by international geographers, including some in the United States, who saw value in the project, but as Pearson and colleagues point out, "A number of commentators doubted whether a single global map made any sense in a divided world where opposing superpowers controlled the cartographic agenda."[131] With the expansion of aerial photography and its utility in creating maps essentially *anywhere*, the project was bedeviled by an "excess of detail" and could never cover the world substantively from such ambitious specifications.[132] Ironically, it was the innovations of the air age itself that may have accelerated the project's demise and lessened its utility. The potential idealism of the air age bringing "one world" together was hamstrung by the sheer amount of knowledge and new technologies that could not be centralized under an international organization. Boggs and his colleagues were caught in the middle of these constraints.

The IMW map, though, did have a notable rhetorical life. The technical specifications of the IMW's scales and projections were adopted by the Army Map Service after 1945 in the extensive Map Series 1301, a staple of Cold War foreign mapping.[133] Thus, it was the U.S. Army, dedicated to advancing American objectives, that became the most successful user of the 1:1,000,000 style. In amassing intelligence for the postwar world, the IMW's techniques were appropriated, but not its values; the IMW's project was viable in mapping global relationships, but its underlying ethic of internationalism could not be sustained.[134] These security objectives required a guardedness that the IMW opposed in principle. Ironically, the adaptation of IMW specifications by the army shows that the new air-age cartographic flexibility actually helped ensure the fragmentation of mapping across nations and agencies.

A related, ill-fated mapping project of Boggs's was his call for an *Atlas of Ignorance*, a comprehensive program of maps that required international cooperation on maps of what was currently unknown in the world and what problems needed to be addressed by the international community. The *Atlas of Ignorance* manifested Boggs's theory that even in the new globally connected world, there were still blank spaces on the map that needed filling in because, as he plainly put it, "for the first time in history there are *world* problems."[135] Boggs proposed here that the international cartographic community come together to reveal the most challenging and underdeveloped areas of study through a full atlas of about

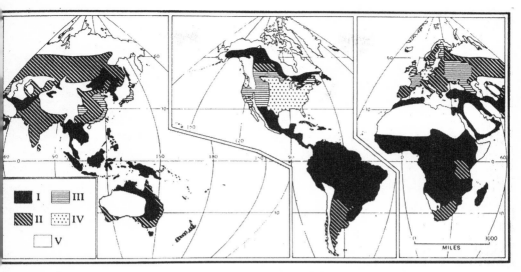

Figure 2.3. S. W. Boggs, Central Intelligence Agency,
"Adequacy of Existing Soil Maps for Agricultural Interpretation," in Proceedings
of the American Philosophical Society, *1949 (Courtesy of Boatwright Library,*
University of Richmond)

a hundred maps in areas as diverse as geology, tides, diseases, folklore, personality types, and cultural values.[136]

In a published article about the *Atlas*, Boggs includes a world map of ignorance in existing soil maps as his example (fig. 2.3). Over a Miller projection, Boggs shows a world divided into different shades based on the degree to which there are world maps adequate for agricultural interpretation.[137] While the subject is ostensibly about soil, the map fluidly frames knowledge, or lack thereof, as a central subject, and every continent is indicted for having pockets of cartographic ignorance. To Boggs, the world is brought closer through its shared gaps: he then accompanies his seemingly apolitical soil map with calls for "orchestrated heterogeneity" and the warning that "if peace is to be conceived dynamically, on a scale commensurate with the emerging realities of the present age, we need to develop a society in which all whose minds and hearts are big enough can find their best expression as citizens of the world."[138]

Projects like the *Atlas of Ignorance* are rich early Cold War artifacts because they express a hope that the postwar world could be drawn together through knowledge and that the silences of maps could be filled in by international alliances and scientific cooperation. Yet, at the same time, Boggs believed those silences and pockets of ignorance could be addressed only by the trained specialist. Boggs was clear that the *Atlas of Ignorance* required a kind of elitism, pointing out that "erudition is required of those who compile these maps of ignorance. Only those mature specialists who, individually or collectively, know the present coverage of the aggregate of human knowledge in one subject, or a selected aspect thereof, can compile one of these maps."[139] Boggs's work was also cognizant of Cold War realities and their constraints, acknowledging that there was a fine line between ignorance and secrecy. "If in any region an 'iron curtain' were to hide from the world the knowledge of its able specialists," Boggs maintained, "the areas they know well would be, not areas of ignorance, but of shrouded knowledge."[140] Unfortunately, the prospects of a collaborative atlas demonstrating a *lack* of knowledge during the beginning of a Cold War era when guarded knowledge was at a premium were doomed from the start. Like the International Map of the World project, the new priority of nationalistic geographic intelligence over collaboration prevailed.[141] Boggs insisted upon the ideal that "when we can hold a globe in our hands and visualize the interrelationships of complete world patterns of physical and social phenomena, we can handle world problems much more intelligently. The increased assurance may help to overcome the 'tragedy of the timidity of statesmanship.'"[142] This timidity of statesmanship, though, was replaced by an increasingly harder line in U.S. foreign relations that constrained Boggs's idealism.

Boggs's sense of cooperative internationalism, for example, was not always matched by his colleagues. In a precursor to his *Atlas of Ignorance* project, he sent inquiries to other mapping agencies in the U.S. government in hopes of establishing a new postwar program to coordinate the foreign mapping needs of the various agencies. As Boggs noted, "Prior to the war, the interest of most of the Government departments with reference to foreign maps and charts had been confined chiefly to nautical charts. . . . It seems that we should consider now what will be the needs of the Government departments and agencies under peacetime conditions, in view of developments that may be anticipated under the various international arrangements which have been made, or which are in prospect, in relation to economic and social development, food and agriculture problems."[143] With this memorandum, he included a blank world map (on a Miller projection) so that each recipient could "draw in" where she foresaw needs for postwar foreign mapping. Included were entreaties to Walter Kotschnig, one of the State Department's main liaisons to the United Nations, to encourage the UN to cover areas "which ought to be mapped within the next few years in the interest of an 'expanding world economy,'" and offer technical mapping assistance to any nation in need.[144] Kotschnig's ensuing negative response to Boggs's appeals evidenced the fears of international cooperation: "It may be assumed that several state members of the United Nations would not be willing to have any of their territories surveyed which might make it difficult to trust the United Nations with any surveying project which would have to be confined to some limited territories" and that "any help this country may be able to offer might be given on the basis of special agreements with specific other countries."[145] This denial shows that foreign policy officials conceived of cartography as part of a more unilateral national strategy and that mapping agreements could be entered into by the United States only in specific cases that would benefit its interests.[146] Boggs's impulse to globalize mapping was tempered by disciplinary boundaries *within* the U.S. government as well as diplomatic power relations between the U.S. government and structures like the UN.

Despite his idealism, Boggs's professional role as an intelligence gatherer for the State Department's postwar sketch of the world mitigated his cartographic activism. During the fateful days of 1946, a banner year in the buildup of Cold War tensions, State Department special assistant Alfred McCormack circulated a memorandum that called for an establishment of an interdepartmental Planning Group to coordinate all government cartographic intelligence under one roof.[147] The memorandum pronounced geographic intelligence as "the most fundamental of all intelligence" and extensively quoted Boggs about the need for more maps to help solve economic and social problems "in order that civilization may survive and that the human race may prosper."[148] At the same time, McCormack's final recommendations indicate that the ultimate goal was to promote and facilitate foreign cartographic and geographic intelligence and to encourage "cooperation between Government departments and agencies, on the one hand, and private institutions in the United States and Governments and private agencies in foreign countries on the other, *as may be advantageous to the Government*."[149] In a sense, Boggs's own conceptions of "one-world" cartographies bringing nations closer together were being directly appropriated during the very design of the Cold War intelligence apparatus that would protect American interests and security above all else.

Around the same time, this new intelligence program was recruiting Boggs in other operations that were informing the character of postwar foreign policy. In August 1945, Boggs was consulted by the State Department's Public Affairs office to provide cartographic objectives for the Special Interrogation Mission to Germany, led by DeWitt Poole, an officer in the State Department who was an expert in anticommunist propaganda and would later head the CIA-funded National Committee for a Free Europe.[150] Boggs requested that Poole's mission bring back maps containing information in regards to Nazi plans for the economic and political organization of Europe and maps regarding the colonial occupation of foreign territories. Most importantly, though, Boggs sought evidence regarding the extent of General Haushofer's influence (the notorious German geopolitical theorist and mapmaker) in Germany's military and diplomatic conduct, mentioning that "copies of maps of a geopolitical nature should be sought."[151] Such exchanges indicate Boggs's concern about the effects of propaganda maps during the reorganization of Europe and demonstrate that it was in the interest of the government to analyze and catalog these maps.

Finally, Boggs's cartographic intelligence work contributed to classified research operations that served early Cold War objectives. In 1946–47, Boggs would commission "map evaluation" studies of Germany, Greece, and Turkey, as well as a comprehensive study of the Hungarian-Czech borderlands.[152] These studies were essentially detailed and exhaustive reviews and critiques of existing map series and atlases that covered each locale, including reviews of maps produced by cartographic agencies *in* each of the countries. Most of the reviews related to the degree of functionality and reliability of maps, both topographic and thematic, highlighting those maps that provide quick and readable evidence of the strategic problem for the user. For example, shortly after the March 1947 declaration of the Truman Doctrine, the map studies on Greece and Turkey were completed, attempting to assess, through maps, the quality of the reconstruction of these nations. Such projects show that the State Department strategy for "reading the world" and its international problems was to amass and catalog as much cartographic data as possible. And in the increasingly walled context of security and intelligence agency research, mapping was being closely guarded and cultivated. Knowledge of the world and its peoples was a high priority, but that knowledge required vigilance, a hallmark of the foreign policy that informed much of the Cold War.

THE INSTITUTIONAL LIVES OF COLD WAR CARTOGRAPHY

In the end, it was that difficult relationship between open and closed knowledge in the cartographic construction of the world that most marked Boggs's work. It is fitting that in his well-known 1947 *Scientific Monthly* article, "Cartohypnosis," Boggs takes the famous 1904 map by Sir Halford Mackinder, influential to both German and American geopolitics during World War II and the early Cold War, and proceeds to show how its Mercator-based assumptions look completely different when viewed through other projections.[153] Thus, Boggs believed the map exerted "hypnotic influence . . . with perversions of the author's original intent" and could be "socially poisonous."[154] Typically, "Cartohypnosis" is cited as one of the main postwar salvos in a growing literature excoriating maps as propaganda, where writers and theorists worried about how simplified journalistic and even academic maps (like Mackinder's) had gained power over the geographic imagination, during a time when the specter of communist propaganda haunted American discourse.[155]

But understanding Boggs in his proper context reveals his appeals as more complex. Rather than offering black and white prescriptions on good and bad maps, he was articulating the important notion that critical interpretation of the world through maps, as well as a variety of new uses for those maps, was something that was destined to be part of U.S. political culture. The idealist overtones are apparent here—that people can be dehypnotized through better maps that offer a greater sense of humanity's interdependency throughout the world, whether through more useful projections or maps that truly account for the revolution in transport and communication. In this same vein is Boggs's strong presence in the development of powerful positivist geographies during the Cold War that prized the role of scientific knowledge and, in particular, America's power to marshal spatial knowledge. Boggs's articulation of cartohypnosis encapsulates the rhetorical complexities of maps in a new world framework and the precarious balance between idealism and realism that he represented in a host of projects throughout his professional life.

In general, S. W. Boggs's cartographic work represents how the global conceptions of the State Department, and its collaborating institutions, both reflected and shaped an emerging postwar visual culture, informed by the contentious disciplinary histories of geography as well as maps' functions as both scientific evidence and artistic projections. The culture around this postwar geographic imaginary provides insights into the strategic design and knowledge production of globalized power. As Bocking has written, "vision" during the Cold War era became more "synoptic" and "managerial," and air-age science created a space where geographical knowledge becomes national authority.[156] The early Cold War was a period of cartographic fragmentation across many government agencies but also saw attempts at consolidation to retain maps as arbiters for national objectives. To know the world was to have a degree of control over it, and thus the potential ideal of internationalism was complicated by the necessities for putting boundaries around knowledge and guarding it with vigilance. By 1988, the geographer of the Department of State, George Demko, speaking to the annual meeting of the Association of American Geographers, was still affirming the need for scientifically viable but artful constructions of the world to reach the hands of policy makers:

> My own experience in Washington with members of Congress, State Department officials, and many other high-ranking members of the nation's decision-making hierarchy confirms my sense of the problem. I have been stunned at the near-total lack of an image, or, at best a hurtful and simplistic image, held of geography by these powerful people. My first reaction now is to give them something to read— geographic analyses and maps produced by my office—the Office of the Geographer. These applications of the geographical perspective to such problems as AIDS, terrorism, environmental issues and more, usually evoke surprise and requests for more. . . . Our problems are not traceable to the art and science of geography, but to its practitioners. The solutions to our problems and our future are also in the hands of its practitioners—*all of us*.[157]

Demko was once again reaching back to the debates of the air-age era around the challenge to "good men" to produce, circulate, and interpret maps—while expressing, too, the kind of anxiety that Boggs and his colleagues had over his bosses' perceived lack of geographic nuance.

As Cold War commitments grew, and the Second and Third Worlds constrained the geographic imagination, the prospect of containing maps would become increasingly unwieldy, as the very flexibility in perspective would turn into a possible liability for policy makers attempting to maintain one consistent image of the world. Out of these cartographic representations in institutional and popular media came a spatial foundation that would gradually come to entrench a bipolar international landscape on the flat pages of maps. Cartography would become militarized more overtly into the peculiar waging of cold war. The actual circulation of maps as material forces in the Cold War visual culture would become even more important, as maps were increasingly appropriated and reappropriated into various public contexts and produced for diverse audiences as *weapons* in the struggle between the United States and the Soviet Union. The sense of "one-world" idealism that Boggs attempted to circulate was mitigated by maps' abilities to draw stark national lines that essentially bounded the world into two ideologies. Through their strategic adoption as tools of authority and authenticity for both popular institutions and government agencies, and through more sophisticated technologies and wider exposure, maps became an indispensable medium for the staging of public opinion battles against the USSR. They lived more active rhetorical lives in the coming years than could have been imagined mere years before. In 1945 the Hough team's trucks drove off with an untold number of maps, hoping that the spatial information they had would never get into the wrong hands. By the early 1950s, maps were being produced and circulated that were meant exactly to get into the wrong hands.

3

IMAGES OF COMMITMENT AND EVIDENTIARY WEAPONS
Maps and the Visual Construction of the Soviet Union

On December 18, 1950, the *New York Times* featured a curious collection of front-page headlines. Most of the headlines announced the unfolding Cold War's increasingly global reach: "Red Chinese Punch at U.S. Beachhead"; "U.S. Will Speed Forces to Europe; Russia Fails to Jar Atlantic Allies"; "U.S. F-86 Jet in First Fight Fells Enemy Plane in Korea." Another nearby headline, almost as prominent as these telegraphs of foreign war and high-stakes diplomacy, read: "Geography Almost Ignored in Colleges, Survey Shows."[1] The accompanying article decried the lack and poor quality of geography education in both colleges and secondary schools across America. The text also connected geography to the question of "good citizenship." Experts quoted in the article concluded that a geographic understanding of the globe, along with an appreciation of American history "should go hand-in-hand as a foundation for citizenship." "The position of the United States as world leader and protector of democracy," the article claimed, "can only be effective if the American citizen, especially if he has a college education, has some geographical knowledge of the rest of the world."[2] The survey mentioned in the article asked educators why geography should be taken more seriously by students, and the statement the majority of respondents chose was "A better knowledge of the world and its people will lead to a better appreciation of foreign policy and will help the United States in its efforts to retain the leadership so suddenly thrust upon us."[3]

Why is this anxiety about geography's plummeting status front-page news, particularly among a host of headlines highlighting the intensely geographic nature of the Cold War conflict? The *Times* geography survey compellingly symbolized the new connections between international political space and public opinion in America. To *know* the world involved consenting to (and participating in) America's new power as world leader, and this new power was accompanied by an anxiety about how to shape, classify, and border such space. In other words, there was an emerging concern in Cold War popular and institutional discourse that if the United States lost its security on the map, it may lose its place as a world power against the Soviet Union.

The emergence of air-age globalism brought a newfound flexibility in ways of viewing the world and a sometimes idealistic hope that the shrinking world would bring the world powers into clearer focus on common goals. As the ideological conflict with the USSR took shape, geography took on the role of an abstract manager of spatial facts. It is noteworthy that the *Times* chose to say that the United States was working to "retain the leadership so suddenly thrust upon us," as if the speed of America's post–World War II rise to international power was something that geographic knowledge could (and must) help manage.[4] Maps visually represented this management process, the ways these anxieties and tensions were drawn out. The immense apparatus of knowledge production in foreign policy, military, academic, and popular discourse was often articulated through cartography both as a medium and as a technology.

In 1951, the same year that the *New York Times* released its survey results, the *National Geographic* put out its first world map since the Cold War began (fig. 3.1).[5] Since 1909, the *Geographic* published eight world maps, and its 1951 edition would serve as the ninth. The map is a massive display on the Van der Grinten projection, which the National Geographic Society (NGS) had been using since 1922 (and would drop in 1988 as the Cold War waned). The Van der Grinten projection is similar to the Mercator projection in that it chooses the accuracy of shape over area, but it uses curved meridians and parallels in order to create the more appropriately air-aged aura of roundness.[6] The Van der Grinten greatly exaggerates size toward the poles, making Canada, Greenland, and particularly the Soviet Union much bigger—as much as 223 percent larger than its actual size. Insets on the top left and right use a polar projection to accurately portray those parts of the map that are too distorted on the larger map. Moreover, in the left corner sits a political map of all UN nations, NATO nations, and Warsaw Pact–Soviet satellite countries.

The NGS map is in some ways the archetypal representation of American Cold War cartography. Jeremy Black writes, "The Society's maps were the staple of educational institutions, the basis of maps used by newspapers and television, and the acme of public cartography for the period when the

Figure 3.1. National Geographic Society, "World Map," 1951

(Courtesy of the Geography & Map Division of the Library of Congress, by permission of the National Geographic Society)

USA was the most powerful nation in the world." And the 1951 version was influential in employing a projection where "a large USSR appeared menacing, a threat to the whole of Eurasia, and a dominant presence in the world that required containment."[7] There is no overt kind of ideological message (there are no Soviet tentacles), as the map disinterestedly displays world relationships with an immense amount of geographic information. At the same time, it offers a self-evident kind of simplicity. The map cleanly contains the world in a frame centering on the United States, and its spatial relationships with the world appear to flow out of the country. In an accompanying introductory article to the map, the editors justify the choice of America as the center because it is the "source of so much of the leadership and aid, so many of the men, machines, and raw materials needed for the preservation of freedom in older lands."[8] Like the *Times*'s arguments about the waning of geographic education, the connection is made between space, nationhood, and citizenship. As the NGS editors put it, "Ignorance of the geography of nations was perhaps excusable a generation ago, but today knowing and understanding the many diverse countries of the world has become urgent and vital for our national survival. . . . What happens in Moscow or Peiping today, or in Korea or divided Berlin, can affect the lives and fortunes of Americans more quickly than the firing on Fort Sumter in South Carolina did 90 years ago."[9] Thus, in a sense, the map asks its readers to *participate* and give consent to America's world leadership; to know *where* the Cold War was being waged, and on what fronts, was to be part of a contributing citizenry.

In addition, the inset of a political map displaying the standoff between UN forces, NATO nations, and Soviet-influenced nations shows how the popular spatial metaphors of the Cold War were concretized on the flat page. The editors write of this inset, "On it one can trace the iron curtain, Communism's 2,000 mile long barrier against free information, travel— and escape." The color contrasts and deep shading on this border fuse a geographic line with an ideological one: the iron curtain is now a traceable barrier and a rigid one that is long enough to partition the world into bipolar camps, actualized as an accurate boundary in the geographic imagination of the Cold War.

The 1951 NGS map is noteworthy not just for what it presents on the page, but the modes of production by which it was compiled. In combination with its text, the entire map is a celebration of Cold War technologies, making the sophistication of its methods part of the actual display. The map itself may appear to hide its origins, but the editors complicate this process, writing that, "although little larger than an opened newspaper, the 41-by-26½ inch map compresses shelves of geographic knowledge. It represents the ripe fruit of some 23 centuries of restless man's investigation of his earth."[10] The NGS map is a culmination of geography and history, coming together in the early Cold War.[11] The editors also laud the explorers, the oceanographers, and the "aerial camera explorations by the United States and Canadian Air Forces" that "have greatly altered the mapped outlines of lands in the Arctic since the war."[12] In the Cold War, the professional and academic geographer was bound up with the U.S. government's military and foreign policy institutions and their attendant technologies. In one comprehensive map resides a host of interweaving interests, institutions, and assumptions *compressed* (in the words of its editors) into one visual package. More so than journalistic maps that simply serve the function of the accompanying story, an NGS map must make its presence known as a *National Geographic* product; its professional and academic connections to the geographic discipline make the production of cartography just as important a subject on the map as what the map actually depicts. This host of interests and technologies triangulate into a portable document that permeated Cold War culture, as the editors proudly point out that the NGS map was in "distribution to 160 countries, to schools, libraries, and government agencies."[13] The finished map circulates and becomes embedded into various contexts for various audiences.

The NGS map is a fitting introduction into how the tensions and tenets that emerged from the discourse of air-age prophets like Richard Edes Harrison and government cartographic policy makers like S. W. Boggs gave way to the cartographic bipolarities of Cold War mapping.[14] Air-age flexibility in the maps that emerged from World War II created the kind of geographic anxiety that allowed space to be seen as alarmingly fluid. Throughout the 1950s, much of the popular and government mapping based on U.S. foreign policy typically accounted for the world in terms of how to locate American power against the Soviet Union. In other words, maps helped *commit* the United States to its ideological conflict with the Soviet Union during the early years of the Cold War. Maps offered compelling ways for policy makers, military strategists, newspaper and magazine cartographers, and citizens to partition the international landscape.

CARTOGRAPHIC CONSTRUCTIONS OF THE COLD WAR: MAPPING THE BIPOLAR 1950S

This chapter highlights the functionality of maps in the early Cold War—how they were used and circulated as active forces with rhetorical lives in the waging of an ideological (and material) conflict. Two major appropriations of maps helped to etch and frame the seemingly rigid bipolarity of the early 1950s. The first use concerns how maps provided *images of commitment,* whereby the various pacts and bloc alliances constructed out of Cold War hostilities and friendships became important spatial markers in popular and institutional maps. Such maps "placed" the Soviet Union in relation to the United States in specific ways, drawing and bounding how Americans were oriented to Cold War space. Second, the maps of the evolving Cold War were increasingly used as *evidentiary weapons.* In other words, they were materially drawn into diplomatic exchanges and embedded into government reports as evidence of the capacities and potentialities that the Cold War superpowers possessed. One particular map unites these various tensions, and thus is used as an extended example: the "'Gulag'—Slavery, Inc." propaganda map produced by the American Federation of Labor. In the process, cartography's unique ability to use art and science to locate and manage political power and edify it on the flat page comes to the forefront. If the cases of Harrison and Boggs show how an "interpretive ground" for the Cold War was laid, then this chapter shows how these interpretations were made, disseminated, and circulated.

Images of Commitment: Journalistic Maps and Cold War Internationalism

The emerging modern, liberal internationalism at the base of Cold War ideology increasingly involved the symbolic *perception* of power as critical to the enactment of foreign policy and the cultivation of public opinion.[15] The entire globe was more flexible and "readable" as a text. With this flexibility came anxiety; America's standing as world power relied on its ability to manage such perceptions. At this time, according to historian Kenneth Osgood, the stakes of what was considered "political warfare," or the means by which the Cold War would be fought through nonmilitary means, were amplifying; the sense that the conflict was a "total war" involving international public opinion was a major part of its militarization.[16] Maps provided a compelling vehicle for this brand of warfare, making spatial sense out of a rapidly changing and potentially volatile international landscape. In particular, political maps accounted for America's commitments in the United Nations and NATO, and the anxieties over such responsibilities often cleaved the United States to an image of bipolarity that would help guide Cold War ideologies throughout the early days of the conflict.

The journalistic cartography of the early Cold War best encapsulated these notions of maps as images of commitment. Following in the wake of popular cartographers like Richard Edes Harrison, magazines and newspapers began to develop their own graphic styles that could account for the new global reach of America. As geographer Mark Monmonier writes, "the news media are society's most significant cartographic gate-keeper and its most influential geographic educator"—they performed a key public opinion function in shaping the Cold War geographic imagination.[17] Walter Ristow noted how the journalistic maps of the era suggest a dynamic and active conflict because of their greater likelihood for experimentation with symbolization.[18] Because of their embeddedness into particular stories and their unique abilities to focus on strategic problems, journalistic maps were prime "placers" in locating Cold War spatial relationships between the United States and the Soviet Union.

For example, the Associated Press (AP) "Background Maps" series that ran from the late 1940s well into the 1960s provides a compelling visual history of America's increasing responsibilities on the world stage vis-à-vis the Soviet Union. After establishing their innovative wire photo service in 1928, AP artists also began to supply maps and other graphic drawings, and such products became particularly important in situating the spatial relationships of World War II in newspaper pages all over America.[19] The AP mailed member newspapers two maps every week, together with a six-hundred-word article, a service that continued throughout the 1950s.[20] The "Background Maps" syndicated series maps were most often drawn by G. W. Braunsdorf and William Rowley, and they were extremely pictorial in style, simplifying typical "scientific" cartographic expectations of shape and size, and converting nation-states into emblematic units. With their simple black-and-white line drawings and uses of shading, they created "political shorthand" for displaying American commitments across the globe and offering stark constructions of the Soviet Union's political space.

The AP Cold War–era maps often centered on the United States and cast the nation anxiously into a world of burgeoning skirmishes and entangling alliances. "The Sun Never Sets on World's Problems," from 1947, offers a standard, Mercator-style projection centered almost exactly on New York City as the "United Nations Capital," while the rest of the map uses iconic badges with letters on them to indicate where crises are taking place (e.g., "P" for political disputes, "I" for internal conflicts, "C" for colonial struggles), accompanied by terse, bolded explanations on placards near major Cold War hot spots (e.g., "TENSION: between U.S. and Soviet Union finds expression in U.N. dispute over atomic arms control").[21] America is visually projected as the eye in a swirling mass of

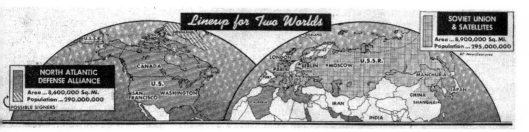

Figure 3.2. Associated Press, "Lineup for Two Worlds," Newsfeatures Series, 1949 (Courtesy of the Geography & Map Division of the Library of Congress, by permission of Associated Press)

entanglements. Other typical AP maps in this series followed events at the United Nations by continually placing America as the central leader and the focus of the viewer's eye. In 1953's "The U.S. Foots the Biggest Bill," the familiar map logo of the United Nations provides the center of the map, with its branches of peace surrounding a polar-projected globe.[22] But the peace logo of the United Nations is subverted, and next to the United States in the center is a number reading "35.12%," indicating how much America contributes financially to the organization. Along the outer margins of the globe are the much smaller percentages of the various member contributions (e.g., "U.S.S.R.: 12.28%"; "Mexico: .70%"). Such a map repurposes recognized cartographic icons in order to question the potential burden of America's economic commitments across the globe.

The AP also used its signature pictorial style to cover the emergence of the "bloc" spatial logic between NATO and the Soviet satellites and helped to create the classic Cold War image of world bipolarity. "Lineup for Two Worlds" (fig. 3.2) from 1949, for example, shows two rounded tops of a globe: on one is the Western Hemisphere, centered on the United States, and on the other the Soviet Union is at the center.[23] Both globes simply indicate which are NATO countries, and which are "Soviet Union & Satellites"; a small infographic next to the maps indicates that the area and population of all the countries in the Soviet Union's camp outweigh the area and population of all the countries in the NATO realm. Nowhere in either map does the viewer see the real existence of a southern hemisphere; thus the two essential worlds are cast as resolutely northern in character.

Other AP maps focus specifically on the extension of the Soviet Union onto the international landscape. The 1950 map, "Russia Thrusts Out from the Center," plants an "X" right in the middle of the Soviet Union, with three flowing arrows (resembling tentacles) that stretch toward

Australia and Oceania, to the bottom tip of Africa, through Europe, over North America, and to the bottom of South America.[24] The map disorients the viewer by placing Australia as the northern point on the map, Africa as the East, and so on, such that the globe appears helpless at the hands of the arrows. Essentially, the entire globe is covered by what the map calls the Soviet's "supposed routes of past migrations," suggesting a natural, historical expansiveness in the Russian people.[25] The thrust metaphor would be a continual cartographic trope, especially through the use of arrows that transcend political borders and traverse bounded spaces. Other maps depicting Soviet aims broke away from the strictly cartographic, and integrated cartoon caricatures and other unconventional elements: in 1953's "Are the West's Defenses against Communism Weakening?," a map of Europe is crossed by a long, winding iron wall, and a cartoon Vyacheslav Molotov (the Soviet foreign minister) behind the wall, with his feet up on his desk.[26] Of course, such fluid relationships between cartoon graphics and mapping have long relegated these styles to the status of "propaganda maps," since the interpretation of the mapmaker is overtly foregrounded. Unfortunately, the "propaganda" label distracts from the fact that these widely circulated newspaper maps were an important part of spatializing the Cold War for citizens and committing American power and responsibility to particular places on the globe.

The AP's maps were constrained by the limitations of the newspaper production processes, while the popular newsmagazines of the time had more freedom for elaborate design in color and iconography. In particular, Henry Luce's journalistic empire at *Time*, *Life*, and *Fortune* created some of the most indelible images of the Cold War.[27] Richard Edes Harrison's work in these periodicals would continue sporadically after his World War II heyday, and another crop of cartographers and graphic designers would take up his mantle. At *Time*, for example, house cartographer Robert M. Chapin developed a signature style that was embedded into the magazine's Cold War offensives. While Harrison used more innovative projections and perspectives, Chapin's novel contribution was his stylistic airbrush techniques. Publisher Luce called Chapin's airbrush "a sort of highpower atomizer with which he sprays paint over his maps in an infinite number of shadings."[28] Chapin used two large floating globes, suspended from the ceiling by pulleys so that they could be photographed from any angle, and "strategy can then be traced from the photos." He also used a "library of celluloid stencils—bomb splashes, flags, jeeps, sinking ships" to create a standardized style.[29] But what most marked *Time*'s cartography was the use of bright, bold reds for lettering and symbols, layered over the black outlines of continents and borders. The red motif became

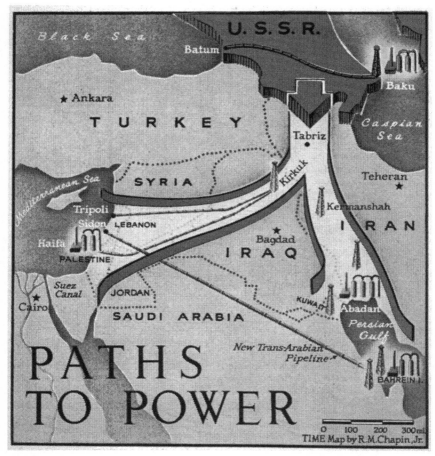

Figure 3.3. Robert M. Chapin Jr., "Paths to Power," Time, 1951 © Time/ Life Publications (Courtesy of Boatwright Library, University of Richmond)

ubiquitous in *Time*: in countless Chapin maps (and others by graphic artist Vincent Puglisi), the color becomes a stand-in for militant infiltration and expansion.[30] In 1951's "Paths to Power," a bright red Soviet Union is depicted at the top of the frame, while seeping ribbons of red flow through Syria, Iraq, and Iran (fig. 3.3).[31] In "Red Rash (after Treatment)" from 1949, the coverage of the Greek civil war shows a grey and white landscape covered in irregularly shaped, blood-red splotches.[32] The reliance on red as a universal symbol of Cold War hostility gave the journalistic maps of the era a master trope that could unite a disparate set of political problems and international conflicts into a cohesive argument against communist ideology.

The red theme also speaks to the increasing militancy of journalistic cartography in committing America to its place in the Cold War. Cartographers like Chapin also covered World War II strategic fronts and battles and carried over many of those themes into maps documenting Cold War skirmishes. This militarization could especially be seen through a frequent trope of Cold War journalistic maps: the use of simple visual metaphor to reduce the spatial information in the map to one striking idea or argument.[33] In covering the Korean War, for example, a 1950 *Time* map used the image of a large c-clamp over a map of the Korean landscape to show the enormous constraints facing forces in the South; in "Korea's Waistland," a red belt crosses the land, to connote a "waist" that is about to burst.[34] Maps like "Eleventh Hour" placed a large clock over the whole of Manchuria with hammers as the hands of the clock.[35] "Clearing & Colder" from 1948 uses an elaborate weather metaphor for the entire Cold War itself, showing the "Russian High" versus the "Western High," with red thunder and lightning in Berlin, steady red drizzle in Greece, and a cartoon red Stalin blowing "cold easterly winds" onto Finland.[36]

Many of the same kinds of militant themes of invasion and encirclement surfaced in magazines such as *Life*, *Fortune*, and *Newsweek*. For example, *Life*'s "Nation's Commitments All around the Earth" detailed an overextended America bound by scores of international treaties and constrained by Cold War alliances.[37] The use of visual metaphors was also a continuing trend. *Newsweek*'s "Western Defense: Where and What NATO Links Are in Danger" dramatically strings a metal chain across the center of Europe with a series of broken links to demonstrate serious breaks with America in Cold War foreign policy.[38] One of the Cold War's most striking metaphor maps is by the illustrator Richard Erdoes from *Life*'s "How Strategic Material Circulates," from 1953 (fig. 3.4).[39] Here, a large curious hybrid between an industrial pump and an octopus, rendered in flame red, hovers over Europe (a hybrid that geographers Cyndy Hendershot and Antony Oldknow call an "impossibly surreal combination").[40] The octo-pump sits over Antwerp, as a defining symbol of the "West," and the pump proceeds to feed icons of bombs, missiles, and other types of arms over a barbed wire fencing running through the center of the continent. Behind the fence lie graphics of factories in East Germany alongside tanks, and small silhouettes of men in trench coats and fedoras next to a cartoon of two shady males whispering. Through Erdoes's depiction of clandestine East-West relationships and arms smuggling, the map is able to instantiate Cold War fears by warning the reader that capitalist gain is contributing to Communist military might in a vicious cycle. The map

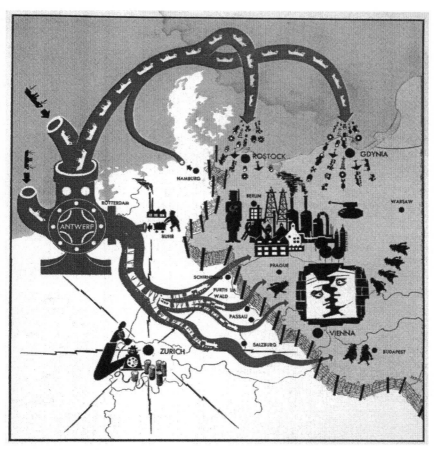

Figure 3.4. Richard Erdoes, "How Strategic Material Circulates,"
Life, *1953 (Courtesy of Boatwright Library, University of Richmond,*
by permission of the Estate of Richard Erdoes)

also proclaims that communist infiltration of European space is part of
a machine-like system involving Western consent, rather than simply a
monstrous octopus.

As the Cold War wore on, these newsmagazines also used cartography
to make future predictions of nuclear standoffs with the Soviet Union,
going beyond maps' propensities to show space merely "as is," and
venturing into the realm of "what could be." *Life*'s multimap spread "How
Could Soviet Attack Come?" continues the politicization of the air from
1940s air-age globalist maps but now projects the ways in which the Soviet
Union would descend upon America and the rest of the world by bomb

carriers in the air.[41] The main map is a spherical, orthographic projection with crisscrossing air routes emanating from the Soviet Union in all directions and with inset maps covering particular regions prime for Soviet infiltration.[42] *Newsweek* maps like "Turning the Tables" also looked to the future with a polar projection of a black Soviet Union hovering over the United States with a series of red arrows thrusting toward cities like New York, Chicago, and Seattle and quantifying the miles it would take to reach and destroy them.[43] Maps in *Fortune*, by the innovative technical designer Max Gschwind, do the reverse and instead project the potential vulnerabilities of the Soviet Union in the face of a future U.S. attack: "Massive Retaliatory Power," for example, is an intricate and provocative map that places a large red Soviet Union in the center, overwhelmed by an army of arrows.[44] The arrows represent missile and bomb trajectories that correspond to points all over the earth surrounding the Soviet Union from which the U.S.–led Strategic Air Command could attack it. Gschwind thus plays with a map's inherent abstractions and reduces world space to one overwhelming field of nuclear arms. The importance of these future-oriented magazine maps lies in how America was navigating Cold War anxieties in trying to locate its knowledge of the Soviet Union's increasing capacities (and its own) into a manageable visual field. Such graphics matched the kind of "future" annihilation projections of behind-the-scenes initiatives like NSC-68 that set the global Cold War landscape as a totalized field of threats. Such predictive measures alarmed diplomats like George Kennan because NSC-68's conception of national security boldly anticipated hypothetical, future scenarios about the potential globally destructive ends of Soviet power, rather than realistically assessing the situation as it was.[45] In the process, NSC-68 broadened the sense of America's militarizing itself for the Cold War, preparing itself from all angles, and accepting the image-making power of its influence in the world vis-à-vis the Soviet Union. Maps provided a graphically simple medium for posing such relationships.

The massive amount of popular, journalistic maps framed the Cold War for millions of American readers during the late 1940s and 1950s.[46] Newspapers and newsmagazines could break out of the technical, formal expectations of cartographic science and geographic objectivity, yet still borrow from the historical authority of the map to place "true" relationships on the page.[47] Because of their reductionistic view of space as equal to pacts, blocs, alliances, and ideologies, they lent themselves well to the bipolar constructions of Cold War discourse. Despite the fact that these maps helped to edify a tense, two-world universe, they were, above all, active and restless, and they dispute that mapping was somehow a static medium that simply "represented" on-the-ground realities.[48] The sum total of these "images of commitment" in newspaper and magazine maps connotes an America continually adapting to the abstract spaces of international conflict.

Cartography as Evidence: Maps and the Depiction of Cold War Capacities

From their journalistic platform, maps were important indexes of Cold War spatial anxieties. As the Cold War commenced, maps' seeming ubiquity went beyond popular newspapers and magazines, as they were also frequently embedded into committee reports, used as testimonial support, and invoked as mediators in diplomatic exchanges between the United States and the Soviet Union. In these various uses, Cold War maps functioned as *evidential weaponry*: a piece of visual evidence marshaled for the strategic purposes of Cold War actors. The rhetorical lives of maps were increasingly extended into staging public standoffs and providing graphic parameters for intense debates around America's sense of how it should extend itself.

Congressional maps provide a representative example of this increasing embeddedness of cartography into Cold War policy making.[49] Historically, since the founding of the Republic, domestic maps were a frequent presence in House and Senate reports, as evidence for districting, population, and land use. In the Cold War, given the pervasiveness of the new internationalism, many foreign policy maps were now circulating in their attachment to various bills, treaties, and committee reports. These foreign policy maps were produced and appropriated from a host of different sources: many were produced in-house by the Library of Congress, others were imported from the Department of State and the Central Intelligence Agency, still others were brought in from the *New York Times* and entered into the record. Congressional reports became a unique medium for the diversity of Cold War mapping; these maps were divorced from their original contexts and producers, and were reappropriated as evidence to serve legislative agendas in the international arena.

Congressional maps were especially noteworthy for projecting the *capacities* of America's commitments in the Cold War. For example, one of the Cold War's essential policy initiatives, the 1951 Mutual Security Act (renewed every year through 1961), which provided billions of dollars in technical, military, and monetary aid to Cold War allies, contained a host of maps in its annual reports to Congress throughout the 1950s. These maps were more technical in style than their contemporary journalistic counterparts, but no less provocative in their ability to reduce places all over the globe into directional spaces for American economic and military power.[50] The *New York Times* map embedded into the 1949 Mutual Defense Assistance Act reduces international space to individual security agreements: the entire "Atlantic Pact Area" and "Rio Pact Area" are indicated by lines and shadings that form a kind of force field against the Soviet Union and its satellites. With a host of bolded "M" icons to indicate Marshall Plan recipients, the Soviet Union appears almost encircled by a united world solidified by pacts.[51] A map that recurs multiple times in the Mutual Security Act reports of the 1950s is "United States Collective Defense Arrangements" (fig. 3.5), designed by Robert Bostick of the Legislative Reference Center at the Library of Congress.[52] The defense arrangement map extends the partitioning theme of the earlier maps and sketches the ultimate spatial argument for containment: circular placards with the name of each major world treaty are connected by pointed lines to their respective members all over the world. The overall effect shows a world that creates a perimeter of alliances to isolate the Soviet Union from the rest of the world. While each treaty (NATO, Rio, Southeast Asia, ANZUS) has different members for different reasons, the map reduces all of the U.S. collective defense agreements to one Cold War purpose: keep the Soviet Union in its place.

These maps also detailed the nature of aid the United States was providing, and the accompanying anxieties of overextension. The "U.S. Postwar Foreign Aid" map centers on the United States, with the statistic "$35.6 Billion" filling the nation's midsection and arrows directing the viewer to all continents with proportional-sized circles, indicating how much military and economic or technical aid each area receives. World geography becomes equated with the power of the dollar.[53] Another frequently used map in the Mutual Security Act reports was the "Cost per Soldier" graphic. The background is a conventional Mercator-style world map, with no political boundaries. But superimposed onto the international landscape is a line of silhouetted black soldier icons holding guns.[54] Like Russian nesting dolls, the line of soldiers goes from tallest to shortest, the last soldier icon being almost too minuscule to discern. The tallest soldier represents the United States, with the cost-per-soldier at more than $3,800, dwarfing the next soldier icon of the United Kingdom at $1,800, all the way down to Korea at $390 and Taiwan at $167. "Cost per Soldier" starkly arranges America as the towering world military power. At the same time, it connotes a lonely, ambivalent power—asking implicitly, "at what cost do we maintain the stewardship of the world?" The juxtaposition of a soldier icon over a flatland of empty continents is a powerful Cold War visual symbol; certainly, the placement of the American soldier over Indochina was an ominous representation of the overextension that would haunt Congress in the coming years.

Finally, Congress also marshaled maps to visually render arguments about how the Soviets were planning an aggressive global-sized war, both militarily and ideologically. The House Un-American Activities Committee (HUAC) released the *Soviet Total War* report in 1956, and its substantial collection of maps includes simple location sketches of communist-influenced regions to show international boundaries, as well as more elaborate maps arguing that the Soviet Union was becoming "uncontainable."[55] "How Communists Menace Vital Materials" (fig. 3.6), for example, is a quintessential use of the map as an evidentiary weapon: produced by the Research Institute of America, HUAC used this map to offer the ultimate penetration or thrust metaphor, a theme that was part of the Cold War at least since George Kennan fired off his Long Telegram in early 1946.[56] A black sickle hovers over Moscow, with militant arrows reaching each continent. Each arrow corresponds to a number in the legend, which indicates "Techniques Being Used in Each Red 'Thrust,'" and how the Soviet Union is contaminating valuable resources across the globe. This gendered visual argument feminizes, in particular, the so-called Third World spaces as being violated, which Cold War historian Frank Costigliola has noted as a frequent rhetorical trope in the era's discourse.[57]

The medium of the "report" itself is significant to the way Cold War congressional maps were interpreted as evidence. The flat surface limitations and their mostly conventional projections are important to their strategic uses. To be effective as evidence, the map had to conform to the expectations of its users; rather than challenge members of Congress with novel perspectives, these maps needed to provide simple spatial relationships and arguments about capacity that could be absorbed in quick, visual glances. The world, as seen through congressional reports, is often shown as a field of simple surfaces that renders foreign policy a process of abstract management.

While congressional maps demonstrate how cartography was used to measure government capacities for waging the Cold War, the map also frequently functioned as supplementary diplomatic evidence in well-publicized exchanges between the United States and the Soviet Union. In such cases, the map was employed more as a kind of weapon for

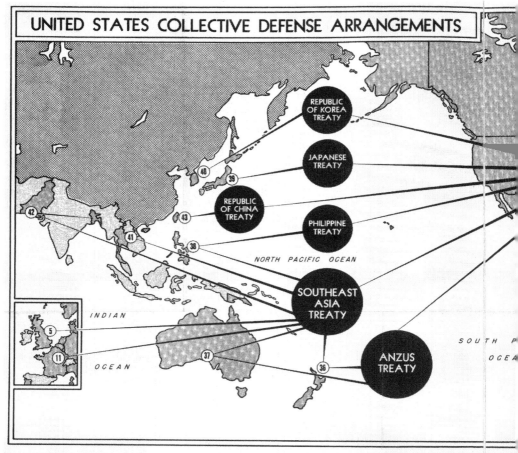

UNITED STATES COLLECTIVE DEFENSE ARRANGEMENTS

REPUBLIC OF KOREA TREATY

JAPANESE TREATY

REPUBLIC OF CHINA TREATY

PHILIPPINE TREATY

NORTH PACIFIC OCEAN

SOUTHEAST ASIA TREATY

ANZUS TREATY

INDIAN OCEAN

SOUTH P OCEA

NORTH ATLANTIC TREATY
(15 NATIONS)

A treaty signed April 4, 1949, by which "the parties agree that an armed attack against one or more of them in Europe or North America shall be considered an attack against them all; and . . . each of them . . . will assist the . . . attacked by taking forthwith, individually and in concert with the other Parties, such action as it deems necessary including the use of armed force. . . ."

1 UNITED STATES
2 CANADA
3 ICELAND
4 NORWAY
5 UNITED KINGDOM
6 NETHERLANDS
7 DENMARK
8 BELGIUM
9 LUXEMBOURG
10 PORTUGAL
11 FRANCE
12 ITALY
13 GREECE
14 TURKEY
15 FED. REPUBLIC OF GERMANY

RIO TREATY
(21 NATIONS)

A treaty signed September 2, 1947, which provides that an armed attack against any American State "shall be considered as an attack against all the American States and . . . each one . . . undertakes to assist in meeting the attack. . ."

1 UNITED STATES
16 MEXICO
17 CUBA
18 HAITI
19 DOMINICAN REPUBLIC
20 HONDURAS
21 GUATEMALA
22 EL SALVADOR
23 NICARAGUA
24 COSTA RICA
25 PANAMA
26 COLOMBIA
27 VENEZUELA
28 ECUADOR
29 PERU
30 BRAZIL
31 BOLIVIA
32 PARAGUAY
33 CHILE
34 ARGENTINA
35 URUGUAY

ANZUS (Australia – New Zealand – United States) TREATY
(3 NATIONS)

A treaty signed September 1, 1951, whereby each of the parties "recognizes that an armed attack in the Pacific Area on any of the Parties would be dangerous to its own peace and safety and declares that it would act to meet the common danger in accordance with its constitutional processes."

1 UNITED STATES
36 NEW ZEALAND
37 AUSTRALIA

PHILIPPIN E TRE
(BILATERAL)

A treaty signed Augu st 30, 1951, b the parties recogniz n "that an arm is the Pacific Area, on either of t Parties would be dan gerous to its that it will act "in meet the comm in accordance with i ts constitutio processes."

1 UNITE D STATE
38 PHILI: PPINES

Figure 3.5. Robert L. Bostick, Legislative Reference Center,
Library of Congress, "United States Collective Defense Arrangements," Senate
Committee on Foreign Relations, Studies on Review of United Nations Charter, 1954
(Courtesy of the Geography & Map Division of the Library of Congress)

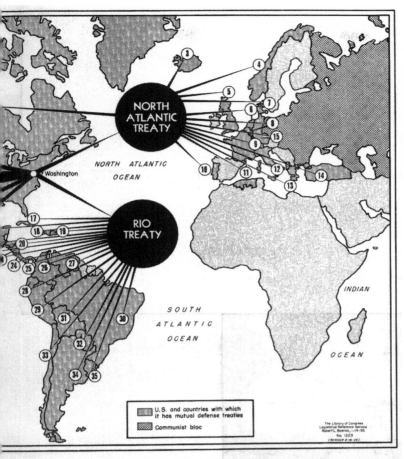

NORTH
ATLANTIC
TREATY

NORTH ATLANTIC OCEAN

○ Washington

RIO
TREATY

SOUTH
ATLANTIC
OCEAN

INDIAN
OCEAN

U.S. and countries with which
it has mutual defense treaties

Communist bloc

The Library of Congress
Legislative Reference Service
Robert L. Bostick, 1-14-55
No. 1223
(REVISED 2-18-44)

PANESE TREATY
(ATERAL)

ty signed September 5, 1951,
y Japan on a provisional basis
ss, and the United States agrees,
intain certain of its armed forces
about Japan . . . so as to deter armed
upon Japan."

1 UNITED STATES

39 JAPAN

REPUBLIC OF KOREA
(South Korea) TREATY

(BILATERAL)

A treaty signed October 1, 1953, whereby
each party "recognizes that an armed
attack in the Pacific area on either
of the Parties . . . would be dangerous to
its own peace and safety" and that each
Party "would act to meet the common
danger in accordance with its
constitutional processes."

1 UNITED STATES

40 REPUBLIC OF KOREA
(SOUTH KOREA)

SOUTHEAST ASIA
TREATY

(8 NATIONS)

A treaty signed September 8, 1954, whereby
each Party "recognizes that aggression by
means of armed attack in the treaty area
against any of the Parties . . . would
endanger its own peace and safety" and
each will "in that event act to meet the
common danger in accordance with its
constitutional processes."

1 UNITED STATES

5 UNITED KINGDOM

11 FRANCE

36 NEW ZEALAND

37 AUSTRALIA

38 PHILIPPINES

41 THAILAND

42 PAKISTAN

REPUBLIC OF CHINA
(Formosa) TREATY

(BILATERAL)

A treaty signed December 2, 1954,
whereby each of the parties "recognizes
that an armed attack in the West Pacific
Area directed against the territories
of either of the Parties would be
dangerous to its own peace and safety"
and that each "would act to meet the common
danger in accordance with its constitutional processes." The territory of
the Republic of China is defined as
"Taiwan (Formosa) and the Pescadores."

1 UNITED STATES

43 REPUBLIC OF CHINA
(FORMOSA)

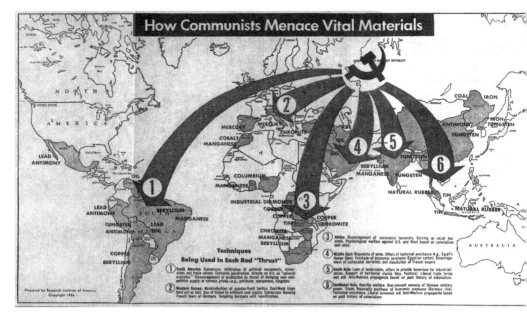

Figure 3.6. Research Institute of America, "How Communists Menace Vital Materials," House Committee on Un-American Activities, Soviet Total War, *1956 (Courtesy of Boatwright Library, University of Richmond)*

TECHNIQUES BEING USED IN EACH RED "THRUST"

1 South America: Subversion. Infiltration of political movements, universities and trade unions. Economic penetration. Attacks on U.S. as "colonial exploiter." Discouragement of production by threat of dumping own competitive supply at ruinous prices—e.g., antimony, manganese, tungsten.

2 Western Europe: Reintroduction of popular-front tactics. East-West trade held out as bait. Use of threat to withhold coal supply. Subversion. Rousing French fears of Germany. Tempting Germans with reunification.

3 Africa: Encouragement of nationalist terrorists. Stirring up racial tensions. Psychological warfare against U.S. and West based on colonialism and color.

4 Middle East: Shipments of arms. Offers of technical assistance (e.g., Egypt's Aswan Dam). Purchase of economic surpluses (Egyptian cotton). Encouragement of nationalist terrorists and dissolution of French empire.

5 South Asia: Loan of technicians, offers to provide know-how for industrialization. Support of territorial claims (Goa, Kashmir). Liberal trade terms and aid. Anti-Western propaganda based on past history of colonialism.

6 Southeast Asia: Guerilla warfare. Ever-present menace of Chinese military power. Trade, especially purchase of economic surpluses (Burmese rice). Technical assistance. Liberal economic aid. Anti-Western propaganda based on past history of colonialism.

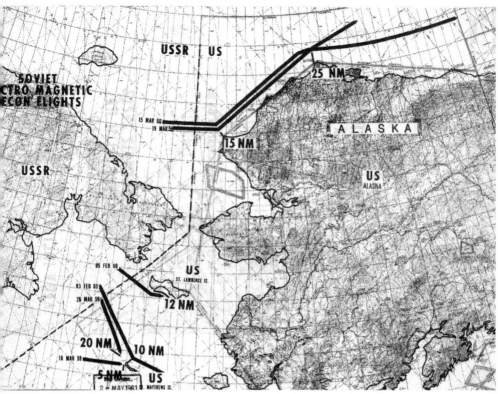

Figure 3.7. U.S. Delegation to the United Nations, "USSR Electro-magnetic Reconnaissance Flights," 1960 (Courtesy of the Geography & Map Division of the Library of Congress)

provocation and response—a way to *perform* the Cold War with the map as a material aid.[58] A compelling demonstration of cartography's higher stakes as diplomatic evidence came in July 1960. In New York, the U.S. ambassador to the United Nations, Henry Cabot Lodge, testified to the UN Security Council in response to the Soviet destruction of an American RB-47 aircraft that had supposedly crossed into Soviet airspace.[59] Lodge activates cartography to prove his point that the United States was not violating international air space and that the Soviets, in fact, tried to lead the plane off course so that it could be shot down. Newsreels of the event show one of Lodge's aides pulling out large poster-sized maps, with Lodge proceeding to walk the audience through the spaces of the map.[60]

More noteworthy than how these fairly straightforward and technical topographic maps actually look (fig. 3.7) is the striking way that Lodge's

use of the maps aesthetically dramatizes the cartographic form as a vehicle for accuracy and an emblem of Cold War.[61] The whole reason Lodge
can dispute the Soviet Union's claims is because of the sophistication of
American science. The RB-47, as Lodge points out, "was equipped with
the most sensitive available radar to tell them—with the degree of accuracy only possible through electronic means—how near they were to any
land mass."[62] Lodge's maps and their abilities to trace the Soviets' "astonishing and criminal" act make cartographic technology itself a central
part of the display.[63] The map is not simply a visual aid for Lodge's accu-
sations; it *is* the accusation. Here, the United States argues that the act of
producing knowledge about Soviet actions and being able to commit that
knowledge spatially to the page is a powerful weapon; to chart the upper
reaches of the Soviet Union with technological sophistication is to anchor
"truth" on the flat page with absolute precision. In addition, the incident
reaffirms the politicization of the air (and cartography itself), as the air
becomes a contested space in a tense war of perceptions.[64] As Lodge
referred to Soviet actions in the air, "We have got them all on a map.
You think we do not know, but we do."[65] In this way, the volley between
the United States and the Soviet Union could be seen cartographically as
attempts to define the world with authority before the other side could.
Beyond merely sitting in a committee report, maps were drafted for
active duty by actors like Lodge into the contested spaces of the Cold War.

The rhetorical lives of maps were, thus, reaching into important venues for public debate and international confrontation. Their conventions
on the page increased both in graphic simplicity and in their ability to
synthesize enormous amounts of data about the destructive capacities of
the Cold War—a potent combination of artistic ingenuity and scientific
innovation. The often metaphoric and iconic renderings of journalistic
cartographers were overlapping with the seemingly objective presenta-
tions by government cartographers about treaty obligations and military
resources. The fluidity of these cartographic discourses shows how both
official and popular discourses were circulating visions of the Soviet Union
as a world aggressor that forced America to a crossroads. On one hand,
maps were supporting the kind of counterforce and vigilance represented
in Kennan-style formulations of containment, but they were also suggesting the possibility of going beyond mere defensive postures. The function of popular and institutional maps as active agitators, as well as the
brand of bipolarity etched into their lines, is well represented by the life
of one extraordinary map of the early Cold War that unites these notions
of commitment and evidentiary weaponry together—the AFL's provocative

map of the Gulag labor camp, an image that reached across popular, journalistic, and government barriers and affirmed cartography as a strategic instrument in an actual Cold War offensive.

" 'GULAG'—SLAVERY, INC." AND THE HAILING OF CARTOGRAPHY INTO THE COLD WAR

In the September 17, 1951, issue of *Time*, the magazine's "News in Pictures" section featured a peculiar and striking image over a two-page spread—a map of the sprawling Soviet Union.[66] The map reveals a network of red circles and pink hammer-and-sickle icons dotted all over the topography of a stark gray and white Soviet landscape, each indicating the location of "Gulag" system prison camps. And in the bottom center of the map, entitled " 'Gulag'—Slavery, Inc." (fig. 3.8), sit three photos of emaciated bodies, with the caption " 'Gulag' Children." The accompanying text details how the map provoked an incident between the United States and the Soviet Union. At the 1951 San Francisco conference to inaugurate a Japanese peace treaty, " 'Gulag'—Slavery, Inc." became a cartographic weapon: "Would the Soviet delegate to the San Francisco conference like to see a map of Russia? 'I'd be delighted,' said Gromyko. Unfolding the map, Missouri's Republican congressman O. K. Armstrong helpfully explained: 'It happens to contain an accurate portrayal of every slave labor camp in the Soviet Union.' Gromyko blinked at the map, mumbled 'No comment,' and handed it to an aide who tossed it into the aisle."[67] Indeed, below the imposing map are before-and-after-style photos of the incident—on the left, Representative Armstrong unfolds the map before a sitting Andrei Gromyko, the Soviet deputy minister of foreign affairs; on the right, a stone-faced Gromyko stares ahead, as the map sits beside him on the floor of the conference room.[68] Together the map, labor camp photos, text, and pictures of the conference on the two-page magazine spread envelop the reader in a Cold War bipolar narrative through both word and image.

Of course, the Armstrong-Gromyko exchange can be added to a long list of minor anecdotes in the history of chilly, Cold War diplomatic relations, and the map seen as simply one small instance of the propaganda battles being waged by both sides. A deeper exploration of the map's active life, however, demonstrates cartography's strategic and ideological functions during the Cold War. Before the map became a kind of diplomatic prank in the hands of Congressman Armstrong, it began as a collaboration in a global labor research project between the AFL-CIO and the United Nations Economic and Social Council, authored by a Russian emigrant

"GULAG"—SLA

THE DOCUMENTED MAP OF FORCED LABO

New Edition (1951) Prepared for the Free

of the American Federation

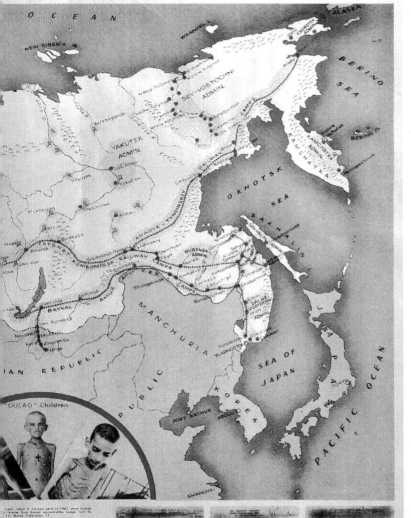

Figure 3.8.
American
Federation of
Labor, Free Trade
Union Committee,
"Gulag'—Slavery,
Inc.," 1951
(Photograph
© AFL-CIO, used
with permission)

ghostwriting journalist, and underwritten by the CIA and the Department of State. After the map's publication in *Time*, Voice of America broadcasts publicized it internationally, leading to frequent requests for reprints across the world, and it would later be used as a training case in psychological warfare for army personnel. The Gulag map also circulated in different versions, sometimes with its camp bodies omitted, sometimes adding photocopies of inmates' official release certificates to the margins, and often including different iterations of accompanying captions and text. The many appropriations of the piece have led to its citation as "one of the most widely circulated pieces of anti-Communist literature."[69]

Thus, the story of "'Gulag'—Slavery, Inc." goes well beyond the borders of the map's frames or its inclusion in a magazine article, as it represents a nexus of institutional interests, audience values, and multimediated usages that adds texture to the display of the map itself. In her study of Farm Security Administration photographs in the 1930s, Cara Finnegan points to the "eventfulness" of the images, which involves consideration of "their *specificity* as rhetorical documents, while accounting for circulation asks us to pay attention to their *fluidity* as material traces of history."[70] This duality of specificity and fluidity also can be used to characterize the rhetorical life of "'Gulag'—Slavery, Inc." The Gulag map is not merely a map, but a network of relationships between cartographic conventions, accompanying text, photographs, and the map's "embeddedness" into the medium in which it appears, whether an AFL pamphlet, a radio broadcast, or a *Time* article.

As such, the Gulag map reflects America's anxieties around its ability to strategically use what historian Susan Carruthers terms "the transatlantic politics of knowledge" in charting enemy space—and, thus, a map of the Soviet Union could say just as much (if not more) about the placement of America on the global stage as it could about the place of Soviet labor camps across Eurasia.[71] And this map absorbed the particular journalistic conventions of venues like *Time* and *Life* to make a simple, graphic argument, while being upheld as an authentic piece of cartographic evidence. In the process, however, the Gulag map commits the United States to a militarized position that goes beyond mere containment. A few months after embarrassing Minister Gromyko, it was Representative Armstrong, speaking at a keynote in front of the Conference on Psychological Strategy in the Cold War, who pointed out that, "Our primary weapons will not be guns, but ideas" and "truth itself."[72] How a map merges such ideologies of truth into informational weaponry in both its visuality and its circulation becomes central to understanding the particular Gulag case but also to the ground laid by this chapter as a whole—to show above all how cartography was an active and collaborative politicized practice.

The Origins and Production of "'Gulag'—Slavery, Inc."

Aleksandr Solzhenitsyn's *Gulag Archipelago* made "gulag" a global household name upon its sensational publication in 1973.[73] But twenty-six years before its popularization, Russian émigré turned crusading anticommunist journalist Isaac Don Levine was certainly trying his best to bring the term to public consciousness. Levine left Russia while in high school before World War I, gained a prominent name at the *New York Tribune* as the leading correspondent on the Bolshevik Revolution, and would go on to pen some of the earliest biographies of Lenin and Stalin. In the late 1930s, Levine collaborated with the famed defector Walter Krivitsky, a Soviet chief of military intelligence, ghostwriting a series of Krivitsky's stories about his escape in the *Saturday Evening Post*.[74] And perhaps most notably, Levine introduced the world to Whittaker Chambers's story of communist infiltration, bringing him to a meeting with Assistant Secretary of State Adolf Berle in 1939, and setting off a chain of events that would reach their full effect in the Alger Hiss trials.[75] Isaac Don Levine was a prominent exposé extraordinaire for anticommunism—the celebrity journalist with government contacts who helped make the "reveal" a staple of popular literature on communism.[76]

It is through Levine's editorship of the anticommunist magazine *Plain Talk* from 1945 to 1950 that cartography becomes a factor in this revelation project. Journalist Eugene Methvin makes the claim that Levine "published for the first time in English the word *gulag*."[77] And in the May 1947 issue of *Plain Talk*, Levine introduced the first version of "'Gulag'—Slavery, Inc.," which, at this stage was titled, "The First Comprehensive Map of Slave Camps in U.S.S.R."[78] Levine's text refers to it as a "Docu-Map" that "is one of the most remarkable compilations of our day, and affords a graphic insight into what has been until now the most carefully guarded secret of current life in Soviet Russia."[79] The label of Docu-Map heightens the focus on authenticity; rather than the human eyewitness that a photograph can provide, the map more closely resembles the expert witness who is called for an impartial opinion that studiously manages facts for the prosecutorial argument at hand.

The year 1947 was also when David Dallin and Boris Nicolaevsky released the influential *Forced Labor in Soviet Russia*, one of the first published offensives against the Soviet Union's prison system.[80] Like Levine, Dallin was a Russian émigré, journalist, and frequent government consultant.[81] His book also included maps of the reported camps; they were much barer in execution than Levine's map, with simple line drawings of the Soviet landscape featuring black and white dots and place names, and without positioning the USSR within the larger Eurasian continent.[82] The *New York Times* praised Dallin's courage in itemizing "the conditions which many deluded men insist on ignoring at the price of their own intellectual honesty" and warned that "the inevitable conclusion which any reader must draw . . . is that the term 'slave state' is not mere abuse, but a precisely accurate description."[83]

This last point about a "slave state" is particularly important, as both Levine and Dallin make a key (re)labeling of Soviet forced labor as slavery, a frame that would take on more and more significance and dramatic weight as the Cold War progressed.[84] As the architects of NSC-68 famously put it in 1950, slavery could be conceptualized in explicitly spatial terms: "The implacable purpose of the slave state to eliminate the challenge of freedom has placed the two great powers at opposite poles. It is this fact which gives the present polarization of power the quality of crisis. . . . The antipathy of slavery to freedom explains the iron curtain, the isolation, the autarchy of the society whose end is absolute power."[85] The Gulag map exemplifies this institutional commitment to a polarized rhetoric of slavery in the Cold War, as it served to organize slavery into a spatial system that demarcated what was free and what was not and to infiltrate the shrouded spaces behind the iron curtain.[86]

The map also participated in a key contextual shift in early Cold War culture where, according to Peter Novick, totalitarianism became a transcendent rhetorical label for industrialized state oppression, allowing for an explicit link between World War II fascism and Soviet communism.[87] As Les K. Adler and Thomas G. Paterson write, "ignoring the widely diverse origins, ideologies, goals, and practices of totalitarian regimes, Americans have tended to focus only on the seemingly similar methods employed by such regimes and to assume that these methods are the basic immutable characteristics of totalitarianism anywhere."[88] "Red Fascism" thus became a useful and widely appropriated label in postwar American foreign policy and popular culture.[89] President Truman, for example, stated in 1947: "There isn't any difference in totalitarian states. I don't care what you call them—you call them Nazi, Communist or Fascist . . . they are all alike."[90] And Rep. Everett Dirksen even suggested that the "red fascists" inspired the German camp system: "Why, it was from Russia that the infamous Hitler got the technique for Dachau. Make no mistake about it, it was borrowed from the people who would create an empire of the mind in the world and destroy freedom in this country."[91] American leaders knew of Russian exile camps as early as the Bolshevik Revolution, but, as Adler and Paterson write, "the German experience . . . seems to have stamped the image of the concentration camp, with all its overtones of mass extermination and unbridled terror, on the Russian camps."[92] Thus, the rhetoric of slavery was politicized under a totalitarian label through the iconic symbol of the camp. Rather than victims of human cruelty, camp laborers were victims of political ideology ("an empire of the mind"), a more abstract formulation that the abstract lines of a map supported well. To place a Russian camp on the map was to fix it inside a war of ideas between the United States and the Soviet Union.

The potential of "'Gulag'—Slavery, Inc." to participate in this unfolding ideological volley quickly became apparent, as Levine's map spread out from its *Plain Talk* origins shortly after its publication. The United Kingdom's *Tribune* adapted it and placed it prominently on its back cover in October of 1947.[93] Next, a November editorial in the *Chicago Tribune* praised the map's overseas circulation, as it "exposed more perfectly than a million words could do the essential character of the rulers of Russia and the creed which they espouse."[94] By validating the use of maps over language, the editors were prizing cartography's ability to visually stand in for a traditional argument. The editorial also sustains Levine's slavery label, reminding the audience of the Soviet Union's profit from a system built on "human material." The Chicago editorial thus situated the map in a powerful narrative about visuality and authenticity, which all came to be seen as necessary tools in the war against Soviet ideology. What *they* hide, *we* are able to locate and display—a powerful claim to authority over Cold War space.

With these rumblings about the specific location of labor camps, the issue began to gather greater attention. In November 1947, the American Federation of Labor made a formal proposal to the United Nations Economic and Social Council (UNESCO), in the hope that the council would begin an international investigation of forced labor.[95] By early 1949, the AFL's Toni Sender made the official presentation of the case against the USSR at a UNESCO convention in Chile, claiming to have volumes of testimony from escapees and marshaled evidence that "some of these labor camps are reported to be grouped together in huge clusters, with hundreds of thousands of inmates."[96] Ultimately, while the AFL's UNESCO project garnered a lot of attention, months passed and no official report or response came.[97] The AFL began to try alternate routes from the UN. Through its Free Trade Union Committee (FTUC), the union decided to wage a specific campaign galvanizing both domestic and international public opinion in a more innovative way, and the Gulag map offered that kind of innovation.[98] The FTUC was covertly funded by the CIA, according to historian Russell Bartley, as a "cold war foreign relations arm of the AFL utilized by successive U.S. administrations to combat communist influence in the international labor movement."[99] Jay Lovestone, head of the FTUC, had been a CIA operative since 1948 and was specifically using agency money to fund the research for the map.[100] Around this same time, the State Department's ongoing campaign since the end of World War II to combat Soviet forced labor converged with the AFL's, and behind the scenes the State Department threw its efforts into supporting the map's production.[101] Lovestone's office then corresponded with Isaac Don Levine throughout 1950 and paid him to commission an update of "'Gulag'—Slavery, Inc."[102] The new edition was finished in early 1951 and was first sent out to union newspapers advertising that copies of the map could be distributed by request.[103]

The production of "'Gulag'—Slavery, Inc." is inextricable from this complex and contentious entry of American organized labor into the U.S. government's anticommunist agenda. A distinct rhetorical tension emerged between domestic and international anticommunism, which material images like the Gulag map had to negotiate. For example, it is not incidental that the AFL referred to the Taft-Hartley Act's (1947) extensive restrictions on labor activism as a "slave labor bill"; yet, while AFL leaders fought the Taft-Hartley restrictions, they also took the opportunity to shore up their anticommunist credentials in the wake of serious challenges by both liberals and conservatives.[104] What resulted was a tenuous alliance between labor and government. Especially as McCarthyism began to shine a spotlight on unions and the Wisconsin senator's investigations increased in scope, the incentive of the AFL to take stances on militant, leftist unionism in its own ranks grew to include hardline anticommunist stances toward its union "brothers" abroad.[105] The AFL was quickly drafted into routing out communists and militant unions all over the world, through initiatives like the FTUC.[106]

The irony is that while, on one hand, the Gulag map was most certainly a bold protest document against oppressive labor practices, it also helped to suppress political dissent by serving as an image of commitment for organized labor to the government's Cold War goals. The black humor in the "Inc." of the map's title is doubly ironic—it places the USSR as a "corporate" slave labor system that perversely apes capitalism, while at the same time the AFL found itself increasingly *incorporated* into government policies. Still, to downplay these official government interests became part of the map's strategy. As William Young, a consultant for Army Operations Research, pointed out: "The authority of the AFL in many ways would probably outweigh the name of the US government, should it have attached its name to the document. It might then have been shrugged off as just another round in the propaganda battle between two governments. But here is a free trade union, the recognized spokesman for millions of American workingmen and associated internationally with many foreign labor organizations, presenting the laboring man's case against the nation that presents itself as the sole international champion of labor."[107] The Gulag map's label as a labor project allowed it to have a more fluid movement through the culture, as it could divorce itself from the top-down objectives of overt, government-sponsored propaganda and mitigate the ironies of its production.

Power and Placement: Reading "'Gulag'—Slavery, Inc."

For geographers Wood and Fels, a map has spatial authority because it makes existence claims and asks for validation and social assent from its users.[108] The Gulag map is an especially potent example of the power of posting: to be able to infiltrate enemy Soviet spaces and claim that "this is there" becomes a way of vying for control through the use of spatial knowledge. As Carruthers writes, "Bound tightly to new geopolitical exigencies, awareness of the Soviet camp system expanded during the early 1950s, encouraged by a state keen to spectacularize knowledge production through dramatic trials, witness testimony, and graphic representations."[109] The "spectacularization of knowledge production" is a fitting name, as the map provided the appropriate aesthetic drama to the statistical information on display.

The first visual choice to note in the Gulag map is simply how the sprawling nature of the Soviet landmass fills the entire frame itself but also features the connection to Eastern Europe and Asia, thus contextualizing the USSR's placement within the Eastern Hemisphere. The landmass is slightly rounded so that the Soviet Union appears uncontainable, spilling off the frame. We also see labor camps as far north as Franz Joseph Land in the Arctic, bordering in the south on Iran and Afghanistan, and stretching all the way to the Chukotsk Peninsula, where Alaska juts into the frame. As Levine explained in *Plain Talk*, "The boundaries of the slave labor regions have been drawn here with a view to understatement. All the territory controlled by GULAG, if consolidated, would make a submerged empire exceeding in area the boundaries of Western Europe."[110]

Such a comparison hints that the Soviet Union is potentially about to spill into the spaces of Western Europe. The higher density of sickles in the western part of Russia divorces the camps from their perceived isolation in the wastelands of Siberia and instead places the camps right inside the highly populated West. This implicitly argues that forced labor plagued the *whole* landscape, even the so-called civilized spaces of Europe. Such a wholeness reinforces the ability of "'Gulag'—Slavery, Inc." to become a *map-as-logo* in Benedict Anderson's terms and associate *all* of Russia and East Europe as one emblematic camp.[111]

In addition to these themes of size and scope, the use of iconography across the spread of the landmass marks an important rhetorical choice. The hammer-and-sickle icons in the AFL map "nationalize" the Soviet gulag as a state system, letting the camp stand in for the nation by mediating it with an iconic Cold War symbol.[112] These iconic choices create a kind of artificiality in the Gulag map. The camps are not to be seen as naturally occurring but as *imposed* by Soviet power on the land. The AFL map also emboldens railroad lines in deep black, with the dotted camps adhering in formation to these lines, thus heightening the focus on the corporate nature of Soviet labor by subtly emphasizing the industrial system that relies on forced labor to perpetuate it. The choices of accompanying text support these themes of artificiality. For example, the captions feature facts about the types of materials that individual camps produce: *Sorokski* produces light metal from nearby mines; *Ussolski* contributes to war industries and "construction of underground airfields."[113] A conventional map might conceal the sources of production for such resources, but the Gulag map subverts those expectations by revealing that it is slave labor that motors these engines of industry. Here, the Gulag map parodies a typical map of industries and natural resources as inhuman—that the effect of these places all over the map is the prizing of communist ideology at real, human cost.[114]

Perhaps most of all what the Gulag map visually demands is that the user affirm its authenticity—to accept that these abstract dots actually correspond to real camps on the ground. The map producers are promoting their very ability to map such forbidden areas, and the viewer is propositioned to consent that the information constituting the map must be authentic and verifiable.[115] But the producers of "'Gulag'—Slavery, Inc." are careful not to arrange their facts in an overly scientistic way. With its hand-drawn place names, simple use of icons, and lack of other geographic information about the Soviet Union, the overall crudeness of the presentation lacks the emphasis on cartographic technique and technology found, for instance, in the *National Geographic*'s rendering of the Cold War.[116]

The map especially supports these arguments for authenticity through its use of passports, photographs, and captions in the marginalia. Here, the Gulag map builds an architecture around the frame that attempts to affirm the material "truth" of forced labor. Thus, the map's production itself becomes a subject of the presentation.[117] While details on each passport are difficult to make out, the documents work together to make claims of existence—that these official papers have been acquired at great peril and affirm our knowledge of what the Soviets are doing.[118] The caption supplements this notion: "A typical 'passport' in the center of the upper left section is of the Soroki Administration. . . . It reads: 'USSR—People's Commissariat of Internal Affairs (NKVD)—Administration of Railroad Construction and Soroki Correctional Labor Camp—December 15, 1951—number 4/58024/16—City of Belomorsk.' The seals and signatures of the commanders, Kliuchkov and Georgeyev, are appended."[119] These almost mundane details of state bureaucracy on the release certificates are strategically used not only to support the authentic, material existence of Soviet forced labor but also to accentuate the autocratic nature of Soviet state power. Highlighting commander signatures, for example, assigns ownership of forced labor to the Soviet leaders. The very existence of these documents and their placement into readers' hands place the United States in the position to infiltrate Soviet space with the power of precise and accurate knowledge itself.

The other key pieces of marginalia, of course, are the photos of camp children, which complicate these appeals to authenticity. In most editions, the viewer sees a half circle marked by a thick red line, containing three pie-slice shaped photographs of what look to be camp prisoners, with the simple title "'GULAG' Children" above the center photo.[120] That central photo features the face of an emaciated child staring straight at the viewer, and the child is wearing a crucifix. The surrounding two photos feature similarly emaciated children. In very small print below the photos is a caption with more information about the photo's young subjects: "The photographs in the insert, taken in Teheran in early 1942, show typical examples of thousands of children upon their release from Soviet concentration camps. Left to right: Barbara Sliwinska, aged 2; Jan Gorski, 14; Monek Finkelstein, 12."

The photographs participate in transferring mediated experiences of fascism onto Soviet communism. As Levine has pointed out, most of the data for the map's compilation came from affidavit testimonies from Polish prisoners, upon being discharged from the camps in late 1941.[121] This "Polishness" of both the map's data and the bodies of the children draws on recent World War II memories that link the Polish nationality with the enactment of genocide. The choice of children is particularly poignant: these are not men who could have been encamped for political purposes or for petty crimes but are innocents who are potentially still free of Soviet ideology, which makes it easier for Americans, in particular, to identify with their victimhood. According to Ziva Amishai-Maisels, the trope of the "child alone" who "stares at the spectator" in Holocaust depictions was "the symbol par excellence of the innocent victim, a prime factor in confronting the world's conscience."[122] The focal point of the crucifix further buttresses this moral identification, infiltrating a Christian symbol into what is seen as an atheistic space. The photos' uncomfortable corporeality disrupts the clean and abstract lines of the map.

In addition, the placement of these photos on the map is a key piece of rhetorical selection. The half circle of photos sits within the map itself, but outside the confines of the USSR, slightly below center and to the right. In this way, the photos do not distract from the map's main focus on the camps; yet the photos are so striking that they cannot be merely supporting evidence—the map and the photos exist in a tense interplay. With the caption of each child's name so small, the photos become more of a generic symbol of oppression. The Gulag map argues that "these bodies can be located anywhere in this landscape," thus equating the entire Soviet landmass with the anonymous, oppressed bodies. So, even as the photographs add specificity and emotional weight to the map, the images ultimately generalize an abstract "moral lesson" about political ideology.[123] For Barbie Zelizer, "the repair work required in the immediate years after the war demanded a unified public, and keeping Nazi brutality at the forefront of public attention" eased the ability of the U.S. government to "move onto postwar agendas."[124] Certainly, "'Gulag'—Slavery, Inc." employs the truth-value of a photograph to document and provide witness but it also complicates this value by politicizing holocaust visuality for the Cold War.

Ultimately, this perpetuation of a wartime mentality is a central part of the whole presentation of the map. Shawn J. Parry-Giles's rhetorical analysis of Cold War propaganda notes a shift from a journalistic paradigm, where propaganda is posited as news, toward a centralized, militaristic paradigm, where propaganda is waged in the visual and linguistic frames of military crisis with the Soviet Union.[125] The Gulag map provides an interesting cartographic extension of this paradigm shift. The producers of the map have worked hard to present the map as an authentic and journalistic eyewitness to the reality of forced labor. Yet the Gulag map's power to cross Soviet borders and map the "unmappable" marks, however subtly, a more militant infiltration of Soviet space—the map goes beyond visualizing a mere containment of Soviet space and engages in an offensive strategy.[126] The juxtaposition of the photos with the system of camps suggests that the horrors of World War II are still ongoing: the enemies may have changed, but there is a still an enemy.[127]

Finally, what compounds these connections between photos, documentary evidence, and captions is a key piece of the "paramap": the centered bolded statement at the bottom of the 1951 edition, which reads: "A Reward of $1,000 Will Be Paid by the Free Trade Union Committee for Evidence Disproving the Authenticity of the Soviet Documents Here Reproduced."[128] The "reward" function redirects the map away from the merely informational and gives it a more overt kind of propositional power—the map now demands a response by issuing a challenge to engage with its claims to authenticity. The map-using audience is asked for its involvement, strengthening the map's function as an arbiter of public opinion. Still, because of the map's bounded completeness and claims to authority, this engagement with public opinion is less about interactivity and more about consensus and social assent.[129]

The Circulation of "'Gulag'—Slavery, Inc."

While an interpretative reading of the Gulag map can assess its ideological values and visual codes, to stop there is to fall prey to the age-old conception of maps as mere products, to assume that they are somehow finished and stable. But, as geographer John Pickles writes, "the whole map is a study in suggestion, in which cartographic techniques are used to depict a particular situation in such a way that both the intrinsic meaning and the suggested meaning resonate with other texts and images beyond [the] single map."[130] Initially, the Gulag map was promoted through union channels to provide information about Soviet forced labor to members. Yet, after newspapers like the *Minneapolis Star Tribune* and the *Baltimore Sun* began to feature it prominently, the demand for the map, and the diversity of that demand, increased substantially.[131] Publications like the *Christian Science Monitor* and the *NEA Daily News* would take the basic Gulag map and then reproduce it in their own particular graphic style.[132] The circulation of the map reached its zenith after sensational reports of the 1951 showdown between Representative Armstrong and Gromyko at the San Francisco conference.[133] The use of photos of the Gromyko-Armstrong exchange in *Time* and the *Los Angeles Times* suggested that the map had concrete effects in the "real" relations of the Cold War. In addition, the *New York Times* prominently highlighted

Gromyko's verbal response: "It would be interesting to know what capitalist slave is the author of this map," adding new complications to the "slave" theme.[134] These uses once again affirmed "'Gulag'—Slavery, Inc." as a Cold War weapon, designed to provoke responses and counterresponses, and thus requiring continual recirculation.

The domestic response to "'Gulag'—Slavery, Inc." wildly exceeded expectations. The AFL fielded requests for reprints from a wide variety of organizations—particularly labor unions, high schools, universities, and churches, but also government and military institutions.[135] The superintendent of the Minneapolis Public Schools wrote that the map "would be used and viewed by upwards of 1100 pupils and teachers."[136] A Methodist pastor in Flemington, Pennsylvania, requested the map "to use it with several study groups in the local church as we study the evils and dangers of communism to our way of life."[137] Martin Berach of Barberton, Ohio, wrote that "my interest in it is to show it to some of my friends who argue that such a thing does not exist in Soviet Russia"; and William Chamberlain of Dayton justified that "I would like very much to have a copy for several reasons; one of the best of these is that it is a very clever way of building up American patriotism."[138]

Such a diverse array of requests cast "'Gulag'—Slavery, Inc." into a new role as an emblem for Cold War citizenship—the kind, perhaps, the *New York Times* had in mind with its surveys of geographic education. Engaging with the map had an educational and civic function, seen as a public duty by many to spread awareness about the oppressiveness of Soviet ideology. For example, the 1951 AFL pamphlet *Slave Labor in Soviet Russia*, which was continually requested by schools and civic groups, activated the map as a living document that was meant to be passed around and displayed. The pamphlet urged the reader to "show this pamphlet to anyone you know who talks of or believes in Soviet 'democracy' and Soviet 'socialism.'"[139] This involved the map's ability to showcase the knowledge production that was central to the Cold War: to *know* (and to quantify) the spaces of the Soviet enemy is to be a consenting participant in the conflict. Yet the map's employment in these various contexts suggests that this cartographic knowledge needed to be actually understood, taught, and disseminated by citizens themselves in meaningful social exchanges.

The map was also growing in utility as an international Cold War weapon, used to break through iron curtains and provoke confrontations. Not only would it find use in "official" diplomacy between actors like Armstrong and Gromyko; the Gulag map would become a key example of "public diplomacy," characterized by Nicholas Cull as "a top-down dynamic whereby governments distributed information to foreign publics using capital-intensive methods such as international radio, exhibitions, and libraries."[140] *Voice of America* broadcasts picked up the Gromyko story and described the map to viewers on the air, even offering to mail it out by request. The story circulated widely in Latin America, and the Voice of America (VOA) received four hundred airmail requests in the first twenty-four-hour period after the broadcast. The Government Printing Office then printed thousands of Spanish-language versions for distribution through the United States Information Services (USIS) offices.[141] As a Chilean miner wrote to the VOA, "Please send me the map you offered so that I may show it to my many co-workers, who, unfortunately, are influenced by the poison of Communism."[142] Thus the Gulag map could serve official government objectives in Latin America by creating the appearance of a public service function.

The map served similar purposes throughout Cold War Europe.[143] In West Berlin, the map was plastered strategically so that it could be seen by people crossing the zonal boundary during a communist youth festival.[144] The AFL contracted for German translations, and five thousand were specifically pressed in Germany, through the Department of State, to be posted on factory bulletin boards.[145] A French-language version was also produced for distribution, and the Swiss weekly *Die Nation* published the map.[146] A commissioner for the U.S. Economic Cooperation Administration's Special Mission in Iceland commented that "personally I think the whole thing is the best piece of propaganda against communism that I have seen."[147] In October 1951, Soviet military police seized 500,000 copies of the map, which were being printed through USIS channels in Vienna for the German-language paper *Wiener Kurier*.[148] Officials reportedly called the map a "filthy pamphlet" and "an effort to slander," which started a war of words with Walter J. Donnelly, the U.S. high commissioner for Austria, who protested for the map's "prompt release" and called the Soviet response "an uncultured piece of sophistry."[149] The contracted printer for the USIS lived in the United States sector of Vienna but sent it across town to be finished by a binder and his wife, who lived in the tenth district of the Soviet sector. That ability of the map to penetrate Soviet space became literalized, working as a material force with the processes of its production, and even its printing becoming part of the Cold War offensive. A *New York Times* editorial about the Vienna incident spoke to this strategic use in engineering a Soviet response: the editors point out that up to now "there has been no effort at refutation, no denial of the map's accuracy, no invitation to foreigners or U.N. observers to visit these places and check for themselves."[150] Yet, with the seizure in Vienna, that original silence now was disrupted by the "brute force of police," which was, as the *Times* argues "the most eloquent proof that the map was irrefutable."[151] The binders' subsequent arrest prompted a letter from AFL's Matthew Woll directly to Dean Acheson at the State Department to protest the unfair treatment of international workers and the suppression of free speech.[152]

Thus, in keeping with the increasingly militaristic propaganda of the early 1950s, the map was being mobilized in more systematic efforts to combat the Soviet Union. As if the map had not penetrated enough into foreign policy initiatives and international incidents, there were attempts to take the map's mediated reach even further. It was reported that a Hollywood motion picture studio was preparing a short film on the map to be released nationally in commercial houses.[153] The American Federation of Musicians even proposed to the AFL a project run jointly with Voice of America to record an album of Russian "slave labor songs" to raise awareness of the issue, complete with the suggestion that the "album should carry the famous AFL slave labor map, as a background."[154]

The public engagement with the Gulag map eventually died down by early 1953, but the forced labor issue continued to be a frequent public and government concern, sparking a series of reports and hearings, and a similar campaign by the AFL against forced labor in China.[155] Still, the map itself continued to leave traces long after its remarkable circulation. During Aleksandr Solzhenitsyn's famed tour of Washington, D.C., in June 1975, after being awarded the Nobel Peace Prize, his speech brought "'Gulag'—Slavery, Inc." back into public memory: "In 1947, when liberal thinkers and wise men of the West, who had forgotten the meaning of the word 'liberty,' were swearing that in the Soviet Union there were no concentration camps at all, the American Federation of Labor published a map of our concentration camps, and on behalf of all of the prisoners of those times, I want to thank the American workers' movement."[156] Here, Solzhenitsyn recasts and (re)remembers the map as a protest document from "brothers in labor," dissociating it from the hand of American state power that sanctioned the map.[157]

And, finally, as the Cold War reignited in the early 1980s, with renewed institutional rhetoric by the U.S. government against the Soviet Union, "'Gulag'—Slavery, Inc." would continue its flow through Cold War culture. In 1982 the U.S. Senate adopted a resolution that expressed fears that human rights violations were being committed in the construction of the trans-Siberian pipeline.[158] The State Department's report included a map detailing the extent of the camps in the Soviet Union, featuring an aerial perspective map of the *inside* of a forced labor camp. In the evolution of the Gulag map, the State Department could now dramatically hyperfocus on infiltrating Soviet space with more sophisticated technologies, a stark departure from the crude but effective hammer-and-sickle propaganda of the old AFL map.[159] And yet, coming full circle, the AFL-CIO devoted a spread to "'Gulag'—Slavery, Inc." in November 1982, reprinting the map, and reminding its members that "American Labor was first to raise its voice against the slave labor system in the USSR." In one of its final public appearances, the Gulag map was being appropriated by the AFL for a new purpose—to reclaim the map as part of its institutional memory and commemorate organized labor's role in waging cold war.[160]

THE EAST-WEST LINES OF COLD WAR CULTURE

"'Gulag'—Slavery, Inc." allows a glimpse into the everyday flow of Cold War culture. This culture actually *draws* the map and gives it meaning beyond what the map simply displays on the page. The State Department could use the Gulag map as a diplomatic weapon in its mission to cultivate international opinion, the AFL could use it as evidence of its commitment to anticommunism around the world (and in its own ranks), and citizens could use it as a frame for Cold War citizenship. The Gulag map was marshaled into Cold War skirmishes both public and private—and reminds us that any reading of a cartographic image must negotiate maps as both product and process. That tension is what gives mapping an explosive dimension in a highly spatialized conflict such as the Cold War.

"Why a map?" remains a viable question in this case. If the focus is on having the authentic evidence to prove the existence of forced labor camps, then why not make the camp photos or the release certificates the main subject of the display? A plausible answer lies in this competition for the power of placement between the United States and the Soviet Union. The photos and the release certificates need the map to anchor them in a particular spatial network—that act of mapping commits the existence of forced labor, as authenticated through photos and documents, into the international, bipolar geopolitics of the Cold War. And in an era of heightened ideological conflict between two nuclear superpowers, the need for scientific abstraction and management grew. Geographer Sanjay Chaturvedi points out that in Cold War geopolitics, often "the singular attributes of a particular place were subordinated to its perceived position in the abstract spaces of the Cold War."[161] A map could manage facts with efficiency and cleanliness in ways that a photograph could not, and could arrange its data through the use of aggregate forms and abstract symbols. In this way, the Gulag map must draw on cartography's own perpetual story of itself as a self-evident reflection of truths about the world. As Wood and Fels write, "The most fundamental cartographic claim *is to be a system of facts*, and its history has most often been written as the story of its ability to present those facts with ever increasing accuracy."[162] The map might poignantly protest the plight of prisoners, but the map is equally situated as a tool of surveillance that affirms the era's essential bipolarity. In the case of "'Gulag'—Slavery, Inc.," by filling Soviet space with points representing labor camps and then circulating the map into actual Soviet territory and at home, the U.S. coalition of labor unions and foreign policy elites spatialized and literally projected their power on to the flat page and into the culture of the Cold War.

Yet the Gulag map has a peculiar relationship to both accuracy and authenticity. The entire story of the map revolves around a constant *defense* of its evidentiary claims and attempts to affirm the validity of the abstract visual evidence (e.g., the reward for disproving its authenticity; the *New York Times*'s defense of the map after its seizure overseas). This consistent reinforcement of the Gulag map's authenticity by a variety of agents leads to an important conclusion that resonates with the cartographic culture of the era: that there existed an obvious anxiety about the potentially provocative artificiality of this map. Producers and audiences were tacitly acknowledging that the Gulag map was a highly charged rhetorical document that bared its ideological convictions, *not* a self-evident scientific aid. The map's agents put in a considerable amount of discursive work to support the map, making for a fascinating, multilayered circulation.

Ultimately, the anxiety around "'Gulag'—Slavery, Inc." reflects a larger anxiety about the artificial, abstract nature of the very Cold War conflict that the map helped (re)produce. The active rhetorical life of this map can be read as a demonstration that the Cold War had to be continually manufactured and readapted, and truly required a dynamic, material engagement with a host of international audiences. The Gulag map emerged from a visual Cold War culture, explored in this chapter, where stark borders were being drawn between ideological forces, and it was part of a fluid exchange of cartographies taking place across popular, government, and private institutional agencies. The Gulag map showed up in *Time* as part of the magazine's journalistic approach to spatializing foreign policy for its readers; and yet its CIA connections and the stamp of authorship by the AFL kept its rhetorical life active and contingent upon its ability to fight the Cold War for "official" actors.

In a certain sense, maps functioned as instrumental technologies to antagonize, survey forbidden spaces, and win public relations battles over the authenticity of information about the Soviet Union. The simplified, powerful, and often metaphor-laden graphics of venues such as *Life* and *Fortune* resonated as part of the same mapping culture that could activate maps' utility in congressional arguments over issues of mutual security and into labor union and intelligence agency collaborations to propagandize our own people and the spheres of Soviet influence. These maps graphed America's newly expanding commitments all over the globe; their very designs *and* circulations etched their lines as self-evident and situated the Soviet Union as a potentially knowable space. American cartographers and foreign policy makers could use the scientific authority of maps to make bold, controversial (and artistic) arguments about the threat and moral bankruptcy of the Soviet Union. Building on the commonsense reinterpretation of the fresh new perspectives by the air-age globalists, the graphic designers of the Cold War saw the map as even more useful and materially substantive in provoking response than ever. That inventive power to say, "We know what you're doing *over there*" not only committed America to the Cold War on the flat page, but it activated maps as viable informational weapons. The journalistic maps, the congressional and government agency maps, and even those unique maps like "Gulag—Slavery, Inc.," which crossed an impressive amount of Cold War spaces, are united by this sense of cartography as part of America's performance of its image in the Cold War. These maps did not sit in reports or magazines as mere backdrops or illustrations for Cold War strategic problems—they were vehicles and media for generating powerful responses and framing the capacities and the future capabilities of Soviet power. Cold War cartography housed a new kind of flexibility of vision as seen in Harrison, a new kind of fluidity between agencies as seen with S. W. Boggs, but also a new kind of usability across media platforms and private and public institutions, as seen in this chapter.

And even as this usability helped to etch these momentous East-West confrontations, a new expansion of the Cold War's spatial reach into the so-called developing world was emerging almost right away to complicate such dichotomies. From almost the very same point that maps were being actively appropriated to instantiate specific visions of the Soviet Union, there were important attempts to write the spaces of the "South" as prime interpretative ground for the Cold War. Maps proved a dynamic and flexible medium for housing the massive projects of modernization and development—decisive moves from mere containment toward an ambitious project to remake the world in the United States' image.

4

FRAMING THE THIRD WORLD

American Visions of "The South" and the

Cartography of Development

The era of decolonization during the Cold War was a busy time for the Department of State's Office of the Geographer. Beginning in the 1950s, the office commenced a series of intra-agency publications called the *Geographic Bulletin* and *Geographic Notes* for circulation to foreign policy specialists, staff researchers, and area specialists in the department.[1] Essentially, these were memo-length updates on volatile or changing world geographic situations, accompanied by a map of the area in question. What was remarkable about the circulation of the *Notes* and *Bulletins* was not the cartography itself (mostly, these were simple political maps of particular nation-states and their major administrative divisions, and the text provided basic geographic, political, and demographic information about that state), but rather the sheer pace at which decolonization was taking place, and the ensuing response that this required in terms of producing geographic knowledge. A new *Notes* would appear any time a state declared its independence, or its boundaries and administrative divisions were reconfigured: in 1966 came Guyana (the fifty-seventh state to announce its independence since World War II), Botswana, and Barbados; in 1968 came Swaziland; 1970 saw Tonga and Fiji; 1971 saw Qatar and Bahrain; 1972 Bangladesh.[2] By December of 1975, as the *Geographic Notes* captioned with its map, Angola marked the eightieth newly independent state since 1943.[3]

With this running tally on each map, it was as if the State Department was quantifying its astonishment about these world developments. As director of the State Department's Bureau of Intelligence and Research (and supervisor of the Geographer's Office), Thomas L. Hughes said at a 1965 lecture at Hamilton College, "already this week we have corporately encompassed about 120 old nations, discovered two new ones, estimated three elections, cast bets on the composition of two cabinets, fretted over one unilateral declaration of independence and another mutiny, noted the decline of two emerging forces and the resurgence of one old established force, and discounted three abortive plots erroneously attributed to the CIA."[4]

In addition to these notes on individual countries, the State Department was continually issuing revisions of the CIA's "Newly Independent States of the World" map, a world map on a Miller projection that simply colored in gray the states that had become independent since 1943 (fig. 4.1). Viewed side-by-side, the 1962, 1963, 1964, and 1965 "Newly Independent States" maps show a growing mass of grays around the equator, almost covering the entire African continent, and filling in Southeast Asia from Pakistan to Indonesia.[5] Visually, the gray creates a kind of dividing line between the states of the North and the states of the South, bringing the world's focus into a kind of top-bottom relationship— and giving an uneasy identity to those considered "Newly Independent." The accompanying memorandum spoke of the need for current, reliable geographic facts, noting the value of "constant monitoring" to define the ever-changing patterns of the world's states and pointing out that "political changes superimposed upon the geography of the globe alter the structure of the international community of nations, in name or by dimension, and they . . . must be reflected in pertinent official maps and documents."[6] Thus, this "community of nations" required continual expert surveillance. A 1968 *Bulletin* explored Africa's "Patterns of Sovereignty" in a map series that attempted to make sense on the flat page of the complex histories of European influence, while accounting for the sequence of how thirty-six African countries gained independence over the course of twenty-five years. The new world order had new dependencies and new shapes, and the "puzzle pieces" of nation-states were not what they used to be. At the same time, the Geographer's Office was continually revising its International Boundary Study (a project since the days of S. W. Boggs) to reflect the international hotspots for political border controversies, a seemingly impossible and interminable task in a world where a new nation-state was defining and redefining itself every week.[7]

The State Department's geographic approach is just one example of a variety of ways that America's Cold War–era cartography interpreted the world in the face of massive disruption. The era of decolonization, during which social scientists, including geographers and cartographers, collaborated on massive projects to turn the world into data, provides a fitting articulation for Bruno Latour's sense of maps as "immutable mobiles." In this way, maps worked in the tensions of being scientific representations

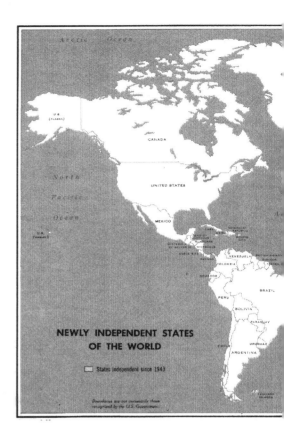

Figure 4.1. Central Intelligence Agency, "Newly Independent States of the World," 1962 (Courtesy of the Geography & Map Division of the Library of Congress)

of spatial data, purported to synthesize and classify "truth" on the page, while at the same time they *moved* flexibly throughout the culture. It is no wonder that the scientific power of maps was growing at the same time they were becoming more and more diverse and useful in their arguments. The ways in which these maps were perceived were also, not incidentally, changing dramatically. The 1950s and 1960s saw the increasing digitization of Cold War mapping, as various users across government agencies, trying to manage immense amounts of data about the decolonizing world, viewed maps more and more on screens. Maps themselves had long served as "screens" for viewing the world, but now that function was re-mediated further with cartography's electrification. In this sense, maps became a kind of interface for monitoring ever-changing patterns in the volatile Cold War. Cartographic experts could now layer the world on the basis of a host of political and socioeconomic data, and manipulate a seemingly pliable global landscape according to models and statistics. The

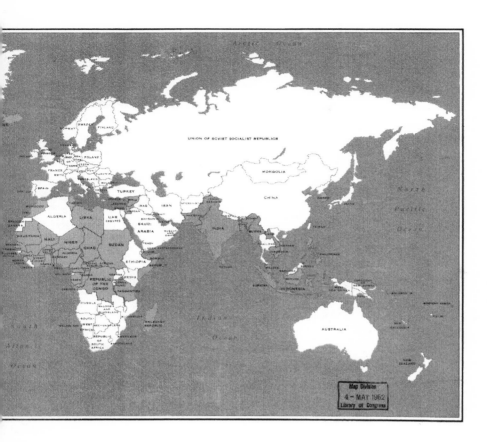

rhetorical lives of maps were now enhanced by cartography's new flexibility to be a portable configuration of ones and zeroes. The irony of a fixed, binary code accounting for the spaces of tumult, revolution, violence, and perpetual unrest is perfectly suited to the essential artifice of the Cold War—an attempt to stabilize a diverse globe into classifiable "worlds" for ideological and material influence (and often control) by superpowers.

The early years of the Cold War had seen a rapid partitioning of the world into blocs and units, bipolar alliances, regional surveillance, and increasingly state-classified uses of sophisticated mapping technology. Within these developments, the so-called Third World had become a central spatial battleground.[8] The State Department was articulating the complex Cold War geopolitical tensions around both the places of the North and the South that had been capturing the geographic imagination since the Cold War's inception. America responded cartographically to such tensions in a variety of compelling ways, and this chapter offers a discussion of these new perspectives that challenged familiar East-West geopolitical binaries. In the Cold War, American maps served as both technical conduits and rhetorical symbols for international development—interfaces that synthesized world data into manageable fields of vision. For Michael Shapiro, "modern 'security' represents the ultimate in leaving nothing to chance. The number and intensity of interests congregated in modern super powers, for example, have resulted in a comprehensive level of surveillance and intervention all over the globe. Within this intensification of the security-oriented gaze, the meanings of landscapes and people everywhere are subjected to an intensified form of objectification."[9] A map provided a fitting medium for a logic of intervention and the objectification of world space, as it abstracts borders, shapes, and area into one readable, intensely concentrated, and sanitized image that can be reproduced and reappropriated.

Not only did maps reflect changes in spatial worldviews during the decolonization and rise of the Third World, but the very *act* of mapping and all of its processes were bound up in the way an array of institutions and actors approached and constructed an increasingly powerful South. As I have noted, the bipolarity of America's placement of the Soviet Union and its capabilities became evident through the ways in which cartography functioned as both images of commitment and evidentiary weapons for waging (and circulating the ideologies of) the Cold War. This chapter builds on these frameworks by exploring how American maps accounted for the expansion of the Cold War into the Third World, and how cartography itself was a mode by which development could be envisioned and practiced. The kind of East-West commitments suggested by maps like " 'Gulag'—Slavery, Inc." were increasingly constrained by North-South relationships, where the Third World became a contested field on the map by which to envision and wage cold war. The volatility, however, of these relationships ensured that challenges would come to these familiar frames of the world—despite the progressive narratives of development imposed by particular institutions, the South could not be easily contained.

To explore these relationships, I first examine the etymology and rhetorical implications of the Third World's emergence as a contested, international concept of world space in the Cold War. Next, I discuss how America placed itself vis-à-vis the emergent South, and how America used cartography as an instrument of development and modernization, and an interface for appointed experts, to further both its security and economic interests. In particular, I highlight the U.S. cartographic collaborations with the United Nations and the multi-institutional medical cartography initiatives to map Third World disease as representative examples of the developing geopolitical tensions between North and South. In these cases, U.S. foreign policy elites and scientists attempted to make America a model of modernization on the world map, while they also surveyed the world for geographic knowledge that would protect U.S. global interests—during a time when decolonization reached its peak and antagonisms between the United States and the Soviet Union reached greater intensity.

SKETCHING THE CONTOURS OF THE THIRD WORLD: ORIGINS AND APPROACHES

The "Third World" is both a fundamentally spatial and Cold War–centric idea. From its conception, it was continually contested and redefined, and it operated as a classification serving a variety of interests.[10] The term itself has been attributed to French economist Alfred Sauvy in 1952 when he used it to demarcate "developing countries" in contrast to the two major Cold War power blocs.[11] The idea, of course, of developed and undeveloped nations was not new. But in the early Cold War, the existence of two international economic systems at such loggerheads was new and thus the "third bloc" became a geopolitically significant, abstract space where the United States and the Soviet Union vied for influence.[12]

Sauvy originally used the term *tiers monde* to mean a kind of "Third Force," emphasizing the "third way" of nonalignment rather than underdevelopment.[13] Certainly, after the famed 1955 conference at Bandung, Indonesia, the idea of an international movement using "Third World" status as a kind of organizing, resistant banner became more and more viable.[14] Thus, from the early etymological origins of the Third World, the idea "served as a hegemonic conceptualization of the world, and of struggles against that hegemony" for both "the paradigms of capitalist modernity" and the "radical advocates of liberation from Euro-American colonialism."[15] According to Carl Pletsch's work defining the complex geopolitics of Third World development, the phrase the "Third World" itself became a kind of "abbreviated ideology" that could represent both state power and its resistance.[16]

Whether the actual term "Third World" was used as a tool of state power or protest, there existed a marked, three-tiered geopolitical framework that powerfully organized Cold War discourse.[17] In Pletsch's estimation "the very thought of three worlds on one planet constrained even those who were opponents of the Cold War or partisans of the third world to do work that contributed both to the strategies of containment and to the exploitation of the third world."[18] Especially from the standpoint of Western elites, the idea of three worlds was inextricable from the modernization doctrines of Cold War social science and public policy. Modernization represented a lineage of development that leads from tradition to modernity; as a discourse, modernization argued that with the right knowledge and instruments, underdeveloped civilizations could advance themselves.[19] In this way, the three worlds concept folded space into time, partitioning the "one world" of 1940s globalism into a continental hierarchy where certain spaces are frozen onto the map as always "arriving."[20] In this process, as Arturo Escobar points out, "to represent the Third World as 'underdeveloped' is less a statement about 'facts' than the setting up a regime of truth through which the Third World is inevitably known, intervened on, and managed."[21] This management of knowledge defined Third World space by what it "lacked" (whether in money, political stability, health—even in developing nations' abilities to properly map themselves).[22] In turn, the First World and the Second World would define themselves and each other around the ways they could meet this lack.

Despite the ways that the Third World was defined as underdeveloped and backward, it is important to note how the South became a powerful geopolitical trope.[23] While this "mass" South was often presented as a passive repository of Cold War interests, it was just as often appropriated (and feared) for its potential strength and threat.[24] As geographer Donald W. Meinig wondered aloud as early as 1956, "Is it not ironic that in this era . . . of unprecedented concentration of military power in the hands of two powerful nations . . . the small nation, the obscure culture group, the wholly non-industrialized people, are able to exert far greater force upon the complexion of events than in the past?"[25] The depth of such force helps explain the massive scale on which modernization projects would be established (as well as the extraordinary violence that often accompanied them).[26]

The tumult of decolonization and the ensuing work by nation-states and global actors to define a postcolonial identity constrained the new spaces of the so-called North and South during the 1950s and 1960s. In defining the spatial relationships between an essentialized East and West, Edward Said noted a "*distribution* of geopolitical awareness" that resulted in "an *elaboration* not only of a basic geographical distinction (the world is made up of two unequal halves, Orient and Occident) but also of a whole series of 'interests' [that]...*is*, rather than expresses, a certain *will* or *intention* to understand, in some cases to control, manipulate, even to incorporate, what is a manifestly different (or alternative and novel) world."[27]

With the politicization of the equatorial masses in the Cold War, the complication of East-West with North-South set up new "processes of subjectification," in Homi Bhabha's terms, where there were constant attempts to "fix" the developing nations' places in the world.[28] What makes the Cold War in the Third World compelling and explosive is that this stability was never reached, and the North-South relationship, just like East-West, was always in flux.[29] For example, the "Third World" and "development" never remained static concepts during the course of the Cold War.[30] For much of the 1950s, development had the optimistic connotation of providing materials and technical knowledge for developing nations to maintain themselves; in the 1960s, as decolonization spread, though, development became more about building stable nations and infrastructures that could withstand communist influence.[31]

Cartographic knowledge provides one entry point into exploring these competing imaginaries, especially the ways the South was envisioned (and bounded) by the North.[32] The rise of geography as a quantitative social science that could aid in political, economic, and social global development during the Cold War is integral to understanding the contextual forces that brought the Third World into view.[33] The social implication of mapping was often downplayed, since a map was frequently seen as an instrument or a confluence of scientific laws. At the same time, mapping was certainly implicated into the race to chart and classify the immense social upheaval of a decolonizing world. In a review of the major cartographic advances in the years 1950 to 1975, for example, cartographer Arthur Robinson cited the explosion of thematic mapping in response to the overwhelming amount of new social phenomena that both *could* be mapped by new technologies (particularly in the digital realm) and, as was increasingly thought, *should* be mapped.[34]

From popular maps to institutional maps to alternative maps of protest, cartography was expanding exponentially into covering a wider range of social and political topics, while still conceived as a system of scientific techniques. This classificatory power of the map was irreparably linked with cartography's history as a colonial project of managing foreign spaces and bounding state control. So even as maps adapted to decolonization, they continued to be, as Graham Huggan writes, marked by a discrepancy, "which marks out the 'recognizable totality' of the map as a manifestation of the desire for control" and had to negotiate "the 'rules' of cartography, both those which function overtly in the systematic organization of the map and those which are implied in the empowering methods of its production."[35] In addition, maps of development often continued to promote a partitioned world of distinct landmasses as an enduring feature of a global geographic imagination, what Martin W. Lewis and Karen E. Wigen call the problematic "myth of continents." This myth advances—in this case, through the visualization of a map—that there are somehow significant cultural groupings denoted by these divisions and that continents are still useful units of analysis. According to Lewis and Wigen, particularly in the international relations of the Cold War, the continental framework served conveniently (and still does) to "structure our perceptions of the human community" but "does injustice to the complexities of global geography, and it leads to faulty comparisons. When used by those who wield political power, its consequences can be truly tragic."[36] This uneasy navigation would mark the U.S. approach to mapping the Third World throughout the Cold War, as maps negotiated the tension between protecting international security interests and idealizing the Third World's capacity to democratize according to America's will and influence.

BRINGING UP THE SOUTH: MAPS, MODERNIZATION,
AND U.S. GLOBAL INTERESTS

At even the earliest stages of the Cold War, the highest halls of American leadership were formulating, with missionary zeal, a spatially conscious global push to modernize the Third World.[37] As a new corollary to the European Marshall Plan, President Harry S. Truman outlined what became to be known as the "Point 4 Program" (so named because it was the fourth plank in his inaugural address on January 20, 1949), which set out to bring "scientific advances and industrial progress" to the world's underdeveloped areas.[38] As Truman offered,

> More than half the people of the world are living in conditions approaching misery. Their food is inadequate. They are victims of disease. Their economic life is primitive and stagnant. Their poverty is a handicap and a threat both to them and to more prosperous areas. For the first time in history, humanity possesses the knowledge and the skill to relieve the suffering of these people. The United States is preeminent among nations in the development of industrial and scientific techniques. The material resources which we can afford to use for the assistance of other peoples are limited. But our imponderable resources in technical knowledge are constantly growing and are inexhaustible.[39]

Truman's Point 4 Program, which morphed into the State Department's Technical Cooperation Administration, was concerned with an interventionism of ideas and knowledge production. Its establishment also

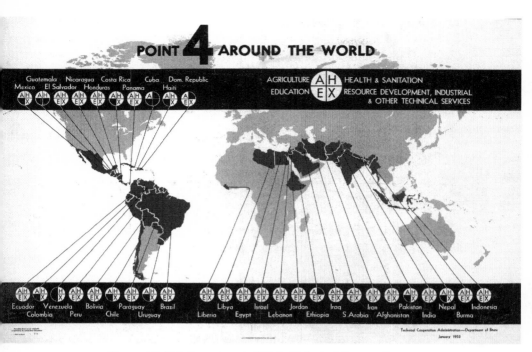

Figure 4.2. U.S. Department of State, Technical Cooperation Administration, "Point 4 around the World," 1953 (Courtesy of the Geography & Map Division of the Library of Congress)

demonstrated that from a point early in the Cold War, the stark East-West binaries were filled out and recolored by the complex, multilayered South. For example, a 1952 map series produced by the State Department to promote the Point 4 Program focused on the darkened countries in Central America, South America, North Africa, the Middle East, and South Asia (fig. 4.2).[40] Black banners cover much of the Northern Hemisphere so that the eye focuses squarely on the equatorial nations. A line traces from each darkened country to a circle in the banner, which contains the letters A, H, E, and X to indicate whether the Point 4 intervention was in Agriculture, Health and Sanitation, Education, or "X" for Resource Development and Other Technical Services. The visual combined with the text of the icons makes for a display in which the countries in dark blue are framed as "arriving" or "in process" relative to the rest of the world.[41]

In addition, though, the push toward development was designed to address the problem of the "dollar gap," according to Curt Cardwell, as U.S. leaders were worried about the inabilities of nations to actually afford the goods that America was exporting.[42] Nations in postwar financial trouble might cut down on trade with the United States and could turn to nationalist economies, or worse, the socialist tutelage of the Soviet Union.[43] The ability to invest in the developing world and turn emerging states into U.S. consumers was considered paramount for the American economy, and leaders found they could make better appeals to Congress and public opinion for foreign aid programs like Point 4 by emphasizing the Cold War benefits.[44] Truman's program, thus, was linked with the rise of modernization theory, which became a major part of the collaboration between the U.S. government and the social sciences in the Cold War. Out of collaborations like these came works such as Walt Rostow's *Stages of Economic Growth*, which was the Cold War hallmark "non-communist manifesto" for modernization.[45] To respond to the Soviet's own brand of modernization, social scientists like Rostow were looking for a logic and a lexicon that expressed U.S. plans for the increasingly southern focus of the Cold War: the push to standardize technical knowledge *of* and *for* the "places" of U.S. influence around the world became the answer.[46]

Of course, this move toward abstract knowledge necessarily involved a rupture and denial of individual Third World nations' pasts and differences.[47] As Kimber Charles Pearce concluded, theories like Rostow's made development a progressive, linear process with an anticommunist pretext whose "argument that all nations pass naturally through the same phases of development convinced U.S. policy makers to homogenize their methods of economic interventionism in the third world, although that view of the evolution of liberal democratic capitalism tended to mask conflict and emphasize the continuities of the development process."[48] This emphasis on continuities also fit with what critical geographers like Simon Dalby referred to as a Cold War narrative where contentious political and social issues are reduced to technical considerations that can be continually improved by better knowledge and instruments (such as maps).[49] Importantly, though, as Cold War historian Odd Arne Westad argues, Washington's objectives to modernize the Third World were not necessarily to exploit but actually involved a deeply rooted social consciousness around aid and improvement.[50] The integration of social science into the waging of the Cold War evidences the driving belief in a liberal modernism that could develop the world to both further American interests and improve the lives of the great masses of the globe.

Cartography played a prominent role in America's social scientific drive to modernize and develop the Third World; maps were uniquely equipped for surveying and improving methods of quantification and visualization. Associated Press maps, for example, like 1962's "Food for Peace Is American

Success Story" and 1966's "Peace Corps—A Hit, and Growing," show the promise of modernization on the international landscape and offer a sense of benevolent paternalism in bringing the Third World up to the standards of the First.[51] "Food for Peace" spatializes the hunger of the Third World using U.S. Department of Agriculture data. Most of Africa and South Asia (and parts of South America) are colored in stark black to indicate which are "diet deficit countries," while the rest of the world is lightly outlined to recede into the map's background. In the margins are grossly stereotypical sketches of "racial types"—an Asian man eating from a bowl of rice, an Arab holding a shepherd's staff, and an African male with a crude rendering of a village hut behind him. The "othering" of the Third World is explicit here: it is the exotic, foreign elements far away that are suffering in terms of diet and hunger, thus putting the "underdeveloped" in their proper place. So, while the map connotes crisis, the implicit argument is that organizations like Food for Peace are working with benevolent goals to improve the health of the less fortunate, thus placing American aid as the real subject of the map.

In "The Peace Corps" (fig. 4.3), a conventional world map is simply covered with numbers that correspond to a legend indicating how many volunteers are serving in a particular country. What anchors the focus of the map, though, are drawings of two young white Peace Corps volunteers (one female, one male) in the bottom left corner of the map, gazing out over the landscape of the map and looking slightly upward toward Africa and Asia. In both AP maps, the cartography is "raced" and the notion of space explicitly linked to notions of "civilization." Visually, the tiers are created between North and South and place the First World as both the surveyor and the model for the Third. Such maps speak to a strong ambivalence about the rise of the South: a wariness of neutrality and an anxious anticipation exists around what choice developing nations would make to join the "right bloc," but there also is a hope that, with the proper U.S. stewardship, international space could be stabilized again.

These tensions around the ideologies of modernization are well represented by two particular U.S. cartographic projects of the 1950s and 1960s. One encompasses the U.S. academic and government collaboration in the mapping of world health, concurrent with Truman's push to understand the "sick" and the "needy"; the second is the "scientific internationalism" of the American cartographic role in the United Nations. Medical cartography provides a compelling example of how maps were used as material instruments to consolidate and manage American interests for both political and economic security; projects like the American Geographical Society's *Atlas of Disease* had rhetorical lives that brought

THE PEACE CORPS--WHERE THEY ARE SERVING*

Country	Number	Country	Number	Country	Number	Country	Number	Country	Number
AFRICA		14. Nigeria	949	24. Thailand	430	34. Ecuador	291	**NORTH AFRICA, NEAR EAST**	
1. Bechuanaland	73	15. Senegal	92	25. Trust Territories	527	35. El Salvador	154	**AND SOUTH ASIA**	
2. Cameroon	86	16. Sierra Leone	237	TOTAL	2,396	36. Guatemala	107	45. Afghanistan	226
3. Chad	41	17. Somalia	102			37. Guyana	50	46. India	1,413
4. Ethiopia	508	18. Tanzania	386	**LATIN AMERICA**		38. Honduras	141	47. Iran	372
5. Gabon	47	19. Togo	40			39. Jamaica	113	48. Libya	23
6. Ghana	131	20. Uganda	102	26. Barbados	28	40. Panama	131	49. Morocco	121
7. Guinea	65	Africa (Regional)	83	27. Bolivia	339	41. Peru	486	50. Nepal	231
8. Ivory Coast	60	TOTAL	3,985	28. Brazil	797	42. St. Lucia	16	51. Pakistan	14
9. Kenya	324			29. Br. Honduras	52	43. Uruguay	67	52. Tunisia	247
10. Liberia	312	**FAR EAST**		30. Chile	482	44. Venezuela	436	53. Turkey	500
11. Malawi	218	21. Malaysia	578	31. Colombia	715	Latin American Regional	115	Regional	76
12. Mauritania	20	22. Philippines	747	32. Costa Rica	223	Volunteer Secretaries	29	TOTAL	3,223
13. Niger	109	23. South Korea	104	33. Dom. Republic	185	TOTAL	4,957	GRAND TOTAL	14,561

*As of Sept. 15, 1966. Source: U.S. Peace Corps. Figures include those in training or en route.

AP Newsfeatures

*Figure 4.3. Associated Press, "Peace Corps—A Hit, and Growing,"
Newsfeatures Series, 1966 (Courtesy of the Geography & Map Division
of the Library of Congress, by permission of the Associated Press)*

spatial information about sickness and underdevelopment into the hands of military planners, influential bodies like the Council on Foreign Relations, and even pharmaceutical companies. In addition, America's leadership in modeling cartographic methods for the UN evidences how the United States believed that the very ability to map was a hallmark of a "civilized," developed nation. The success of development and interventionism in the Third World was absolutely dependent on the right modes of perception and, therefore, the ability of maps to synthesize a world of data and provide an expert interface for foreign policy makers.

Diagnosing the Third World: America's Mapping of World Health in the Cold War

The relationship of disease to physical location and region was not a new line of inquiry, of course: the writings of Hippocrates in *On Airs,*

Waters, and Places established this connection.[52] In America, studies of disease (particularly alcoholism) and geography in the early frontier West appeared in public discourse, and U.S. census data were used to produce "Sanitary Maps" of preventable diseases in areas such as Louisiana and Texas.[53] During the Civil War, early work in medical geography was published discussing the relationship of disease and race to geographic location.[54] Still, U.S. efforts at an international program of study in medical geography and cartography did not really take place until the push toward globalism in the 1940s. In 1944, Dr. Richard Light proposed, at an American Geographical Society (AGS) conference (with geographers, medical scientists, military medical officers, and influential government public health officials in attendance), that the AGS board should produce a comprehensive *Atlas of Diseases*.[55] A pilot project was started, and by 1948 it reached full steam. Dr. Jacques May, a French surgeon who had taught surgery and practiced in Hanoi, was chosen by Light and the AGS to take over the project.[56] With funding from the Office of U.S. Naval Research and with grants from pharmaceutical companies, May was able to establish a Medical Geography Department based out of the AGS's New York office, in order to create the atlas.[57] The full color map plates (seventeen would be produced by the end of the 1955) for the *Atlas of Disease* would eventually be distributed to various U.S. government institutions and world health organizations throughout the 1950s.

May was especially innovative in his work that connected the cultural aspects of particular regions to the outbreaks of disease—going beyond merely pointing out where such outbreaks were taking place. For example, a 1954 *Newsweek* profile of May, which referred to him as "The Map Doctor," highlighted his disease maps and their ability to make connections between disease and "soil, air, water, foodstuffs, modes of living, and religious customs and habits that contribute to these ailments."[58] The specific examples used in the article are direct connections between sickness and religious beliefs: "The daily ablutions of Moslem rites are usually performed in polluted water, causing infection. The common bowls for washing the hands in Buddhist temples are a prime source of eye and skin diseases. In Asia, pilgrims are frequently the carriers of cholera and plague."[59] May's work examining the prevalence of disease in North Vietnam due to cultural factors of land tenure laws and house-building materials makes a similar case.[60] And accompanying May's maps on starvation is text that bears out how seemingly "backward" habits have a ripple effect on Third World societies: "The social structure of the society, chiefly exemplified in Egypt and China, is a serious cause of food shortage. In

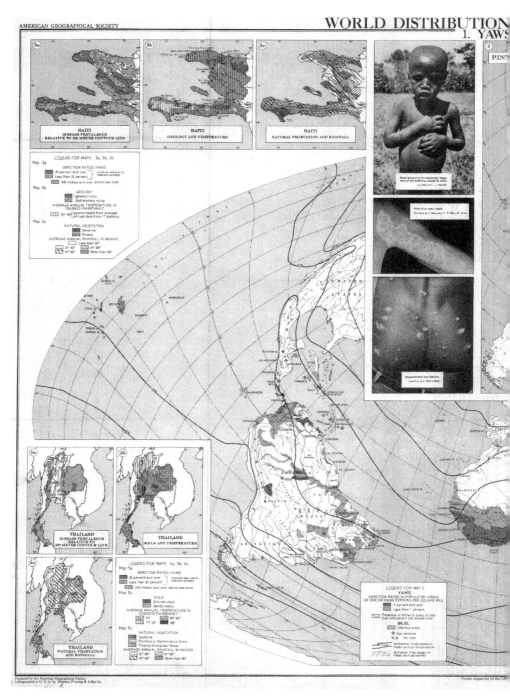

Figure 4.4. American Geographical Society, "World Distribution of
Spirochetal Diseases," Atlas of Disease, 1955 (Courtesy of the American Geographical
Society Library, University of Wisconsin–Milwaukee, by permission of the
American Geographical Society)

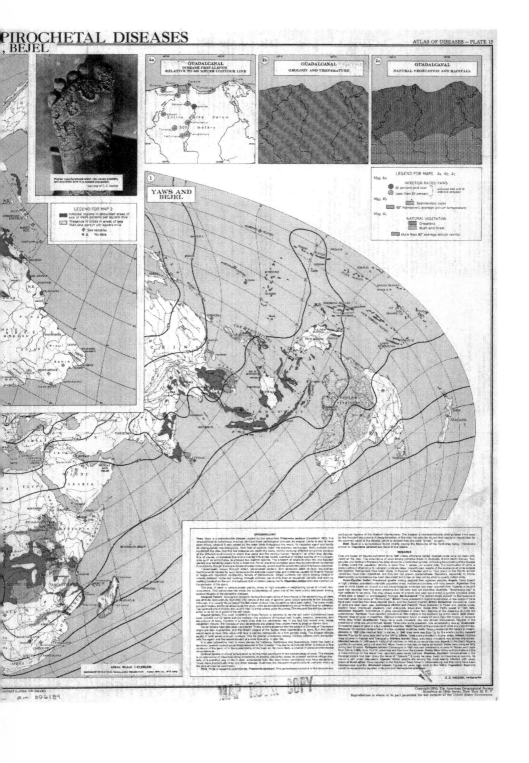

some places the customs governing inheritance divide the land to such a degree that it can no longer be worked profitably. Yet the people refuse to migrate because they have heard frightening tales about the places where they could migrate, or because there are no such places within their reach, or because they cannot afford transportation, or because they are bound by religious belief to stay near the place where their ancestors are buried."[61] The focus on culture in these maps of world disease is telling because it parallels the Cold War discourses around foreign aid and development in Third World countries, as seen in Truman's Point 4 initiatives. As international relations scholar Roxanne Doty notes, these foreign aid discourses "suggest that the danger was not in poverty itself, but in the identities of those who were impoverished, those who could not take a long-range view of their situations."[62] Similarly, in combating world health issues, sickness would be equated not only with particular world regions but also with the people who filled those regions. Cartography provided the means to visually edify these dangers—the way by which the "long-range view" could be taken.

The *Atlas of Disease* spatializes this cultural and medical knowledge together in a colorful way that is packed with a "paramap" full of information. For example, the *Disease* map of the tropical skin diseases Yaws, Pinta, and Bejel features a world map focused on Africa, where splotches of brilliant red and orange mark outbreaks of the affliction (fig. 4.4).[63] Since Europe has almost no incidence of them, the map simply covers that continent with a closer inset of South America and displays several provocative photos of what looks to be African children with skin lesions who function as symbolic stand-ins for an entire "diseased" continent. Surrounding the frame of the world map are insets of countries like Haiti and Thailand that display their infection rates relative to vegetation or soil, for example. On this global scale, the combination of world map, photos, and regional insets overwhelms the map user with the graphics of infection: the white spaces of either so-called healthy spots or those with "no data" stand in stark contrast with the bright colors of those that are affected, as the map plays temporally with the idea that it is only a matter of time before more color seeps into these spaces.

The overall effect of these displays is the empowerment of America's medical expertise as a form of knowledge and visuality. Cartography's historical power of linking entire territories with particular traits and relating them *in total* to other territories with those same traits is especially powerful when the subject is sickness, epidemics, and plagues. In May's cartographic study of cholera epidemics, for example, a main world map uses different colored lines to depict the worldwide spread of the disease during different eras of the nineteenth century, while the insets show how cholera was isolated to the Middle East and India by 1950. Over the map spread, the viewer sees a worldwide pandemic slowly becoming a specifically Third World concern in the postwar; the spaces of the North had "progressed" beyond it.[64] The map's ability to partition world spaces creates a kind of quarantine effect, seeking to isolate the problem areas from the rest of the world.

Mediating this display is the important political choice of projection that the *Atlas of Disease* uses. May's maps were drawn by the American Geographical Society's senior cartographer William Briesemeister.[65] First developed in 1948, the Briesemeister projection was a notably prominent representation of the increasingly popular use of equal area on world maps in the postwar era. Briesemeister himself billed it as a "world equal-area projection for the future . . . most suitable . . . for the purpose of plotting worldwide statistics in this present day of super speed, jet planes and intercontinental missiles."[66] The overall display of the Briesemeister uses an elliptical egg shape, and in the top center of the map, the entire North Pole can be seen, with Alaska and the Bering Strait region forming the northernmost point.[67] Importantly, except for Antarctica, the continents are grouped without being cut; thus, the map has a fluidity and "one-world" quality.[68] Most striking is the prominence of Africa and South America, and the two continents' large area in comparison to North America and Europe. Using the Briesemeister projection, *Atlas of Disease* maps like "Distribution of Helminthiases" make particularly prominent use of Africa as the focal point, where the comparatively few other instances of this parasitical disease stand in contrast to the deep colors and thick, crisscrossed lines plaguing the African landscape.[69] The projection contributes to the effect of the visual field "clearing up" around Africa and creates the impression that Africa is a sick continent. For Cold War space, the new focus on comprehensive, global knowledge called for maps that lent themselves well to statistical distribution. In the process, Third World spaces increased in size and centrality; shapes may have been slightly distorted, but cartographers and policy makers placed a higher premium on accuracy to pinpoint areas for economic and social development in the emerging nations.

While May's background and credentials gave the *Atlas of Disease* an international flair, it was resolutely American in its concerns about security and economic modernization. Historical geographers Tim Brown and Graham Moon use May's background as a physician during Indochina's last vestiges of colonialism to show his approach to medical geography as a benevolent, triumphalist spin on an "imperial history that views the unfolding of events from the perspective of the dominant culture."[70] At the same time, though, this brand of imperialism was complicated by a more "rational, scientific view of disease causality."[71] One particularly compelling illustration of this view, and its effects on U.S. strategy, is through May's involvement in the Council on Foreign Relations, which he was invited to join in 1954 for a new project on "Climates and Economic Development in the Tropics."[72] A confidential conference was held in June 1954, attended by May and a slew of other key academics from research foundations and universities, military representatives, and corporate executives of entities such as the United Fruit Company and Standard Oil Corporation. Here was an influential gathering of prominent strategic elites working to advance persuasive, scientifically grounded rationales for development of the Third World, and their policy committee established a clear purpose: "We are convinced that the United States has an important interest in far more general and more dynamic economic, social and political progress in the underdeveloped areas of the free world than has been achieved to date. . . . The additional factor of the aggressive thrust of international communism backed by Soviet imperialism, with the clear indications that it has focused upon the subversion or conquest of the underdeveloped areas as the soft underbelly of Western civilization, increases the urgency."[73]

At the ensuing conference, Dr. May had *Atlas of Disease* maps distributed to all the participants and led the discussions on research and development, laying out what he found were the central problems: "It is assumed that the reasons which motivate our work are to find out what makes tropical populations 'backward.' . . . No ethical considerations have their place here. The problem is not to discover what makes people happy. . . . The problem is to discover how a condition which is detrimental to the well-being of the United States can be remedied."[74] Backed by the "self-evident" scientific power of his maps, May visualized the world in civilizational terms—where Cold War realities precluded an altruistic view of development, and priorities rested in advancing American superiority. While he "hoped that the solution found will be profitable also to the populations and to the territories to which it will be applied," he employed his geographic facts as a kind of a realist evidence of the necessity of a tiered world, with the advancement of U.S. security as most integral.[75] And the Council of Foreign Relations' interest in May's research ultimately showed that this was a "security" in which spatial knowledge was held at a premium.

May's brand of knowledge also had a hand in development as defined by the spread of American private capital abroad. Throughout the twelve-year duration of the AGS medical mapping initiative, various pharmaceutical corporations were committed to sponsoring the work, including Upjohn and Lederle.[76] Pfizer, in particular, corresponded with the Medical Geography Department about having disease maps specially designed to show data for diseases that were specifically treatable by Pfizer medicines, and bound copies of the *Atlas of Disease* plates were commissioned by Pfizer to use as Christmas presents for its physician clients.[77] May was also using his expertise as a consultant for these same companies on the side, concurrent with but separate from his work for the American Geographical Society. For example, developing medical geography reports for Mead Johnson and Lilly (looking to expand in Argentina) about the viability for their drug products in particularly disease-ridden parts of the world.[78] In a 1955 speech to medical professionals and pharmaceutical reps about "American Stake in Foreign Diseases," May remarked that global disease "can be cured by the simple administration of products that are manufactured in this country in enormous quantities. . . . This would mean salvation for hundreds of millions of people, and undoubtedly, if the ways and means to carry these drugs to these markets were found, it would mean profit for American industry."[79] Maps provided, for May, the medium by which the fates of the North and South could most clearly be drawn together. Cartography not only projected the facts of world disease but also drew the parameters of the American market and projected its infiltration all across the developing world. That conflation of Third World pestilence with First World profit speaks compellingly to the complexities of international altruism and national interest in development discourse, and how the hierarchies of space in the Cold War created rigid, civilizational divisions.

The *Atlas of Disease* compounded its economic functions with its implications for military security, as it was consistently contextualized as part of a comprehensive U.S. program of surveillance of Third World space. Not only did U.S. Naval Research underwrite the work, but May also forged key collaborations with the Office of the Surgeon General of the Army, suggesting that medical geography had strategic defense potential. One of his main projects in the *Atlas of Disease*, for example, was mapping the various forms of viral encephalitis, particularly in response to the hemorrhagic encephalitis epidemic that ravaged U.S. troops in the Korean War.[80] In general, the *Atlas* motivated the charting of poverty and food shortage trouble spots as well as environmental facts for the U.S. armed forces that "would help in global military encounters."[81] As May stipulated in his naval grant application of 1952, "Under the threat of war we have to sum up our knowledge of the distribution of diseases, existing or potential, throughout the world to protect our men who may be called upon to establish themselves in any of the infected areas and also to defend ourselves against unfounded charges that we spread diseases which can be proved to have always existed in that place."[82] Thus, in a sense, this mapping initiative was continually justified on its ability not only to contribute to development but also to provide preemptive defense in the war of knowledge production. To be able to visually display the knowledge of the world was to have power over its dissemination and interpretation in the Cold War. The United States could inoculate itself from its subjects of intervention through the sheer force of scientific fact and the ability to classify it across the globe. It is no wonder then that, shortly after completing his tenure at AGS, May was appointed as Chief Medical Education Adviser to the U.S. Operations Mission in Vietnam.[83]

The ensuing appropriation and adaptation of the *Atlas of Disease* reveals that the U.S. government's interest in this global mapping project was inseparable from its interests in world economic development. The Mutual Security Act of 1958, originally enacted in 1948, set forth a policy plank stating: "The Congress of the United States, recognizing that the diseases of mankind, because of their widespread prevalence, debilitating effects, and heavy toll in human life, constitute a major deterrent to the efforts of many peoples to develop their economic resources and productive capacities, and to improve their living conditions, declares it to be the policy of the United States to continue and strengthen mutual efforts among the nations for research against diseases."[84] The issue of world disease is rhetorically situated under the umbrella of America's conception of mutual security in the Cold War, as well as the drive toward modernization in the Third World. To supplement this policy, in 1959 the Committee on Government Operations in the Senate, headed by Senator Hubert Humphrey, produced a report called *The Status of World Health*, which included more than thirty maps and charts, most of which were adapted versions from the AGS's *Atlas of Disease*. Humphrey's introduction to the report makes special reference to the need for a "big picture" approach to medicine rather "than piecemeal views of world health, such as may have been seen in times past" and "requires a total, not a segmented view," as "U.S. responsibilities under world health programs continue to mount."[85]

Maps, appropriately, served as the main instruments of vision for Humphrey's proposed big-picture approach, able to capture a total snapshot of world health. Using world regions as the basis of study, world maps of issues such as life expectancy at birth and the ratio of population to physicians sketched the stark contours of an unequal world.[86] To make this case succinctly and unequivocally, the adaptations of the AGS maps are made much simpler than their referents. For example, the layers of colors and shades that distinguished the *Atlas of Disease* maps are replaced by the simple black, white, and gray dots of the typical congressional report. Quite literally, world health and the Western response to it were depicted as a black-and-white issue. In this way, the diseases stand in for the regions on these maps (India equals smallpox; Egypt equals low life expectancy).[87] In page after page of maps, whether depicting hookworm, yellow fever, or leprosy, the darkest-colored areas of the world are concentrated underneath a kind of invisible horizontal line drawn just north of Mexico, Turkey, Iran, Afghanistan, India, and North Vietnam.[88]

To accentuate this line, *The Status of World Health* actually forgoes the innovative, Third World–centric projections like the AGS's Briesemeister projection for the more conventional Mercator projection. With the audience for this report limited mostly to other U.S. lawmakers and government health officials, the map's projection eschewed statistical accuracy and scientific innovation in order to support the more officially sanctioned view of the world during the Cold War of the East-West bipolar superpower relationship. Thus, the North-South divisions are constrained by the East-West ones, and *The Status of World Health* situates world health from the global perspective of American security interests. While the intent of mappers like May might not have been to advance a crude cultural and environmental determinism of geographic area to disease and poverty, in the appropriation of them by the Senate, the maps instantiate a deep boundary between the "above" world and the "under" world. Without surveillance, containment, and management, these volatile areas could spread beyond their boundaries and displace the centrality of the United States and its allies.

Importantly, the *Status of World Health* report showcases that the ability to map world health is only as good as the availability of data, and this fact is used in the report to make a distinction between the First World and the Second and Third Worlds. As Humphrey points out, the main conclusion of the report is that "more statistics are needed. . . . Regrettably, an analysis of the world health situation is difficult due to the lack of accurate, current statistical data, particularly from the less developed countries."[89] Instead of specific conclusions as to what can be done with such statistical information to improve world health, the implied argument is that the "full and accurate" documentation of world health is enough. In that way, disease is not the enemy: it is the lack of knowledge about such diseases in foreign areas that becomes the enemy.

Thus, medical cartography was not just a scientifically significant Cold War artifact but a rhetorical one as well: the world on the flat page, through the bounded lines of the map, could now be "diagnosed" and its weak spots and sicknesses absorbed in a glance.[90] As David Campbell writes, "Foreign policy might be likened to an 'ethical power of segregation,' whereby moral distinctions can be made through spatial and temporal delineations, constituting a 'geography of evil' that allows dangers to be understood as originating from distinct and distant places."[91] The visual charting of health (or lack thereof) of developing nations became an important representation of North-South relations through this power of segregation in the expansion of the Cold War. Cartography provided the necessary abstraction of individual human suffering from disease, an interface that could manage bodies and suffering, so that health could be aggregated as a strategic world problem to be solved through development by powerful, intervening world actors. As the entire medical geography initiative reminds us, too, maps powerfully triangulated the interests and the considerable stakes of U.S. foreign policy elites, Congress, private corporations, and academics into one visual field.

Decolonizing the Map: The United States, the United Nations, and the Scientific Internationalism of Cartography

While projects like medical cartography exemplified maps as interfaces for world data, there was also continual emphasis on the use of cartography as a Cold War teaching medium to help newly developing nations achieve self-sufficiency. Such projects were often framed under the banner of "scientific internationalism," a term coined early in the Cold War to articulate the belief that science should transcend geography and politics for the good of all.[92] In terms of cartography, one example of this internationalism was found in the postwar push to dramatically increase the amount and accuracy of topographic maps of the earth. Such an effort required collaborations with "friendly countries all over the world," and it resulted in projects like the U.S. Army Corps of Engineers' Inter-American Geodetic Survey (IAGS), which drew on State Department, army, and navy support to work with various Latin American countries to map the entire continent. Out of this collaboration came the Alaska-to-Chile line, the longest measured line in the world, "an arc of triangulation [that] will eventually lock the maps of North and South America into a unified whole."[93] As Colonel Robert R. Robertson of the Army Corps of Engineers remarked in a 1956 *Life* profile, "An important thing to remember about the IAGS is that we are not mapping Latin America. We're helping the Latin Americans to do it themselves. It's their program. . . . You can see what a terrific thing it is for furthering inter-American relations."[94] Cartography was framed as both a way to protect national security (having the most accurate survey of the Western Hemisphere possible would help missile accuracy) and a symbol of self-determination and spatial identity for developing nations. As Albert Lieber, writing for the American Congress on Surveying and Mapping, offered in 1954, institutions like the Corps of Engineers had mapping agreements with practically every country outside the Iron Curtain because, "aside from their military importance, adequate maps provide the information required for the rapid economic and industrial development required by the free world today."[95] In this way, cartography was posited as a facilitating force for global development that could aid security and economic ideologies—but still under a unifying rhetoric of scientific internationalism.

As the case of the American Geographical Society's medical geography program demonstrates, with its maps circulating through halls of the Defense Department and the boardrooms of multinational corporations, this scientific internationalism was also always bound up in national security and other partisan interests. Marie Tharp's brilliant cartography of the ocean floor (along with geologist Bruce Heezen) during the 1950s at Columbia, for example, was a quintessential Cold War project in that its internationally renowned scientific achievements were underwritten by the defense considerations of the U.S. Office of Naval Research (and faced the constraints of its often classified data) while also sponsored by Bell Laboratories in the hopes of finding commercial opportunities for transatlantic telephone lines.[96] Similar constraints befell the transnational collaborations of the famed International Geophysical Year of 1957–58, which witnessed unprecedented exchange of earth science data among sixty-seven countries (including the Soviet Union and many so-called developing nations).[97] IGY's dramatic advancements made in satellite technology (including Sputnik's launch and the ensuing response and public relations panic in America) had profound effects on the surveillance abilities for military cartography and for the development of the polar regions as Cold War bastions. This "scientific Olympics," thus, transcended its idealistic origins and was hailed into the Cold War (while also expanding air-age globalism with the "eye in the sky" of satellites going higher than any human pilot).[98]

The United Nations, though, was especially where cartography was conceived as an ideal of scientific internationalism for development—and yet one still constrained by Cold War realities. The UN's initiative to centralize international mapping projects in the late 1940s marked the first major attempt to systematically define cartography for its capacity to aid international development efforts. A UN Economic and Social Council resolution of 1948 stated that "accurate maps are a prerequisite to the proper development of the world resources which in many cases lie in relatively unexplored regions."[99] This resolution set the tone for the official start of a comprehensive international cartography program, for which U.S. actors like S. W. Boggs had been lobbying for years, at a two-week conference in March 1949.[100] The participants were able to agree on a galvanizing direction: a specific UN branch for cartography that would further stimulate national programs of surveying and mapping by promoting the exchange of technical information and other means; coordinate the plans and programs of the UN and specialized agencies in the field of cartography; and develop close cooperation with cartographic services between interested member governments.[101]

In addition, the resolution broke the world down into six cartographic regions (Asia and the Far East, Central and South Africa, the Middle East, Western Europe and the Mediterranean, Eastern Europe, and the Americas—a typical geographic partitioning during the Cold War). Out of these six regions, government representatives who shared a community of interests in mapping that area would hold periodic meetings for each region, supervised and supported by the United Nations. Despite the idealist overtones of its calls for global cartographic cooperation, the resolution was not without its partisan controversies. The delegations of the Soviet Union and Poland opposed joining the resolution on the grounds that it would lead to "the establishment of international cartographic standards and therefore to the eventual modification, through a difficult and costly process, of laboriously built up national cartographic systems which were designed to satisfy specific national needs."[102] Thus, the tensions between national interests and internationalism were bound up in the ways maps were situated in the Cold War landscape.

From the outset of the UN cartographic program, the focus on economic and social advancement through mapping was critical. The delegates to this first map conference produced a manifesto that represents well the conundrums of cartography in an era of a rapidly shifting political and economic landscape. For one, they noted how decolonization was changing and expanding cartography's role. While topographic maps may remain a responsibility of national governments, "we are now living in a period when the principle of absolute national sovereignty is losing some of its strength, a political development which may be considered as the hallmark of our time," the document concluded.[103] Thus, maps had to meet more fluid needs that required international efforts. The report also attacked the lack of exchange of cartographic information, particularly between more highly developed countries and lesser-developed countries: "In an advancing civilization there is increasing and urgent need for more power, more food, and better communications. The means of producing these essentials are various, but in every case they can be produced more cheaply and more quickly with adequate maps than without them."[104] Maps were supposed to speed the pace of development and equalize the playing field—and governments had an actual *duty* to serve their publics by producing them. More than merely technical instruments, they were foundational for international progress. As the conference delegates' recommendations note,

> Not only is cartographic service a tool to the United Nations and its specialized agencies, but, in the broad sense used here, cartographic knowledge is the basis for any program for social and economic development.... Human history, especially the recent records and particularly in the more highly developed nations, is full of examples of things that have been done, large structures intended for human betterment, which have completely or partly failed for lack of ordinary cartographic facts.... It would seem to be the responsibility of those charged with the consideration of social values to protect peoples and communities from unconsidered—or not sufficiently considered—economic developmental projects.[105]

Maps, in other words, can also visually reveal where development can go wrong, thus serving as a protective device for communities that are in upheaval. In turn, the UN cartographic branch was offering an interpretive function in its services, helping nations not only to get the right tools but to "read" maps better. In 1955, the same year as the summit at Bandung, the United Nations held its first regional cartographic conference for Asia and the Far East in Mussoorie, India. The conference's inaugural address by a popular Indian politician (and former member of India's Non-Cooperation movement), Dr Sampurnanand, upheld the idea that a lack of adequate mapping was a sign of global inequality that required rectification. As he reminded the delegates, "Fairly accurate maps showing political sub-divisions and the positions of the principal seas, rivers and mountains are still luxuries in certain parts of the civilized world."[106] The age-old connection of maps to "civilization" was especially heightened here in a Cold War context. To participate in the new global world order, a nation had to know itself; maps, thus, were important not just for their geographic information but for their utility as a development symbol. The very act of mapping allowed nations' entries into a global conversation. This spirit of development would carry forward into the United Nations' regional cartographic conferences held every couple of years, which began in 1955 and continued into the 1980s, for areas such as Africa and the Near East.

The U.S. role in this cartographic program of the United Nations particularly provides some unique insight into the discursive role of mapping on an international scale and what development meant in terms of U.S. global interests. The successful U.S.-led Pan-American collaborations to map the Western Hemisphere became the kind of go-to examples for how a spirit of scientific internationalism could work for UN cartography, and it gave the United States a dominant role in setting the tone for the collaborative mapping of the entire world.[107] In the report of the U.S. Delegation to the UN Regional Cartographic Conference for Asia and the Far East, State Department geographer G. Etzel Pearcy (S. W. Boggs's successor) pointed out: "National developmental organizations must rely on the surveyor and cartographer for support in order to discover, evaluate, and utilize resources, and to foster the economic and social developments of the region."[108]

Such development was also increasingly tied to developing states' access to better mapping technologies—particularly the emergent digital methods that had originated in defense quarters but now were expanding to unclassified realms. As Pearcy noted, "The increased demands to exploit our resources to meet man's needs make it mandatory to develop improved cartographic production techniques. Emerging states, however, should not wait for the utopia computer, but arrange their data and plan their programming techniques for today's computers. Consideration should be made by affluent nations to include the emerging countries as recipients of computers and automatic systems suitable for their applications."[109] Mapping was clearly an activity to be brought into the tide of modernization—the notion that with the right instruments from the established North and the right interface by which to see the world, the South had a chance to catch up. At a UN Regional Cartographic Conference for Africa, a report to Secretary of State Dean Rusk by Delegate H. Arnold Karo (from the U.S. Coastal Survey) proposed that any kind of successful "rational economic development" in Africa depended on the credibility of technical specialists who could come in and help standardize the continent's disparate mapping methods.[110] Karo bemoaned how aerial photography needed for mapping was in danger in the face of decolonization. He reported that "a majority of the aerial photography in the New Africa states has been provided by the British and French governments through commercial contracts or government-owned survey air-craft. As the influence of these governments on the new countries wanes, the support for aerial mapping and surveying will diminish in like proportion."[111] In a peculiar way, decolonization here is framed as inciting chaos, with the employment of American technical knowhow as a way of establishing order.

While the report depicts the United States as a benevolent provider of technical assistance, the specter of Cold War competition for influence lingered not far behind. For example, Karo's version of the conference notes that "the African nations displayed much interest in the U.S. [geodetic] system and discussed it at considerable length," but it also observed that "the mapping system proposed by the Soviet Union . . . could have a strong appeal to the African nations which are desperately seeking ways and means for mapping and survey assistance. Technically, however, the Soviet system entails cumbersome methods" and "could in effect only be operated and maintained by a large contingent of Soviet technical specialists."[112] In this way, the actual presence of Soviet cartographers to run this equipment connoted an infiltration of African areas that could prove dangerous for American interests. Responding to the anxieties, Karo's final recommendations to Rusk indicated that the United States needed to take the lead in providing mapping support for Africa, as "these same maps and data are necessary for the security of individual property rights, to the security of an individual nation, and the collective security of the region" as well as "worldwide security and defense of freedom everywhere." "As such," continued Karo, "adequate and accessible cartographic intelligence on a worldwide scale is a necessary part of our national policy."[113]

THE MILITARIZED CONUNDRUM OF
DEVELOPMENT MAPPING

These examples speak to a continual conundrum in the American approach to development in the Third World. According to Westad, for American Cold War ideology, decolonization provoked two very different kinds of responses: "On the one hand, American elites welcomed the breakup of the European colonial empires because it meant opportunities for extending US ideas of political and economic liberties. . . . On the other hand, however, decolonization increased the threat of collectivist ideologies getting the upper hand in the Third World. . . . If that was the case, then a covert strategy for influence would make more sense than open attempts at gaining friends through aid and trade."[114] The dualism between opportunities for open exchange and the need for covert secrecy found its way into the development of cartography and the production of geographic knowledge in the era. Extraordinarily fluid lines appeared between economic and social development and militarization. The push toward development and modernization encompassed the efforts of the United States to lead UN initiatives in providing technical knowledge to Third World nations all over the earth. Promotional maps of the Peace Corps missions around the world, for example, showed a kind of benevolent intervention across the globe that idealized America's development spirit.[115] Still, despite the idealism inherent in some of America's cartography of development, the most prodigious and vigorous mapping of the Third World during the Cold War era was done primarily by the Department of Defense and the Central Intelligence Agency.[116] Also, the rise of area studies, funded by U.S. intelligence agencies and major foundations, saw the Third World mapped into particular regions that minimized local differences in the face of finding larger trends.[117] As geographer Jim Glassman said, this kind of area expertise tended to "otherize" regions like Southeast Asia and helped to legitimize interventions.[118] A strange relationship thus developed between cartography and what Frank Ninkovich has called the "symbolic interventionism" of the domino-theory era. Maps served as the symbol of technical expertise that aided in lifting allies out of poverty and backwardness, while simultaneously serving as tools of surveillance that monitored Third World sites for their strategic placement in the potential for global skirmishes and new fronts.[119] Geographer Matthew Edney has written of this concept of "disciplining cartography," where the map serves not just as a tool of state power but also to perpetuate a progressive narrative about the worth of cartography as a practice.[120]

A quintessential example of this dualism in terms of U.S. Cold War cartography of the Third World came through the use of maps in the infamous Strategic Hamlets program in Vietnam.[121] The Hamlets program was, arguably, modernization theory's ultimate project, where, according to James C. Scott, social science blended seamlessly into military science.[122] The program, which essentially involved removal and relocation of Vietnamese families from their villages to evade communist propaganda and to cut down on civilian casualties, even saw Robert McNamara defending it as an opportunity for community building for rural Vietnamese.[123] The program used a system of map overlays that evaluated population and area to determine the stability of particular strategic sites for relocating villages. Because of the task's scope, the military outsourced some of this cartographic work to the civilian United States Geological Survey (USGS). In the process, USGS cartographers were given classified CORONA aerial satellite photographs to make their maps but were not notified that they were classified or where they came from. An interview with USGS director Roy Mullen, by historian John Cloud, reveals that "USGS was commissioned by the State Department to prepare civilian land reallocation maps for South Vietnam, and we were commissioned by Army Map Service to prepare battle maps of North Vietnam. They were the same maps. *They were the same maps!*"[124] In Cloud's terms, "the spatial relationships, the geographic 'truth' between hamlets was identical, but the maps validated different political concepts, and the ways they were used to literally 'target' the populations were quite distinct."[125] The fact that the same cartographic data was literally being used to both save and destroy Vietnamese communities speaks to the ultimate tension between Cold War military prerogatives and social science.

Such conundrums were on display even in the most public uses of maps as evidential weaponry in this era. In his televised address of April 30, 1970, on the U.S. "incursion" into Cambodia, President Nixon frequently referred to and engaged with a striking cartographic visual aid.[126] Several times, Nixon pointed to a poster-sized map of a Cambodian border outflanked by the North Vietnamese forces in alarming shades of red over a pale yellow background, calmly asking Americans to follow along on the map as he argued that his only tenable position was to make a military strike against the North Vietnamese in Cambodia.[127] He kept his viewers with him by saying repeatedly, "as you see here on this map," and using his finger to gesture at the kind of encirclement he was accusing the North Vietnamese of making. Nixon was drawing on the presidency's long-standing rhetorical position as chief geographic educator, in ways that resonated with the old fireside chats of President Franklin Roosevelt.[128] Here, however, the simplified, self-evident presentation of this map belied a cartographic silence around the complicated and violent position facing the U.S. mission in Southeast Asia during a period when public opinion was deeply divided. A mere five days after Nixon's speech, four students at Kent State University lay dead from National Guard gunfire in the wake of a demonstration against U.S. actions in Cambodia. Certainly, cartography could still be marshaled at the highest levels for the purposes of strategy, but its ideological function as a contested discursive process had become, arguably, more complex in the U.S. move toward international intervention in the spaces of the so-called Third World. By this time, with the United States in the throes of the conflict in Vietnam, the weight of what maps *could not* order, classify, and simplify in the Cold War was just as heavy as the weight of what maps could—and radical geographers would take notice.

These spatial tensions quickly inspired a movement of "countergeopolitics." In 1972, for example, French geographer Yves Lacoste, visiting North Vietnam on a commission to investigate war crimes, wrote a piece (published in the *Nation* and expanded for the radical geography journal *Antipode*) about the systematic, premeditated bombing by the United States of the irrigation system on the dikes of the Red River Delta—a bombing (and ensuing public relations disaster in America) that flooded the homes and crops of tens of millions, an effect tantamount to a hydrogen bomb.[129] Strategic geographic knowledge of mass projects like an irrigation system to modernize and aid local populations could also be conversely used as a weapon to drown and starve them. As Lacoste wrote, "Today, more than ever, one has to become aware of the political and military function which geography has always had since its inception. In our time this function has assumed greater magnitude, and takes on new forms because of increased information, more technically-sophisticated means of destructions, and also because of progress in scientific knowledge. The title of an article in *Newsweek* . . . 'When the landscape is the Enemy' is indeed significant."[130]

During this period, an ambivalence and anxiety accompanied U.S. cartographic constructions of the developing world, both in terms of its ongoing competition with the Soviet Union and in its processes of geographic knowledge production. There was no easy reconciliation between "winning hearts and minds" through the teaching of cartography to help nations develop and the use of classified mapping technologies to capture hard data that may be used for the potential destruction of terrain. Geographer D. W. Meinig in 1956 decried the oversimplified view of the world that was arising during the dissolution of colonialism: "While we sincerely promoted the general ideal of political freedom and economic well-being for all mankind—and a marvelous and powerful ideal it is—we have ignored the inevitable corollary that that freedom and development would not find a singular, uniform pattern of expression."[131]

It was perhaps not surprising that around the same time that Vietnam was shattering these dreams of modernization, and while nations were still decolonizing in significant numbers, the infamous "Peters projection" became a worldwide sensation as a cartographic icon.[132] Arno Peters was a German socialist historian who repurposed a long-forgotten nineteenth-century equal-area projection that shrunk the Northern Hemisphere and enhanced the image of the subequatorial world.[133] His map emphasized accuracy in area at the expense of the familiar sense of continental shapes; thus, South America and Africa appeared distorted and stretched but larger and more central than before. Peters voiced this shift as a challenge to Western powers' colonialism and exploitation of the Third World.[134] While many critics deplored Peters's "worthless" and "absurd" use of cartographic science and his openly ideological stance (still often shunned in the field), the map took on an active rhetorical life for the remainder of the Cold War. The UN, transnational development organizations like Willy Brandt's famed Independent Commission on International Development Issues, international education groups, and even religious missionary outfits took up the map as a symbol of how a "third way" was needed in the rigid Cold War.[135] However, while Peters's radicalism opened up new avenues for cartography as a force of social change, the Peters projection also represented the complexities and contradictions of Cold War cartography's influence on development and modernization. Even those who used the map genuinely to articulate a sense of independent, "nonaligned" identities for decolonizing nations still perpetuated a three-tiered world where some nations were seen as always in need of "becoming" and catching up to civilization.

As the Peters projection reminds us, the Third World was by no means a stable entity—it was continually contested, redefined, and remapped by superpower nation-states, international mediators like the United Nations, and even challengers like Arno Peters. As demonstrated in this chapter, the developing world and the cartographic South were a force in Cold War geopolitics since the conflict's inception in the late 1940s. The notions of development and modernization went hand in hand with the way America synthesized world data and projected the emerging international framework: the United States defined itself (and its security) in terms of its ability to expand its influence. Such a concept dovetails with what Ned O'Gorman has called "political-economic adventurism" in the development culture within the U.S. government, wherein key leaders and bureaucrats saw that "with creative world political and economic action, the United States could restore its ideological hegemony over the free world and 'expand the area of freedom.'"[136] Failure to take bold and global-size actions would be seen not only as a strategic problem but also as an *aesthetic* one. In other words, to not seize the opportunity for the

United States to perform on the world stage was a failure to uphold a particular image that was seen as necessary.[137] Not only did mapping participate in this image-making process; cartography itself was "hailed" into the rhetorical battleground of the Cold War. The very practice of mapping was seen as a progressive method of bringing the Third World up to the standards of the First, as an attempt to validate not only the capitalist system but American ideology as a whole.

Overall, the imaginative geographies of North and South evolved, adapted, and were contested throughout the course of the Cold War, making for profound tensions on the map between internationalism and nationalism, shape and area, and developed and undeveloped. The volatility of spatial concepts like the Third World anchored the spatial relations between the United States and the Soviet Union but also opened up the possibilities of radical challenges to those relations. Walter Mignolo has written of "cosmopolitanism" as one global objective during the Cold War era, where international spatial relationships were redefined by Western elites in terms of interdependency, and human rights were redefined through the "master discourse" of political economy.[138] In this move to interdependency among global actors, the "language of developing under-developed nations as an alternative to communism" became integral. The problem, though, was that during the Cold War's three-world system, "human rights were caught in the middle of the transformation of liberal into neoliberal democratic projects" while "decolonized countries were striving for a nation-state, at the same time that the ideologues of the new world order no longer believed in them."[139] Thus, the ways the North was envisioning the South on the flat page were decidedly at odds with the ways in which developing nations were self-identifying.

The anxieties of the binary framework between the United States and the Soviet Union helped fuel the use of cartography both to modernize potential allies and to offer a stable place on the map for an American state, whose role as superpower was being challenged more than ever before. That binary, however, would receive a jolt of energy in the increasingly digitized world of nuclear cartography. If development mapping saw an immense mobilization of all kinds of new data about the potential to improve the world, nuclear cartography zeroed in on data pertaining to the capacity for destruction of the world. Particularly in the origins of the so-called Second Cold War in the late 1970s and early 1980s, with its stockpiling of armaments for deterrence, maps made for flat, abstract planes of nuclear surveillance. In this realm, the three tiers of spatial development became irrelevant; *all* was potential target ground. This was a shrinking world of air-age globalism *in excelsis*, a terrifying kind of internationalism where distinctions between North and South, East and West, were flattened by the power of the nuclear missile to obliterate international space. Nuclear maps, despite their often classified uses, had to consistently translate this sense of both fear and strength to publics. Their function as expert interfaces for the world still had to account for international public opinion, and institutions like the Department of Defense, as we will see, used cartography to manage such opinion and consolidate its ability to win, not just maintain, the Cold War.

But as with development mapping, challenges to this kind of cartographic management were taking place. As the Cold War entered a fifth decade, more and more mappers were finding the state's waging of a potentially world-ending standoff unacceptable. They also found maps too often an easy instrument for dispassionately counting and offering targets for nuclear missiles. These activist cartographers would build on a small but important tradition of protest mapping, and even use the very tools of abstraction that Cold War government maps used so well, to forecast what the "end of geography" might look like if the spaces on the maps were ever to become actual targets.

5

THE END OF CARTOGRAPHY

State Control and Radical Change in the
Nuclear Geopolitics of the Second Cold War

On February 27, 1984, Secretary of Defense Caspar Weinberger made good on a promise to debate Marxist historian E. P. Thompson in front of the famed Oxford Union Debating Society.[1] The resolution? "That there is no moral difference between the foreign policies of the U.S. and the U.S.S.R." This was one curious Cold War confrontation: the appearance of Weinberger, as a major, high-ranking U.S. official and the prominent face of deterrence and nuclear policy, opposite one of the most significant leaders of the antinuclear movement in Europe, was not only startling but in some ways courageous.[2] The U.S. Embassy in London, the State Department, and even members of his own Defense Department staff warned Weinberger that this trip was a fool's errand, a debate that was unwinnable, and may even damage the Reagan administration's "ability to hold anti-Communist allies together."[3]

As Weinberger would later quip, "I had been on my feet in the Union only five minutes when I decided the Embassy was absolutely right."[4] Students from both the university and Oxford Polytechnic protested outside the Union, shouting "Weinberger warmonger, Britain out of NATO!"[5] Colin Powell, a senior military assistant to Weinberger at the time, remarked that "the students in the packed house reminded me of Romans at the Colosseum waiting for a Christian to be thrown to the lions."[6] Five hundred attendees voting on the motion crowded around the two debaters in their three-plus hour exchange, which was also broadcast live over BBC radio and eventually premiered on PBS in June across the United States. The clash of rhetorical styles was stark; Thompson's impassioned and dramatic approach, representative of the notorious Oxford Union style, stood in contrast to Weinberger's quiet, calm, even "dispassionate" demeanor, "almost as if . . . believing his argument was self-evident, [he] has decided not to extend himself."[7] Overall, a tense and confrontational atmosphere hung over the exchange; Thompson's case posited the two superpowers as "towering terrorist states" and "mutually exacerbating military structures." He singled out the United States, in particular, for its imperialistic nuclear occupation of Europe with Cruise and Pershing missiles as "symbols of menace, of 'posture.'"[8] Thompson joked to loud applause, "When friends come to help us it's fine for them to stay in the house for three or four days. When they stay for three weeks we get a little bit restive. But after 35 years . . ."[9] Weinberger's case, in turn, offered the morality of American ideology as the key difference between the foreign outlook of the two superpowers: "It is very simple. It's all about freedom. Individual, personal, human freedom and whether we and our children will be allowed to exercise it. . . . Who among the Soviets voted that they should invade Afghanistan? Maybe one, maybe five men in the Kremlin. . . . Nobody else. And that is, I think, the height of immorality."[10] To much surprise, "Cap" Weinberger was declared the winner by a decisive margin of 271 to 232. His simple "civics lesson" drew on a well of sympathy from the audience after Thompson's brutal harangue, although as Grafstein added, "it was the presence of about a hundred Americans in the debating chamber that proved decisive."[11]

Forgotten in the novelty of the proceedings was the fact that Professor Thompson built his case on two peculiar visual aids: at one point during the debate, he brought forward two defense booklets, one produced by the U.S. Department of Defense (with a foreword by Weinberger), the other by the Soviet Union.[12] The professor called the U.S. pamphlet, *Soviet Military Power*, a "Sears-Roebuck catalogue of all the deadly military equipment" possessed by the USSR, while the Soviet book, *Whence the Threat to Peace*, was filled with the "usual half-lies and propaganda statements."[13] Pointing to the books, Thompson argued, "They have even copied each other in maps. Here is a power projection in the United States catalogue, with a *huge* Soviet Union, with arrows going in every direction around the world. And in the Soviet catalogue, the Soviet Union is rather smaller and all the arrows are spreading out from the United States towards the five continents of the world" (figs. 5.1 and 5.2 display the two dueling maps to which Thompson referred).[14] Reaching the climax of his speech, Thompson railed, "Bind these two together and they make the most evil book known in the whole human record . . . an inventory of the matched evils of this accelerating system, a confession of absolute human failure. What moral difference is there between these two catalogues? . . . The first

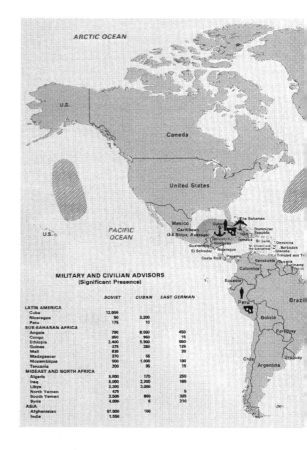

Figure 5.1. U.S. Department of Defense, "Soviet Global Power Projection," in Soviet Military Power, *1981 (Courtesy of Boatwright Library, University of Richmond)*

moral difference that will appear will be when either superpower makes an actual *act* of disarmament. Then we can start to talk about morality. Until that happens I rest my case on these two odious books."[15] Remarkably, the five-hundred–plus members of the audience, and the millions tuning in across various media, were witnessing a radical socialist peace advocate directly lecturing a top U.S. leader about the moral evil of his maps in promoting a potential nuclear apocalypse.

Weinberger's very presence at the debate displayed the sizable investment of America's foreign policy makers and defense strategists in international public opinion. But more than a minor public relations victory for the Reagan administration's defense of its nuclear arms policies, the Oxford event represented the increasingly moral terms of the nuclear arms debate. Through his appearance at the Oxford debate and through his commissioning of literature such as *Soviet Military Power*, Weinberger

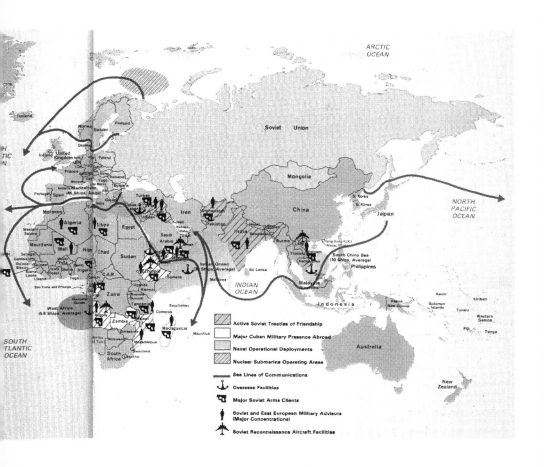

was clearly reaching beyond the balance-of-power pragmatism of 1970s détente and offering a bold rationale for the deployment of new arms to maintain peace, a rationale that relied on perception and moral fortitude.

G. Thomas Goodnight has noted the Reagan administration's rhetorical rekindling of a so-called Second Cold War through its reformulation of the rhetoric of war.[16] For example, in early policy-defining speeches such as "Zero Option" (1981), President Reagan argued that new nuclear missiles are needed not because they will correct the overall imbalance of power; rather, "the reality of force balances do not matter precisely because deterrence depends upon the 'perceived ability of our forces to perform effectively.'"[17] Nuclear weapons are "symbols of commitment" and "all weapons deficits are construed as signs of appeasement, and the danger of appeasement in a nuclear age is attached to an infinite risk."[18] Thus, Reagan and his defense representatives like Weinberger emphasized the value of

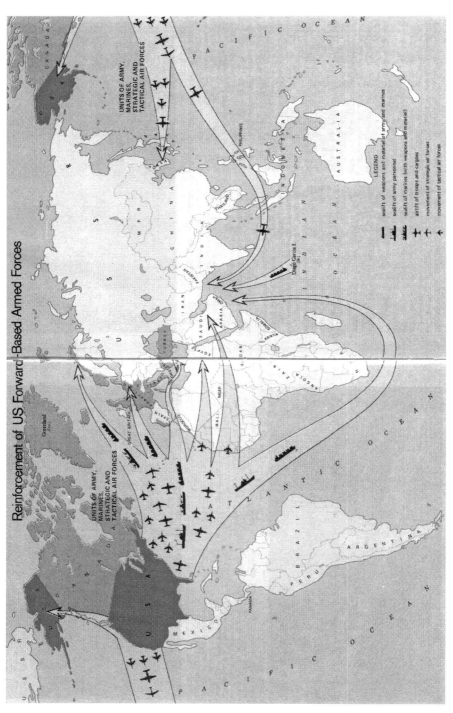

Figure 5.2. U.S.S.R. Ministry of Defense, "Reinforcement of U.S. Forward-Based Armed Forces," in Whence the Threat to Peace, *1982 (Courtesy of Boatwright Library, University of Richmond)*

perception and each side's ability to persuade the other of its strength—hence the need for exceeding the Soviet Union in nuclear capacities. In addition, this reformulation hearkened back to traditional definitions of war before 1945; the Soviet Union as an "Evil Empire" made the nuclear struggle an age-old moral battle between the forces of light and darkness. The Cold War strategies of containment and the asymmetrical development of counterforces had posited the United States and the Soviet Union as two superpowers linked on the same road to doom, requiring, in Ira Chernus's terms, a careful calibration of "apocalypse management."[19] The Reagan and Weinberger of the Second Cold War sought to go beyond mere management with the startling claim that *nuclear war is winnable*. Weinberger's presence on the stage at Oxford affirmed the seriousness of conviction with which both morality and the perception of intentions informed the defense policies of the United States.

At the same time, however, by discussing nuclear policies on moral terms, Weinberger was opening up an opportunity for Thompson's radical brand of moral outrage. This allowed for Thompson's damning depiction of the Soviet Union and the United States as the same evil face of destructive state power. The *Wall Street Journal*, in fact, scolded Weinberger on this point: "Western governments should not raise the credibility of 'peace' movement spokesmen by giving them the same status. . . . Commitment to democratic values does imply tolerance and a civilized attitude toward one's opponent—but it does not require that you act as his publicity agent."[20] Thompson, thus, was given a platform for moral dissent, and maps became an important plank in that platform.

The improbable debate between Thompson and Weinberger points to, in a larger sense, how maps offered a compelling and contested mode of visual perception for the complex nuclear tensions of the Second Cold War and how questions of morality constrained such cartographic discourse. Certainly, the debate represents cartography's continuing evidentiary power during the Cold War to spatially define and *envision* the world, as well as the prominence of maps in the arena of public opinion. And "nuclear geography" had some unique properties.[21] Maps had to account for the prospect of nuclear war—to project a present world of state power armaments while also sketching a future world of potential destruction. In addition, most of this brand of cartography was produced through increasingly digital methods—the already abstract projections of nuclear capacity were doubly abstracted through screens that could be manipulated by sanctioned experts. The entire experience of the map was changing alongside its methods. In the process, nuclear weapons substantially changed notions of space in international relations by sparking a new emphasis on, in James Der Derian's terms, "rapidity and totality."[22] In a way, this focus on the immense speed of nuclear weaponry and the total miniaturization of the earth was the ultimate extension and outcome of the air-age globalism of the 1940s. Like the air-age global maps, nuclear cartography depicted a dramatically shrinking earth, where time had replaced distance (i.e., how fast a missile could reach a target) as the measure of power, but now the map foretold the total destruction of global space.

Through considerations of the speed and *scale* of nuclear war, I explore cartography in this chapter through the Second Cold War's expansion of armaments and the responding calls for disarmament. In terms of the expansion of armaments, the volley of defense propaganda that incensed Professor Thompson and that *Time* referred to as the "Battle of the Booklets" supported arguments for a nuclear arsenal buildup.[23] Each year throughout the 1980s, map-laced pamphlets like the U.S. *Soviet Military Power*, the USSR's *Whence the Threat to Peace* and *Disarmament: Who's Against?* were updated, revised, and reprinted, providing a compelling visual record of the reignited Cold War and, more importantly, promoting a kind of *hyperinternationalism* where defense technologies mark every corner of the globe as a potential target.[24] Hyperinternationalism is my term for the spectacular collapse of distance during the nuclear arms race. With missile technology bringing nation-states so close together, the United States and the Soviet Union overlapped so as to become almost copies of one another. International relations were thus based on a surreal absurdity around quantitative projections of force that sanitized the mega-destructive effects of the weapons. Particularly, as the maps of the late Cold War were being increasingly designed on and seen through interfaces and mediated screens controlled by defense experts, the evolution of cartographic abstraction dramatically accelerated.

While these developments posed both technical and moral challenges to those seeking to use maps as subversive challenges to state power, important examples of activist cartographies surfaced to echo the kind of moral challenge made by E. P. Thompson. The radical geographer William Bunge and his *Nuclear War Atlas* project was one particularly flamboyant challenge that supported the nuclear freeze movement with its graphic cartography of nuclear destruction and the moral bankruptcy of state power during the arms race of the early 1980s. This disarmament cartography envisioned the end of the Cold War by trying to subvert the abstraction of space by superpower forces. By heightening their own ideologies and moral values in the lines of the map, these cartographers defied the expectation that Cold War maps uphold standards of rationality and scienticity. At the same time, radical mapping was constrained by cartography's continuing struggle between its expectations to present space "as is" and its traditional role of providing a means for state power and control. As political scientist Michael Shapiro writes, "The alternative worlds destroyed and suppressed within modern cartography become available only when the global map is given historical depth and alternative practices are countenanced. In sum, although the dominant geopolitical map appears uncontentious and nonnormative, it constitutes what I am calling a moral geography, a set of silent ethical assertions that preorganize explicit ethicopolitical discourses."[25] The defense maps of works like *Soviet Military Power* and *Whence the Threat to Peace* organize the world through these dominant lenses, while diatribes like the *Nuclear War Atlas* constitute the "alternative practices" that attempt to graph the silences of these ethical assertions and expose their powerful assumptions.[26] This chapter details how nuclear cartography negotiates uniquely explosive tensions between social change and social control.

NUCLEAR GEOPOLITICS AND THE
"SCREENING" OF THE COLD WAR

The Second Cold War was accompanied and sustained by a long-evolving nuclear geopolitics that dates at least back to the flights over Hiroshima and Nagasaki in the dead of summer 1945. Nuclear geopolitics rested on a complex conundrum, as its tenets simultaneously employed both an intensely spatial outlook and a denial of space. As John Agnew writes, "the advent of the capacity to deliver nuclear weapons over great distances almost instantaneously both devalued the military importance of territorial space through a new emphasis on virtuality and yet reinforced the sense of being targeted because of where you happened to live."[27] As seen in chapter 4, the ascendance of development cartography during the course of the Cold War was predicated on regional consciousness, continental imaginaries, and expertise on particular areas. Concurrently, the rise of nuclear geopolitics mitigated the impact of that expertise; the prospect of nuclear war reasserted the familiar security of East-West superpower politics and totalized the Cold War. For Ciro Zoppo, nuclear geopolitics revolves around the "intercontinental projection of nuclear firepower" and the "extension of land and sea space to atmospheric space and from the latter into the stratosphere and beyond."[28] This extension ironically created a "closed world," which in Paul Edwards's terms was "a dome of global technological oversight . . . within which every event was interpreted as part of a titanic struggle between the superpowers," a war of information management.[29]

The architects of nuclear geopolitics in the Second Cold War were part of a long lineage running back to the construction of massive defense projects in the 1950s, which were designed to create a vast border of satellites, radars, and alert systems that could demarcate superpower control of space. Iconic early Cold War nuclear projects, for example, such as the building of the DEW Line in northern Canada (the Distant Early Warning system), relied on important cartographic technological advances triangulated from commercial, academic, and military interests, while almost literally drawing boundaries between the nuclear power of the Soviet Union and that of the United States. Matthew Farish has noted how projects like these were not just "ramparts" in a physical sense, but ideological as well, writing that with DEW, "the fruits of the military-industrial-academic complex were on display. And those ramparts, while increasingly material, were, just as importantly, imaginative constructions, flexible enough to accommodate the boundaries of both scientific knowledge and strategic destiny."[30] The imaginative constructions of such complex technologies always involved the preparation for probable disasters, and thus saw a constant need for tests and future projections. In Philip Mirowski's terms, "The entire Cold War military technological trajectory was based on simulations, from the psychology of the enlisted men turning the keys to the patterns of targeting of weapons to their physical explosion profile . . . to the behaviour of the opponents in the Kremlin to econometric models of a postnuclear world."[31] Security discourse, thus, became a world of theories, simulations, and models.

Since nuclear deterrence itself was a projection, the map provided a fitting vehicle for its presentation, allowing for the simple and reliable display of complex calculations and quantifications. By showing a flat world over which missiles could be projected, cartography allowed for the necessary detachment and abstraction of nuclear planning. As early as 1955, for example, a textbook manual on the "principles of guided missile design" produced by the Naval Research Laboratory assured its readers:

> There is no question that, with presently available techniques, it would be possible to send an aircraft to a predetermined point on the globe, have it drop its bombs, and return to the starting point without the assistance of a human pilot in the aircraft. . . . The practical question

is: where do we start the automatic operations in the chain of offense or defense? The obvious answer is that when man becomes the weak link in the chain, for any reason, he must be replaced by a specialized automatic device.[32]

Richard Edes Harrison's air-age pilot was replaced by a revival of the omniscient cartographic perspective—except now, the perspective was most often produced by machine.

Not only did the data of such defense maps reflect this technological quantification, but the actual production of the maps in this era was becoming increasingly automated.[33] There can be no overstating the profound effects of digitization on mapping as a whole in the Cold War, and particularly in the realm of nuclear geography. The metaphor of a map as "interface" became more and more a literal one, as world space would come to be charted and surveyed through the electronic screen.[34] Cruise missiles, for example, contained special radars in their nose cones that allowed them to monitor the layout of the ground below them against the information from satellite maps that were digitized and stored in a built-in computer.[35] While digitized mapping was still largely used for classified security objectives during the majority of the Cold War, the overall technofied air of digitization would come to implicate even more traditional printed maps and cartographic materials. Ambassador Lodge's bold accusation of Soviet air aggression through his cartographic visual aid at the United Nations in 1960, for instance, was produced only through the latest in America's air satellite technology. He drew a specific line on the militarization of U.S. knowledge in his speech, remarking that "the difference between the United States and the Soviet Union is that we shoot their places with cameras. They shoot ours with guns and rockets."[36] Those classified photographic and cartographic methods came to the surface at key flashpoints to become a provocative part of public diplomacy.

Of course, the GIS revolution in cartography did not fall out of the skies in the late 1960s; the provenance of innovative digital overlays typically came out of classified, defense-related origins going back to the very beginning of the Cold War.[37] As John Cloud writes, "An array of technologies were developed to rectify and geo-position top-secret panoramic photography and later imagery into standard and novel map making and geographic analysis systems. A major part of the analog-to-digital transition in the American military and intelligence communities was precisely the development of these capabilities."[38] In the process, a tension arose between the strategic geopolitical benefits that could come from such technologies and the often precarious stability and accuracy of these systems as they were still developing. Particularly as nuclear fears intensified during the late 1950s and early 1960s, the rapidly progressing production methods for maps existed alongside an uneasy anxiety about whether these untested systems would actually secure America in the event of an attack.

The abstractions of the cartographic process were especially amplified during this increasing digitization of the Cold War. A growing detachment brought the cartographer even further away from the object of the map, increasing the prospects for efficiency and surveillance but problematizing cartography as fragmented, "managed," and neutral. As Patrick McHaffie puts it, "A 'new' cartographer was created, one laboring in dark rooms using complicated optical-mechanical instruments, embedded within a process that was more easily watched, more easily controlled" but a process that nonetheless "progressively devalues the human contribution to the map."[39] The mapmaker was in a sense, a "cybernetic" manager central to the construction of a "vast strategic grid" across the globe, which "a universal man-machine had to *recognize* but could then *regulate* as much as possible."[40]

The nuclear cartography of the U.S. Air Force's Strategic Air Command (SAC) in the late 1950s and early 1960s, for example, compellingly demonstrates this premium on cybernetic technocratic control (and the fear of its loss) that presaged the defense propaganda of the Reagan era. SAC was one of the best-funded nuclear projects of the Eisenhower and Kennedy eras, as it coordinated a vast network of bases that could activate missile-carrying nuclear bombers while also monitoring the air for signs of impending danger. The mostly digital maps of SAC are not as easily archived as the "material" traces left by a circulating map like "'Gulag'—Slavery, Inc.," as SAC maps were most often circulating through screens. Thus, perhaps one of the best ways to see these maps in action was through the periodically produced SAC films, some of which were produced for public consumption, others for classified, interagency briefings.[41] Like many newsreels and TV documentaries of the time, maps provided important graphic interfaces for complex data: the films consistently rely on maps to present arguments for both the efficacy of SAC and the high stakes of nuclear surveillance.

The *SAC Command Post* film of 1964, for example, was designed for a public audience in the wake of the Cuban Missile crisis, in order to explain to Americans how SAC would successfully manage a real nuclear threat.

The beginning of the film shows a silhouetted shot of a guard dog as the male narrator proclaims, "There is only world peace where there is power to preserve order among nations" and touts SAC as the "greatest deterrent" to world war that exists across the globe. The film argues for SAC's expert control, over montages of impressive computer technology and visual details of a potential nuclear threat as it might pass through the chain of command at an underground SAC headquarters. In one shot of a huge command center control room, an anonymous group of air force technicians sits at computer interfaces under massive, wall-size screens displaying data and maps, as the narrator notes, "Critical data from the computers can be displayed quickly on screens in the command post. Displays are vital for briefing the commander and the battle staff on daily operations, exercises, or national emergencies." Elsewhere, digital target maps show the world in gridded quadrants to track incoming missiles: one sequence traces on the map how an attack from Cuba would be intercepted by SAC technicians.[42]

The many shots of SAC men (the gendered implications remain important) sitting in front of these imposing maps reveal the kinds of structures that contemporary films like *Fail-Safe* and *Dr. Strangelove* exploited for both drama and satire.[43] Those films remarked on the fear of the loss of control inherent in Cold War nuclear technology. *SAC Command Post*, instead, through the ubiquitous medium of the map, attempts to reassert control and answers that American technical expertise will keep the continent safe. Combined with the film's focus on experts pushing buttons, answering red telephones, and feeding data to computers, the air force "man" becomes a cyborglike figure with human faculties always connected to complex machines and communications networks.[44] And yet, despite this closed-off technological underground world of the command post depicted in the film, the fact that the documentary was designed for public consumption shows that even the most classified of institutions in this era were concerned with the notion of public image and perception. In response to the popular sense of a shadowy "military-industrial-*academic* complex" and the accompanying nuclear dread, institutions like SAC saw worth in communicating their mission (and a sense of their expertise in the face of potential nuclear panics) to broader audiences.[45] Nathan S. Atkinson has demonstrated how visual-rhetorical control over nuclear technology was part of policy makers' and military institutions' goals during the Cold War—to persuade "viewers to cede control over the development of nuclear technology to an unelected, technocratic elite," and to promote assent for deterrence and nuclear stockpiling.[46] Films like *SAC*

Command Post and their use of cartography show important attempts to achieve that sense of technocontrol.

While *SAC Command Post* assures viewers that U.S. management plans for nuclear threats is sound and strong, other SAC films like 1959's *Operation Head Start* and 1960's *Development of the Soviet Ballistic Missile Threat* were more conventional briefing and training films kept classified inside the Air Force and collaborating agencies. However, their appropriations of cartography focus on the quantification of threat that, say, Weinberger would circulate publicly on a much larger scale. *Operation Head Start* tracks how a successful airborne alert would take place for the deployment of nuclear missiles, complete with maps animating the bomber routes off the coast of Maine. Here, the air-age globalism of the airplane is in its transitional mode toward the globalism of the missile, as the shrinking world takes on more devastating implications.[47] *Development of the Soviet Ballistic Missile Threat* engages in a controversial argument over whether the Soviet Union is winning the Cold War by outstripping the U.S. in the so-called "missile gap"; this film answers that question with a resounding "yes."[48] The film intercuts a host of maps and charts that attempt to confirm the fears of increasing Soviet superiority in nuclear bombs. In fact, the cartographic style of these maps is not far off from the Defense pamphlet cartography of the 1980s; much of what we see on the screen are world or regional snapshots with missile trajectories, black and red missile icons, and bases and cities as targets. The sense of capacity and totality is what is perhaps most striking about the maps, as their range of coverage and relentless sense of numerical threat are constantly onscreen. The mapping is sleek, bloodless, and seemingly commonsense around the menace of the Soviets; but the very impressiveness of SAC's ability to synthesize such secret data is also a major part of the displays. With the maps as expert interfaces for SAC technicians, the stockpiling of knowledge and our surveillance abilities become central to the implied answer to the problem of Soviet superiority: we must outmatch.

In Farish's words, a "new age of information had replaced one of materialism"; while the end consequences of a nuclear war were no doubt seriously feared in these contexts, the clean grids of the digitized cartographic displays abstracted the world into fields of perception management.[49] These visuals would only become more sophisticated as the Cold War waged on. While periodic diplomatic thaws in the 1960s and 1970s would dramatically calm the hotheaded rhetoric of nuclear proliferation, the apparatus for the arms race, built by institutions like SAC, continued to strengthen. And as the military-industrial-academic complex grew, so did the capacities for its ability to synthesize and digitize the space below. By the time the nuclear tensions resurfaced with gusto, new forms of cartography were marshaled to plot them for a wide audience.

"BATTLE OF THE BOOKLETS": NUCLEAR ARMAMENTS AND (LATE) COLD WAR STATE POWER

Soviet Military Power, what Thompson called "the most evil book of our time," appeared in 1981, as part of an informational offensive that accompanied the Reagan administration's intense calls for nuclear expansion to achieve not simply *parity* but missile superiority. While this kind of rhetoric was resonant in earlier Cold War discourse like that of SAC, Reagan's brand of deterrence reached back to the 1970s anti-détente discourse of influential political lobby organizations like the Committee on Present Danger (CPD), which shared key members with CIA director George H. W. Bush's "Team B," an independent group convened to advise President Gerald Ford on Soviet intelligence. Members included past Cold War luminaries like NSC-68 architect Paul Nitze, conservative Democratic intellectuals like Eugene Rostow, and many future members of the Reagan Administration such as Richard Perle, Paul Wolfowitz, and Jeane Kirkpatrick. Once President Jimmy Carter took office, the group challenged his administration by bringing its strategic ideas to the public, producing manifestos and various publications constructing a dark picture of Soviet superiority and calling for a much stronger security apparatus.[50]

This more militant security discourse was also marked by what Simon Dalby called a revival of geopolitical thinking. Intellectuals and policy makers constructed the threat of the USSR in explicitly spatial terms, and publicized the potential effect of Soviet weapons on the global landscape.[51] Coupled with the perceived failure of SALT II and the Soviet invasion of Afghanistan, this discourse contributed to the Reagan administration's resuscitation of a bipolar Cold War. In historian Fred Halliday's estimation, Cold War II was defined by a "concerted and sustained attempt by the USA to subordinate the various dimensions of its foreign policy, and that of its allies, to confrontation with the USSR . . . the postulation of an external threat was combined with alarm about the erosion of pre-existing values to foster mobilization for a new Cold War."[52]

Defense Department initiatives like *Soviet Military Power* had to first establish that the Soviet Union enjoyed a destructive advantage over the United States. To achieve this, the booklet constructs a verbal and visual rhetoric that perpetuates "crisis."[53] Weinberger's introduction constructs this crisis by focusing on how Soviet power has become uncontainable: "There is nothing hypothetical about the Soviet military machine. Its expansion, modernization, and contribution to projection of power beyond Soviet boundaries are obvious. A clear understanding of Soviet Armed Forces, their doctrine, their capabilities, their strengths and their weaknesses is essential to the shaping and maintenance of effective U.S. and Allied Armed Forces."[54] Weinberger underlines the premium on a "clear understanding," thus setting up the self-evident proposition that the visual displays presented in the booklet will correct any misperceptions. He then takes his readers through a comparative litany of the Soviet Union's numerical advantage in nuclear capabilities; in the 1983 edition, the Secretary of Defense pointedly referred to America's disadvantage as heightened "by a decade of our neglect coupled with two decades of massive Soviet increases."[55] This implicit reference to the détente period of nuclear rollbacks set a line in the sand for the military posture of the Reagan administration. Of course, while such pamphlets served as an inventory of capacities, their public opinion function was equally important. The same data were available, for example, in the secretary of defense's annual report, but the booklets allowed high-tech visual persuasion, based on digital methods, to set the new nuclear geopolitics. Weinberger wrote of *Soviet Military Power* in his autobiography that "it helped us measure and adjust our own forces and capabilities in relation to the Soviets'—an ongoing exercise that was crucial for realistic planning and budgeting. It was also most useful in persuading some of our allies that they needed to increase their defense efforts."[56]

The Soviet Union responded in kind, setting off a back-and-forth exchange in the pamphlet series from 1981 until the beginning of the Cold War's end in 1989. The Soviets' first response came in 1982 with *Whence the Threat to Peace*, which was launched in conjunction with a news conference featuring the chief of staff of Soviet Armed Forces, General Valentin Varennikov. The *New York Times* called the news conference "the first opportunity in years for foreign reporters to put questions directly to a member of the [Soviet] military hierarchy." Varennikov announced that "the Soviet Union has never sought and does not seek military superiority" but the book would provide "objective factual material" on "who is responsible for the arms race."[57] The introduction to *Whence the Threat* is more confrontational, accusing Weinberger and the U.S. of " inciting military psychosis" and promising that the "unprejudiced reader will find answers in it to the anti-Soviet intentions that abound in the propaganda pamphlets of the USA and NATO."[58]

The public relations offensive resulted in wide distribution of the book-let in six languages and an extensive amount of American press coverage. Congressman Thomas J. Downey of Long Island commented to the *New York Times*: "For the ordinary person, it's useful to see that the Soviets regard us with the same hostility we view them."[59] An *Economist* review reproduced one of the Soviet maps (a map claiming America as a techno-logical belligerent) with the caption, "They're catching up in pamphlets too." The *Economist* also noted the lavish maps as products of "Madison-sky Avenue," and the *Times* called it the "most sophisticated effort yet to persuade public opinion . . . that the Reagan Administration's arms buildup is a threat to peace."[60] *Time* declared that while many of the claims are false, "the production represents a quantum leap in Moscow's mastery of military propaganda."[61] While the first edition of Weinberger's booklet contained only a few maps, the Soviets used cartography extensively. In response, the U.S. Department of Defense notably increased the number of maps used in future editions. Further reprints of *Whence the Threat* and other tracts like 1983's *Disarmament: Who's Against?* escalated this numbers-and-maps war between the two powers.

The maps in the "Battle of the Booklets" detail this escalation by reducing the conflict to a zero-sum game of numbers with the world as the playing board. The metaphor of the "zero sum" in the Second Cold War was an important "symbolic enclosure within which the (il)logic of nuclear politics played itself out."[62] Both sides in the pamphlet wars, as the *New York Times* points out, share the "same penchant for quantitative measurement" that came to especially characterize the era's defense dis-course and its sophisticated, computerized technologies.[63] A central map in *Soviet Military Power* entitled "Soviet Military Forces" uses an outline of the USSR and fills the landscape with stark black icons (over a pink background) of missiles such as ICBMs, IRBMs, SLBMs.[64] The map rep-resents ground forces with a silhouetted icon of a soldier, and its resem-blance to a toy soldier minimizes the human element and equates Soviet fighting men with the missiles and submarines surrounding them. Just as the Soviet Union became one emblematic labor camp in the Gulag map, here the USSR became one emblematic logo of a missile base. The power of cartography draws on the recognizable lines of the Soviet Union's shape and makes them synonymous with the equally recognizable shape of a nuclear missile. In addition, the map is simply a large puzzle piece over a white background, divorcing the Soviet Union from its relationship with the rest of the world. Its outline is shaded in such a way that it appears to be a plateau coming off the page, appearing as a detached, abstract surface on the page. And like the Gulag map, the "Soviet Military Forces" map emphasizes the process of knowledge production around enemy spaces and serves as a militant brand of propaganda, while still making use of the map's representational power to reliably showcase statistical truth.

One particular map in *Soviet Military Power* extends this concept by alarmingly transposing Soviet space *onto* American space. The "Area of Nizhniy Tagil Tank Plant" map (fig. 5.3) uses an aerial view of the Washington, D.C., area, centered on the National Mall, and outlines in red the size of the Soviet tank plant at Nizhniy Tagil over the symbolically hallowed ground of the U.S. capital.[65] The red outline of the plant's dwarfing of the entire landscape of downtown D.C. connotes that the Soviet Union can destroy the infrastructure of its American enemy with the sheer immensity of its military power. The striking detail of familiar roads, buildings, and parks on the ground is also key to the map's function: those streets and their famous landmarks are now contained by the capacity of military power to essentially target them. Obviously, the map stops short of arguing that the Soviets are specifically targeting D.C., but the choice of using an aerial map (typically used to assess military targets from the air) with a kind of blueprint-style motif inevitably makes that case implicitly, and the symbolic center of "freedom" and American power becomes a kind of militarized zone. Most importantly, though, the detailed realism of the satellite perspective is striking. Prefiguring the immersive cartography of, say, Google Maps, this viewpoint validates the Department of Defense's very ability to use digital computers and satellites to quantify and spatialize the capacity of its enemy. The impressive power of the technology itself is on display in such a map.

In *Whence the Threat*, the Soviets simply reproduce the exact same map scheme but now use a large blue outline of the Detroit Tank Armory, superimposing it over the red Tagil plant to show how America subsumes the Soviet Union in terms of military capacity.[66] In the process, their map accuses the Americans of omission and concealment in their use of cartographic evidence. No small part of the "paramap" here is that the Soviets include a photograph of U.S. nuclear-fitted howitzers (large cannons mounted on wheeled motor vehicles, similar in look to a tank) across the page from their adaptation of the D.C. map, helping to concretize the abstract nature of the tank plant outlines. Both of these maps also speak to the techniques of surveillance that mark Cold War superpower technologies. As Der Derian has written, this surveillance regime defined a superpower contest wracked by "hyper-vigilance, intense distrust, rigid and judgmental thought processes, and projection of one's own repressed

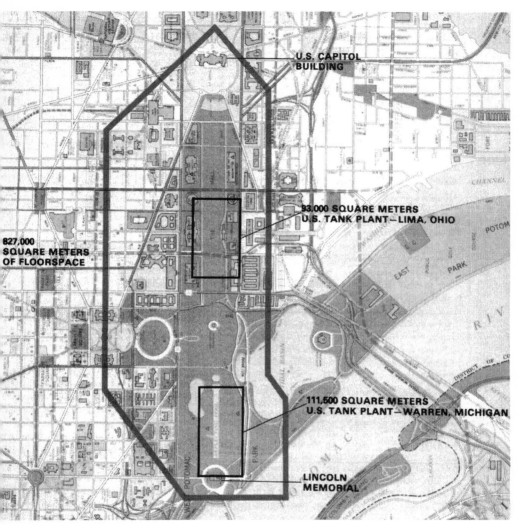

Figure 5.3. U.S. Department of Defense, "Area of Tagil Tank Plant over Plan of Washington, D.C.," in Soviet Military Power, 1981 (Courtesy of Boatwright Library, University of Richmond)

beliefs and hostile impulses onto another."[67] The tank plant maps literally project the enemy's hostility onto our own internal spaces. In addition, the use of the aerial map emphasizes, once again, the complex production of the "view from above." The problem is that this surveillance "normalizes relations by continuing *both* war and peace by other, technical means. The same satellite that monitors and helps us verify whether the Soviets are conforming to the Intermediate-Range Nuclear Forces Treaty simultaneously maps the way for low-level, terrain-following cruise missiles."[68] The choice of whether to use cartographic technology for good or evil is thus drawn into the lines of the map.

Other U.S. maps in *Soviet Military Power* such as "Soviet Global Power Projection" do place the Soviet Union back into context with the rest of the world, using a conventional Mercator projection (thus exaggerating the size of the Soviet Union and Eastern Europe), and demonstrating the global locations of Soviet treaties of friendship, military presence abroad, and nuclear submarine operating areas. These maps even use pistol icons to show where major Soviet arms clients can be found.[69] Altogether, the map spread reveals an extensive network of Soviet influence. By contrast, the Soviet answer in *Whence the Threat* maps such as "Reinforcement of US Forward-Based Armed Forces" employ a projection that shrinks the Soviet Union and increases the size of Africa and South Asia.[70] A large brigade of arrows aggressively protrudes forth from the United States and besets the Eurasian heartland from all sides. The arrow had been a frequent theme in so-called propaganda cartography since at least World War II, able to suggest directionality and movement on the static page. Here, the presence of the arrows carrying various weapons of destruction connotes a feeling of constant, unending flow. The actual locations are less vital than the message that this movement of arms from the United States all around the world against the Soviet Union will be continuous and relentless. In the introductory text, the Soviet Ministry of Defense even invokes an old Cold War cartographic standby, noting: "Like the tentacles of a gigantic octopus, American imperialism's bases—springboards for aggression—reach to all corners of the globe. The network of military bases and installations is being constantly extended to new regions . . . with the obvious intention of creating a palpable threat from all sides to the Soviet Union and its allies."[71]

Elsewhere, maps like "Concept of Operations of US Strategic Offensive Forces on the Basis of Major Military Exercises" steal a page out of the U.S. journalistic cartography of the 1940s and 1950s. The map employs a polar projection anchored around the Arctic, except *now* the United States hovers above the pole and the USSR sits below.[72] A series of thick, imposing arrows filled with jet and missile icons descends over the pole and infiltrates the Soviet Union.[73] The accuracy of targeting used to matter more in early Cold War cartography. In the Second Cold War, however, it was less about the specificity of the target and more about the totality of coverage, thus making a foray into the hyperinternational. Nuclear weaponry can be launched from any direction, as the earth is reduced to a simple flat plane that weapons can fly over; all space is rendered vulnerable. By bringing all of international space into a platform for a theoretical war, the scale is both infinitely large and small at the same time. No longer abstracting "real" scenarios on the ground, the map becomes an abstraction of nuclear war, an event that was already a significant abstraction of warfare in itself.

In this way, Soviet military power is mapped as menacingly global and total. The maps of the early Cold War that used boundaries to partition NATO and Warsaw Pact countries became increasingly irrelevant when the trajectory of the nuclear missile came to encompass more and more ground. In U.S. Defense maps of Soviet SS-20 missile sites in Europe, a pink shading covers all of Europe (even into Greenland) and the upper Atlantic Ocean, an ambit representing the full trajectory of advanced nuclear strike capabilities.[74] In a map of the Soviet Union's missile detection and tracking system, a series of overlapping radar systems, including locations in outer space, cover the earth in searchlight-like streams that come from all directions and wrap around the continents.[75] In both of these maps, the distinction between geographic features such as land and ocean is tangential, as a kind of radar-like dome covers the sky and subsumes everything beneath. According to Paul Virilio, "In the ballistic progress of weapons, the curvature of the earth has not stopped shrinking. It is no longer the continents that become agglomerated, but the totality of the planet that is diminished . . . a world wide phenomenon of terrestrial and technological contraction that today makes us penetrate into an artificial topological universe: *the direct encounter of every surface on the globe*."[76] The internationalism of the nuclear-based Second Cold War is thus built on radii, circles, and waves rather than lines and edges, and this marks a key shift in cartographic techniques—encompassing a totality that implicates all surfaces of the earth.

Cartography becomes an ideal visual medium for the display of state power during a nuclear arms race because of its ability to reduce space and create the illusion of a manageable surface for weapons. In this process of reduction, the specifics and uniqueness of particular places are subsumed by the homogenizing character of the nuclear weapon. Writing around this same time, geographer Doreen Massey was concerned about these developments, particularly "that maps (current Western-type maps) give the impression that space is a surface—that it is the sphere of a completed horizontality."[77] Much of the media coverage of the defense booklets, for example, notes that most of the actual data presented are relatively true; what makes them reflective of the official space of the Second Cold War, though, is how they direct perception.[78] What the maps in the "Battle of the Booklets" do not do is suggest the potential of nuclear destruction; rather, they suggest the potential loss of national influence in an international arms race. The consequence of this escalating race is not death but more of an abstract loss of security. As Der Derian notes, the technological premium on acceleration resulted in an "urgent need" to "accurately see and verify the destruction of the enemy at a distance."[79] Such a "collapse of distance" shifted the aim of battle "from territorial, economic, and material gains to immaterial, perceptual fields" where "the war of spectacle begins to replace the spectacle of war."[80] The data sources of all the negative comparisons in the maps of *Soviet Military Power* and *Whence the Threat to Peace* are, at least in this light, irrelevant. The form of perception makes the argument, not the so-called real disparities in arms between the two powers.[81]

The abstract power of the state over the future is critical to the persuasive power of these maps. Rachel Holloway, for example, has noted the use of a "technological sublime" in the Cold War, particularly in how agents like Reagan place a high value on the vision of military and scientific expertise, where nuclear force takes on an almost metaphysical overtone.[82] And with nuclear weaponry, citizens do not have the chance to test the claims of their leadership; the very idea of projecting nuclear war is to take its waging on faith by those who possess that power to project.[83] Weinberger makes the point that "the greatest defense forces in the world are those of free people in free nations well informed as to the challenge they face, firmly united in their resolve to provide fully for the common defense, thereby deterring aggression and safeguarding the security of the world's democracies."[84] Here, he emphasizes perception and information management, defining nuclear deterrence and security in abstract terms, as a way to protect American democratic ideology. The maps serve such abstractions by framing the irrationality of nuclear war within the bounds of cartographic rationality. In addition, this brand of cartography displays the implications of some key shifts from the analog to the digital. Designed for public consumption, the maps themselves in these booklets are not terribly complicated or sophisticated, not appearing much different from the *Time/Life* propaganda cartography of the early 1950s. And yet that ability to quantify, survey, and convert such an immense amount of complex data about weapons systems into a simple display is the hallmark of the move toward a digital, synoptic view of space. The Defense cartographers' abilities in the Second Cold War to convert enemy space into ones and zeroes becomes a significant projection and validation of power, which the SAC films hinted at in the early 1960s. In the process, numbers themselves (and the ability to manage them) become synonymous with American values.

Altogether, the immense state power on visual display in *Soviet Military Power* and *Whence the Threat to Peace* is an important attempt by the Cold War superpowers to control the "identity and the interpretation of space."[85] What the pamphlets ultimately do is affirm the need for superpowers at a time when the stability of such bipolar organization was collapsing; they reproduce the Cold War and uphold its values, while ironically assuring a kind of security in their suspension of crisis and conflict.[86] As historian Norman Graebner has written of the Cold War, "The prodigious investment of human and physical resources assumed a fundamental international security, one that, despite the recurrence of limited aggression and war, permitted the evolution of the complex, dynamic, technology-driven civilization."[87] Even with their alarming depiction of potential aggression and antagonism, Weinberger's maps assure that the Cold War could comfortably keep progressing as is.

The overall phenomenon of the pamphlet wars is especially compelling if viewed longitudinally throughout the 1980s. Every year, a new edition would map this insulated, abstract universe of defense, as budgets and stockpiles fluctuated. Benjamin Bratton wrote that "history progresses at the speed of its weapons systems . . . that is, at the speed of the competitive capacities to envision, draw, map, curtail, mobilize, contour, stabilize and police the polis."[88] Each reprinting and remapping of the progress of nuclear offense and defense systems in the 1980s can be seen as part of an attempt at stabilization by Cold War state power. Since the effect of nuclear weapons is often unfathomable, nuclear arms are frequently "discourse-defying," according to Bryan C. Taylor and thus can be used by the state as a means to suppress resistance and control public dialogue.[89] This unfathomable nature of nuclear war is integral to the silences of the maps contained in the Department of Defense's propaganda of the Second Cold War. The maps are not necessarily scrubbed free of morality; it is simply that their moral questions are constructed as self-evident. The value of superiority in technoscience, digitization, and the abstract notion of security become the moral architecture of the map. In the end, the maps' reduction of the globe to a playing field for armaments serves to suppress any challenges to the bipolar spatial framework of the Cold War.

And yet cartographic challenges to this forty-plus-year standoff would indeed surface. As if to echo the outrage of Professor Thompson, activists and scholars were manipulating the unique qualities of maps to showcase the immensity of state power in the nuclear age and to highlight the sense of moral and human cost that they saw hidden in the boundaries of works like *Soviet Military Power*. The complex power of these maps that dared to assess the "end of geography" articulated the destruction of world space in the face of nuclear war; in the process, such cartographic activism also foresaw the end of the Cold War itself in compelling ways.

"MISSILES AS MISSIVES": WILLIAM BUNGE AND THE RADICAL CARTOGRAPHIC CHALLENGE TO THE SECOND COLD WAR

In 1982, around the same time that Weinberger and the Soviets were engaging in their booklet volley, expatriate geographer William Bunge was distributing, through his Canadian collective the "Society of Human Exploration, a poster-pamphlet, containing twenty-eight maps, called simply the *Nuclear War Atlas* (*NWA*).[90] A project realized during the rise of the intercontinental nuclear freeze movement (and eventually published in 1988 as a full-length book), "Wild Bill" Bunge's angry salvo ambitiously set out to map the latitude and longitude of the potential for human suffering in the face of nuclear attack. Labeled recently by Nik Heynen and Trevor J. Barnes variously as a "disciplinary bad boy," "cult hero," and "spatial scientist," Bunge was a long-standing radical geographic crusader, who had drawn the idea of the polemic into mappers' imaginations ever since the upheaval of the late 1960s attracted geographers into a new socially active role.[91] Perhaps his most ambitious polemic yet, the *Nuclear War Atlas* graphically charted a teetering apparatus of death in the hands of what he saw as a morally bankrupt state system. As Fraser MacDonald has written, "Bunge's *Atlas* maps out a post-apocalyptic terrain, without any attempt to soften the theme of 'unremitting and sense-numbing disaster.' Few geographers have offered their readers such a bleak cartography."[92] A macabre map of Chicago uses simple "emoticon" faces as icons that are melting from third-degree burns. Another map, entitled "The Sea of Cancer" renders the United States in lines of red across most of the page (and only a few white spaces) with a caption that reads, "In a full nuclear war, not only will most of the United States be washed in immediate radiation, but even the white areas on the map will be safe only in the sense that people in the open escape short-term damage but not long term. The cancer is everywhere."[93] The message of Bunge's maps is both crude and devastating. Most of the maps are skeletal and simple in content, awash in black and blood-red dots and lines; the simple carnage of the most complex technology ever devised is on display. The *NWA*'s introduction declares, "Many geographers now understand, and the general public itself is gradually getting the idea, that we cannot sustain nuclear war. It is a geographical impossibility."[94]

Bunge himself embodies the tensions of postwar Cold War academic geography and its attempts to define itself and its role as it engages with various publics. On the one hand, Bunge helped spark the quantitative revolution that transformed geography into a *science*, advancing cartography specifically as a mathematical practice (as well as a digital one), and a steadfast believer in using theoretical knowledge to produce objective spatial prediction, generalization, and quantification. On the other hand, he was a vociferous critic of the loss of the human in geography—a radicalized, impassioned preacher for exploring the very specificity of particular regions and peoples. Bunge railed against "armchair academics" who did not use their tools and expertise to help improve the human condition.[95] The so-called quantitative revolution, thus, was peculiar in that it aided the kind of increasingly automated military-academic cartography that supported the U.S. efforts against the Soviet Union, while also embodying a critical movement that would question the appropriation of spatial knowledge for the benefit of state power.[96] By arguing for a new visual language of cartographic proximity, the *Nuclear War Atlas* uses the ultimate fear of annihilation ironically as a catalyst for social change. What went hidden in Weinberger's maps is now put on display, accentuated, and made uncomfortably present, thus creating a future geography of "place annihilation and post-nuclear landscapes."[97]

The ways in which the cartography of such projects as Bunge's foregrounded the artifice of mapping exhibit how maps can then function simultaneously as a rhetoric of social change and social control. As Jeremy Black asserts, "Radical cartography . . . offers the possibility of problematizing generally accepted notions of progress" and opening "the politically charged question of social justice."[98] At the same time, as he also points out, the emancipatory function of cartography has its limits, as mapping is constrained by our desire to "explain, classify and organize space," entailing a significant degree of control.[99] Although maps with radical messages can eloquently challenge the status quo, these messages contend with a cartographic impulse for convenient efficiency, simplicity, and objectivity. Maps still share the age-old problem of many rhetorical forms of social change: the difficulty of challenging a system while working from within it. In this way, Bunge's maps of disarmament represent a unique argument against the Reagan-era conception of world space as a platform for force calculation but still face the difficulty of being tied to conventions and disciplinary histories that for so long had supported the power of the state to control and classify.

The Emergence of Radical Cartography and the
Origins of the Nuclear War Atlas

The story of Bunge's development remarkably mirrors the emergence of a new brand of social consciousness in postwar geography. Bunge was born in 1928 in Milwaukee to a family of relative privilege. As Bunge notes in the preface to the *Nuclear War Atlas*: "As a boy, my father would take me on business trips through southern Wisconsin and explain the region, the farming, the industry and all that we were passing through between calls on small-town banks. Both he and I thought he was teaching me his business, but it turned out that he was teaching me his geography."[100] For Bunge, "the primary effect of the Depression was not hunger or fear, but loneliness from those who were hungry and fearful."[101] He would draw on this sense of social inequity and spatial isolation as he became increasingly radicalized in the 1960s.

As a student of William Garrison at the University of Washington, Bunge was at the forefront of the quantitative revolution in geography.[102] His first major work, *Theoretical Geography* (the first edition completed in 1962), was a landmark move toward establishing geography as a spatial science, conceiving of maps specifically as mathematical models.[103] According to Michael Goodchild, *Theoretical Geography* appeared "between the old analog world of crude, imprecise tools and the modern world of abundant data and powerful techniques of analysis, visualization, and simulation."[104] This, for example, would go on to influence the digital applications of GIS technology that would come to revolutionize the field even further.[105] According to Kevin Cox, after Bunge's work, "the spatial became the central organizing concept of the field," as the premise of the uniqueness of places that marked much of the first half of the century in geographic research was abandoned in favor of work that sought generalizability.[106]

This new world in the American academy was inescapably tied to the state power interests of the Cold War, and this never quite sat well with Bunge. Out of many research universities' contracts with the defense establishment came a focus on the increasing importance of the "spatial model," particular for nuclear defense purposes. New "cyborg forms" of science "offered through their rigour, analytical purchase, and generalizations, the means to exceed mere description. Models lay exactly between the worlds of high theory and empiricism," serving as "mediators, and consequently seized upon" to achieve specific ends."[107] Bunge's adviser, Garrison, for example, was enlisted by the Washington State Highway Commission to use spatial models for highway planning with the objective of providing ways for Seattle citizens to exit the city in case of a nuclear emergency.[108] His friend and contemporary at Washington, Waldo Tobler, contributed to mapping technology for one of the most important computer-based early warning systems for nuclear attack, SAGE, which Farish has referred to as a series of Cold War "laboratories in which the connection to an exterior space was negotiated through machines."[109] Tobler's innovative "analytical cartography" and its digital applications worried Bunge in their tendency toward detachment, as he admitted in 1966: "To see region construction, one of the last preserves of the non or anti-mathematical geographers, crumble away before the ever growing appetite of the computing machines is a little unnerving even for a hard case quantifier."[110]

Bunge also worried about the increasing compartmentalization and professionalization of Cold War geographers. Like-minded contemporary David Smith wrote that, "There were sessions in urban and economic geography which gave the clear impression that more than a decade of . . . running regression models, factor-analyzing census data, and the like, has done little to help us improve the quality of life for real people in real cities or real economically declining regions."[111] Smith even used an example of a local university atlas that had "a section of thirty-four maps of the United States which includes dot maps of the location of turkeys, hogs, and chickens, but no maps of any human material or social conditions."[112] Bunge's response to these developments was to bring the field closer to humanist concerns; in his philosophy of scientific activism, "There exist objective ways to judge police states. Map them."[113]

Bunge became truly radicalized alongside the student protesters outside his office doors, crediting Vietnam with forever taking him out of abstract work altogether and "headlong into peace work."[114] As Bunge has said about this immersion, "Betty [his wife] and I are a couple of rich white kids no longer rich, certainly not kids and I'm not so white any more . . . when I confront the physical aspects of The Movement, my family's money falls away and I find my ultimate legitimacy."[115] In 1968, after denial of tenure at Wayne State for obscenity charges, Bunge was one of sixty-five names listed by the United States Anti-Subversive Committee not to speak on campuses. As Bunge notes, "To my eternal glory, I was alphabetically placed between H. Rap Brown and Stokely Carmichael and not far from philosopher Angela Davis."[116] John Pickles notes that Bunge became the archetypal "nomad cartographer," moving from visiting lectureships to periods of unemployment to working with underground publishers and organizing on the streets.[117]

At this time, Bunge became a proponent of a new kind of fieldwork, reviving the geographic concept of the "expedition," where he engaged deeply in charting crumbling neighborhoods.[118] He was a resident of a Detroit ghetto, Fitzgerald, and his most controversial project was the radical *Fitzgerald: The Geography Revolution* (1971). *Fitzgerald* takes up the largely black Detroit community threatened by slum and shows how everyday community inhabitants were using geographic knowledge to take back the neighborhood. As Bunge noted in *Fitzgerald*'s introduction, "In this radioactive age, these are signs of Life itself."[119] According to Rich Heyman, the Detroit expedition "represented a wholesale reconceptualization of the social role of geographical knowledge production" where "the direction of the flow of knowledge and power is outward into civil society not oriented . . . towards policy elites."[120] Around Bunge arose a loose cadre of geographers and cartographers that formed a movement of socially progressive practitioners, which Bunge's friend Richard Peet defined as a radical attempt by mappers to contribute to the "evolution of a non-destructive society."[121]

By the time *Fitzgerald* appeared, though, Bunge left Detroit for the landscapes of Canada, after "displeasing the national political police too severely to remain in other than a permanently horizontal and motionless position."[122] The *NWA* was produced out of the tumult of Bunge's long (and still ongoing) expatriate period. During this exodus, Bunge's locational focus broadened significantly into the realm of the atomic, and he came to see the "nuclear question" as vital to the future contribution of geography to society. Bunge's stance on these questions had been germinating at least since Bunge had been drafted into the Army during the Korean War, and spent his service working at the Chemical, Biological, and Radiological Wartime School at Camp McCoy in Wisconsin, ironically, in his words, "teaching atomic war."[123] As he said while promoting the atlas,

Normally socialism, nuclear war protest and academic freedom are not directly linked, so how did this happen in me? Each generation of geographers produces a few of us who walk off campus to serve the people, returning to our glorious field tradition of exploration in the process. . . . I am a Martin Luther King American driven out of my native land in November of 1970 and away from the faculty of Wayne State University. I am fiercely loyal to my home, the Fitzgerald community in Detroit, a Dr. Martin Luther King community. I am a socialist by the classic definition of 'holding the means of production in common,' but I do not prefer socialist H bombs to capitalist ones. I simply hate all H bombs implacably.[124]

As the geographic "impossibility" of nuclear war became the driving focus in this nomadic period, Bunge used both his background in mathematical modeling and urban exploration to build his case. *NWA's* maps contrast superpower nuclear antagonism with much smaller-scale renderings of cities and surrounding areas laid to waste by atomic blasts and waves of radiation. Bunge helped resurrect the works of mid-twentieth-century German geographer Walter Christaller, whose "Central Place Theory" cast cities as settlements of hierarchical systems that, if attacked, would set off a kind of "chaining out" of nuclear disaster.[125] In Bunge's explanation, "When the major centres are destroyed, so are all skilled workers, the artists, the diamond cutters. If the 'primate city'—the city in each nation that tops the hierarchy—is destroyed, then all the national centres are destroyed. . . . The nation is not only decimated, it is decapitated."[126] For Bunge, reflecting on the identity of urban populations was a central way to situate the physical and moral consequences of nuclear weaponry directly into the map. He was recasting geography as a science of survival and often used what he called the "steel-hard hammer of humanism" to describe his perspective.[127] This vision was uncompromising in its moral absolutism: "If the earth is finite and fragile, and geography clearly proves the total destructibility of the human race, then one cannot be relative about all things . . . and still claim a humanism. If cockroaches and not humans survive the radioactivity, biologists might be interested, but geographers and other humanists are not. A humanist . . . must be singularly absolute about the species continuation."[128]

This brand of moral absolutism, though, is a complex one. Only fairly recently have scholars dealt with the implications of some of the roots of geography's quantitative revolution on a critical and cultural level, and these critiques raise important questions about the development of space, maps, and geographic expertise in the Cold War. Walter Christaller's central places theory, for example, was developed out of his bureaucratic service to the Nazi regime, and his ultrarational, modernist spatial ideas, particularly around urban development, were used in the violent resettlement of Poland. The problem was that such work was conceived of, according to Trevor J. Barnes and Claudio Minca, "as merely a scientific exercise, an innocent laboratory experiment."[129] The objective of Christaller's geometric modeling was "to allow for production and the establishment of a form of territorial order that corresponded to a stable and 'proper' social, cultural, economic, and political arrangement," taking for granted that there was somehow a "united and internally consistent human consortium."[130] The sinister side of Christaller's Nazi utopianism seemed all but forgotten when his theories were adopted by the quantitative geographers and cartographers of the 1960s, receiving a warm embrace of citations and even awards from a new generation bent on a different vision of social change from Christaller's.[131]

Of course, an uncomfortable irony remains around the moral responsibility of cartography, one that speaks to the difficulty of separating models from men. Both Christaller's and Bunge's projects, in a sense, shared a zeal around the power of spatial theory and the promise of the orderly perfection of mapping. Scientific activists like Bunge were drawing on the "dark geographies" of Christaller but also subverting and reappropriating those dark visions of sanitized and ordered World War II Eastern European cities in order to show the geometry of nuclear destruction across the cities of the world.[132] Bunge seemed to be both adopting and resisting, in equal measure, the statistical data, theoretical models, and the increasingly digital computations of the era—drawing on the benefits of these methods while also indicting their dehumanization. This tension in Bunge's work, and in that of the larger quantitative movement, made for an uneasy kind of idealism around the power of science in geography and cartography. To challenge the militarized geographic apparatus of defense professionals like Weinberger was, in many ways, more straightforward and easier to reconcile than to challenge the difficult histories of the very geographic discipline that one is a product of.

Such thorny questions around maps, space, and the morality of science also energized Bunge's antinuclear contemporaries, who were trying to grapple with the conundrum of challenging one form of scientific power and expertise by replacing it with another. Geographer Michael Curry, for example, emerged out of the same quantitative revolutionary hopes as Bunge did but by the early 1980s, was railing with disillusionment at the failure of "scientific professionalism" in the battle against nuclear weapons. For Curry, well-meaning scientists raised on quantitative models were missing the moral responsibility behind their employment of positivist, so-called objective ways of looking at disarmament. To trust in such science, wrote Curry, was to "deny there are good reasons other than factual ones for ending the arms race, and in doing so it is to defer to 'experts' on issues on which we are all, if we admit it, expert."[133] Curry balked at the risk of "turning over" the debate to scientists based on the misperception that "science is seen as providing an overwhelming and objective case against the development of these weapons, and a case untainted by values."[134] To forcefully and unabashedly announce those values through the seemingly objective medium of maps was a bold contribution. At the same time, the work by activist-scientists like Bunge risked repeating that powerful narrative that a scientific expert is always needed by everyday citizens to speak *for* them about the dangers of nuclear weapons in the Cold War.

Still, those experts did play a prominent role in the attempts to offer a coherent case against nuclear armaments from a geographic and cartographic perspective. Gilbert White, arguably the most famous postwar environmental geographer, who contributed innovative flood-planning measures to the Johnson administration, argued that nuclear policy demanded input and activism from geographers and cartographers. As White wrote, "The world is condemned to living with them. As long as the missiles are present and ready to launch in large numbers, there will remain the hazard, to which no probability is assigned, that their detonation would massively disturb atmospheric and biologic systems."[135] In particular, nuclear disarmament movements in Britain and Canada, such as the Campaign for Nuclear Disarmament (CND) and Women Strike for Peace, drew heavily on activist geographers. Stanley Openshaw, for example, charted and mapped the geography of hypothetical nuclear attacks on the British Isles and particular cities, using the kind of map modeling pioneered by Bunge and Tobler to predict the effects of this future geography. As Openshaw warned, "Some people may find it difficult to think about the unthinkable and some may even feel that spatial models concerned with the prediction of 'mega-deaths' are even more distasteful," but government figures in the throes of nuclear policy decisions needed to *visualize* the consequences of their actions.[136] Similarly, Canadian geographers such as Kenneth Hewitt advanced the notion of "place annihilation," accentuating how nuclear extermination is "literally to kill by geography, not necessarily damaging an organism, but driving it beyond the bounds," potentially turning nation-states into *non-places*.[137] A policy like Cold War civil defense becomes "a token gesture, an abstract, statistical notion of survivability," and state leaders divert publics with their "'nuclear diplomacy,' a high-class and very secretive game."[138]

Bunge especially challenged nuclear policy in terms of how it approached the notion of scale and charged, like Curry, that even some of his progressive colleagues underestimated the issue's full import. The scale of the problem, wrote Bunge, "is invariably missed by most strategists, who nibble away at it by concentrating on issues such as . . . the capability of a civil defence programme. They look at the war at a scale below its true one—which is the planet itself; and they come up with conclusions that the human species will not be completely destroyed."[139]

Bunge also emphasized the three-dimensionality of the human race, to prove that "the 'zoning' of the battlefield away from the nurseries of the world would be impossible. The battlefield is everywhere due to the collapse of topological space."[140] This concept of three-dimensionality was borrowed from Ronald Horvath, who theorized the rise of "machine space" in the Cold War, where the habitable space for humans dramatically shrunk because of the sheer amount of space that machines covered—including nuclear weapons and the industries that built them.[141] Air-age globalism's contraction of the earth was again on display; as Bunge lamented: "Already, national sovereignty over the earth's surface and atmosphere has been lost—the United States with its satellites knows more about what is happening in Canada than do the Canadians. Loss of sovereignty over the earth below would be the final destruction of geography. . . . In geographical terms, this planet is not too small for peace but it is too small for war."[142]

Bringing Nuclear War Home: Radical Proximity and the End of Binaries in the NWA

The actual maps of the *NWA* bear these principles out particularly in terms of how they treat cartographic distance. After the original broadsheet was distributed at peace rallies in 1982 and 1983, the *NWA* was expanded and eventually featured a total of fifty-seven maps and in-depth textual analysis.[143] While a perusal through the *NWA* may give a horrifically visceral first impression about the sheer enormity of nuclear warfare, its most lingering suggestion is the immediacy of the weaponry. On the map entitled, "The Closest Neighbours Ever," the Soviet Union's and the United States' borders are missing on the map, while the rest of the world is filled in as normal. The legend at the bottom of the map reads "National boundaries," indicating the border of the USSR in three red diagonal lines, while those of the U.S. are three red diagonal lines going the other way. Over the map are crisscrossed red lines, displaying that the two superpowers intersect everywhere in the nuclear age, since, as Bunge claims, they are volumetric powers that "cannot be contained by lines, but only by surfaces."[144] Bunge is indicting familiar geopolitical frameworks: since the concepts of Cold War realists like George Kennan hinged on clear separations between Soviet and American spheres, Bunge argues that "'containment' has been a mathematically proven bankruptcy for almost twenty years."[145] Not only does Bunge bring the proximity of the powers into close range; he also overlaps them, essentially making them share in destructive capability. The maps of Weinberger's Defense Department and his

Soviet counterparts sought to advance moral distinctions and inequities between the two powers; Bunge erases any distinction between the two.

The separation of containment is rendered meaningless in maps like "Nuclear Proliferation."[146] On this world map, countries belonging to the "Nuclear Club" are marked in solid red, countries that could develop nuclear weapons in five years are striped in red, and countries that could develop them in ten years are marked by red dots; this leaves only a few white spaces on the map (those with no hope of nuclear development), most prominently in Africa and Central America. Rather than the typical ocean space on world maps being left empty or colored in blue, wavy red lines cover the entire surface of the world's oceans. These lines correspond on the legend as "aquatic launching pads," with Bunge's point being that, in the Second Cold War, "all the oceans are launching platforms: this constitutes two-thirds of the earth's surface for a start."[147] This seemingly typical political map equalizes the world as a nuclear launch site. Still, the map does include some specific references to places, noting the locations of famous nuclear detonation sites such as Hiroshima, Nagasaki, Alamogordo (New Mexico), Eniwetok Atoll, and even Stagg Stadium in Chicago, along with their explosion dates. Contrasting these iconic sites with the flattened surface of the entire world (as one nuclear launch pad) draws on the collective memory of those nuclear tests and projects them into a future where, Bunge suggests, even more detonations will dot the landscape. Traditional arrows and distance lines are nowhere to be seen; the maps connote that nuclear weapons have already arrived at their destinations and exist essentially everywhere.

Bunge's nuclear maps resonate with early Cold War air-age globalism, except now the airplanes have become nuclear missiles. "Space: The Disputed Volume" (fig. 5.4) actually uses a Harrison-style perspective map with a bird's-eye view, although much more crude in design. Here, Bunge sketches a perspective of the Northern Hemisphere, where we see a piece of the United States as well as the Soviet Union. Instead of seeing, say, mountains appearing three-dimensionally off the page, the map displays the red lines of a missile trajectory curving from both superpowers above the earth in the top space of the map. Surrounding this trajectory is a bevy of floating American and Soviet flags, again showcasing the idea that warfare takes place in "national boundary *surfaces*, not boundary lines."[148] The dispute becomes that of volume in the air, rather than lines on the ground. As Bunge explains in the caption about the worthlessness of borderlines, "You cannot hold water with sticks."[149] The consequence of the nuclear-age "one-world" is a loss of familiar national autonomies. Bunge

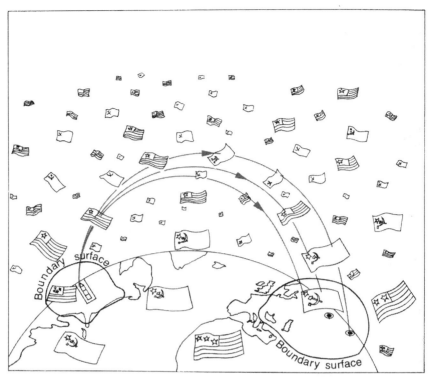

Figure 5.4. William Bunge, "Space: The Disputed Volume,"
Nuclear War Atlas *(New York: Blackwell, 1988)* © *William Bunge 1988*
(Courtesy of Boatwright Library, University of Richmond)

even reproduces S. W. Boggs's 1941 air-age map of world transportation, which shows the new ease of movement in the progressive development of transport technologies.[150] However, Bunge appropriates it for a more sinister purpose—to show how the nuclear missile has sped up transportation to such a radical degree that there essentially *is* no strategic distance anymore between warring powers. To argue for disarmament is to decelerate, according to Virilio, "the speed of means of communicating destruction"; thus, for Bunge, the first step is revealing and putting those means on display.[151]

Bunge's radical proximity also surfaces in the way he accentuates the power of specific locations in the prospects of nuclear war. Instead of simply relying on large-scale maps of Cold War superpowers, Bunge resurrects his *Fitzgerald* approach in certain maps by showing the effects of nuclear war on regions and real neighborhoods, namely his

Midwest heritage grounds. His two "ring" maps "The Explosion" and "The Firestorm" use the space around Lake Michigan, with Chicago as the center, to show the effects of a twenty megaton hydrogen bomb blast.[152] By drawing a series of rings around Chicago, Bunge shows the extent in miles where people would become vaporized (four miles), where most frame buildings and trees would collapse (fourteen miles), where extreme radiation would carry (twenty miles), where second-degree burns would occur (twenty-three miles), and where incidences of blindness would occur (forty miles).

The depiction of miles on these maps radicalizes distance as a vehicle of destruction; after a nuclear blast, the migration from the core to the periphery is a trail of death.[153] In addition, Bunge's rings serve as a kind of ironic comment on the use of the radius and concentric circles in Cold War urban planning for the purposes of civil defense against possible nuclear war and to decentralize urban blight.[154] The rings of Cold War urban planning designed the center of the city as empty, only for transient use, whereas the inhabitants of the city would live in successive rings on the outer edges.[155] Bunge's rings had the ultimate in atomic activity at the city's core, with destruction emanating outward—serving as a reminder that the urban centers are still filled with people, often poor and African-American. Bunge localizes the suffering of a region he is intimately familiar with; the abstraction and theoretical nature of much nuclear cartography is made startlingly concrete by placing human symptoms and disease into the lines of the map.

Bunge's heightening of air-age globalism's intensity, as well as the contrast of intensive local hotspots, reveals how the *NWA* works to strip away at the binaries of the Cold War. Many of the maps point to the number of times nuclear arms can destroy the world over, making a dualism between red and red, white, and blue meaningless. In the Harrison-style map, "Edge of Debris from the Fifth Chinese Nuclear Detonation," the Arctic is placed in the center. The United States and the Soviet Union are pictured on the map, but the focus of the map is on a red dot in China. A large red path circles out from the dot, around the Arctic through Europe, the United States, Asia, and all the way back to the other side of the dot. As Bunge writes in the caption, "The northern mid-latitudes have prevailing westerlies which circumnavigate the globe, so it is possible, as in the Chinese test shown in the map, to sail radiation around the planet to finally return home."[156] Bunge's map is one of suicide, an argument that nuclear war cannot be reduced to a binary antagonism with helpless standbys, but a war that the mapped nations are waging on themselves. Similarly, in "Patriotic Poisoning," Bunge shows a red wave of radiation originating from a 1965 cratering event in Nevada, with winds carrying it across the northern United States. Bunge refers to this as the "radioactive poisoning of your own nation by its own patriotic generals," accompanying the map with the adage of "we have met the enemy and he is us."[157]

In addition, part of Bunge's activism was not just concerned with nuclear disarmament but with the destabilization of state power in general. In maps like "American Domino Theory," Bunge mocks the traditional Cold War geopolitics of the domino theory: a map of eastern Asia and the Pacific shows an arrow moving in one direction from Moscow to Hawaii (representing Soviet aims), superimposed exactly over an arrow going in the opposite direction (representing American aims).[158] The overall visual presentation accuses both sides not only of imperial conquest but, more importantly, of being stuck in a standoff with identical aims, one no nobler than the other. On a larger scale, "Regions of Recent and Often Repeated Genocide" eliminates the Cold War binary and shows a whole world united in the act of genocide as "a universal final solution for one's enemies."[159] The "victims" are in red, while the "victimizers" are in white; almost the entire world is awash in red, including both the United States and most of the USSR, both being victims at one time or another of genocide. The map blends a sense of outrage at the liquidation of enemies with an acknowledgment of identification with those lost; in other words, the spaces of victimhood are simultaneously the spaces of victimizing, showing how the Manichaeism of the Cold War does not the fit the complicated histories of state violence.

A final (and perhaps best) example of Bunge's cartographic protest against binaries comes from "Moscington," which is a map that combines the landmarks, medical centers, atomic energy research institutes, and government buildings of Moscow and Washington together, as if the two were united as one city.[160] In "Moscington," the White House is down the street from the KGB, while the CIA and the Kurchatov Atomic Energy Institute follow each other on the Potomac River. Bunge's map provides a perfect addendum to the "Tank Plant" maps in *Soviet Military Power* and *Whence the Threat to Peace* that compared the capacity for destruction over an aerial map of Washington, D.C. By highlighting military, science, and government institutions in both capitals, the map also argues that these spaces are detached from the "everyday" lives and places of Soviet and American citizens. The world in this map is reduced solely to state power; all else is left out. This isolation connotes that these governments lack control of anything outside of these hermetic spaces. Furthermore, by blending these symbols of state power together, the map destabilizes each government's uniqueness and ability to isolate itself from the "other": the new, radical proximity has forever brought them together.

Days After: The Use of Rhetorical Vision in the NWA

The themes of proximity are part of an overall perspective on space/time in the NWA that cohere as a rhetorical *vision* of nuclear war, one that inevitably looks forward to the future. Spencer R. Weart comments that "by the 1980s it was clear to all careful thinkers that nuclear policy had less to do with the physical weapons than with the images they aroused."[161] Bunge's atlas serves less as a representation of Cold War realities than it does as a bleak image of the nuclear future. A temporal aspect is integral here: a resonant rhetorical vision of nuclear war has to contrast the image of life now with the after-vision of a post-atomic age.[162] That vision has to conform to an acceptable narrative of what we expect nuclear war to look like. In some ways, Bunge represents the nightmarish flipside to Reagan and Weinberger's ideology of a "technological sublime," wherein the fear and awe brought about by nuclear weapons give way to a reenergized commitment to using such weapons for the good of mankind.[163] Whereas Reagan and his administration invoked an almost spiritual rhetoric of "awe" to promote defense technologies like the Strategic Defense Initiative, Bunge inverted such visions of techno-superiority into one of awe at technology's penchant for destruction.

Of course, the challenge for Bunge is the attempt to inject "The Real" into something utterly unimaginable like nuclear war, with a cartographic medium that relies on inherent abstractions. Sam Dragga and Dan Voss have called for "a humanistic ethic of visuals," indicting technical graphics for their lack of attention to human elements. To Dragga and Voss, the typical "graphic isn't so much deceptive, however, as it is plainly inhumane—insensitive or indifferent to the human condition it depicts."[164] Bunge's choice of icons seems to almost overexaggerate the sense of humanity and presents a contrast with the dehumanization of weaponry. Faces with "X"s for eyes in "The Firestorm" map show the effects of blindness alongside icons of jagged red lightning bolts to denote radiation; in "The Explosion" map, droplets melt from emoticon-style faces.[165] Elsewhere the standard nuclear mushroom cloud is used; unlike the almost cartoonish faces in the other maps, "Nuclear Weapons Accidents in the United States" uses the realistic cloud to represent a more culturally familiar icon of nuclear war.[166] In other maps, even mere dots provide iconic power to the NWA's crude simplicity. The figure entitled "Nuclear Firepower" presents a grid of 121 boxes all filled with red dots, except for the center box, which has only one. The center dot represents all firepower used in World War II, whereas the other 120 boxes filled with dots represent the firepower of existing nuclear weapons.[167] The contrast between red dots is overwhelming visually and invites a reading of the map's provocative caption that three dots "represents the weapons on one Poseidon submarine. It is equal to the firepower of three world wars."

In terms of color, the stark contrast between black and red is the staple of the atlas's presentation of nuclear vision. Through the use of *simultaneous contrast*, when a light color is engulfed by dark color, the light seems lighter and the dark seems darker, and thus can draw deep and often dualistic distinctions between elements being mapped.[168] Bunge employs such contrasts in almost every map; the red sears and burns through the pages to represent the destructive capability of state weapons. Color is also tied to temporal concerns; red represents the "future hell," while the isolated spots of green represent a "future heaven." "The Native Plan for Toronto" map is one of the few without any red, representing an American Indian–style revision of Canada's most famous city centering around parks and cultural centers rather than business and government, bringing in the cool greens as a respite from the red covering the rest of the maps.[169] But these are isolated moments: Bunge's skepticism is apparent in the sheer quantity of red bleeding on the pages of the *NWA*. Red in Cold War maps usually meant the spreading menace of Soviet communism, but in his explosion of binaries Bunge awards red to all who exist in the nuclear age. In "Nuclear Poison Gas Cloud," for example, the brash red paint of potential bloodiness covers all of Europe.[170] Most importantly, the map uses the red to project a bleak vision of how the hope for peaceful uses of nuclear technology is a deceptive one. Here, black dots all over Europe indicate the places of nuclear power plants; as Bunge warns, "Nuclear war inevitably makes peaceful atomic power into a war weapon."[171] Bunge twists the vision that many Cold War–era policy makers and activists had for a future of clean nuclear energy and rhetorically subjugates the peaceful uses of nuclear technology to its militaristic ones.

To make the unreal, the unhappened, believable, Bunge falls back on the map's privileged position as a frame of reality, even while he tries to subvert those very same conventions of reality. One of the key elements of Bunge's "New Chicago" map (fig. 5.5) is its horrific depiction of sickness and insanity, tracking migration patterns of the "sick, maimed and insane," and complete with arrows tracking "marauding zombies" and

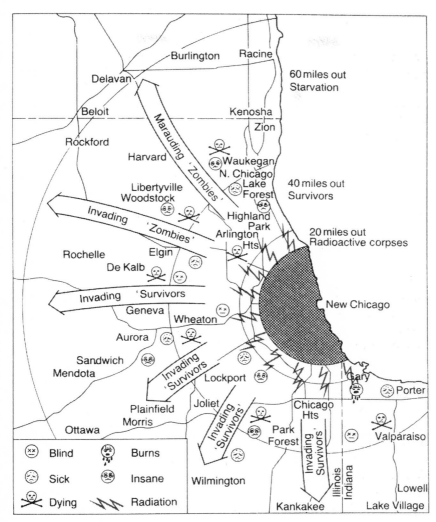

Figure 5.5. William Bunge, "New Chicago," Nuclear War Atlas (New York: Blackwell, 1988) © William Bunge 1988 (Courtesy of Boatwright Library, University of Richmond)

"invading zombies."[172] J. Michael Hogan was unsparing in his criticism of this kind of "rhetoric of doom" outlined by leaders and supporters of the nuclear freeze movement, where he chided privileged experts for going so far as to paralyze (and ultimately stifle) debate through the use of "images, synoptic phrases, and fear appeals."[173] Here, the use of an exaggerated pop-culture icon like a zombie risks that condescension by turning the potential loss of life and land into a mediated, voyeuristic fantasy. Bunge's utter disregard for standards of cartographic taste allows him to destabilize the usually clean and scientific form of the map, but it also risks a kind of detachment without responsibility for a solution.[174]

On the other hand, Bryan C. Taylor defends the desire for a more radical aesthetic in nuclear activism, suggesting that such appeals can have a certain open-endedness that invites a healthy ambiguity.[175] Because the maps simultaneously indict the nuclear arms apparatus, while also showcasing a malleable, self-reflexive attitude about the objective truth of their making, a space is drawn for other readings and interpretations. This subversion of expectations is best summed up through the important connection between irony and nuclear vision. The *NWA* reflects a kind of horrified detachment from nuclear war, but detachment, according to Karen Foss and Stephen Littlejohn, does not have to mean uninvolvement. As they write, "Irony works paradoxically: the superiority of detachment enables one to see clearly own one's involvement as a potential victim."[176] This irony brings into clearer focus the final major theme of Bunge's atlas: the *NWA*'s subversive, absurdist use of humor.

Wit and Weaponry: The Absurdity of Space in the NWA

Bunge's brand of nuclear cartographic righteousness takes it to an extreme level that exposes the apparatus of power behind mapping. His maps explicitly radiate with ideology and thus call into question all other maps that mask their intentions. Bunge bases much of his impassioned polemic on this absurdity of nuclear technology; his rough, unsophisticated cartography is a protest against the massive and slick technical impressiveness of the subject it maps. The content of "Space: The Disputed Volume," for example, serves to heighten the enormity and proximity of the nuclear weapons being exchanged between superpowers, but the form of the cartoon flags of the United States and the Soviet Union, scribbled onto the space of the page, deflates the importance of the state powers and renders their battle of missiles childish.[177] Elsewhere, Bunge's comically simple map of Reagan's SDI program ("Nuclear Shields") shows a world map with the famous three-grid Star Wars shields. Simply imposed in red over the map, the grids look humorously flimsy and imprecise: the most sophisticated and complex military technology ever devised is constructed as an absurd, almost video game–like projection.[178] In an important sense, Bunge indicts the shift of cartography toward the detached and the digital, as he reduces the "awe" around technological, militarized progress to a visual joke. Juxtaposed with other maps in the atlas that depict "real" potential effects of nuclear war, this map of Reagan technology emphasizes artificiality; the state is charged with being "unreal."

Bunge's maps thus function as a kind of parody of what an ordinary map might look like. His use of exaggerated cartoon-face icons to depict burns and insanity heighten the sense of humanity, hence parodying the normally staid pages of typical atlases and accentuating the structures of ideology and power in state cartography.[179] Typically, parody is a kind of ridiculing imitation that often mocks the form of an original source and draws ironic humor at the expense of the text being parodied. Literary critic Linda Hutcheon's expansion of parody, however, foregrounds the entire process of meaning making in the creation and reception of art, making parody a "double-voiced discourse" that points out the differences between itself and the original text.[180] Unlike satire, though, parody does not have to be an aggressive rhetorical strategy; it exaggerates but also conserves "an aesthetic impression of rationality."[181] The *NWA* suggests that rational standards for mapping are suspect by featuring exaggeratedly absurd icons and graphics, yet it simultaneously holds onto such standards so that readers will believe that nuclear war is a dangerous possibility.

Despite the potential of parody to serve as a radical critique, its use in the *NWA* also suggests a possible problem. The atlas cannot simply destabilize the process of mapping altogether; it has to uphold the traditional idea that the form of mapping can help recapture a more ideal political world and effect change, or Bunge could not advance the content of his message that the nuclear world needs mending. Bunge's messiness exposes the barbarism behind nuclear technology, but he also may be in danger of rendering that nuclear threat ridiculous, a potential that could undermine the radical message of the *NWA*. Robert Hariman highlights both the radical and the conservative functions of parody's rhetorical "doubling." On the one hand, he notes the momentous political shift in parody's dependence on a "prior conversion of some part of the world into an image."[182] Once the parodic discourse is recognized as an image, the "weight of authority" of the original discourse is destabilized, and more avenues of resistance are thus opened. On the other hand, the parodic double is immersed in the rituals of its source material; as Hariman writes, "Everything is left as it was, because the original discourse is not itself subject to any change."[183] In this case, Bunge's cartography foregrounds the absurdity of, say, maps like those in *Soviet Military Power*, by converting cartography to an image, even as his work faces the conundrum of how to channel those absurdities into a coherent vision of how the Cold War landscape should be changed.

THE PROJECTION OF THE COLD WAR'S END

Like a cartographic *samizdat*, the *Nuclear War Atlas* was Bunge's home-made attempt at propagating a movement. However, even though the atlas was written for both a lay audience and policy makers (Bunge's introduction optimistically asks that "after the hour or two it takes to study this atlas, act for peace as if the lives of the children in your family, and your very own personal life too, depended upon it"), it is difficult to get a sense of the text's reception or circulation beyond the academy.[184] Donald Fryer excoriated Bunge for his *inhumanity*, writing that "survival in Bunge's world is not likely to be pleasant," while John Whitelegg believed "the sheer good common sense of Bunge make[s] a deep impression."[185] Overseas, researchers at the Geography Institute at the Soviet Academy of Sciences used the *NWA* as an exemplar for their own goals: "There is a recognition at the highest levels within the institute that geographers have much to contribute as scientists in the context of war and peace. Geographers can help to identify and publicise the impact of nuclear war, an approach exemplified by William Bunge's *Nuclear War Atlas*."[186] Denis Wood referred to it as a "grim imperative" but somewhat lovingly as "an anti-atlas in the form of a Marxist tabloid, a document one could well imagine run off after hours on a hand-cranked press and thrust at nervous yuppies on street corners, or nailed to a senator's door."[187] In the same year the *NWA* was published, Susan Cutter made a call for geographers to band together and make more of a difference in nuclear policy, and she lauded the atlas for its intentions, "despite some failings."[188]

This ambivalence in the *NWA*'s reception is a microcosm of the tentative support cartographers and geographers have given their colleagues who make their maps overtly political.[189] Bunge suffered no ambivalence, though, in the confidence of his science and his message, as he declared, "'Professional' geographers deny the world of reality. There are important maps to be made about, for instance, the spatial realities of nuclear war and, by this token, the recently published *Nuclear War Atlas* is one of the most important geography works ever written, because it is about the most important subject ever addressed. The prospect of a war so terrible that it threatens to eliminate our species: 'The war to end all wars'—at last. . . . It is filled with terrible maps, horrific maps."[190]

But the conundrum presented in the pages of the *NWA* is: How do we deal with these "horrific maps" and the potential elimination of space and place as we know it? Nuclear war is the ultimate in fantastic vision and abstraction—and difficult to represent as a concrete, future "reality," to use Bunge's term. Thus, Bunge's red and black lines, insistent and haunting, reveal a compelling intersection between art and science in the nuclear age, making his maps a unique example of the forces that strategies of social control and social change exert on each other. Denis Wood writes of activist maps in general: "Their *subversion* of the power of [rhetoric] amounts to a bold proclamation of their rhetorical stance (cartographic nudism, cartographic streaking, cartographic punk), the very opposite of the position occupied by the United States Geological Survey, which . . . obscures its stance beneath a rhetorically orchestrated *denial* of rhetoric (dressing itself in the style of science)."[191] Such a radically revisionist message ultimately places Bunge in a new cartographic tradition where structures of ideology and power are brought into the foreground. Not only do the maps speak through angry ideology about a new world order; they also reflexively question the function of Cold War state cartography as a whole. By heightening its ideological viewpoints in such visually evocative ways, Bunge makes "process" a central feature of mapping.[192] This movement helps eliminate the fixed position of maps and puts them on a shifting and more contested ground.

Still, despite such radical revisionism, William Bunge was no postmodernist: he remains steadfastly a product of the Cold War's often idealistic scientific positivism, mired in the modernist belief that "science, not policemen, has created what order man has achieved."[193] John Pickles, in fact, used Bunge as the quintessential example of the way the "discursive practices of modernist cartography are to be deconstructed and read differently."[194] Similarly, Wood termed Bunge's style of cartography as "oughtness maps," and thus, in this way, it is important to examine the visual displays of the *Nuclear War Atlas* maps as a moral projection of how Bunge believed the world *ought* to be read, which Caspar Weinberger might have identified with.[195] Thus, one larger question left unanswered in this chapter regards the cartographic relationship between problem and solution. In representing space, this connection is tenuous. The social change map reduces the world to a particular temporal and spatial rendering and contains it. It cannot necessarily offer solutions to the problems it highlights: the map's frame can encapsulate only the spatial relationships and the exigencies of the new political landscape. The complex mixture of militancy and moderation may lessen the overall coherence of the message, exhibiting the potential limits to advocacy that can be achieved through cartography.

These issues come back to that night in Oxford when the morality of the Cold War and cartography as a practice were a subject for public debate. The contrast of the *NWA* with the "Battle of the Booklets" maps speaks not only to the complex geopolitical imagination of the Second Cold War but also to the dynamic between revelation and concealment. While Bunge put both nuclear weapons and the mapmaking process on display, the Defense Department maps hid that process from view. According to Gordon Mitchell, "Excessive secrecy locks in Cold War patterns of public discourse, where defense officials and industry representatives monopolize arguments, sealing their positions with the unassailable proof of classified evidence. Threat assessments drift toward worst-case scenarios generated from simulation and speculation, rather than more sober appraisals. . . . Military officials who see the idea of public debate as a superfluous luxury skirt critical arguments, removing issues of grave national importance from arenas of democratic deliberation."[196] What makes the Defense pamphlets most compelling is how Weinberger's maps reveal what he deemed worthy of going declassified and up for deliberation—what he was willing to be mapped and put on display. The map is expected to be reliable and all-encompassing, while the methods of production behind those maps can remain classified. And particularly, as maps were more and more becoming computerized, digital interfaces, defense professionals had incentives to downplay the element of human choice in the maps' constructions. Thus, the dynamic between what is revealed and what is concealed on the map is based here on what state representatives are willing to show, and the means by which that cartographic data are produced can remain silent and outside the margins of the map. Bunge has the tougher position of fighting these conventions of the map. As Fischoff, Pidgeon, and Fiske write, "Military proposals typically promise to solve specific narrow problems (e.g., defending a particular weapons system against a particular form of attack), whereas peace proposals stress more nebulous actions (e.g., having a more robust, resilient, and ethical society)."[197] Bunge, thus, had to push at the very edges of what cartography as a medium could be expected to accomplish.

Despite their differences, though, what both mapping projects share is what Barry Brummett has termed the "symbolic perfection" of nuclear discourse.[198] Weinberger and his colleagues are attempting to perfect the technology, to progress toward greater control and mastery of the missiles and radars. Bunge, for his part, tries to perfect society and the world at large in the face of this technology. Weinberger's maps make the atomic bomb more palatable and conventional, with missiles as game pieces in a progressive escalation; Bunge uses the maps as visions of how the world has progressed too fast and lost its moral bearing. The cartography of both remain part of the Cold War's brand of liberal, modern internationalism: in a shrinking world, we can use scientific expertise and the promise of better perception to improve the world. Even though Bunge and Weinberger had significantly different visions, maps provided them with images of commitment that placed Cold War values into the realm of public opinion. For Weinberger, the danger of the nuclear weapon was a loss of the security of national values, and a blow against the power to control and define Cold War spaces before our enemies could. For Bunge, the danger of the nuclear weapon was a loss of humanity's material place in an increasingly abstract, technologized world.[199] The superpower pamphlets, and Bunge's radical disarmament challenge to them, provided not only compelling visualizations of America's power in a rapidly changing world but also a chance to reflect on the nature of the expert in a world of nuclear weaponry. Perhaps it was Bunge's colleague, Michael Curry, who best expressed the difficulties of such expertise when he asked, "If we accept the word of scientists who tell us that it is not all right to build nuclear weapons, ought we then to accept their word if they change their minds and tell us that it is all right?"[200] Both projects thus are implicated in the rhetorical problem of militarized science and how it was presented to the public in the Cold War.

Finally, while Bunge prophesizes the "end of geography" in the nuclear future, both his maps and those of the defense pamphlet wars also foretell of the end of the Cold War itself. In a new era of revolutionary missile speed, the Second Cold War embodied an overdetermined globe, a place of hyperinternationalism.[201] Bunge collapses the familiar U.S.-Soviet binaries to show the tenuousness of the spatial frameworks that had so long defined the Cold War, thus foreshadowing a future where the world system would have to be redefined (unless it was destroyed first). At the same time, Weinberger's maps indicate a system outquantifying and overextending itself, where ideology outstrips the actual means by which either side could fight such a war. Sure enough, by the end of the 1980s, the Soviet system was unable to support itself under the weight of its arms economy. Thus, the "future cartography" of both projects reflects the cracks in Cold War space. It is perhaps fitting that E. P Thompson rested his debate case with this entreaty: "I ask Oxford to support this motion in the name of a universalism at its very foundation in the Middle

Ages: a universalism of scholarship which owed its duty to the skills of communication and learning and not to those of the armed state."[202] In the Second Cold War, cartography uniquely framed the capacities of the armed state, while also offering a universal mode of communication for those attempting to challenge that state. Nuclear mapping had come full circle, beginning with the end of World War II as the bombs hit Japanese ground, now attempting to project the twilight of the long Cold War itself. The airmen that Roald Dahl had envisioned anxiously charting the ground below were now the expert technicians in front of digital interfaces, immersed in the intricacies of the ground below with a degree of technical detail that could never have been imagined in World War II. However, they were also detached from that same ground.

CONCLUSION

From Globalism to Globalization

The Afterlives of Cold War Maps

Three years after Gorbachev and Bush debated a crumbling Cold War system on their map, former dissident turned Czechoslovakian president Vaclav Havel, in the midst of his own country's dissolution, spoke to the World Economic Forum in Davos in March 1992 about the challenges of an era's end. Havel characterized the Cold War as "an era of systems, institutions, mechanisms and statistical averages. It was an era of ideologies, doctrines, interpretations of reality, an era in which the goal was to find a universal theory of the world, and thus a universal key to unlock its prosperity."[1] Havel's worry, though, was that in the face of a new era, the leaders of the world were not learning their lessons: "We are looking for new scientific recipes, new ideologies, new control systems, new institutions, new instruments to eliminate the dreadful consequences of our previous recipes, ideologies, control systems, institutions and instruments. We treat the fatal consequences of technology as though they were a technical defect that could be remedied by technology alone. We are looking for an objective way out of the crisis of objectivism."[2] For Havel, the Cold War was the ultimate modern project: two world systems united in the "proud belief that man, as the pinnacle of everything that exists, was capable of objectively describing, explaining and controlling everything that exists, and of possessing the one and only truth about the world."[3]

The Cold War's end required a new mode of envisioning the world, and Havel wondered aloud if the same familiar frameworks of superpowers and scientific control were being erected once again. A week after Havel spoke in Davos, a Pentagon draft memorandum of the "Defense Planning Guidance for the Fiscal Years 1994–1999" was leaked to the *New York*

Times. The report presented an America coping with an uncertain international political landscape and offering prescriptions:

> First, the U.S. must show the leadership necessary to establish and protect a new order that holds the promise of convincing potential competitors that they need not aspire to a greater role or pursue a more aggressive posture to protect their legitimate interests. Second, in the non-defense areas, we must account sufficiently for the interests of the advanced industrial nations to discourage them from challenging our leadership or seeking to overturn the established political and economic order. Finally, we must maintain the mechanisms for deterring potential competitors from even aspiring to a larger regional or global role. . . . There are other potential nations or coalitions that could, in the further future, develop strategic aims and a defense posture of region-wide or global domination. Our strategy must now refocus on precluding the emergence of any potential future global competitor.[4]

As *Harper's* editor Lewis Lapham pointed out, the contrast between Havel's new world vision and that of the Defense Planning Group could not have been starker. While Havel hoped for some kind of international pan-humanistic collaboration of nation-states, America was still defining the world in terms of balances and competitors, forces and threats— all from a geopolitical, strategic vantage point and clinging to the old Cold War map of superpower competitions. This notion was not lost on Lapham, who wrote of the Pentagon report: "Within the Washington conference rooms where the strategic theorists decorate their maps with lines of force and arcs of crisis, the Pax Americana remains as it was in 1947, as permanent and serene as the dome on the Capitol or the stars in the flag. . . . The Cold War imprisoned the nations of the earth in the attitudes of fear. It wasn't only the threat implicit in the weapons, although the weapons were many and terrible; it was also the pattern of thought bent to the service of abstraction."[5]

Ultimately, in *Mapping the Cold War*, I have followed Lapham's sentiments and interrogated how these abstract Cold War patterns were materialized into the lines of maps and were hailed into the contexts and conflicts of an international standoff. A map remained a vibrant frame by which America attempted to project its power and stabilize its identity in the face of global-scale spatial change. Both popular and institutional maps can be seen as management systems that reduce and universalize, flatten and make round, reveal and conceal. Space, in short, matters—and the visual, material ways in which we vie for control over the right to envision and chart that space matter as well.

The story of cartography in the second half of the twentieth century is a microcosm of the narrative of the Cold War itself: the drive to incorporate and devise *better* and clearer perceptions of the world, the development of technologies that encompass more facts and wider spaces, the negativity of containment placed against the ideal of scientific internationalism in economic and social development. While Lapham may have mentioned the maps decorating defense office walls as a kind of literary device, this book has advanced that those map-covered walls have actual ramifications in helping to produce and enact the U.S. imaginary of itself and the world. A map is not placed in a congressional report thoughtlessly; the choice of a mapmaker to frame subequatorial Asia in a particular way is not arbitrary. These maps were produced, displayed, and entered into exchanges and debates according to the dictates of the Cold War and the dictates of the historical conventions of the map as a medium. Cold War maps are, if anything, a fitting barometer of the modern era, gauging the climate for state progress but also measuring the storms of state upheaval. Havel's "crisis of objectivism" started well before the end of the Cold War; cartography was bound up in these conundrums of science, art, and ideology since the conflict's beginning, adapting and readapting to tumultuous changes. Most importantly, the very materiality and rhetoricity of maps, from production, to display, to circulation and reappropriation, reveal active rhetorical lives in a seemingly fixed geopolitical conflict. The function of *Mapping the Cold War* is not simply to detail the diverse usages of maps in the American-Soviet conflict but also to affirm that the waging of the Cold War was a fundamentally cartographic enterprise.

Fixing and Unfixing: Maps as the "Immutable Mobile"

One implication of the history of Cold War cartography is the need to characterize Cold War maps as an uneasy balance between fixing and unfixing. Situating maps in this dynamic helps create a better understanding of America's recent cartographic history and potentially strengthens a sense of the contingencies of world space as the twenty-first century barrels ahead. Arguably, the map's ability to fix and freeze relationships onto the page is its most pervasive and powerful characteristic: to say not only that *this is there* but also that *this is the world*. The international landscape was not simply in flux during the Cold War; America was powerful enough that its frameworks of world space were often immovably rigid. Thus, the maps of the Cold War have displayed the various ways by which, in Shapiro's words, "dominant territorialities have daily helped to reproduce the international imaginary."[6] This reproduction is particularly important, as it helps to critically assess the contentious process by which certain dominant views of the world become fixed and powerful. In the words of international relations theorist Kennan Ferguson, cartographic practices have "served as a sense-making machinery for the United States and other geopolitical entities in the form of the taxonomies that make placing the American self in the world possible. . . . To map is to 'do' politics: to make political judgments, to place people in different worlds, to grant and deny opportunities—but also to attempt to depoliticize and naturalize these judgments."[7] What makes maps important in the visual politics of the Cold War is not just how the maps politicized space, but also how their power of scientific authority and authenticity removed politics from the map, often smoothing out the wrinkles of inequities and struggle that forging an abstract space can create.

Still, while the bipolar image of the U.S.–Soviet Union was (and in some ways remains) powerful, it is entirely too easy to claim forty-plus years of a static geopolitical landscape. The maps of the Cold War era have demonstrated that this is far from true. Even as they were used to fix the world, maps were dynamic, continually contested, circulated and recirculated, drawn and redrawn; they often were unfixing our sense of the world as well. Denis Cosgrove points out that a map, in the tradition of Latour's "immutable mobile," is "a container of information gathered at specific locations, returned to a 'centre of calculation,' and then placed once more into circulation as a vehicle and instrument of scientific knowledge."[8] The map freezes and commits particular relationships to the page but then becomes a circulatory medium that has movement in the culture, as certain projections will be redesigned and refashioned or particular mapping projects designed for one purpose will be (re)appropriated for other uses. All the while, the map has to, in a sense, perform—to constantly promote itself as a credible expert witness to the world space it abstracts. Because of this, maps also have a recursive quality, referring back to themselves by pulling on past conventions, while arguing for future realities.[9] The wide scope of *Mapping the Cold War* was used to show this restless sense of movement.

Projecting Internationalism: The Spatial Image of American Power

I have primarily focused on world political maps that project American power (and its perceptions) across a global field, making the modern, liberal conception of internationalism a central concern. The Cold War introduced the tension between an acceptance that horizontal distance on the ground is no longer the primary measurement of space and the fact that the horizontal, flat map still reigned supreme. These changes in distance had profound implications for the character of America's international image-building and foreign relations. Richard Edes Harrison, for example, sketched the opportunities, limitations, and ambivalences that come with the visual presentation of America as a steward of the world. His acceptance of maps as a discourse prefigured the fact that, during the Cold War, cartographers and policy makers from a wide array of institutions accepted that maps had strategic properties and could no longer be static. The rise of the air as a new cartographic perspective, the technological advances in missiles, and the accompanying digitization of maps transcended familiar political boundaries. To maintain America's "place" on the map, Cold War cartography had to successfully project the labyrinth of new commitments and frame the geopolitical reasoning behind blocs and pacts. Perspectives from airplanes and later satellites could allow the cartographer (and the user) a vantage point by which to powerfully synthesize and manage the space below, most often from a privileged place outside of that area (e.g., in an office or a control room). And as the Cold War reached its final decade, the world had shrunk on the map to the point of hyperinternationalism, where the United States and the Soviet Union overlapped so much in destructive power that international distance, at least in a horizontal sense, became meaningless. The fear that familiar cartographic methods of explaining the world were becoming obsolete was expressed in attempts to enforce and protect those methods. Hence, it is clear why the Weinberger defense maps of 1981, which cataloged a new arsenal of the most sophisticated weapons technology in American history, were projected on maps that could have come out of *Time* magazine in 1947, with their arrows of Soviet aggression and arguments for spatial containment.

The search for disciplinary truth and scientific rigor both vied against and aided the defense needs and the programs of U.S. international relations. Particularly, the rise of social science as a modernizing force was inseparable from the geopolitical internationalism of Cold War security and foreign policy discourse. Producers understood that a map had an instrumental purpose and could be marshaled and circulated as evidential weapons against the USSR. "Gulag—Slavery, Inc.," for example, constructed a powerful vision of America's place vis-à-vis the Soviet Union, infiltrating its borders with "authentic" knowledge; yet, the map's full influence is not seen until it is shown how "Gulag—Slavery, Inc." was used as a strategic force by international labor unions, congressional representatives, the CIA, and even everyday citizens.

These usages lie at the heart of what makes Cold War mapping compelling: most mapmakers, policy analysts, and defense representatives responded to the new malleability of mapping to represent America's international interests, yet this was not always accompanied by a critical understanding of maps as ideological constructs. More often, any problems with the map were seen as technical; a map could be reconceived and redrawn to get a better perception, but there usually was not a question about maps themselves as a form of vision and what those implications might be. This conundrum explains why outsiders like Arno Peters and William Bunge were often met with extreme reactions of hostility and adulation. The anxiety of America's leap into internationalism made familiar cartographic conventions even more important to maintain. The borders on the map were not simply legal-political lines and military barriers; they were powerful ways to maintain and defend a particular vision of the world and a method of ordering and containing international chaos.

Imagining and Reimagining: The Choice to Map in the Cold War

Despite their sophisticated technology and abstract qualities, maps are, in a sense, unfailingly *human*. As part of a more artistic "imaginary" in Cold War visual culture, cartography was drawn with particular value systems, setting spatial hierarchies and politicizing the flat page and the digital screen. The Cold War did see an unprecedented technologization of cartography and a transition of mapping into a highly sophisticated science, but it also saw an explosion of social-political issues that fell under the mapping umbrella, from health to economics to religion to poverty and beyond. When popular cartographers were hailed into the Cold War, government policy makers absorbed and recirculated their artistic perspectives, reductionistic visual metaphors, and the appreciation of public opinion's role in creating visions of the world. When S. W. Boggs brought Boris Artzybasheff of *Time* to render map graphics for State Department propaganda films, or representatives entered *New York Times* maps of Cold War international problems into the Congressional Record, these actors were reaching out for novel perspectives and signifying the importance of the "audience" as a factor in their use of cartography. Taken together, this melding of art and science made for maps as unique sources of both authoritative expertise and visionary inspiration.

Agency, thus, remained a central factor in the development of Cold War maps, as the individual choices of cartographers and the interests of particular institutions bounded and framed the map's presentational power. The way in which William Bunge comes of age during both the tumult of Vietnam and the rise of quantitative geography and digitized mapping, or the function of Isaac Don Levine as defector journalist who chooses cartography as one medium of fighting communism, or Boggs's frustration behind the scenes as America drops its commitments to international mapping collaborations—all speak to cartography as a confluence of human forces, not simply a by-product of history.

This relationship between the ideologies of maps and their strategic, instrumental uses reveals the power of the map as an inventional resource. President Franklin Roosevelt understood this when he ordered Americans to become World War II participants by tracing strategic routes on maps, while President Nixon also tacitly understood this as he used the simplicity of a map to order a complex, contested war for his audience. Richard Edes Harrison acknowledged this function when he discussed the importance of "user requirements" for training Army personnel to absorb the importance of the new pilot perspectives. S. W. Boggs certainly responded to this power as he sent a new state-of-the-art globe to Secretary of State George Marshall around the time the general was blueprinting a vision for a postwar Europe. Hubert Humphrey distributed maps of world disease, and Caspar Weinberger chose cartography as a central medium to rekindle an arms race. All of these actors understood, at least implicitly, the map's importance as a writ of commitment and a source of evidentiary power. These agents' maps populate a network of interests and ideologies constrained by the rhetorical choices that inform (and are informed by) the larger Cold War. It is no coincidence that the map continually infiltrated its way into high-level summits and conferences or stirred up overseas reactions. Maps provided Cold War actors with a political vision of the world but also one that was tangible, to be held in one's hands, passed around, and argued about.

The role of a map's circulation also comes to the forefront here: the map is not just a rendering of its cartographer's artistic vision or its institutional origins; it also accrues further political meaning and ideological value through its rhetorical life in circulating through various contexts and interpretations. This critical approach removes the map from its status as detached visual aid or a mere reflector of historical change—a kind of historical wall decoration. Maps are points of human communicative action, not empty containers of ideology. To approach them in this way first involves reading the actual maps for their internal grammars *and* their external ideologies—seeing the map and the "paramap" as working in tandem.

Of course, the danger of doing a historical study of Cold War mapping is that it risks reducing, as has happened all too often, space to time. Stringing together a narrative around cartography may create the appearance of a neat chronology, when there is actually messiness and loose ends. Worse, it may suggest, once again, that maps simply serve as reflectors of historical circumstances. What I argue, instead, is that what makes maps particularly important sites of study in this era is their inherently fragmentary nature—that here and there they are embedded in a report for statistical evidence, used as emblems for internationalism at other points, and circulate as provocative arguments elsewhere. Mapping thus finds its way into some of the most heightened and dramatic of Cold War situations, as well as the more mundane, everyday politics of the Cold War. The performative drama of Henry Cabot Lodge hailing cartography into a direct confrontation with the Soviet Union at the United Nations exists alongside the routine conference reports of State Department representatives made at UN cartographic summits about developing nations. Both provide equally important representations of not only the strategic uses of mapping but also the way cartography was understood as a practice. That Richard Edes Harrison was a State Department consultant, that the same specifications for International Map of the World maps were being used by the Army Map Service to chart foreign areas, that Dr. May's maps of disease for the American Geographical Society were circulating in congressional debates—each connection points to how Cold War space edified itself into U.S. government, academic, and popular identity. Maps engaged constantly with other maps, creating a complex web of relations between values and practice. In this way, the enhanced fluidity of maps remains one of the most enduring legacies of Cold War cartography.

MAPPING BACK, MAPPING FORWARD: RESITUATING COLD WAR CARTOGRAPHY

In some ways, the cartographic icons of Soviet octopi and slave camps, the widely distributed educational maps showing America as the center of the world, and the congressional and Defense reports filled with endless security projections of America's power all over the globe all seem like antiquated, historical curios. The mapping impulse and spatial assumptions of the Cold War, however, remain very much alive and relevant—the concept of closed, absolute spaces on the map, the continental frame-work of power lines between developed and underdeveloped, and the acceptance that the world is continually shrinking through rapidly chang-ing technology and communication still hold sway. In March 2003, as the U.S. military prepared to enter Iraq, a military strategist at the U.S. Naval War College, Thomas P. M. Barnett, made waves with an article in *Esquire*, entitled "The Pentagon's New Map."[10] Barnett sought to define a post–Cold War, post-9/11 American geopolitics that finally confronted the expanding tides of globalization. In short, Barnett's thesis is that in this new era, "disconnectedness defines danger"—those nations that are plugged into the globalizing capitalist networks are safe, while those states that stay outside of these networks are threats. Barnett wrote in *Esquire*: "Show me where globalization is thick with network connectivity, financial transactions, liberal media flows, and collective security, and I will show you regions featuring stable governments, rising standards of living, and more deaths by suicide than murder . . . . But show me where globalization is thinning or just plain absent, and I will show you regions plagued by politically repressive regimes, widespread poverty and disease, routine mass murder, and—most important—the chronic conflicts that incubate the next generation of global terrorists."[11] Included was a map (fig. C.1) depicting a deeply divided world between the connected and the functioning (the "core": the United States, the European Union, parts of South America) and the disconnected and dysfunctional (the "gap": almost all of Africa, the Middle East, most of Southeast Asia).[12] Barnett's bold map landed him a position as a special strategist for Donald Rums-feld with the Department of Defense, and his multimediated PowerPoint presentation of the piece, entitled "The Brief," was required viewing by all Air Force members who attained the rank of general, and was given hundreds of times to various private and public organizations. The project became a book (*The Pentagon's New Map*) in 2004, Barnett became a pop-ular media pundit who parlayed his work into his "Glo*blog*ization" project on the Web, and his map was widely circulated as a new geopolitical vision for the twenty-first century.[13]

Certainly, Barnett's vision was different from that of the Defense Plan-ning Group in 1992, which was still mired in a world of superpower pol-itics. Rather than simply an arms-wielding power or world cop, the U.S. was posited by Barnett as a "systems administrator" helping manage the world toward peace through connectivity. As Simon Dalby pointed out, though, Barnett was assuming that globalization was a benevolent, U.S.-led process that all would want to partake in, and within Barnett's vision

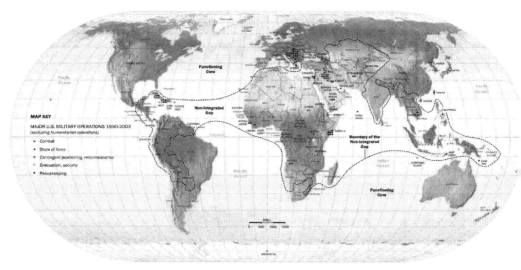

Figure C.1. William McNulty, "The Pentagon's New Map,"
in Thomas P. M. Barnett's The Pentagon's New Map, *2004*
(© Thomas P. M. Barnett, used with his permission)

was the age-old ideology of American exceptionalism and manifest destiny.[14] Furthermore, Barnett's geopolitical imaginary involved the legitimation of U.S. military intervention wherever it may be needed to ensure that the "gap" would shrink ("Show me a part of the world that is secure in its peace and I will show you a strong or growing ties between local militaries and the U.S. military").[15] So, while Barnett's project defined itself as resolutely post–Cold War, Barnett uneasily synthesizes the promise of the "shrinking world" bringing connectedness and peace with the calculus of security and counterforce into a package that engages with, and relies on, America's recent cartographic history. Barnett's own agency as strategist and cartographer mixed popular, academic, and government-defense assumptions in ways that Richard Edes Harrison and S. W. Boggs would understand. His geopolitical reasoning spoke to the kind of "world divided" that Sir Halford Mackinder's World War I cartography inspired in the move toward containment and bipolarity, which mapped American constructions of the Soviet Union. The multimediated circulation of Barnett's maps may have been more sophisticated than the AFL's Gulag labor map, but the importance of how a map is produced amid institutional collaborations through a multitude of forms rings true in both cases. Barnett's map also drew civilizational lines that reinstantiated notions of inside-outside and center-periphery in ways that resonate with the cartography of development and modernization during the Cold War's realignment toward the South in the Third World (except now framed in twenty-first century neoliberal management-speak—"functioning" vs. "non-integrated"). Ultimately, the "Pentagon's New Map" phenomenon once again shows cartography being called into a global debate around America's continually shifting place in the world. The map of globalization is haunted by the complex globalism of the Cold War past. Barnett's work reminds us that to see the map forward, we have to see the map back as well.

While Barnett reemphasizes the artistic agency and fluidity of the cartographer-strategist exemplified by Cold War maps, more recent developments reestablish the evidentiary power, interface technology, and scientific authority that underwrote such maps. In January 2013, headlines began highlighting a particularly provocative new achievement by the ambitious Google Earth project—the formerly white space of North Korea in Google maps was now replaced by a detailed map including hospitals, monuments, institutional buildings, and, of all things, gulags.[16] From one's home computer, a user could access satellite-procured, bird's-eye views above areas such as Camp 14 in central North Korea and Camp 22 in the northeast.[17] So-called "citizen cartographers" and human rights groups had furthermore been able to label parts of these camps, such as guard posts, gates, and even alleged burial grounds.[18] The red dots of "'Gulag'—Slavery, Inc." had reached the twenty-first century with new immersive views that simulated the user almost *into* the spaces of a shrouded ideological enemy.

Of course, the two Gulag maps exist in very different worlds: this new graphing of North Korea enters into a world without clear superpower bipolarities, and without the clandestine support of the national security and intelligence apparatus that the first Gulag map received.[19] The revelation of Google's map accompanied reports of CEO Eric Schmidt making a private trip to North Korea to discuss both "humanitarian" and social media connectivity and openness issues. Such a trip received public criticism from the State Department around Schmidt's timing, potentially complicating diplomatic processes at a time when North Korea was reportedly testing potential satellite technology for ballistic missiles.[20] The Cold War–era collaboration of private organizations and the government here seemed, at least on the surface, not to be operable.

The important history, however, of Cold War cartography still announces itself in the Google Earth North Korea project: the evidentiary weaponry of a map's ability to penetrate bordered space with scientific authority is palpable here.[21] The sense of immersion, of course, is much more literal with the North Korea map, as the user can infiltrate the camps in a way that "'Gulag'—Slavery, Inc." never promised, but the ability to transcend borders and politicize "place" in the form of a labor camp reengages with a Cold War past. The digital technology that arose out of military necessity in the Cold War has certainly given way to public and commercial uses in exciting and complex new ways, but that essential militarization of the map that was activated in the Cold War remains.[22] Just as "'Gulag'—Slavery, Inc." was appropriated and reappropriated in a long rhetorical life by labor unions, congressional activists, and everyday citizens, Google's North Korea map is already being drawn into an eventful circulatory tour through twenty-first-century international culture, human rights groups and Bunge-like protest work, commercial attempts to prove Google's viability, and even diplomatic exchanges over North Korea's future relations with America and the world. And the North Korea map, and whatever other politicized, electrically charged functions that immersive digital cartography creates in the future, still has a rhetorical trajectory that remains to be traced.[23]

Cartographic surveillance as power promises only to grow in the coming decades, and thus its Cold War roots remain strong and relevant. As Cold War geography reminds us, the borders between war and peace are not often as clear-cut as the lines of the maps we use. And if Michael Shapiro is correct that "the primary contestations in current global instabilities are over identity and spaces," then the visual artifacts that shape and contain such identities and spaces must continue to be situated as potent instruments of power and knowledge production.[24] The map simultaneously reveals and conceals its ideological commitments to the user, and that process of display is especially heightened in intensity during times of global reorganization and changes in the nature of state power. In a world supposedly marked today by the fluid lines of globalization, there is a benefit from sharper critical vocabularies on the "producers" of space and the output of their production. This requires a perspective that productively brings history and geography together in a way that, according to critic Peta Mitchell, "is at all times attentive to the stratification of history, memory, language, and landscape."[25] Or, in historian Edward Ayers's terms, recognition is constantly needed of a world mired in "deep contingency": if geography is "about patterns and structures; history is about motion; by integrating the two, we can see layers of events, layers of the consequences of unpredictability."[26] My approach to reading such stratification and contingency in *Mapping the Cold War* is not just a way of looking back into recent history. Critically reaching into that history allows for the useful interpretation of uncertain, unfolding spaces (as well as the powerful attempts at stabilizing them) in the future.

In terms of situating U.S. power, the Cold War and its maps remain an explosive site of inquiry. For the Cold War was not simply a war of missile trajectories and political treaties but a war of symbols; ensuring that maps are framed as integral articulations of this war of symbols remains a vital task. In Ferguson's eloquent terms, "The United States' imaginary in the twentieth century was conceivable primarily in reference to the communist 'threat.' A world was designed where the geographic and the ideological could be superimposed on one another to create a powerful map with both horizontal depth and interpretive depth, explaining what the world meant as well as how it looked."[27] Furthermore, for America "the instability of its own geographic identity, its plurality of history, and its character as a method of thought rather than an ideologically secure territory have long provoked a strong need to map. Yet simultaneously, these characteristics have allowed a plurality and an instability of mappings."[28] The anxiety of Roald Dahl's pilot anxiously traversing over the blank pages of an atlas represents that instability. Looking toward the prospect of mapping the future, the trap is to fall into prescribing what will be good maps and what will be bad maps with the promise that we will make cartography more accurate and responsible. Such a trap succumbs to Boggs's "cartohypnosis" that haunted the Cold War and could risk replacing the world of today with the world of 1947. Rather, I would argue that we can (and should) continue to interrogate the processes by which we see and envision our place in the world and engage with the contentious cartographies that sketch such visions. In other words, we would do well to rewrite the histories of spaces at the same time as we remap the spaces of history.

Notes

INTRODUCTION

1. Roald Dahl, *The BFG*, 193–96. Katherine Harmon also fittingly closes her fascinating collection of art maps with this *BFG* quote and, of course, includes the obligatory blank atlas pages. See Harmon, *You Are Here*, back flap.

2. This notion of space and legibility is perhaps best theorized by anthropologist James C. Scott in *Seeing Like a State*. In this work, he posits legibility as a central problem of modern statecraft, with the goal of creating a synoptic view of land. In particular, his discussions of early cadastral maps (tax collection maps) evidence the complexity of a state attempting to catalog its landscapes and people for the sake of national interest. See Scott, *Seeing Like a State*.

3. A discussion on the shifts from an open space to a closed space, particularly in a Cold War context, can be found in Henrikson, "Maps, Globes, and the 'Cold War,'" 445–46. Gearóid Ó Tuathail goes even further into the roots of America's closed spaces in his discussion of the development of twentieth-century geopolitics. See Ó Tuathail, *Critical Geopolitics*, 15–16.

4. Harley discusses the importance of signification in bird's-eye views of the earth. See Harley, *The New Nature of Maps*, 45.

5. See Frank Ninkovich's thesis in his introduction to *Modernity and Power*, xi–xv.

6. John Berger, *Ways of Seeing*, 9–10.

7. The amount of contested definitions of "space" can scarcely be recounted in this chapter, but some of the best expressions of its complex nature can be found in Harvey, *Social Justice and the City*, 13–14; Lefebvre, "Reflections on the Politics of Space," 31; and Soja, "The Socio-spatial Dialectic (1989)," 246–47, 255.

8. For more details on this summit, see the previously classified documents and analysis released by the Central Intelligence Agency on the end of the Cold War. Fischer, *At Cold War's End*, ix–xxii, xlvii.

9. Henrikson, "Power and Politics of Maps," 57.

10. Ibid.

11. Harley, *The New Nature of Maps*, 67.

12. To evidence America's shift into Cold War space, I focus on the contestable functions of maps as *representations*—because perhaps, above all, maps are entangled in the problems of representing "what is," while making visual arguments about "what should be." Michael Shapiro's work offers an introduction to the overall complexities of space and representation. See, as a representative example, Shapiro, *The Politics of Representation*. For the problems of representation and maps specifically, see Vujakovic, "'A New Map Is Unrolling before Us,'" 43–57; Denis Wood, *The Power of Maps*, 4–26; Barnes, "Obituaries, War, 'Corporeal Remains,' and Life," 693–701; and Pickles, "Texts, Hermeneutics and Propaganda Maps," 193–230.

13. On "rhetorics of display," see Prelli, *Rhetorics of Display*. On maps as selective and reductive, see Tyner, "Persuasive Cartography," 141–44.

14. Pickles, "Texts, Hermeneutics and Propaganda Maps," 194.

15. More explicit discussion of the geopolitical implications of *Time* publisher Henry Luce's declaration of the so-called American Century can be found in chapter 1. See Luce, "The American Century," 61–65. See also Smith's introductory discussion of Luce in Neil Smith, *American Empire*, 17–21.

16. One of the best sources on the symbolic and semiotic design functions of maps remains MacEachren, *How Maps Work*.

17. The important subfield of international relations known as "critical geopolitics" has been particularly forceful and persuasive in making this argument. See especially Ó Tuathail, *Critical Geopolitics*; Ó Tuathail and Luke, "Present at the (Dis)Integration," 381–98; Ó Tuathail and Agnew, "Geopolitics and Discourse," 190–204; Ó Tuathail, "(Dis)Placing Geopolitics," 525–46; Dalby, *Creating the Second Cold War*.

18. Olson, Finnegan, and Hope, *Visual Rhetoric*, 18.

19. For more on the role of space in the development of American history, see especially Driver, *Geography Militant*; Bruckner and Hsu, *American Literary Geographies*; Baker, *Heartless Immensity*; Levander and Levine, *Hemispheric American Studies*.

20. See especially the work done by Martin Bruckner on the geographic imagination of America's early days, in Bruckner, *The Geographic Revolution in Early America*.

21. Cited in Neil Smith, *American Empire*, 21.

22. For more on the relationship between space-time and geography-history, see Agnew, *Geopolitics*, 36; and Godlewska and Smith, *Geography and Empire*, 7.

23. Schulten remains the leading source on the rise of cartography in America during the nineteenth and early twentieth centuries; see Schulten, *The Geographical Imagination in America*; and Schulten, *Mapping the Nation*.

24. Robert L. Scott, "Cold War and Rhetoric," 4.

25. The field of rhetorical studies has been particularly active in arguing the Cold War as a rhetorical worldview. See especially Mary Stuckey's discussion of the Cold War as powerful interpretive schema in Stuckey, "Competing Foreign Policy Visions," 214–27; also note Thomas Kane's discussion of the Cold War as a kind of commanding lens by which to view the world in Kane, "Foreign Policy Suppositions," 80–91.

26. Henrikson, "The Power and Politics of Maps," 64, 51.

27. As Jeremy Black has written, mapping is constrained by our desire to "explain, classify, and organize space," entailing a significant relationship between the cartographic impulse and control itself. Black, *Maps and Politics*, 95.

28. See especially Huggan, "Decolonizing the Map," 115–31.

29. Borges, *A Universal History of Infamy*, 141.

30. The imperial foundations of cartography are well explored in Edney, *Mapping an Empire*.

31. See the chapter on "How Mapping Became Scientific," in Crampton, *Mapping*, 49–61. See also McMaster and McMaster, "A History of Twentieth-Century American Academic Cartography," 305–21; and Barnes and Farish, "Between Regions," 807–26.

32. Heffernan, "The Politics of the Map," 223.

33. Cook, "The Historical Role of Photomechanical Techniques," 137–54; Collier, "The Impact on Topographic Mapping," 155–74.

34. Crampton, *Mapping*, 60.

35. Cloud, "American Cartographic Transformations," 262.

36. One of the best works that reflects critically on the development of digital mapping is Pickles, *Ground Truth.*

37. For the cartographic notion of state power as natural and transparent, see Biggs, "Putting the State on the Map," 399.

38. Extension of the Cold War into the Polar North, for example, represents this key decentering, becoming another defining dynamic of Cold War geographic science, defense mobilization, and foreign policy. See Bocking, "A Disciplined Geography," 288–90; Chaturvedi, *The Polar Regions*, 83–104.

39. Ninkovich, *Modernity and Power*, xiv.

40. Gaddis, *Strategies of Containment*, 276.

41. Hart and Kendall, "Lyndon Johnson and the Problem of Politics," 93, 96, 97.

42. See Harley, *New Nature of Maps*, 35; Biggs, "Putting the State on the Map," 374. See also Benedict Anderson, *Imagined Communities*; and Randviir, "Spatialization of Knowledge," 230–31.

43. The label of propaganda was frequently used against any map that had an overtly biased political agenda. For more on this, see Ager, "Maps and Propaganda," 1–15; Alan Burnett, "Propaganda Cartography," 60–89; Hall, "A Geographical Approach to Propaganda," 313–30.

44. This idea is expressed well in Cohen, *Geography and Politics in a World Divided*, xiv.

45. Sparke, *In the Space of Theory*, 9–11.

46. Richard Edes Harrison, unpublished book manuscript, 1943, Publications Box, Part IV, Richard Edes Harrison Collection, Geography & Map Division, Library of Congress, Washington, D.C. Hereafter, the Geography & Map Division is abbreviated as GMD and the Library of Congress as LOC.

47. Dickinson, Blair, and Ott, *Places of Public Memory*, 23.

48. Tuan, *Space and Place*, 6.

49. Massey, *Space, Place and Gender*, 5. For more on the conceptualization of maps as processes, see Barton and Barton, "Ideology and the Map," 62.

50. Neil Smith, *American Empire*, xvii–xviii.

51. Spykman, *America's Strategy in World Politics.*

52. For a discussion on the implications of these ideas, see Nijman, "The Limits of Superpower," 681–95.

53. Neil Smith, *American Empire.*

54. Agnew, *Geopolitics*, 36.

55. Chilton, "The Meaning of *Security*," 210.

56. An illuminating discussion of the discourses of containment and liberation is found in O'Gorman, "'The One Word the Kremlin Fears,'" 389–428.

57. Agnew, *Geopolitics*, 103.

58. This notion of maps and abstractions is eloquently described in Winichakul, *Siam Mapped.* In terms of the specific context of this project, Matthew Farish discusses

these kinds of spatial abstractions in the spatial changes of World War II and the early Cold War; see Farish, "Archiving Areas," 663–79. Ninkovich also makes arguments about how abstraction and space took on important connections during the rise of Wilsonian internationalism and traces its roots into the Cold War. Ninkovich, *Modernity and Power*, xvi, 133–202.

59. See the chapter on "Regional Intelligence," in particular, in Farish, *The Contours of the Cold War*, 51–99.

60. Two important works on modernization include Latham, *Modernization as Ideology*; and Pearce, *Rostow, Kennedy, and the Rhetoric of Foreign Aid*.

61. Cloud, "American Cartographic Transformations," 277–78.

62. Medhurst, "Rhetoric and Cold War," 25.

63. Wander, "The Rhetoric of American Foreign Policy," in *Cold War Rhetoric*, 156.

64. Prelli, *Rhetorics of Display*, 1–38.

65. Sparke, *In the Space of Theory*, 9.

66. Ibid., 9–11.

67. Ibid.,12.

68. See, for example, U.S. Delegation to the United Nations Regional Cartographic Conference, *Official Report of the United States Delegation to the United Nations Regional Cartographic Conference for Africa*.

69. Westad, *The Global Cold War*, 5.

70. The original pamphlet was U.S. Department of Defense, *Soviet Military Power* (1981).

71. O'Gorman, *Spirits of the Cold War*, 6.

72. Parry-Giles, *The Rhetorical Presidency*, xix–xx.

73. Bunge's influential work in quantitative spatial science can be found in Bunge, *Theoretical Geography*. His later more radical work is best represented by Bunge, *Nuclear War Atlas*.

74. Brunn, "Geopolitics in a Shrinking World," 131–32.

75. Latour, "Drawing Things Together," 26.

76. Raffestin, "From Text to Image," 9.

77. Harley, "Deconstructing the Map," 242–43.

78. Hartnett, "Michel de Certeau's Critical Historiography," 287–88.

79. De Certeau, *The Practice of Everyday Life*, 121.

80. Pickles, "Texts, Hermeneutics, and Propaganda Maps," 219–20.

81. Finnegan, *Picturing Poverty*, xii; Finnegan, "Studying Visual Modes of Public Address," 250–70.

82. Wood and Fels, *The Natures of Maps*, 8–9.

83. Ibid., xvi.

84. Derek Gregory has provided a full theoretical treatment of this "geographic imagination" concept. See Gregory, *Geographical Imaginations*. Another rich historical application of these notions can be found in Schulten, *The Geographical Imagination in America*. See also Holleran's review of Schulten for more discussion of this concept in Holleran, "America's Place in the World," 419–24. Other instructive treatments of the concept can be found in Cosgrove, *Apollo's Eye*; and Schwartz and Ryan, *Picturing Place*.

85. See especially the conclusion in Parry-Giles, *The Rhetorical Presidency*, 183–86.

86. Harley, *The New Nature of Maps*, 37; Pickles, "Texts, Hermeneutics, and Propaganda Maps," 219; Barnes and Duncan, *Writing Worlds*, 8.

87. American Federation of Labor, Free Trade Union Committee, "'Gulag'—Slavery, Inc.," 1951, Graphics Collection, American Federation of Labor, George Meany Memorial Archives, Silver Spring, Md.

88. The various documents establishing the project are discussed further in chapter 4; most of the materials are from the Jacques May Papers Collection and the American Geographical Society Medical Geography Archives at the American Geographical Society Library (AGSL), University of Wisconsin–Milwaukee.

89. The quote is from Young, "Gulag—Slavery, Inc.," 601. On the subject of the *Atlas of Disease*, see the review in Koch, *Cartographies of Disease*, 216–20.

90. Letter from A. Larkin to Jacques May, June 22, 1953, folder 1: Plates 8 and 9, Correspondence 1952–54, box 3, series 1: Professional Records, 1943–1960, Jacques May Papers, AGSL.

91. Häkli in Herb et al., "Mapping Is Critical!," 335.

92. Barnes, "Geography's Underworld," 7.

93. This approach is modeled in Farish, *The Contours of America's Cold War*.

94. Kitchin and Dodge, "Rethinking Maps," 335.

95. Ibid., 337. See also Crampton, *Mapping*, 60.

96. Wood and Fels, *The Natures of Maps*, xvi.

97. See especially Cloud, "Crossing the Olentangy River," 371–404; Cloud, *Hidden in Plain Sight*; and Cloud, "Imaging the World in a Barrel," 231–51.

98. Schulten, *Mapping the Nation*, 2.

99. Schulten, *The Geographical Imagination in America*, 241.

100. Wood and Fels, *The Natures of Maps*, 7.

CHAPTER ONE

1. Louis H. Powell, "New Uses for Globes," 49.

2. Ibid.

3. Ibid., 53.

4. Henrikson, "Maps, Globes, and the 'Cold War,'" 445–46.

5. Roosevelt, "Fighting Defeatism," 209.

6. W. H. Lawrence, "Roosevelt to Warn U.S. of Danger; Asks All to Trace Talk on Maps," *New York Times*, February 21, 1942.

7. Roosevelt, "Fighting Defeatism," 207–8.

8. Ristow, "Air Age Geography," 333.

9. See especially the classic propaganda series, *Why We Fight*, by Frank Capra, which included animated map sequences produced by Walt Disney.

10. Henrikson, "The Map as an 'Idea,'" 46.

11. See Ninkovich, *Modernity and Power*, xiv.

12. Ibid., xv.

13. Ibid.

14. For a representative contemporary academic analysis of the new "bird's-eye view" and the notion of expanding three-dimensional space due to changes in technology

and communication, see Whittlesey's presidential address to the Association of American Geographers. Whittlesey, "The Horizon of Geography," 15–27.

15. For more on the stoicism of Kennan's articulation of America's national security, see O'Gorman, *Spirits of the Cold War*, 38–69.

16. George Kennan, *Realities of American Foreign Policy*, 50.

17. George Kennan, "Telegram: The Charge in the Soviet Union to the Secretary of State, 22 February 1946," National Security Archive, George Washington University, http://www.gwu.edu/~nsarchiv/coldwar/documents/episode-1/kennan.htm (accessed June 5, 2014); Kennan (X), "The Sources of Soviet Conduct," 575.

18. U.S. Department of State, "NSC-68," 253.

19. For a contemporary review of new air-age projections and a critique of Harrison, see Hinks, "Some New Effects in Map Projection," 123–27.

20. Harrison, *Look at the World*. For an exploration of Harrison's process, see "Perspective Maps: Harrison Atlas Gives Fresh New Look to Old World," *Life*, February 28, 1944, 56.

21. For more on this idea of Wilsonianism, see Meinig, *The Shaping of America: Global America 1915–2000*, 299–369.

22. De Seversky, *Victory through Air Power*. See also De Seversky, *Air Power: Key to Survival*.

23. Disney, *Victory through Air Power*.

24. Packard, Overton, and Wood, *Our Air-Age World*.

25. Representative Clare Boothe Luce of Connecticut, "America in the Post-War Air World," *Congressional Record*, 78th Cong., 1st sess., 1943, vol. 89, pt. 1, 760.

26. General H. H. Arnold, "Air Power for Peace," *National Geographic Magazine*, February 1946, 137–93.

27. Cooper, *The Right to Fly*.

28. See Pearcy, "The Air Age: Fact or Fantasy?," 304–12.

29. Ristow, "Air Age Geography," 333.

30. Barnes and Farish, "Between Regions," 811–13; Ristow, "Air Age Geography," 334.

31. Ristow, "Air Age Geography," 334.

32. Ibid.

33. Ibid.

34. Henrikson, "The Map as an 'Idea,'" 28.

35. Ristow, "Air Age Geography," 334.

36. Ibid., 334–35.

37. Ibid., 335.

38. For more information on the development of mapping ocean basins in the early Cold War era, see Doel, Levin, and Marker, "Extending Modern Cartography," 605–26.

39. Speier, "Magic Geography," 310–11, 316.

40. John K. Wright, "Map Makers Are Human," 528.

41. Ibid., 527.

42. De Seversky, *Air Power*, 12.

43. Soffner, "War on the Visual Front," 467.

44. Henrikson, "Maps, Globes, and the 'Cold War,'" 447.

45. Schulten, *The Geographical Imagination in America*, 229.

46. Soffner, "War on the Visual Front," 465.

47. Quam, "The Use of Maps in Propaganda," 22.

48. Weigert, "Maps Are Weapons," 529.

49. Whittlesey, "The Horizon of Geography," 20.

50. Malin, "Space and History," 107.

51. Ashley, "The Geopolitics of Geopolitical Space," 413–15. Also of interest is the work done by Mary Dudziak on the wider history of Cold War civil rights and its effects on foreign policy. See Dudziak, *Cold War Civil Rights*.

52. For a good discussion of the "new internationalism" in terms of its advancement by international organizations, see Iriye, *Global Community*.

53. Luce, "The American Century," 64.

54. MacLeish, "The Image of Victory," 10–11.

55. Henrikson, "The Map as an 'Idea,'" 42.

56. De Seversky, *Air Power*, 394.

57. For a discussion on this duality of despair and triumph from an "air" perspective, Hannah Arendt's exploration of the "Archimedean Point" is a fitting expression of these new choices; in it, she writes about the abolishment of the "old dichotomy between earth and sky" and points out, "We always handle nature from a point in the universe outside the earth. Without actually standing where Archimedes wished to stand . . . we have found a way to act on the earth and within terrestrial nature as though we dispose of it from outside, from the Archimedean point." Such a powerful perspective, she writes, encompasses both "despair and triumph" simultaneously, and this certainly speaks to the air-age's new anxieties and opportunities. Arendt, *The Human Condition*, 237–38.

58. Schulten, "Richard Edes Harrison and the Challenge," 187. Willkie, *One World*, 202. See also Henrikson, "The Map as an 'Idea,'" 28.

59. Other figures such as Vice President Henry Wallace were extolling a postwar universe marked by global cooperation over air space. See Henry Wallace, "What We Will Get Out of the War," *American*, March 1943, 104.

60. *Triumph of the Will*, dir. Leni Riefenstahl. For a discussion of the scene's spatial significance, see Cosgrove, *Apollo's Eye*, 242.

61. Many contemporary academics and government technicians were concerned about the use of "geopolitics" and, in particular, the employment of maps for strategic ends; the most representative include Weigert, "Maps Are Weapons," 528–30; John K. Wright, "Map Makers Are Human," 527; Powell, "New Uses for Globes," 49–58; Soffner, "War on the Visual Front," 465–76; Quam, "The Use of Maps in Propaganda," 21–32.

62. Bowman, "Geography vs. Geopolitics," 646–58.

63. "Albatross," *New Yorker*, July 9, 1960, 23–24.

64. See also "Friends," *New Yorker*, February 4, 1967, 24–25.

65. Wolfgang Saxon, "Richard Harrison, Avid Bird-Watcher, and Map Maker, 92," *New York Times*, January 7, 1994.

66. For more discussion of the "geographical imagination" concept, see Schulten, *The Geographical Imagination in America*; Schwartz and Ryan, *Picturing Place*.

67. Another of Harrison's obituaries spoke of his cartographic influence: "Indeed it is fair to say that he was *the* critical actor in a process that culminated some years later with publication and impact of that stunning image of our 'blue marble' as glimpsed from outer space." Zelinsky, "In Memoriam: Richard Edes Harrison," 190.

68. "Perspective Maps," 56.

69. Schulten, "Richard Edes Harrison and the Challenge"; Farish, *The Contours of the Cold War*, 9–19.

70. Harrison and Strausz-Hupe, "Maps, Strategy, and World Politics," 65; Harrison, "Art and Common Sense in Cartography," 27–28.

71. See Henrikson, "America's Changing Place in the World," 73–100.

72. Zelinsky, "In Memoriam: Richard Edes Harrison," 187–88.

73. Schulten, "Richard Edes Harrison and the Challenge," 178.

74. Monmonier, *Maps with the News*, dedication page.

75. Zelinsky, "In Memoriam: Richard Edes Harrison," 188.

76. Ristow, "Journalistic Cartography," 375.

77. Monmonier, *Maps with the News*, 23.

78. Cosgrove and Veronica della Dora, "Mapping Global War," 373–74.

79. Ristow, "Journalistic Cartography," 374; Schulten, *The Geographical Imagination in America*, 3.

80. Richard Edes Harrison, "The War of the Maps: A Famous Cartographer Surveys the Field," *Saturday Review of Literature*, August 7, 1943, 26.

81. See Richard Edes Harrison, *Fortune* 1938: Czechoslovakia, part 1, file 19, Richard Edes Harrison Collection, Geography & Map Division, Library of Congress, Washington, D.C. Hereafter, the Geography & Map Division is abbreviated as GMD and the Library of Congress as LOC. Also worth looking at for more on Harrison's process is a 1985 interview with Monmonier, *Maps with the News*, 167. For a categorized list of all of Harrison's *Fortune* output, see Perry, "Harrison's *Fortune* Maps, 1933–1938," 46–56 and Perry, "Harrison's *Fortune* Maps, 1939–1945," 13–20.

82. For more on the history of the Mercator projection, see Monmonier, *Rhumb Lines and Map Wars*.

83. "Perspective Maps," 56.

84. Joan M. Schwartz and James R. Ryan posit photography as a key piece of the "picturing impulse" of geography, a "means of observing, describing, studying, ordering, classifying and, thereby, knowing the world." See Schwartz and Ryan, *Picturing Place*, 6, 8.

85. "Perspective Maps," 61; Schulten, "Richard Edes Harrison and the Challenge," 180.

86. Henrikson, "The Map as an 'Idea,'" 23.

87. Monmonier, *How to Lie with Maps*, 8.

88. For a discussion of the connection of map projections and politics, see Black, *Maps and Politics*, 29–59.

89. Harrison, *Look at the World*, 30–31.

90. Mackinder, "The Round World," 601.

91. Lippmann, *U.S. Foreign Policy*, 145. Stoler covers some archival correspondence between Joint Chiefs of Staff members like Henry Stimson on Lippmann's book as well

as some letters to Lippmann praising his take on foreign policy. Stoler also comments on the potential influence of Mackinder's and Spykman's theories on the waging of foreign policy. See Stoler, *Allies and Adversaries*, 129–32.

92. For the origins of the critical discussions in cartography around the "silences" of maps and their role in power relations, begin with Harley, *The New Nature of Maps*.

93. For a discussion of "common sense" philosophy and geopolitical reasoning, see Ó Tuathail and Agnew, "Geopolitics and Discourse," 194–99. See also Boria, "Geopolitical Maps," 304–5.

94. Harrison, *Look at the World*, 12.

95. Prelli, *Rhetorics of Display*, 15.

96. Olson, Finnegan, and Hope, *Visual Rhetoric*, 7, 9, 16.

97. Harrison, *Look at the World*, 52–53.

98. Consolidated Vultee Aircraft Corporation, *Maps . . . And How to Understand Them*, 9.

99. Harrison, *Look at the World*, 52.

100. Ibid.

101. Ibid., 53.

102. Visualizing global space typically places the observer outside of space and features the "world-as-a-picture," framing the "world as apart from and prior to the places and people it contains." See Agnew, *Geopolitics*, 15. Also see Henrikson, "America's Changing Place in the World," 73–100.

103. Cosgrove, *Apollo's Eye*, 13.

104. Richard Edes Harrison, *Fortune* 1942: Southeast to Armageddon, part 1, file 82, Richard Edes Harrison Collection, GMD, LOC.

105. Richard Edes Harrison, *Fortune* 1943: Not-So-Soft Underside, part 1, file 97, Richard Edes Harrison Collection, GMD, LOC.

106. Ibid.

107. Harrison, *Look at the World*, 11.

108. Ibid.

109. Richard Edes Harrison, *Fortune* July 1941: U.S.S.R., part 1, file 70, folder 2, Richard Edes Harrison Collection, GMD, LOC.

110. Aforementioned works by Neil Smith and the Barnes-Farish collaborations discuss this movement. See also McMaster and McMaster, "A History of Twentieth-Century American Academic Cartography."

111. See especially Bowman, "Geography vs. Geopolitics."

112. Harrison, *Look at the World*, 50–51.

113. Ibid., 10–12.

114. Ibid., 12.

115. S. W. Boggs, "Cartohypnosis," *Scientific Monthly*, June 1947, 469.

116. Harrison, "War of the Maps," 24.

117. Harrison, "Art and Common Sense in Cartography," 27–28.

118. See Barney, "Power Lines," 412–34.

119. Ninkovich, *Modernity and Power*, 4.

120. Harrison, *Look at the World*, 8–9, 12; Consolidated Vultee Aircraft Corporation, *Maps . . . And How to Understand Them*, 11.

121. Harrison, *Look at the World*, 9.

122. Ibid., 9.

123. Richard Edes Harrison, *Fortune* 1941: World Divided, part 1, file 74, Richard Edes Harrison Collection, GMD, LOC.

124. Ibid.

125. For more on color conventions in mapping, see Kress and van Leeuwen, "Colour as a Semiotic Mode," 343-68; Kimball, "London through Rose-Colored Graphics," 353-81; Monmonier, *How to Lie with Maps*, 170-71.

126. Wood and Fels, "Designs on Signs," 54-103.

127. Richard Edes Harrison, *Fortune* 1952: U.S. Commitment, file 205, Richard Edes Harrison Collection, GMD, LOC.

128. Richard Edes Harrison, "Atlas for the U.S. Citizen," *Fortune*, September 1940, 58.

129. Spykman, *America's Strategy in World Politics*. See also Sempa, *Geopolitics*, 75-76.

130. Spykman, *America's Strategy in World Politics*, 457.

131. Chaturvedi, *The Polar Regions*, 88-89.

132. Ibid.

133. Harrison, "Atlas for the U.S. Citizen," 44-45.

134. Ibid., 42.

135. Ibid., 56-57.

136. Ibid., 57.

137. Harrison, *Look at the World*, 54.

138. Ibid., 54-55.

139. Along similar lines, an interesting Harrison map drafted for *Compass of the World* in 1944 portrays South America covered in foreign broadcasting lines from all over the globe, with the caption: "Scarcely any other region is so thickly overspread with foreign broadcasting as this continent." Richard Edes Harrison, Macmillan, February 1944: Compass of the World, part 1, file 112, Richard Edes Harrison Collection, GMD, LOC.

140. Richard Edes Harrison, "World According to Standard," *Fortune*, March 1940, 84-85.

141. Richard Edes Harrison, PanAm, September 1946: Aitoff World Map, part 1, file 156, Richard Edes Harrison Collection, GMD, LOC.

142. Harrison, *Look at the World*, 9.

143. Harrison goes on to even compare this approach to a Dali painting, thus showing his acknowledgment of cartographic abstraction. Richard Edes Harrison, Publications Box, part IV, Richard Edes Harrison Collection, GMD, LOC.

144. Lawrence Prelli's work on maps discusses the complexities of their function as metaphors. See especially Prelli, "Visualizing a Bounded Sea," 90-120.

145. Marshall, *General Marshall's Report*.

146. Richard Edes Harrison, *Life* October 1949: U.S.S.R.'s First Atom Bomb, part 1, file 179, Richard Edes Harrison Collection, GMD, LOC.

147. Richard Edes Harrison, *Fortune* 1950: The Communist Fastness, file 180, Richard Edes Harrison Collection, GMD, LOC. See also Leland Stowe, "Satellites in Arms," *Life*, December 17, 1951, 98-99.

148. Richard Edes Harrison, *Life* April 1954: The Fatherland Is Again Divided, part 1, file 229, Richard Edes Harrison Collection, GMD, LOC.

149. Weigert, Stefansson, and Harrison, *New Compass of the World*, xiii–xiv.

150. Cloud, "American Cartographic Transformations," 261–82.

151. Bunge, *Nuclear War Atlas*, 1, 9.

152. Olson, Finnegan, and Hope, *Visual Rhetoric*, 18.

153. Dodds, "Cold War Geopolitics," 206–7.

154. Gaddis, *Strategies of Containment*, 276.

155. U.S. Department of State, "NSC-68," 241.

156. Gaddis, *Strategies of Containment*, 276.

157. Ibid., 273.

158. Kennan, *Realities of American Foreign Policy*, 50.

CHAPTER TWO

1. John Dille, "The Missile-Era Race to Chart the Earth," *Life*, May 12, 1958, 132–33.

2. Cloud, "American Cartographic Transformations," 266. See an account of Hough's story in Dille, "The Missile-Era Race," 124–38.

3. Dille, "The Missile-Era Race," 135.

4. The Hough Team Materials are available at the National Archives II in College Park. See specifically File 11, Records of the Office of Chief Engineers, RG77, National Archives and Records Administration II, College Park, Md. The National Archives II is hereafter abbreviated as NARAII.

5. See especially Lieber, "International Cooperation in Mapping," 71–74.

6. For more on this "hailing" and "mangling" idea in World War II and early Cold War mapping, see Barnes and Farish, "Between Regions," 807–26.

7. Cloud, "Imaging the World in a Barrel," 233.

8. Barnes and Farish, "Between Regions," 821.

9. For explorations of mapping and the power relations behind maker and user, see especially Pickles, "Texts, Hermeneutics and Propaganda Maps" and Harley, "Deconstructing the Map" in *Writing Worlds*; and Denis Wood, *The Power of Maps*.

10. Lefebvre, *The Production of Space*, 33.

11. Ibid., 38–45.

12. James Anderson's work on the role of ideology in geographic studies is particularly important, as he posits that geography is too often seen as a transmitter of ideologies, rather than as a producer of them. James Anderson, "Ideology in Geography," 3.

13. Gaddis, *Strategies of Containment*, 103. See also Ninkovich's description of "symbolic interventionism" in *Modernity and Power*, xv.

14. Neil Smith, *American Empire*, 4.

15. Bocking, "A Disciplined Geography," 288–90.

16. Paul A. Smith, "Aviation Development and Its Mapping Needs," 67.

17. Lieber, "International Cooperation in Mapping," 71.

18. For rhetorical definitions of realism, see Beer and Hariman, "Realism and Rhetoric," and "Strategic Intelligence and Discursive Realities."

19. Ó Tuathail and Agnew, "Geopolitics and Discourse," 191.

20. Bowman also wrote the introduction to Boggs's book on international boundaries. See Boggs, *International Boundaries*.

21. Isaiah Bowman, "The Geographical Situation of the United States," 130.

22. Ibid.

23. Ibid., 129, 132.

24. See Barnes and Farish, "Between Regions," 808–12.

25. Ninkovich, *Modernity and Power*, xv.

26. Ibid., xiv.

27. Henrikson, "Geographical 'Mental Maps,'" 496.

28. Ashley, "The Geopolitics of Geopolitical Space," 423.

29. Gaddis, *Strategies of Containment*, 27–33.

30. George Kennan, "PPS/23: Review of Current Trends—U.S. Foreign Policy," U.S. Department of State, *Foreign Relations of the United States: 1948*, vol. 1, 527.

31. For example, the State Department geographer during the 1950s and 1960s, G. Etzel Pearcy, referenced Mackinder's theory as inextricably bound up with the American concept of containment. In a series of political maps, Pearcy shows the world from various perspectives and projections through maps to demonstrate the extent of American commitments circa 1964, with an obvious focus on the geopolitical aspects of Southeast Asia and their role in American interests. See Pearcy, "Geopolitics and Foreign Relations," 318–30.

32. Gaddis and Nitze, "NSC-68 and the Soviet Threat Reconsidered," 167–68.

33. Wilson, "Geographic Training for the Postwar World," 575–89; Wilson, "Lessons from the Experience of the Map Information Section," 298–310.

34. Herbert Block to Assistant Director, Economic Studies Group, Department of Research, "Evaluation of German Geopolitics," August 3, 1944, box 5, Records of the Geographer, U.S. Department of State, RG59, Cartographic & Architectural Records Division, NARAII. The U.S. Department of State hereafter is referenced by its record group, RG59, and the Cartographic & Architectural Records Division is abbreviated as CARD.

35. *Map 2: Haushofer's Latest Theory: Imperialist Expansion along the Meridians*, in Herbert Block, "Evaluation of German Geopolitics," 17.

36. Kimble, "The Role of Surveying and Mapping," 108.

37. Crittenberger, "The Relationship of Mapping and Charting," 8.

38. See the quote from Colonel Robert R. Robertson: "During World War II, we learned the hard way that adequate maps just didn't exist for most parts of the globe. Even in the United States, only 37 percent of the land is covered by really accurate topographic maps. When the war ended, the President started a long-range plan to promote map making, with United States technical help, in friendly countries all over the world. The Army, Navy, and State Department were directed to cooperate." Robert Leslie Conly, "Men Who Measure the Earth: Surveyors from 18 New World Nations Invade Trackless Jungles and Climb Snow Peaks to Map Latin America," *National Geographic*, March 1956, 338.

39. Loper, "The Role of Surveying and Mapping," 365.

40. Andrew Kirby points out that eventually, the prominent political geographers who served the government like Bowman and Hartshorne became increasingly rare,

and political geography and geopolitics were more practiced by international relations experts, representing "a division of academic labor between political science and geography." Kirby, "What Did You Do in the War, Daddy?," 314.

41. The official report, coming out of research sponsored by the Army Map Service, can be found in Chovitz and Fischer, "A New Determination of the Figure of the Earth," 534–45.

42. "It's a Smaller World," *Scientific American*, July 1956, 50; "Taping the Earth," *Time*, May 14, 1956, 75.

43. Conly, "Men Who Measure the Earth," 335. See also Deborah Jean Warner, "From Tallahassee to Timbuktu," 393–415; and Deborah Jean Warner, "Political Geodesy," 363–89.

44. U.S. Aeronautical Chart and Information Center, *Geodesy for the Layman*, 1.

45. Some other contemporary treatments of this concept can be found in the annals of the American Congress on Surveying and Mapping. See particularly Skop, "The Effects of User Requirements," 315–18; Diercks, "The Role of the Topographic Map in the Missile Age," 349–54.

46. Dille, "The Missile-Era Race," 130.

47. Chaturvedi, *The Polar Regions*, 103.

48. Bocking, "A Disciplined Geography," 267.

49. See Cloud, "Crossing the Olentangy River," 371–404; Rostow, *Open Skies*; Hall, "From Concept to National Policy," 107–25.

50. Brugioni, *Eyes in the Sky*, 1. For other historical and critical anthologies on these technologies, see Day, Logsdon, and Latell, *Eye in the Sky*; and Peebles, *The Corona Project*.

51. Day, Logsdon, and Latell, *Eye in the Sky*, 177. See also Cloud, "Hidden in Plain Sight," 203–9.

52. Cloud, "Crossing the Olentangy River," 402.

53. S. W. Boggs to George C. Marshall, January 21, 1947, box 20, Records of the Geographer, RG59, CARD, NARAII.

54. Boggs was often consulted by government agencies, particularly the military, about strategic uses of the "roundness" concept and how globes could be used to solve policy and intelligence problems. See S. W. Boggs, "Memorandum of Conversation," March 8, 1949, box 3, Records of the Geographer, RG59, CARD, NARAII.

55. Boggs, "Global Relations of the United States," 910. Boggs's statement here was actually a play on the famous dictum of Sir Halford Mackinder in 1919:

Who rules East Europe commands the Heartland:

Who rules the Heartland commands the World-Island:

Who rules the World-Island commands the World.

See Mackinder, *Democratic Ideals and Reality*, 106. For critical readings of Mackinder's work, see especially Ó Tuathail, *Critical Geopolitics*, 24–38; Sidaway, "Overwriting Geography," 163–70.

56. Pearcy, "The Air Age: Fact or Fantasy?," 304–12; and Richard Edes Harrison, "The Face of One World: Five Perspectives for an Understanding of the Air Age," *Saturday Review of Literature*, July 1, 1944, 5.

57. Boggs, "Cartohypnosis."

58. S. W. Boggs, Memorandum of Conversation, February 4, 1946, box 7, Records of the Geographer, RG59, CARD, NARAII.

59. S. W. Boggs to Richard Edes Harrison, August 31, 1944, box 19, Records of the Geographer, RG59, CARD, NARAII.

60. Wright, "Map Makers Are Human," 527.

61. Williams, "Lawrence Martin, 1880–1955," 357–64.

62. Alexander, "Samuel Whittemore Boggs," 237.

63. American Congress on Surveying and Mapping, "Obituaries: Samuel Whittemore Boggs," 517.

64. See especially Boggs, *International Boundaries.*

65. S. W. Boggs, Memorandum, "The Program of Geographical Studies and Maps," February 2, 1943, box 20, Records of the Geographer, RG59, CARD, NARAII.

66. S. W. Boggs to J. S. Dickey, Memorandum, "Activities of the Division of Geography and Cartography," December 28, 1944, box 20, Records of the Geographer, RG59, CARD, NARAII.

67. Postwar geopolitical planning was a notable focus of Boggs among other geographers, academics, and policy makers during the course of World War II. Some representative publications include George Renner, "Maps for a New World," *Collier's* 53 (June 1942): 14–21; Spykman, "Frontiers, Security, and International Organization," 436–47; Bowman, "Geography vs. Geopolitics," 646–58.

68. Boggs, "The Program of Geographical Studies and Maps."

69. Ibid.

70. Ibid.

71. Eagleton quoted in Christian Parenti, "The World Was Not Enough," *In These Times*, July 28, 2003, http://www.inthesetimes.org/article/87/the_world_was_not_enough/.

72. Alexander, "Samuel Whittemore Boggs," 242.

73. See especially Barnes and Farish, "Between Regions"; and Neil Smith, *American Empire.*

74. Neil Smith, *American Empire*, xviii.

75. Boggs, "Global Relations," 903.

76. Boggs, "A New Equal-Area Projection," 241–45.

77. Ibid., 241.

78. Ibid., 243.

79. See Charles A. Thomson to S. W. Boggs, February 8, 1943, and Boggs to Charles A. Thomson, February 20, 1943, box 20, Records of the Geographer, RG59, CARD, NARAII.

80. Charles A. Thomson to S. W. Boggs, February 8, 1943.

81. Boggs to Charles A. Thomson, February 20, 1943. A noteworthy aspect of this memo, and a trend that would become part of the postwar move in State Department geography toward intelligence gathering, is the call for more specific area experts.

82. Boggs, "National Claims in Adjacent Seas," 185–209; Boggs, "An Atlas of Ignorance," 253–58.

83. Boggs, "National Claims in Adjacent Seas," 185.

84. Barnes and Farish, "Between Regions," 808.

85. Alexander, "Samuel Whittemore Boggs," 238. See also Boggs's correspondence with the Nystrom Company through the State Department in S. W. Boggs to C. A. Burkhart, August 24, 1949, box 4, Records of the Geographer, RG59, CARD, NARAII. On an interesting note, Boggs's memorandum from July 1945 talks about using the eumorphic or Miller projection on the Foreign Service post maps that would become a staple of the State Department map program and mentions "probably the United States should be somewhere near the middle of the map so that Eastern Asia is to the left and Europe to the right." S. W. Boggs, Memorandum, July 31, 1945, box 4, Records of the Geographer, RG59.

86. Baar also noted the contributions of Charles H. Deetz and Oscar S. Adams of the United States Coast and Geodetic Survey in working with Boggs on developing the projection—showing some of the cross-agency cartographic cooperation that was part of the State Department's outreach. Baar, "The Manipulation of Projections for World Maps," 112–13.

87. O. M. Miller, "Notes on Cylindrical World Map Projections," 424.

88. United Nations, "A Student Map of the United Nations," Map (New York: United Nations, 1953); Civic Education Service Inc., "The World: Headline Focus Wall Map," Map (Washington, D.C.: Civic Education Service, 1965); Scholastic Magazine, "Economic Map of the World, 1966-67," Map (Springfield, N.J.: Hammond, 1966). All are located in the World-International Relations Folder, Title Collection, Geography & Map Division, Library of Congress, Washington, D.C.

89. Alexander, "Samuel Whittemore Boggs," 242. Some examples of Boggs's Miller proselytizing can be found in S. W. Boggs, Memorandum, February 12, 1946, box 20; S. W. Boggs to Max Horn, September 1, 1943, box 19, Records of the Geographer, RG59, CARD, NARAII.

90. See S. W. Boggs, Memorandum, January 6, 1948, box 19, Records of the Geographer, RG59, CARD, NARAII. See also Crawford to Boggs, December 26, 1947, box 19; and Boggs to Crawford, January 12, 1947, box 19, Records of the Geographer, RG59, CARD, NARAII. Also interesting to note is that Boggs sent air-route globes and plastic hemispheres over to the office of Chip Bohlen, who would come to be one of the main architects of State Department Cold War policy. See S. W. Boggs to Charles Bohlen, January 12, 1945, box 20, Records of the Geographer, RG59, CARD, NARAII.

91. Colonel Desloge Brown to S. W. Boggs, November 24, 1948, box 3, Records of the Geographer, RG59, CARD, NARAII.

92. Ristow, "Air Age Geography," 334.

93. Boggs to Secretary of State Cordell Hull, April 10, 1944, box 20, Records of the Geographer, RG59, CARD, NARAII.

94. Boggs, "This Hemisphere," 850. The article was reprinted as S. W. Boggs, "This Hemisphere," *Journal of Geography* 44 (1945): 345-55.

95. Boggs, "This Hemisphere," 848–49.

96. Boggs, "Global Relations of the United States," 908.

97. Wright, "Terrae Incognitae," 1–15. Also, Denis Cosgrove does an analysis of Wright's theories and their ramifications in Denis Cosgrove, "Book Review Essay," 202–9.

98. Lippmann, *Public Opinion*, 11, 18.

99. Wright, "Terrae Incognitae," 7.

100. Ibid., 5, 7, 11–12.

101. Cosgrove, "Book Review Essay," 207.

102. Luce, "The American Century," 61–65.

103. The William F. Eisner Museum of Advertising & Design in Milwaukee houses an online exhibit of Artzybasheff's work. See William F. Eisner Museum of Advertising & Design, "Boris Artzybasheff."

104. Harrison, "The Nomograph," 655–57. A scale diagram can be found in Harrison to Boggs, April 17, 1946, box 19, Records of the Geographer, RG59, CARD, NARAII.

105. Schulten, "Richard Edes Harrison and the Challenge," 178; S. W. Boggs to Richard Edes Harrison, March 3, 1943, box 19; Boggs to Harrison, December 22, 1943, box 19; Boggs to Harrison, April 17, 1946, box 19, Records of the Geographer, RG59, CARD, NARAII.

106. Boggs to Harrison, July 21, 1941, box 19, Records of the Geographer, RG59, CARD, NARAII.

107. George Renner, "Maps for a New World," *Collier's* 53 (June 1942): 14–21.

108. For a history and critique of this controversy, see DeBres, "Political Geographers of the Past IV," 385–94. DeBres discusses the excoriation of Renner by popular press writers such as Lippmann, as well as the academic community. *Time* reported that a group of University of Minnesota professors even petitioned President Roosevelt to oust Renner from his advisory position at the Civil Aeronautics Administration.

109. Harrison to Boggs, March 9, 1943, box 19, Records of the Geographer, RG59, CARD, NARAII.

110. Boggs to Harrison, October 22, 1943, box 19, Records of the Geographer, RG59, CARD, NARAII.

111. An interesting side note to the correspondence of Boggs and Artzybasheff is that Boggs was working with Artzybasheff, ultimately unsuccessfully, to design the logo for the United Nations. S. W. Boggs, Memorandum of Conversation, March 15, 1945, box 19, Records of the Geographer, RG59, CARD, NARAII.

112. S. W. Boggs to Boris Artzybasheff, March 18, 1942, box 19, Records of the Geographer, RG59, CARD, NARAII.

113. Boggs, "Global Relations," 905–6.

114. S. W. Boggs to Boris Artzybasheff, January 3, 1944, box 19, Records of the Geographer, RG59, CARD, NARAII.

115. Boggs to Artzybasheff, May 27, 1944; Boggs to Harrison, August 31, 1944, box 19, Records of the Geographer, RG59, CARD, NARAII.

116. United States Information Agency, *Expanding World Relationships*, filmstrip, Special Media Archives Division, Records of the U.S. Information Agency, RG306, NARAII.

117. Boggs to Artzybasheff, May 27, 1944.

118. Boggs, "Mapping the Changing World," 119.

119. Kaiser and Wood, *Seeing through Maps*, 86.

120. Boggs, "Mapping Some of the Effects of Science and Technology," 187, 185.

121. See especially Pearce, "Narrative Reason and Cold War Economic Diplomacy," 395–414.

122. Boggs, "Geographic and Other Scientific Techniques," 224–5.

123. Several contemporary comments on this project include Crone, "The Future of the International Million Map of the World," 36–38; Gardiner, "A Re-appraisal," 31–47. For a good general history, see Pearson et al., "Cartographic Ideals and Geopolitical Realities," 149–76.

124. Colonel D. I. Burnett to S. W. Boggs, June 15, 1949, box 6, Records of the Geographer, RG59, CARD, NARAII.

125. Heffernan, "The Politics of the Map," 209.

126. Burnett to Boggs, June 15, 1949.

127. Pearson et al., "Cartographic Ideals and Geopolitical Realities."

128. S. W. Boggs, Memorandum, October 1, 1937, box 11, Records of the Geographer, RG59, CARD, NARAII.

129. Army Map Service, "Index Map: Carte du Monde au Millionieme," to S. W. Boggs, 1936, International Map of the World Folder, box 11, Records of the Geographer, RG59, CARD, NARAII. See also United States Department of Interior Geological Survey, "International Map of the World: Arrangement of Sheets for the United States," June 5, 1947, International Map of the World Folder, box 6, Records of the Geographer, RG59, CARD, NARAII.

130. Boggs's archive reveals considerable movement on his part to work with the UN to keep up the project. See S. W. Boggs, "Report to the Meeting of Experts on Cartography to the Secretary-General of the United Nations," March 29, 1949, box 6; United Nations Economic and Social Council, "Relations with Inter-Governmental Organization: Report by the Secretary General," June 18, 1951, box 6; S. W. Boggs to J. D. Tomlinson, Memorandum, July 3, 1951, box 6; Dean S. Rugg to S. W. Boggs, May 20, 1952, box 6, Records of the Geographer, RG59, CARD, NARAII.

131. Pearson et al., "Cartographic Ideals and Geopolitical Realities," 162.

132. Gardiner, "A Re-appraisal"; Crone, "The Future of the International Million Map of the World."

133. Pearson et al., "Cartographic Ideals and Geopolitical Realities," 161. For an online collection of this Cold War series of Army Map Service maps, see Perry Castañeda Library Map Collection, University of Texas at Austin, http://www.lib .utexas.edu/maps/imw/.

134. Also, the IMW would find itself competing with millionth-scale maps produced by the International Civil Aviation Organization, whose charts were designed solely for air travel; yet, owing to aviation's huge commercial value, nation-states (including the United States) were more energetic in this organization than they were with the IMW. Commercial and military objectives thus triumphed over the lofty ideals of the IMW's idea of a scientific consortium. See Gardiner, "A Re-appraisal," 32.

135. Boggs, "Atlas of Ignorance," 254.

136. Ibid., 256–58.

137. Ibid., 257.

138. Ibid., 258.

139. Ibid., 256.

140. Ibid., 253.

141. S. W. Boggs to Dr. Odegaard, American Council of Learned Societies, October 18, 1948, box 4, Records of the Geographer, RG59, CARD, NARAII.

142. Boggs, "Atlas of Ignorance," 258.

143. S. W. Boggs to W. R. Wrather, Director of the Geological Survey, Dept. of the Interior, August 29, 1945, box 19, Records of the Geographer, RG59, CARD, NARAII.

144. S. W. Boggs to O. A. Sandifer, August 28, 1945, box 19, Records of the Geographer, RG59, CARD, NARAII.

145. O. A. Sandifer to S. W. Boggs, October 4, 1945, box 6; W. M. Kotschnig to S. W. Boggs, September 10, 1945, box 6, Records of the Geographer, RG59, CARD, NARAII.

146. Boggs would meet similar difficulties with the domestic cartographic agencies—in his requests for foreign mapping needs, for example, representatives at the Department of Agriculture would bristle at what they perceived as the State Department trying to push a global agenda beyond its institutional powers. One official wrote Boggs that "considerable reluctance was evidenced by all agencies of this Department to registering a 'need' for maps, when no Congressional authority existed within this Department to create such a need in foreign countries." A cartographer at the Soil Conservation Service was less tactful, writing that "it is erroneous to think that the Soil Conservation Service is isolationist and not interested in anything outside of the United States" but that it helps foreign countries only on a case-by-case basis, not as part of some worldwide initiative from an outside agency. Marshall S. Wright to S. W. Boggs, October 3, 1945, box 19; J. M. Snyder to S. W. Boggs, September 26, 1945, box 19, Records of the Geographer, RG59, CARD, NARAII.

147. The memorandum actually came six days before McCormack's resignation. He had drawn fire for trying to create a stand-alone intelligence agency that gave too much power to the State Department and did not properly address the needs of the military agencies. Much of his basic plan, though, would be filtered into Truman's eventual directive to create the CIA. See Central Intelligence Agency, "The Birth of Central Intelligence."

148. Alfred McCormack, Memorandum for the Director of Central Intelligence, April 16, 1946, box 2, Records of the Geographer, RG59, CARD, NARAII.

149. Ibid., emphasis added.

150. Poole, interestingly enough, was also a founder of *Public Opinion Quarterly* and had worked for the Foreign Nationalities Branch of the OSS during the war.

151. S. W. Boggs to Dangerfield, August 6, 1945, box 20; Dickey to Poole, "Interrogation Mission to Germany," August 19, 1945, box 20, Records of the Geographer, RG59, CARD, NARAII.

152. The Cartographic Branch of the National Archives II holds an assortment of these cartographic intelligence reports from 1946–47. Each was produced under Boggs's direction through the Office of Intelligence Collection and Dissemination. See "The Borderlands of Hungary and Czechoslovakia, Including Carpatho-Ukraine," January 31, 1947; "Evaluation of Maps Pertaining to Reconstruction in Greece," May 1, 1947; "German Cartographic and Map Collecting Agencies: The Geodetic Bases of German Cartography," July 17, 1947; "Evaluation of Map Coverage of Spain," December 30, 1946; "Hatay Province, Turkey—An Evaluation of Map Coverage," August 4, 1947. All can be found in Records of the Geographer, RG59, CARD, NARAII.

153. Boggs, "Cartohypnosis," 472.

154. Ibid., 471.

155. For contemporary air-age literature on cartography as propaganda, see chapter 1.

156. Bocking, "A Disciplined Geography," 272, 288–89.

157. Demko, "Geography beyond the Ivory Tower," 577, 579.

CHAPTER THREE

1. Benjamin Fine, "Geography Almost Ignored in Colleges, Survey Shows," *New York Times*, December 18, 1950, 1.

2. Ibid., 28.

3. Ibid. A similar study was reported on (again as front-page news, and again alongside headlines about American power in Europe and the Pacific) by the *Times* in June of 1951. See Benjamin Fine, "U.S. College Students 'Flunk' in Knowledge of Geography," *New York Times*, June 11, 1951.

4. Fine, "Geography Almost Ignored," 28.

5. National Geographic Society, "World Map 1951," Map (Washington, D.C.: National Geographic, 1951), World-International Relations Folder, Title Collection, Geography & Map Division, Library of Congress, Washington, D.C. Hereafter, the Geography & Map Division is abbreviated as GMD and the Library of Congress as LOC.

6. Monmonier, *Rhumb Lines and Map Wars*, 138.

7. Black, *Maps and Politics*, 31.

8. "Our Narrowing World: The Story of the New National Geographic Map," *National Geographic*, December 1951, 751.

9. Ibid., 751.

10. Ibid., 752–53.

11. For more on the important relationship between geography and history in this era, see Schulten, *The Geographical Imagination in America*, 240; Agnew, *Geopolitics*, 36.

12. "Our Narrowing World," 752.

13. Ibid., 751.

14. Commercial map companies like A. J. Nystrom and Denoyer-Geppert also provided this function through their extensive educational maps. See especially A. J. Nystrom, "The Cold War and the Search for Security 1960," Map (Chicago: A. J. Nystrom, 1960), World-International Relations Folder, Title Collection; Denoyer-Geppert, "World Relationships Today," Map (Chicago: Denoyer-Geppert, 1958), World-International Relations Folder, Title Collection, GMD, LOC.

15. See especially Gaddis and Nitze, "NSC-68," 164–70.

16. Osgood, *Total Cold War*, 32–45.

17. Monmonier, *Maps with the News*, 19.

18. Ristow, "Journalistic Cartography," 369.

19. For an early history of the Associated Press, see Gramling, *AP: The Story of News*.

20. Monmonier, *Maps with the News*, 85.

21. Associated Press, "Background Map: Sun Never Sets on World Problems," Map (New York: Associated Press, 1947), World-International Relations Folder, Title Collection, GMD, LOC.

22. Associated Press, "Background Map: The U.S. Foots the Biggest Bill," Map (New York: Associated Press, 1953), World-International Relations Folder, Title Collection, GMD, LOC.

23. Associated Press, "Background Map: News 1949 Lineup for Two Worlds," Map (New York: Associated Press, 1949), World-International Relations Folder, Title Collection, GMD, LOC.

24. Associated Press, "Background Map: Russia Thrusts Out from the Center," Map (New York: Associated Press, 1950), World-International Relations Folder, Title Collection, GMD, LOC.

25. Ninkovich's discussion of Kennan's essential containment concept is instructive on this point about Russia's cultural tradition. See Ninkovich, *Modernity and Power*, 140.

26. Associated Press, "Background Map: Are the West's Defenses against Communism Weakening?," Map (New York: Associated Press, 1953), World-International Relations Folder, Title Collection, GMD, LOC.

27. For a history of Luce's impact on Cold War culture, see especially Swanberg, *Luce and His Empire*; Baughman, *Henry R. Luce and the Rise of the American News Media*; and Herzstein, *Henry R. Luce, Time, and the American Crusade*.

28. "A Letter from the Publisher," *Time*, December 14, 1942, 27.

29. Ibid.

30. Ristow offers an extended discussion of *Time*'s cartographic style in Ristow, "Journalistic Cartography," 384–85.

31. "Paths to Power," Map, *Time*, February 5, 1951, 20.

32. "Red Rash (After Treatment)," Map, *Time*, May 23, 1949, 27.

33. For a discussion of Cold War metaphors in cartography, see Hendershot and Oldknow, "Virtual Slide Set #1."

34. "Squeeze," Map, *Time*, October 2, 1950, 15; "Korea's Waistland," Map, *Time*, October 16, 1950, 26.

35. "Eleventh Hour," Map, *Time*, October 20, 1947, 34; "Eurasian Heartland," Map, *Time*, September 22, 1947, 28.

36. "Clearing & Colder," Map, *Time*, April 19, 1948, 27.

37. "Nation's Commitments All around the Earth," Map, *Life*, December 23, 1957, 20–21.

38. "Western Defense and What NATO Links Are in Danger," Map, *Newsweek*, December 17, 1956, 28–29.

39. Richard Erdoes, "How Strategic Material Circulates," Map, *Life*, January 26, 1953, 27.

40. Hendershot and Oldknow, "Virtual Slide Set #1." For more specifically on octopus imagery in Cold War maps, see Pickles, "Text, Hermeneutics and Propaganda Maps," 211–17.

41. "How Could Soviet Attack Come?," Map, *Life*, February 27, 1950, 20–22.

42. See also *Life*'s "Attack on U.S.," which inverts this by making the spherical projection focus on the U.S., and showing potential airborne attacks from all sides of the earth. "Attack on U.S.," Map, *Life*, January 22, 1951, 78–79.

43. "Turning the Tables: How Far the Russians Must Fly to Hit U.S. Cities," Map, *Newsweek*, October 3, 1949, 26.

44. "Massive Retaliatory Power," Map, *Fortune*, May 1954, 105.

45. Gaddis and Nitze, "NSC-68," 165–66.

46. See also magazine cartography's focus on the Arctic as a field of spatial concern in U.S.-Soviet relations, especially in "Arctic Strategy," Map, *Life*, January 20, 1947, 55–56; "The Coldest Cold War," Map, *Newsweek*, November 15, 1954, 54.

47. A good source of the "social role" of newspapers and magazines in this era can be found in Gilmartin, "The Design of Journalistic Maps," 1–18.

48. See also Davies, "Interpretative Cartography," 121–22.

49. The Congressional Serial Set has collected and published all House and Senate documents and addenda to bills and reports since 1817.

50. See especially "Regional Security," Map, Committee on Foreign Relations, Foreign Assistance Act of 1949, 81st Cong., 1st sess., 1949, S. Rep. 1068, serial 11294, 8.

51. "As the U.S. Bolsters the Position of the Western World," Map, Committee on Foreign Affairs, Mutual Defense Assistance Act of 1949, 81st Cong., 1st sess., 1949, H. Rep. 1265, serial 11301, 24.

52. "United States Collective Defense Arrangements," Map, Committee on Foreign Relations, *Studies on Review of United Nations Charter*, 83rd Cong., 2nd sess., 1954, S. Doc. 164, serial 11760, 204–5.

53. "U.S. Postwar Foreign Aid," Map, Mutual Security Act of 1952, 82nd Cong., 2nd sess. 1952, S. Rep. 1490, serial 11567, 15.

54. For a few examples of these, see "Cost per Soldier 1960," Map, Committee on Foreign Affairs, Mutual Security Act of 1961, 87th Cong., 1st sess., 1961, H. Rep. 851, serial 12341, 56; "Cost per Soldier 1959," Map, Committee on Foreign Affairs, Mutual Security Act of 1960, 86th Cong., 2nd sess., 1960, H. Rep. 1464, serial 12244, 20; and "Cost per Soldier—Pay, Allowances, Subsistence and Clothing," Map, Committee on Foreign Affairs, Mutual Security Act of 1959, 86th Cong., 1st sess., 1959, H. Rep. 440, serial 12160, 12.

55. Committee on Un-American Activities, *Soviet Total War*, 85th Cong., 1st sess., 1956, H. Doc. 227, serial 12017.

56. Research Institute of America, "How Communists Menace Vital Materials," Map, ibid., 550.

57. Costigliola, "'Unceasing Pressure for Penetration,'" 1309–39. For other graphics on this fear of Third World penetration, see "Africa," Map, Committee on Un-American Activities, *Soviet Total War*, 587; "Areas of Communist Influence," *Soviet Total War*, 561.

58. Historian Walter LaFeber recounted a particularly salient 1951 incident at a Japanese peace treaty signing with John Foster Dulles. At the conference, Dulles had attempted to exclude Russia from the early negotiations. When the Soviets were eventually allowed to participate, Dulles interpreted their proposal as an attempt to dominate the area around Japan. Dulles gave a speech and demonstrated this effect of the Soviet plan on a large map; as one participant recalled, he "took the map dramatically and held it up . . . and then threw it on the floor with the utmost contempt. And that made a tremendous impression." See LaFeber, *America, Russia, and the Cold War*, 120.

59. U.S. Department of State, "Security Council Rejects Soviet Complaint," 235–44.

60. British Pathé, "U.S. Declares Reds Pushed RB-47 Off Course."

61. The Library of Congress houses copies of the actual maps that Lodge used in the presentation. See "Detailed Flight Path (Planned and Actual) of the RB-47 Aircraft, 1 July 1960," "Planned Route of the RB-47 Aircraft," "Vega Incident," and "USSR Electromagnetic Reconnaissance Flights," Maps (New York: United Nations, 1960), U.S.-International Relations Folder, Title Collection, GMD, LOC.

62. U.S. Department of State, "Security Council Rejects Soviet Complaint," 236–37.

63. Ibid., 237.

64. For a good source on this politics of the air in the Cold War, see Walt Rostow's account of his involvement in Eisenhower's Open Skies proposal, also containing a great collection of primary documents surrounding the matter. Rostow, *Open Skies*.

65. U.S. Department of State, "Security Council Rejects Soviet Complaint," 242.

66. "News in Pictures: 'Gulag'—Slavery, Inc.," *Time*, September 17, 1951, 28–29.

67. Ibid., 29.

68. See also the photo in "Gromyko Given Russ Map with Slave Camps," *Los Angeles Times*, September 7, 1951, 2.

69. Young, "'Gulag'—Slavery, Inc.," 601.

70. Finnegan, *Picturing Poverty*, xii.

71. Carruthers, *Cold War Captives*, 101.

72. Rep. O. K. Armstrong, "A Crusade of Truth and Freedom," *Congressional Record*, February 28, 1952, appendix: A1237.

73. Levine, *Plain Talk*, 235–39.

74. Methvin, "Isaac Don Levine," 247.

75. Levine would also provide character testimony on Chambers's behalf during the Hiss hearings. See Chambers, *Witness*, 457–66; Levine, *Eyewitness to History*, 179–212.

76. Levine, *Eyewitness to History*, xii.

77. Methvin, "Isaac Don Levine," 247.

78. The distributed version of Levine's *Plain Talk* map can be found at the George Meany Memorial Archives, which house the historical records of the AFL-CIO. See "'Gulag'—Slavery, Inc.: *Plain Talk* Version," folder: Slave Labor 1919–1950, box 55, Vertical Files 1881–1999, RG98, American Federation of Labor, George Meany Memorial Archives, Silver Spring, Md. Hereafter, these archives are referred to as GMM.

79. Levine, *Plain Talk*, 238.

80. Dallin and Nicolaevsky, *Forced Labor in Soviet Russia*.

81. Carruthers, *Cold War Captives*, 76, 109, 117.

82. Dallin and Nicolaevsky, *Forced Labor in Soviet Russia*, 55–57, 60, 64–65. It is difficult to say whether Dallin or Levine influenced each other's map, but it is clear that both maps are based on the map in the 1945 volume *La justice sovietique* by two Polish military officers, Sylvester Mora and Pierre Zwierniak—one of the first books to bring in firsthand accounts by prisoners and to feature attempts at quantifying slave labor. The etymology of the Polish map's origins and how it came to influence Levine is unclear. Dallin directly cites *La justice sovietique*; his map of "The Corrective Labor Camps, 1942" contains a note that simply says, "After Mora and Zwierniak, *La Justice Sovietique*." And in his suggestions for further reading, Dallin mentions *La justice* as "one of the most important books ever to appear on

Russian prison camps" and that "the map attached to the book is of great interest and value." Levine never explicitly cites Mora and Zwierniak but does mention that most of his sources are Polish. To make the matter more confusing, a *Catholic Digest* article from 1952 says that the "map had been compiled by a former Soviet citizen and was first published in Rome in 1945 in a book, *La justice sovietique.* American Federation of Labor investigators revised it the next year to include information obtained by questioning inmates and officials." This article makes no mention of Levine. And none of these sources indicate how the design firm Sigman-Ward compiled and drew its version of the map that ended up in *Plain Talk*. See Dallin and Nicolaevsky, *Forced Labor in Soviet Russia*, 60, 313; Paul Wohl, "Seven Million Soviet Slaves," *Catholic Digest*, March 1952, 44. The only available copy of *La justice* is the Italian version at the Law Division of the Library of Congress: Mora and Zwierniak, *Giustizia Sovietica.*

83. Orville Prescott, "Books of the Times," *New York Times*, August 26, 1947, 21.

84. A good example of the cross-flow between popular and government perspectives on the forced-labor issue is in Representative John E. Rankin of Mississippi speaking on April 15, 1947, about the need to make a complete break with Communist Russia, where he also inserts Max Eastman's 1947 *Reader's Digest* article "The Truth about Soviet Russia's 14,000,000 Slaves," one of the earliest exposés, along with Levine's, in American popular journalism. See Hon. John E. Rankin, "Break with Communist Russia," *Congressional Record*, April 15, 1947, Appendix: A1684–87.

85. U.S. Department of State, "NSC-68," 239–40.

86. For a critical analysis of NSC-68 and its slave language, see Newman, "NSC (National Insecurity) 68," 56–90.

87. Novick, *Holocaust in American Life*, 86.

88. Adler and Paterson, "Red Fascism," 1048.

89. See also MacDougall, "Red, Brown and Yellow Perils," 59–75.

90. Truman, "The President's Special Conference," 238. This quote is also cited in Adler and Paterson, "Red Fascism," 1046.

91. Rep. Everett Dirksen, "Red Fascism: Freedom Is in Jeopardy," *Congressional Record*, January 23, 1947, 547.

92. Adler and Paterson, "Red Fascism," 1053.

93. Carruthers, *Cold War Captives*, 267.

94. "Slavery in Russia," *Chicago Daily Tribune*, November 14, 1947, 20.

95. In the meantime, the AFL issued various manifestoes and editorials protesting Soviet labor camps at its various conferences and in several of its publications and also worked on a controversial "International Bill of Rights" for the UN to outlaw involuntary servitude and concentration camps all over the globe. Young, "'Gulag'—Slavery, Inc.," 599. See also Folder: Slave Labor 1919–1950, box 55, Vertical Files 1881–1999, RG98, GMM.

96. American Federation of Labor, *Slave Labor in Russia*, 32.

97. Young, "'Gulag'—Slavery, Inc.," 599.

98. For more on the Free Trade Union Committee and its work during this time, see folders 19–27, box 35, series 1, RG18, GMM.

99. Bartley, "The Piper Played to Us All," 585. For a comprehensive history of the so-called cultural Cold War waged by the CIA, see Saunders, *Who Paid the Piper?*. From a rhetorical perspective, see Parry-Giles, *The Rhetorical Presidency, Propaganda, and the Cold War*, 92–96.

100. Lovestone's biographer claimed that Lovestone was playing "a board game on the map of the world that made him one of the masterminds of the Cold War." Morgan, *A Covert Life: Jay Lovestone*, 144, 196–99. See also Dan Kurzman, "Lovestone's Cold War: The AFL-CIO Has Its Own CIA," *New Republic*, June 25, 1966, 17–22; Ranelagh, *The Agency: The Rise and Decline of the CIA*, 248–49; and Michael Warner, "Origins of the Congress for Cultural Freedom."

101. Folder 861.064, box 5157, U.S. Department of State Decimal Files 1950–1954, RG59, NARAII, College Park, Md.

102. The Free Trade Union Committee's correspondence with Levine can be found in folder 11, box 47, International Affairs Department, Jay Lovestone Files, 1939–1974, RG18, GMM.

103. American Federation of Labor, Free Trade Union Committee, "'Gulag'—Slavery, Inc.," Second Edition, Graphics Collection, GMM.

104. "National Affairs: Barrel No. 2," *Time*, June 23, 1947, 19.

105. In particular, see Oshinsky, *Senator Joseph McCarthy and the American Labor Movement*. For a specific study of anticommunism's effect on local unions, see Meyer, *Stalin over Wisconsin*.

106. Ronald Radosh, "Labor and Foreign Policy," *Nation*, September 8, 1969, 210; Hill, "The CIA in National and International Labor Movements," 405–7; Bernard Nossiter, "Labor and McCarthy: A Showdown Must Come," *Nation*, July 24, 1954, 70–72; "Labor and the Cold War," *Nation*, December 10, 1955, 506–10. See also Fure-Slocum, "Housing, Race, and the Cold War in a Labor City," 173.

107. Young, "'Gulag'—Slavery, Inc.," 601.

108. Wood and Fels, *The Natures of Maps*, xvi.

109. Carruthers, *Cold War Captives*, 133.

110. Levine, *Plain Talk*, 237.

111. Benedict Anderson, *Imagined Communities*, 175.

112. For a discussion of how iconography works in the internal "codes" of maps, see Wood and Fels, "Designs on Signs," 73–78.

113. Levine, *Plain Talk*, 238–39.

114. For a discussion of how parody has been used in maps of social change, see Barney, "Power Lines," 421–22.

115. Pickles, "Texts, Hermeneutics and Propaganda Maps," 217–19.

116. A representative example can be found in National Geographic Society, "World Map 1951," World-International Relations Folder, Title Collection, LOC.

117. American Federation of Labor, *Slave Labor in the Soviet World*, 16–17.

118. The George Meany Archives contain a sizable amount of these original documentary passports and testimonies from former prisoners. For example, see folders 14 and 15, box 59, International Affairs Department, Irving Brown Files 1943-1989, RG18, GMM.

119. See the caption in American Federation of Labor, Free Trade Union Committee, "'Gulag'—Slavery, Inc."

120. The pictures of the camp victims were omitted from the AFL's *Slave Labor in the Soviet World* pamphlet, and a few of the newspaper reprints would also omit the photos.

121. Levine, *Plain Talk*, 238.

122. Amishai-Maisels, *Depiction and Interpretation*, 143–45.

123. Ibid., xxxii.

124. Zelizer, *Remembering to Forget*, 155.

125. Parry-Giles, *The Rhetorical Presidency*, xx–xxi, 49–51.

126. For more on the dualities of containment and liberation, see Ivie, "Cold War Motives," 74–75; O'Gorman, "'The One Word the Kremlin Fears,'" 389–428.

127. A story from the *AFL Weekly News Reporter* from 1953 extends this Polish connection to slave labor even further, noting that the International Federation of Free Journalists had created a map showing the location of seventy-four forced labor camps in Poland and noted that "escaped Poles said the food and organization of the camps are very similar to the original Nazi system." The actual map, though, in reference, could not be found. See "Modern Slave Camps Exposed," *AFL Weekly News Reporter*, January 2, 1953, folder: Slave Labor 1951–1984, box 55, Vertical Files 1881–1999, RG98, GMM.

128. AFL, "'Gulag'—Slavery, Inc."

129. Wood and Fels, *The Natures of Maps*, xvi.

130. Pickles, "Texts, Hermeneutics and Propaganda Maps," 209–10.

131. "Workers of Free World 'Spotlight' Red Slave Labor," *Minneapolis Star*, March 7, 1951, found in folder: Slave Labor, Newspaper Reactions, 1951, box 59, International Affairs Department, Jay Lovestone Files 1939–1974, RG18, GMM.

132. "Soviet Secrecy Shrouds Widespread Chain of Slave-Labor Camps," *Christian Science Monitor*, December 13, 1951, 17; "14 Million Slaves: Soviet Union Is Vast Labor Camp," *NEA News*, June 6, 1951. For an in-depth exploration of "newspaper style" in cartography, see Monmonier, *Maps with the News*.

133. "Gromyko Given Russ Map with Slave Camps," *Los Angeles Times*, September 7, 1951, 2.

134. "Gromyko Gets Answer on Map of Slave Camps," *New York Times*, September 9, 1951, 34.

135. For example, the diplomatic mission in the Netherlands, the U.S. Air Defense Command, even the mayor of Atlanta all requested maps. See folder: Slave Labor-Maps, Requests For, 1951, box 59, International Affairs Department, Jay Lovestone Files 1939–1974, RG18, GMM.

136. Ibid.

137. Ibid.

138. Ibid.

139. AFL, *Slave Labor in the Soviet World*, 31.

140. Cull, *The Cold War and the United States Information Agency*, xv.

141. Young, "'Gulag'—Slavery, Inc.," 601.

142. Ibid., 602.

143. See especially the International Confederation of Free Trade Unions, *Stalin's Slave Camps: An Indictment of Modern Slavery* (Brussels: ICFTU, 1951), folder 15, box 8, International Affairs Department, Country Files 1945–1971, Soviet Union Printed

Materials 1942–1970, RG18, GMM. The fact about the CIA's sponsorship can be found in Iriye, *Global Community*, 53.

144. See Young, "'Gulag'—Slavery, Inc.," 601; "News in Pictures," 29.

145. Memorandum, Wolf Von Eckardt to Free Trade Union Committee, folder: Slave Labor in Russia 1949–1951, box 59, International Affairs Department, Jay Lovestone Files 1939–1974, RG18, GMM. Also, the archive indicates that the International Graphical Federation was being contracted for German translations of the map from a June 28, 1951 memo. See folder: Slave Labor-Maps, Requests For, 1951, box 59, RG18.

146. The French translation of the map and the Swiss version (published in the July 29, 1951, issue of *Die Nation*) can be found in folder: Slave Labor-Maps, Requests For, 1951, box 59, International Affairs Department, Jay Lovestone Files 1939–1974, RG18, GMM.

147. Letter, M. H. Hedges to Jay Lovestone, March 21, 1951, folder: Slave Labor-Maps, Requests For, 1951, box 59, International Affairs Department, Jay Lovestone Files 1939–1974, RG18, GMM.

148. "Soviet Map Seizure in Vienna Protested," *New York Times*, October 20, 1951, 5.

149. "Soviets Seize Map of Labor, Call It Filthy," *Washington Post*, October 22, 1951, 3.

150. "Moscow Finds an Answer," *New York Times*, October 23, 1951, 28.

151. Ibid.

152. Letter, Matthew Woll to Dean Acheson, October 19, 1951, folder: Slave Labor—Newspaper Reactions, 1951, box 59, International Affairs Department, Jay Lovestone Files 1939–1974, RG18, GMM.

153. "Russians Arrest Austrian Binder of AFL Slave Map," *AFL Weekly News*, October 19, 1951, folder: Slave Labor 1951–1984, box 55, Vertical Files 1881–1999, RG98, GMM.

154. Letter, Arnold Beichman to Matthew Woll, May 15, 1952, folder 22, box 35, International Affairs Department, Jay Lovestone Files 1939–1974, series 1, RG18, GMM.

155. See especially *U.S.S.R. Labor Camps*, Hearings before the Subcommittee to Investigate the Administration of the Internal Security Act and Other Internal Security Laws of the Committee on the Judiciary, U.S. Senate, 93rd Cong., 1st sess., February 1973. The archives reveal several references to Chinese slave labor maps, but I could not locate any copies. Press Release, Free Trade Union Committee, June 25, 1952, folder 6, box 59, International Affairs Department, Jay Lovestone Files 1939–1974, RG18, GMM.

156. See Solzhenitsyn, *Warning to the West*, 10.

157. And Isaac Don Levine himself would continue to take ownership and pride in his connection to the map; Methvin's interviews with Levine before his death in the late 1970s revealed that he "kept a copy of that map hanging on the wall of his study in his Maryland home, and often pointed it out to the stream of distinguished visitors who came to enjoy his company and hospitality and conversation." See Methvin, "Isaac Don Levine," 247.

158. Senate Subcommittee on International Finance and Monetary Policy, *Human Rights Consequences of the Proposed Trans-Siberian Natural Gas Pipeline: Hearings*

before the Subcommittee on International Finance and Monetary Policy, 97th Cong., 2nd sess., June 18, 1982.

159. "American Labor Was First to Raise Its Voice against the Slave Labor System in the USSR," *AFL-CIO Free Trade Union News* 37 (November 1982): 1, folder: Slave Labor 1951–1984, box 55, Vertical Files 1881–1999, RG98, GMM.

160. "Forced Labor Remains on the Map in the Soviet Union," *AFL-CIO Free Trade Union News* 24 (April 1968): 4–5. Later, publications like *U.S. News & World Report* were drawing their own maps of the Gulag camps, continuing to emphasize the spatiality of forced labor and circulating the importance of being able to invade Soviet borders with the power of knowledge. See "A New Report: Soviets' Record on Slave Labor," *U.S. News & World Report*, November 22, 1982, 31.

161. Chaturvedi, *The Polar Regions*, 85.

162. Wood and Fels, "Designs on Signs," 63.

CHAPTER FOUR

1. Selected copies of *Geographic Notes* and *Geographic Bulletin* from 1961 up until 1989 can be found in Records of the Geographer, U.S. Department of State, RG59, Cartographic & Architectural Records Division, National Archives and Records Administration II, College Park, Md. The U.S. Department of State hereafter is referenced by its record group, RG59, the Cartographic & Architectural Records Division is abbreviated as CARD, and the National Archives II is abbreviated as NARAII.

2. See the following *Geographic Notes* issues: GE-17, GE-28, GE-33, GE-48, GE-68, GE-72, GE-81, GE-83, GE-88, Records of the Geographer, RG59, CARD, NARAII.

3. *Geographic Notes* issue GE-152, Records of the Geographer, RG59, CARD, NARAII.

4. Hughes, "Scholars and Foreign Policy," 199–214.

5. Central Intelligence Agency, "Newly Independent States," Map, 1962, Title Collection, Geography & Map Division, Library of Congress, Washington, D.C. Hereafter, the Geography & Map Division is abbreviated as GMD and the Library of Congress as LOC. See also "Newly Independent States" Map, *Geographic Bulletin*, May 1963, Records of the Geographer, RG59, CARD, NARAII. The map was revised in July 1964 and May 1965.

6. "Profiles of Newly Independent States," *Geographic Bulletin*, May 1965, Records of the Geographer, RG59, CARD, NARAII.

7. "Status Map of International Boundaries," *International Boundary Study*, March 15, 1963, Records of the Geographer, RG59, CARD, NARAII.

8. See especially the main thesis in Westad, *The Global Cold War*.

9. Shapiro, *The Politics of Representation*, 106.

10. For a critical discussion of the etymology of the uses of "Third World" as a term and a concept, see especially Randall, "Using and Abusing the Concept of the Third World," 41–53.

11. Pletsch's critical discussion of Sauvy's use of the Third World in the context of Cold War social science is particularly important. See Pletsch, "The Three Worlds," 567–73.

12. For a historical discussion, see Mark T. Berger, "The End of the 'Third World'?," 257–75.

13. Wolf-Phillips, "Why Third World?," 105–6.

14. For contemporary histories of the Bandung conference, see the journalistic account in Richard Wright, *The Color Curtain*. See also the more academic account by George McTurnan Kahin of the influential Southeast Asia Area Studies Program at Cornell in Kahin, *The Asian-African Conference*. In addition, for an account of Bandung's relationship to U.S. policy, see Parker, "Small Victory, Missed Chance," 153–74.

15. Dirlik, "Spectres of the Third World," 132–33.

16. Beloff, "The Third World and the Conflict of Ideologies," 12–13.

17. B. R. Tomlinson's account covers a wide amount of ground succinctly on the impact of the Third World on Cold War discourse. See Tomlinson, "What Was the Third World?," 307–21.

18. Pletsch, "The Three Worlds," 572.

19. Ibid., 571.

20. Agnew, *Geopolitics*, 47.

21. Escobar, "Culture, Economics and Politics in Latin American Social Movements," 62.

22. Slater, "Geopolitical Imaginations across the North-South Divide," 642.

23. A representative example of scholarship reconfiguring the Cold War around notions of the South can be found in Saull, "Locating the Global South," 253–80.

24. A revealing contemporary account of the Third World by geographer Keith Buchanan draws on this duality between a passive and an influential Third World. Buchanan's cartogram maps on a variety of development subjects related to developing nations are particularly fascinating. See Buchanan, "Profiles of the Third World," 97–126.

25. Meinig, "Culture Blocs and Political Blocs," 220.

26. A representative example of decolonization on the map from a popular perspective can be found in Hammond Inc., "Emerging Nations," Map (Springfield, N.J.: Hammond, 1966), World-International Relations Folder, Title Collection, GMD, LOC.

27. Said, *Orientalism*, 12.

28. Bhabha, "The Other Question," 37–38.

29. For a discussion of the essentialization of North-South, particularly in terms of Cold War developmentalism, see Power, *Rethinking Development Geographies*, 95–118.

30. For a historical review on decolonization in Cold War scholarship, see Suri, "The Cold War, Decolonization, and Global Social Awakenings," 353–63.

31. See especially Painter, "Explaining U.S. Relations with the Third World," 525–48.

32. Ó Tuathail, *Critical Geopolitics*, 14–15.

33. McMaster and McMaster, "A History of Twentieth-Century American Academic Cartography," 305–21.

34. Robinson, Morrison, and Muehrcke, "Cartography, 1950–2000," 3–18.

35. Huggan, "Decolonizing the Map," 117, 119.

36. Lewis and Wigen, *The Myth of Continents*, 1.

37. For a collection of essays from a geographic standpoint exploring this sense of "mission" in American ideology, see Slater and Taylor, *The American Century*.

38. "Background of Point-4," *Congressional Digest*, January 1952, 4–11.

39. Truman, "Inaugural Address," 114.

40. Technical Cooperation Administration, U.S. Department of State, "Point 4 around the World," Map, January 1953, World-International Relations Folder, Title Collection, GMD, LOC.

41. See also U. S. Department of State, "Technical Cooperation Administration," Map, July 1952, World-International Relations Folder, Title Collection, GMD, LOC.

42. Cardwell, *NSC-68*, 115–16.

43. Ibid., 65–66.

44. Ibid., 58–59.

45. Rostow, *The Stages of Economic Growth*.

46. Pearce, "Narrative Reason and Cold War Economic Diplomacy," 399.

47. Slater, "Geopolitical Imaginations across the North-South Divide."

48. Pearce, "Narrative Reason and Cold War Economic Diplomacy," 399.

49. Dalby, *Creating the Second Cold War*, 10–11.

50. Westad, *The Global Cold War*, 5.

51. Associated Press, "Background Map: Food for Peace Program Is American Success Story," Map (New York: Associated Press, 1962); Associated Press, "Background Map: The Peace Corps—A Hit, and Growing," Map (New York: Associated Press, 1966), both in World-International Relations Folder, Title Collection, GMD, LOC.

52. John K. Wright, *Geography in the Making*, 265.

53. See, for example, Dorn, "(In)temperate Zones," 256–91; John K. Wright, *Geography in the Making*, 265.

54. See also Meade and Erickson, *Medical Geography*.

55. John K. Wright, *Geography in the Making*, 267.

56. "The Map Doctor," *Newsweek*, May 3, 1954, 84–86. See also May's contemporary memoir in May, *Siam Doctor*.

57. John K. Wright, *Geography in the Making*, 268.

58. "Map Doctor," 86.

59. Ibid. See also May's own descriptions of cultural factors in his articles accompanying the *Atlas of Disease* plates. May, "Map of the World Distribution of Poliomyelitis," 646–48; May, "Map of the World Distribution of Cholera," 272–73; May, "Map of the World Distribution of Malaria Vectors," 638–39; May, "Map of the World Distribution of Helminthiases," 98–101.

60. May, *The Ecology of Human Disease*, 29–35.

61. "The Health Problem," report by Jacques May to the Council on Foreign Relations, Study Group on Climate and Economic Development in the Tropics, March 18, 1954, folder 8: Council on Foreign Relations Study Group, box 5, series 1: Professional Records, 1943–1960, Jacques May Papers, American Geographical Society Library, University of Wisconsin-Milwaukee. Hereafter the American Geographical Society Library at UWM is referred to as AGSL.

62. Doty, *Imperial Encounters*, 131.

63. American Geographical Society, "World Distribution of Spirochetal Diseases: 1. Yaws, Pinta, Bejel," Map (New York: AGS, 1955), GMD, LOC.

64. May, "Map of the World Distribution of Cholera."

65. John K. Wright, *Geography in the Making*, 268. See also Briesemeister, "A New Oblique Equal-Area Projection," 260–61.

66. Briesemeister, "A World Equal-Area Projection for the Future," 60–63.

67. The first use of Briesemeister's projection was in H. Duncan Hall, "Zones of the International Frontier," 615–25.

68. See the discussion of the Briesemeister in Snyder, *Flattening the Earth*, 239.

69. May, "Map of the World Distribution of Helminthiases."

70. Brown and Moon, "From Siam to New York," 752.

71. Ibid.

72. See folder 7: Council on Foreign Relations Correspondence 1953–57, box 5, Jacques May Papers, AGSL.

73. Meeting Digest June 2–4, 1954, folder 6: Council on Foreign Relations Conference on Climates and Economic Development in the Tropics, box 5, Jacques May Papers, AGSL.

74. Jacques May, "The Health Problem," report, March 18, 1954, folder 8: Council on Foreign Relations, Study Group on Climate and Economic Development in the Tropics, box 5 Jacques May Papers, AGSL.

75. Ibid.

76. Minutes, Atlas of Disease Steering Committee, May 10, 1946, folder 9: Atlas of Disease Steering Committee Minutes 1944–46, box 1, Medical Geography Archives, AGSL.

77. Letter from William Adams Littell to J. Bruce Swigert, January 30, 1952; Letter from William Adams Littell to Roger Varin, March 17, 1952, folder 1: Plates 8 and 9 Correspondence 1952–54, box 3, Jacques May Papers; Letter from Jacques May to Roger Varin, June 11, 1954, folder 1: Medical Geography, Atlas of Disease Correspondence, 1948–54, box 1, Medical Geography Archives, AGSL.

78. See the exchange of correspondence with chemist Erwin Di Cyan (his consulting partner) in folder 5: Professional Correspondence Erwin Di Cyan 1954–56, box 5, Jacques May Papers, AGSL.

79. Jacques May, "American Stake in Foreign Diseases," *MD* 11 (1956): 77. See also folder 7: Related Articles and Publications 1955–59, box 3, Medical Geography Archives, AGSL.

80. "Map Doctor," 86.

81. Brown and Moon, "From Siam to New York," 759.

82. AGS application to Office of Naval Research, April 2, 1952, folder 1: Atlas of Disease Correspondence, 1948–54, box 1, Medical Geography Archives, AGSL.

83. Jacques May to Charles B. Hitchcock, January 17, 1962, folder 1: Medical Geography, Ecology of Human Disease Correspondence, 1960–62, box 2, Medical Geography Archives, AGSL.

84. Committee on Foreign Relations, *The Mutual Security Act of 1958*: *Report of the Committee on Foreign Relations on H.R. 12181*, 85th Cong., 2nd sess., 1958, S. Rep. 1627, serial 12062, chap. 3, sec. 6, 67.

85. United States Senate Committee on Government Operations, *The Status of World Health in Outline Text and Chart: Report of the Committee on Government Operations, United States Senate and Its Subcommittee on Reorganization and International Organizations*, 86th Cong., 1st sess., 1959, S. Rep. 161, serial 12149, v.

86. "Life Expectancy at Birth: Map," 18–19; "Ratio of Population to Physicians: Map," 70–71, both in U.S. Congress, *Status of World Health*.

87. "Life Expectancy at Birth: Map," 18–19; "Smallpox Endemicity, 1954–1957," 54–55, both in U.S. Congress, *Status of World Health*.

88. "Distribution of Hookworm," 44–45; "Distribution of Yellow Fever," 43; "Distribution of Leprosy," 48–49, all in U.S. Congress, *Status of World Health*.

89. U.S. Congress, *Status of World Health*, vi, viii.

90. May, "Medical Geography: Its Methods and Objectives," 9–41.

91. Campbell, *Writing Security*, 88.

92. An excellent review of the complexities of scientific internationalism and its evolution into a bipolar, Cold War–constrained discourse can be found in Manzione, "'Amusing and Amazing and Practical and Military,'" 21–55.

93. Conly, "Men Who Measure the Earth," 361–62.

94. Ibid., 362.

95. Lieber, "International Cooperation in Mapping," 71.

96. Doel, Levin, and Marker, "Extending Modern Cartography," 620–21. A fascinating biography of Marie Tharp was recently published, which sheds important light, too, on the gender imbalances of scientific work in the era, as Tharp's contributions were always subordinated (if not omitted) to her partner Heezen. See Felt, *Soundings*.

97. For a contemporary popular account of the IGY, see Chapman, *IGY: Year of Discovery*.

98. The best recent source on the Cold War implications of the IGY is in Collis and Dodds, "Assault on the Unknown," 555–73.

99. United Nations Department of Public Information, *Yearbook of the United Nations, 1947–48*, 653.

100. The history of relations between UNESCO and the United States is actually a tumultuous one, reflecting contentiousness over development and Cold War contexts; see Joyner and Lawson, "The United States and UNESCO," 37–71.

101. United Nations Department of Social Affairs, *Modern Cartography*, 1–7.

102. Ibid., 93.

103. Ibid., 22.

104. Ibid., 13.

105. Ibid., 33.

106. United Nations, *Official Report on United Nations Regional Cartographic Conference for Asia and the Far East, 1955*, 23–24.

107. U.S. Delegation to the United Nations Regional Cartographic Conference, *Official Report of the United States Delegation to the United Nations Regional Cartographic Conference for Africa*.

108. U.S. Delegation to the United Nations Regional Cartographic Conference, *Report of the United States Delegation to the Fifth United Nations Regional Cartographic Conference for Asia*, v.

109. Ibid., 58.

110. U.S. Delegation to the United Nations Regional Cartographic Conference, *Official Report of the United States Delegation to the United Nations Regional Cartographic Conference for Africa*, 20.

111. Ibid., 34.

112. Ibid., 35.

113. Ibid., 42.

114. Westad, *The Global Cold War*, 26–27.

115. For a good example, see United States Peace Corps, "Peace Corps around the World," Map (Washington, D.C.: Government Printing Office, 1967), U.S.-International Relations Folder, GMD, LOC.

116. The Cartographic & Architectural Records Division at the National Archives II in College Park houses an extensive collection of Cold War–era CIA and Defense Maps. The Geography & Map Division at the Library of Congress also has CIA maps that have been digitized. In addition, the Perry-Castaneda Library at the University of Texas has made an impressive amount of CIA and Defense maps available on its website: http://lib.utexas.edu/maps/.

117. Farish, *The Contours of America's Cold War*, 110–20. See also Wallerstein, "The Unintended Consequences of Cold War Area Studies," 195–231.

118. Glassman, "On the Borders of Southeast Asia," 788.

119. Ninkovich, *Modernity and Power*, xv.

120. Edney, *Mapping an Empire*.

121. For a contemporary "area studies" assessment of the strategic hamlets, see Osborne, *Strategic Hamlets in South Viet-Nam*. For a critical discussion, see Cullather, "'The Target Is the People,'" 29–48.

122. James C. Scott, *Seeing Like a State*, 97–98. See also Farish and Lackenbauer, "High Modernism in the Arctic," 523.

123. Westad, *The Global Cold War*, 37; Latham, *Modernization as Ideology*, 81.

124. Cloud, "American Cartographic Transformations," 277–78.

125. Ibid., 278.

126. Nixon, "Address to the Nation."

127. Miller Center, "Video: Address to the Nation."

128. Nixon, "Address to the Nation," 405–6.

129. See the critical discussion of Lacoste's work in Ó Tuathail, *Critical Geopolitics*, 160–68. "Countergeopolitics" is Ó Tuathail's term.

130. Lacoste, "An Illustration of Geographical Warfare," 2. See also Yves Lacoste, "Bombing the Dikes: A Geographer's On-the-Site Analysis," *Nation*, October 9, 1972, 298–301.

131. Meinig, "Culture Blocs and Political Blocs," 221.

132. See especially Sriskandarajah, "Long Underwear on a Line?," 236–44; Crampton, "Cartography's Defining Moment," 16–32.

133. The original projection comes from Gall, "Use of Cylindrical Projections," 119–23.

134. See Peters, *Die Neue Kartographie/The New Cartography*; Kaiser, *A New View of the World*.

135. Some of the most notable critiques of Peters include Robinson, "Arno Peters and His New Cartography," 103–11; Porter and Voxland, "Distortion in Maps," 22–30; Vujakovic, "Arno Peters' Cult of the 'New Cartography,'" 1–6. For its appropriation as development icon, see especially the Independent Commission on International Development Issues, *North-South: A Program for Survival*.

136. O'Gorman, *Spirits of the Cold War*, 161.

137. Ibid.

138. Mignolo, "The Many Faces of Cosmo-polis," 737–38.

139. Ibid., 738.

CHAPTER FIVE

1. "Weinberger Victor at Oxford Debate," *New York Times*, February 28, 1984.

2. Gaddis, "On Moral Equivalency and Cold War History," 131.

3. Weinberger, *In the Arena*, 318.

4. Weinberger, *Fighting for Peace*, 169.

5. Carolyn Milner, "Yank in Oxford—Weinberger versus Thompson in Nuclear Battle," *Cherwell—Independent Oxford University Student Newspaper*, March 2, 1984.

6. Powell, *My American Journey*, 302.

7. John Corry, "TV Reviews: Morality in Policies," *New York Times*, July 3, 1984; Milner, "Yank In Oxford."

8. A full transcript of the debate is unavailable currently, as it is accessible only to members of the Oxford Union. However, enough of the debate can be pieced together through video clips, news reports, and Thompson's own (edited) transcript in his book of essays. See E. P. Thompson, *Heavy Dancers*, 53, 55. Also see Gerald Frost, "Europe: Disarmament Crowd Gets an Unexpected Boost," *Wall Street Journal*, March 7, 1984.

9. E. P. Thompson, *Heavy Dancers*, 60; Corry, "Morality in Policies."

10. Gaddis, "On Moral Equivalency and Cold War History," 131–32; Glennon, *Constitutional Diplomacy*, 71. See also Weinberger, *In the Arena*, 321.

11. Laurence Grafstein, "Oxford Diarist: Moral Differences," *New Republic*, April 2, 1984, 42.

12. U.S. Department of Defense, *Soviet Military Power* (1981); U.S.S.R. Ministry of Defense, *Whence the Threat to Peace* (1982).

13. E. P. Thompson, *Heavy Dancers*, 54.

14. Ibid.

15. Ibid., 54, 60.

16. For a historian's take on the etymology of the so-called Second Cold War, see Halliday, *The Making of the Second Cold War*. For a critical geographer's assessment of Second Cold War discourse, see Dalby, *Creating the Second Cold War*.

17. Goodnight, "Ronald Reagan's Re-formulation of the Rhetoric of War," 396. Reagan's quote within Goodnight's is from Reagan, "Remarks to Members of the National Press Club," 1276.

18. Goodnight, "Ronald Reagan's Re-formulation of the Rhetoric of War," 396.

19. See Chernus, *Apocalypse Management*.

20. Frost, "Disarmament Crowd."

21. For an introduction to the relationship of geographers to nuclearism, see Cutter, "Geographers and Nuclear War," 135–36.

22. Der Derian, "The (S)pace of International Relations," 308.

23. "Soviet Union: Battle of the Booklets," *Time*, February 1, 1982, http://www.time.com/time/magazine/article/0,9171,954993,00.html.

24. For more on this concept, see also Dalby, "Geopolitical Discourse: The Soviet Union as Other," 421.

25. Shapiro, *Violent Cartographies*, 16.

26. On the antagonisms between discourses of disarmament and deterrence, see especially Bryan C. Taylor, "'A Hedge against the Future,'" 2.

27. Agnew, *Geopolitics*, 31.

28. Zoppo and Zorgbibe, *On Geopolitics: Classical and Nuclear*, 8.

29. Edwards, *The Closed World*, 1.

30. Farish, *The Contours of America's Cold War*, 189.

31. Mirowski, *Machine Dreams*, 15.

32. Locke, *Guidance: Principles of Guided Missile Design*, 713.

33. See both of Waldo Tobler's landmark essays on these phenomena: "Automation and Cartography," 526–34; "Analytical Cartography," 21–31.

34. For an important recent discussion of the relationship of satellites, maps, and the notion of the "interface," see Brannon, "Standardized Spaces."

35. Freedman, *Atlas of Global Strategy*, 16–17.

36. U.S. Department of State, "Security Council Rejects Soviet Complaint," 242.

37. The best historical introduction to GIS can be found in Foresman, *The History of Geographic Information Systems*. However, Cloud's critique explicitly targets such histories as diluting the military roots of GIS.

38. Cloud, "The Case of the Missing Overlays," 4.

39. McHaffie, "Manufacturing Metaphors," 119, 122.

40. Farish, *The Contours of America's Cold War*, 149.

41. The online National Security Archive at George Washington University recently collaborated with the National Archives II to digitize some of these films for public access. The films, as well as analyst William Burr's excellent commentary on them, can be accessed at the National Security Archive, "The Air Force versus Hollywood," The Nuclear Vault: Resources from the National Security Archive's Nuclear Documentation Project, 2010, http://www.gwu.edu/~nsarchiv/nukevault/ebb304/#film03 (accessed June 5, 2014).

42. United States Air Force, *SAC Command Post*, film documentary, 1964, National Security Archive, http://www.gwu.edu/~nsarchiv/nukevault/ebb304/film03 .htm (accessed June 5, 2014).

43. For an important piece on the masculine rhetoric of defense professionals, see Cohn, "Wars, Wimps, and Women: Talking Gender and Thinking War," 227–46.

44. Barnes, "Geography's Underworld," 8.

45. The military-industrial-academic complex is a term from Senator J. William Fulbright. See Fulbright, "The War and Its Effects: The Military-Industrial-Academic Complex," 171–78. The concept is historicized well in Leslie, *The Cold War and American Science*.

46. Atkinson, "Newsreels as Domestic Propaganda," 71.

47. United States Air Force, *Operation Headstart*, film documentary, 1959, National Security Archive, http://www.gwu.edu/~nsarchiv/nukevault/ebb304/film01 .htm (accessed June 5, 2014).

48. United States Air Force, *Development of the Soviet Ballistic Missile Threat*, film documentary, 1960, National Security Archive, http://www.gwu.edu/~nsarchiv/nukevault/ebb304/film02.htm (accessed June 5, 2014).

49. Farish, *The Contours of America's Cold War*, 148.

50. Dalby, *Creating the Second Cold War*, 46–47.

51. Ibid., 41. See also Ó Tuathail's critique of Dalby's concept in Ó Tuathail, *Critical Geopolitics*, 178–85.

52. Halliday, *The Making of the Second Cold War*, 16–17.

53. "Soviet Union: Battle of the Booklets." For a recent discussion of the crisis theme in rhetorical studies, particularly in reference to the Cold War, see Bostdorff, *Proclaiming the Truman Doctrine*.

54. Weinberger, preface to U.S. Department of Defense, *Soviet Military Power* (1981), 3.

55. U.S. Department of Defense, *Soviet Military Power* (1983), 3.

56. Weinberger, *In the Arena*, 307.

57. John F. Burns, "Cut in Arms Urged by Soviet General," *New York Times*, January 26, 1982.

58. U.S.S.R. Ministry of Defense, *Whence the Threat to Peace* (1982), 5.

59. Wayne Biddle, "Moscow Asserts Strategic Parity," *New York Times*, August 28, 1984.

60. "Down Madisonsky Avenue," *Economist*, February 6, 1982, 43; John F. Burns, "Soviet Booklet Attacks U.S. Arms Policy," *New York Times*, January 8, 1982.

61. "Soviet Union: Battle of the Booklets." *Whence the Threat* is also advertised in the April 1982 issue of the *Atomic Bulletin of Scientists*, 53.

62. Edwards, *Closed World*, 118.

63. Biddle, "Moscow Asserts Strategic Parity."

64. U.S. Department of Defense, *Soviet Military Power* (1981), 6–7. Future versions of the map would also document the weaponry's ballooning expansion. See U.S. Department of Defense, *Soviet Military Power* (1983), 8–9.

65. U.S. Department of Defense, *Soviet Military Power* (1981), 11.

66. U.S.S.R. Ministry of Defense, *Whence the Threat to Peace* (1982), 11.

67. Der Derian, "The (S)pace of International Relations," 305.

68. Ibid.

69. U.S. Department of Defense, *Soviet Military Power* (1981), 84–85.

70. U.S.S.R. Ministry of Defense, *Whence the Threat to Peace* (1982), 26–27, 56–57.

71. U.S.S.R. Ministry of Defense, *Whence the Threat to Peace* (1984), 3.

72. U.S.S.R. Ministry of Defense, *Whence the Threat to Peace* (1982), 68.

73. See the important discussion of nuclear cartography in the Second Cold War era in Burnett, "Propaganda Cartography," 64.

74. U.S. Department of Defense, *Soviet Military Power* (1981), 26.

75. U.S. Department of Defense, *Soviet Military Power* (1983), 28.

76. Virilio, *Speed and Politics*, 151–52.

77. Massey, *For Space*, 107.

78. Polelle, *Raising Cartographic Consciousness*, 46.

79. Der Derian, "The (S)pace of International Relations," 307.

80. Ibid., 308.

81. See also the reprint and critique of the maps in the French publication, Chaliand and Rageau, *A Strategic Atlas*, 216–17.

82. Holloway, "The Strategic Defense Initiative," 219–27. Also contributing to this line of argument is Tietge, *Flash Effect*.

83. Holloway, "The Strategic Defense Initiative," 211; Fischoff, Pidgeon, and Fiske, "Social Science and the Politics of the Arms Race," 168.

84. Weinberger, preface to U.S. Department of Defense, *Soviet Military Power* (1981), 3.

85. Shapiro, *Violent Cartographies*, 20.

86. Robert L. Scott, "Cold War and Rhetoric," 4.

87. Graebner, "Myth and Reality," 34–35.

88. Bratton, "Introduction: Logistics of Habitable Circulation," 11. Virilio's famous pronouncement, "History progresses at the speed of its weapon systems," can be found in *Speed and Politics*, 90.

89. Taylor, "Nuclear Weapons and Communication Studies: A Review Essay," 303.

90. William Bunge, "Ban the Bomb: Nuclear War Atlas," Map (Quebec: Society for Human Exploration, 1982), Geography & Map Division, Library of Congress, Washington, D.C.; Bunge, *Nuclear War Atlas*.

91. Heynen and Barnes, "Foreword to the 2011 Edition," viii.

92. MacDonald, "Geopolitics and 'The Vision Thing,'" 58. The quote within a quote is from Bunge. See Bunge, *Nuclear War Atlas*, 178.

93. Bunge, *Nuclear War Atlas*, 54; Bunge, "Ban the Bomb: Nuclear War Atlas."

94. Bunge, *Nuclear War Atlas*, xiii.

95. Bunge, "Geography Is a Field Subject," 209. See also Royal Geographic Society, "Dr W Bunge," 254.

96. A good introduction on both the history and theory of "radical geography" can be found in Peet, *Modern Geographical Thought*.

97. The phrases "future geography" and "place annihilation and post-nuclear landscapes" are borrowed from Cutter, "Geographers and Nuclear War," 135–36.

98. Black, *Maps and Politics*, 77, 78.

99. Ibid., 95.

100. Bunge, *Nuclear War Atlas*, xxvii.

101. Bunge, *Fitzgerald: Geography of a Revolution*, 137.

102. An excellent recent review of Bunge's background can be found in the new edition of *Fitzgerald*, published by the University of Georgia Press. See the foreword by Heynen and Barnes, "Foreword to the 2011 Edition," vii–xiii.

103. Bunge, *Theoretical Geography*.

104. Goodchild, "Theoretical Geography (1962): William Bunge," 14–15. See also Macmillan, "Classics in Human Geography Revisited," 74.

105. Goodchild, "Theoretical Geography (1962): William Bunge," 13.

106. Cox, "Classics in Human Geography Revisited," 71.

107. Barnes, "Geography's Underworld," 9.

108. Ibid., 13. See also Garrison's landmark work on the geography of the new highway system, considered a classic work in the field: Garrison, *Studies of Highway Development*.

109. Farish, *The Contours of America's Cold War*, 169. See Tobler, "Automation and Cartography," 526–34.

110. Bunge, *Theoretical Geography*, xiv. See also Clarke and Cloud, "On the Origins of Analytical Cartography."

111. David M. Smith, "Radical Geography," 154.

112. Ibid., 155.

113. Bunge, "Comment in Reply to Donald W. Fryer," 483.

114. Bunge, *Nuclear War Atlas*, xviii.

115. Bunge, *Fitzgerald*, 135.

116. Peet, "The Development of Radical Geography," 14; Bunge, *Nuclear War Atlas*, xx. Another source of interest is the collection of essays in Nystuen, *The Philosophy of Maps*, 31–33.

117. Pickles, *A History of Spaces*, 184.

118. Bunge, "The First Years of the Detroit Geographical Expedition," 31–39.

119. Bunge, *Fitzgerald*, xv.

120. Heyman, "Who's Going to Man the Factories," 106–7.

121. Peet, *Radical Geography*, 1–6; Bunge, "The First Years of the Detroit Geographical Expedition," 31–39. Bunge's work in this vein was part of the larger push in the geography discipline, beginning in the early 1970s, to incorporate newfound interests and insights in social conditions, Marxist economics, and urban planning. This movement was centrally concerned with the privileged place of the geographer and how the nature of political upheaval all over the world begged the geographer to be actively involved. David Harvey's 1973 landmark *Social Justice and the City*, for example, accuses fellow geographers of being apologists for the status quo and calls for a revolution in geographic thought, in his case "to design a form of spatial organization which maximizes the prospects of the least fortunate region." Harvey, *Social Justice and the City*, 118, 148–49, 110.

122. Bunge, *Nuclear War Atlas*, xx; Goodchild, "Theoretical Geography (1962): William Bunge," 14. See also Fryer, "A Geographer's Inhumanity to Man," 479; Bunge, "Geography Is a Field Subject," 209.

123. Bunge, *Nuclear War Atlas*, xi; Heynen and Barnes, "Foreword to the 2011 Edition," 9.

124. Royal Geographic Society, "Dr W Bunge," 254.

125. Christaller, *Central Places in Southern Germany*.

126. Bunge, *Nuclear War Atlas*, 28.

127. Bunge, *Fitzgerald*, xv; Bunge, "The Geography of Human Survival."

128. Bunge, "Comment in Reply," 484.

129. Barnes and Minca, "Nazi Spatial Theory," 681.

130. Ibid., 682.

131. Ibid., 678.

132. Ibid., 669.

133. Curry, "Beyond Nuclear Winter," 265.

134. Ibid., 258.

135. White, "Geographers in a Perilously Changing World," 13.

136. Openshaw and Steadman, "The Geography of Two Hypothetical Nuclear Attacks," 193.

137. Hewitt, "Place Annihilation," 259.

138. Ibid., 279, 280.

139. Bunge, "Epilogue," 290.

140. Bunge, "Geography Is a Field Subject," 209.

141. Horvath, "Machine Space," 167–88.

142. Bunge, "Epilogue," 291.

143. Much of the *NWA*'s early foundation can be found in Bunge, "The Geography of Human Survival," 275–95.

144. Bunge, *Nuclear War Atlas*, 93.

145. Bunge, "Ban the Bomb: Nuclear War Atlas."

146. Bunge, *Nuclear War Atlas*, 108.

147. Ibid.

148. Ibid., 84.

149. Ibid.

150. Boggs, "Mapping the Changing World," 119–28.

151. Virilio, *Speed and Politics*, 153.

152. Bunge, *Nuclear War Atlas*, 18–19.

153. Ibid., 21.

154. Larabee, "Ground Zero," 269. See also Farish's chapter on "Anxious Urbanism" in *The Contours of America's Cold War*.

155. Larabee, "Ground Zero," 270.

156. Bunge, *Nuclear War Atlas*, 40.

157. Bunge, "Ban the Bomb: Nuclear War Atlas"; Bunge, *Nuclear War Atlas*, 44.

158. Bunge, *Nuclear War Atlas*, 82.

159. Ibid., 147.

160. Ibid., 128.

161. Weart, *Nuclear Fear, 383.*

162. Foss and Littlejohn, *"The Day After,"* 326.

163. Holloway, "The Strategic Defense Initiative," 220–21.

164. Dragga and Voss, "Cruel Pies," 266.

165. Bunge, *Nuclear War Atlas*, 19.

166. Ibid., 132.

167. Ibid., 12.

168. Monmonier, *How to Lie with Maps*, 172.

169. Bunge, *Nuclear War Atlas,* 184.

170. Ibid., 53.

171. Ibid.

172. Ibid., 21.

173. Hogan, *The Nuclear Freeze Campaign*, 187.

174. Hogan, "Apocalyptic Pornography," 547.

175. Taylor, "Nuclear Pictures and Metapictures," 591.

176. Foss and Littlejohn, "*The Day After*," 328–29.

177. Bunge, *Nuclear War Atlas*, 84.

178. Ibid., 4.

179. For more on the use of parody in radical maps, see Barney, "Power Lines."

180. Hutcheon, *A Theory of Parody*, xiv.

181. Lynch, "Pictures of Nothing?," 18. See also McClure and McClure, "Postmodern Parody," 81–82.

182. Hariman, "Political Parody and Public Culture," 255.

183. Ibid., 254.

184. Bunge, *Nuclear War Atlas*, 10.

185. Fryer, "A Geographer's Inhumanity," 482; Whitelegg, "William Bunge," 266.

186. David M. Smith, "New Directions in Human Geography in the USSR," 21.

187. Denis Wood, *The Power of Maps*, 132.

188. Cutter, "Geographers and Nuclear War," 138.

189. The quintessential example of this is in the Peters controversy. See chapter 4, n. 132, for a brief discussion and list of contemporary sources.

190. Bunge, "Geography Is a Field Subject," 209.

191. Denis Wood, *The Power of Maps*, 115.

192. Barton and Barton, "Ideology and the Map," 62.

193. Bunge, *Fitzgerald*, 137.

194. Pickles, *A History of Spaces*, 184.

195. Denis Wood, *The Power of Maps*, 189.

196. Mitchell, "Japan-U.S. Missile Defense Collaboration," 99.

197. Fischoff, Pidgeon, and Fiske, "Social Science and Politics," 167.

198. Brummett, "Perfection and the Bomb," 85. Brummett, of course, comes to this discussion through the works of Kenneth Burke.

199. See Derrida, "No Apocalypse, Not Now," 23–24.

200. Curry, "Beyond Nuclear Winter," 246.

201. Der Derian, "The (S)pace of International Relations," 306.

202. E. P. Thompson, *Heavy Dancers*, 60.

CONCLUSION

1. Vaclav Havel, "The End of the Modern Era," *New York Times*, March 1, 1992.

2. Ibid.

3. Ibid.

4. "Excerpts from Pentagon's Plan: 'Prevent the Re-emergence of a New Rival,'" *New York Times*, March 8, 1992.

5. Lewis H. Lapham, "Apes and Butterflies," *Harper's*, May 1992, 11, 12.

6. Shapiro and Alker, *Challenging Boundaries*, xx.

7. Ferguson, "Unmapping and Remapping the World," 165, 179.

8. Cosgrove, *Geography and Vision*, 167–68.

9. Ibid.

10. Thomas P. M. Barnett, "The Pentagon's New Map," *Esquire*, March 2003, 174–79, 227–28.

11. Barnett, "The Pentagon's New Map," 174.

12. William McNulty, "The Pentagon's New Map," Map, in Barnett, *The Pentagon's New Map*.

13. See Barnett, *The Pentagon's New Map*; and Barnett, *Glo*blog*ization* (blog), http://thomaspmbarnett.com/weblog/ (accessed June 5, 2014).

14. Dalby, "Imperialism, Domination, Culture," 429. See also Dalby, "The Pentagon's New Imperial Cartography," 295–308.

15. Barnett, "The Pentagon's New Map," 229.

16. See Paul Eckert, "Google Earth Helps Put North Korea Gulag System on Map," Reuters, January 9, 2013, http://www.reuters.com/article/2013/01/09/korea-north-google-idUSL1E9C7CYD20130109 (accessed June 5, 2014); Julian Ryall, "Google Earth Exposes North Korea's Secret Prison Camps," *Telegraph*, January 25, 2013, http://www.telegraph.co.uk/news/worldnews/asia/northkorea/9826125/Google-Earth-exposes-North-Koreas-secret-prison-camps.html (accessed June 5, 2014); Chico Harlan, "Google Releases Detailed Map of North Korea, Gulags and All," *Washington Post*, January 28, 2013, http://www.washingtonpost.com/blogs/worldviews/wp/2013/01/28/google-releases-detailed-map-of-north-korea-gulags-and-all/ (accessed June 5, 2014).

17. In addition to Google Earth's application, the U.S. Committee for Human Rights has contracted with the company DigitalGlobe to track the development of the prison camps. See especially Hawk, *The Hidden Gulag*.

18. See especially Evan Ramstad, "Gulags, Nukes, and a Water Slide: Citizen Spies Lift North Korea's Veil," *Wall Street Journal*, May 22, 2009, http://online.wsj.com/article/SB124295017403345489.html (accessed June 5, 2014).

19. An important early debate on this can be found in U.S. Congress, *The Hidden Gulag: Putting Human Rights on the North Korea Policy Agenda*.

20. See especially, Michael R. Gordon, "2 Americans Are Advised Not to Visit North Korea," *New York Times*, January 3, 2013, http://www.nytimes.com/2013/01/04/world/asia/bill-richardson-and-googles-eric-schmidt-are-advised-not-to-visit-north-korea.html?_r=0 (accessed June 5, 2014); Drew Guarini, "Google Earth Is Key to Revealing North Korea's Prison Camp System, Activists Say," *Huffington Post*, January 22, 2013, http://www.huffingtonpost.com/2013/01/22/google-north-korea-prison-camp_n_2526539.html (accessed June 5, 2014).

21. For some important recent scholarship on the cartographic implications of Google Earth technology on global politics, see Mittman, "Inverting the Panopticon"; Kumar, "Google Earth and the Nation State"; and Kingsbury and Jones, "Walter Benjamin's Dionysian Adventures."

22. For representative explorations of these new functions of cartographic technologies, see Harris and Weiner, "Empowerment, Marginalization, and 'Community-Integrated' GIS," 67–76; Miller, "A Beast in the Field," 187–99.

23. Some recent work by geographers, cartographers, and communication critics have been emphasizing the importance of how digital maps can change and enhance local communities from the ground up—the antithesis of the top-down state-centered approach. Eloquent essays on geography's and cartography's integration into the digital humanities can be found in Dear et al., *GeoHumanities*. In Chicago, Daniel

Makagon has been engaging in "sonic mapping," combining cartography with audio documentaries, where neighborhood inhabitants tell their own stories of the urban landscape and take listeners along a sonic journey as they walk through parts of the city with their map, allowing citizens and tourists to piece together and collaborate in an alternative story of Chicago and participate together in urban life, in ways that would resonate with the immersive approach of William Bunge. Jeff Rice takes a fragmentary approach to contemporary Detroit in some complementary ways and works through exciting new methodologies of "networking" city spaces together through critical invention. On an international level, Joan Faber McAlister recently studied how maps of shack settlements in South African Townships, commissioned out of government attempts to resettle the inhabitants, have been marked by repressive racial reordering that "marginalize the lived practices that constitute the places that more than 2 million black citizens currently call home." In response, McAlister has been working with shack settlers to draw their own maps as resistance techniques to resettlement plans. Such projects evidence the potential of today's space-minded practitioners and scholars to challenge the still-powerful Cold War frameworks of abstract space. See Makagon, "Mapping the City through Sound"; Rice, *Digital Detroit*; McAlister, "Going Off the Map."

24. Shapiro and Alker, *Challenging Boundaries*, xx.

25. Mitchell, "'The Stratified Record,'" 77.

26. Ayers, "Mapping Time," 223.

27. Ferguson, "Unmapping and Remapping the World," 166–67.

28. Ibid., 167.

Bibliography

ARCHIVE COLLECTIONS

American Federation of Labor. George F. Meany Memorial Archives, Silver Spring, Md.

Associated Press. Background Maps Series, 1947–68. Geography & Map Division. Library of Congress, Washington, D.C.

Perry Castañeda Library. Digital Map Archive. University of Texas, Austin. http://lib.utexas.edu/maps/.

Richard Edes Harrison Collection. Geography & Map Division. Library of Congress, Washington, D.C.

Jacques May Papers. American Geographical Society Library. University of Wisconsin–Milwaukee.

Medical Geography Department Archives. American Geographical Society Library. University of Wisconsin–Milwaukee.

Nuclear Vault. National Security Archive. The George Washington University, Washington, D.C. http://www.gwu.edu/~nsarchiv/nukevault/index.htm.

Title Collection, 1940–1968. U.S. and World-International Relations Folders. Geography & Map Division. Library of Congress, Washington, D.C.

U.S. Department of State. Records of the Geographer. Cartographic & Architectural Records. National Archives II, College Park, Md.

U.S. Information Agency. Special Media Archives Division. National Archives II, College Park, Md.

NEWSPAPERS AND MAGAZINES

American
Chicago Daily Tribune
Collier's
Congressional Digest
Esquire
Fortune
Geographical Magazine
Guardian
Harper's
In These Times
Los Angeles Times
Nation
National
National Geographic
New Internationalist
New Republic
Newsweek
New Yorker
New York Sun
New York Times
Plain Talk
Saturday Review of Literature
Scientific American
Scientific Monthly
Time
UN Secretariat News
U.S. News & World Report
Wall Street Journal
Washington Post

GOVERNMENT DOCUMENTS AND PUBLICATIONS

Boggs, S. W. "Global Relations of the United States." *Department of State Bulletin* 30 (1954): 903–12.

———. "Mapping Some of the Effects of Science and Technology on Human Relations." *Department of State Bulletin* 12 (1945): 183–88.

———. "This Hemisphere." *Department of State Bulletin* 12 (1945): 845–50.

Central Intelligence Agency. "The Birth of Central Intelligence." CIA Historical Review Program, September 22, 1993. https://www.cia.gov/library/center-for-the-study-of-intelligence/kent-csi/vol10no2/html/v10i2a01p_0001.htm.

Fischer, Benjamin B., ed. *At Cold War's End: US Intelligence on the Soviet Union and Eastern Europe, 1989–1991.* Washington, D.C.: Central Intelligence Agency, 1999.

Kennan, George. "PPS/23: Review of Current Trends—U.S. Foreign Policy." U.S. Department of State. *Foreign Relations of the United States: 1948.* Vol. 1, 510–29. Washington, D.C.: Government Printing Office, 1948.

Nixon, Richard M. "Address to the Nation on the Situation in Southeast Asia, April 30, 1970." *Public Papers of the Presidents of the United States, Richard M. Nixon, 1970,* 405–10. Washington, D.C.: Government Printing Office, 1971.

Pearcy, G. Etzel. "Geopolitics and Foreign Relations." *Department of State Bulletin* 50 (1964): 318–30.

Reagan, Ronald. "Remarks to Members of the National Press Club on Arms Reduction and Nuclear Weapons, November 18, 1981." *Weekly Compilation of Presidential Documents* 17 (November 23, 1981): 1273–78.

Truman, Harry S. "Inaugural Address: January 20, 1949." *Public Papers of the Presidents of the United States, Harry S. Truman, 1949,* 112–16. Washington, D.C.: Government Printing Office, 1964.

———. "The President's Special Conference with the Association of Radio News Analysts." *Public Papers of the Presidents of the United States, Harry S. Truman, 1947,* 238–41. Washington, D.C.: Government Printing Office, 1963.

U.S. Aeronautical Chart and Information Center. *Geodesy for the Layman.* St. Louis, Mo.: United States Air Force, 1962.

U.S. Congress. *Congressional Record.* 1943–52.

———. House. Committee on Foreign Affairs. *Mutual Security Act of 1959: Report of the Committee on Foreign Affairs on H.R. 7500.* 86th Cong., 1st sess., 1959. H. Rep. 440. Serial 12160.

———. House. Committee on Foreign Affairs. *Mutual Security Act of 1960: Report of the Committee on Foreign Affairs on H.R. 11510.* 86th Cong., 2nd sess., 1960. H. Rep. 1464. Serial 12244.

———. House. Committee on Foreign Affairs. *Mutual Security Act of 1961: Report of the Committee on Foreign Affairs on H.R. 8400.* 87th Cong., 1st sess., 1961. H. Rep 851. Serial 12341.

———. House. Committee on Un-American Activities. *Soviet Total War.* 85th Cong., 1st sess., 1956. H. Doc. 227. Serial 12017.

———. Senate. Committee on Foreign Relations. *The Mutual Security Act of 1958: Report of the Committee on Foreign Relations on H.R. 12181.* 85th Cong., 2nd sess., 1958. S. Rep. 1627. Serial 12062.

———. Senate. Committee on Foreign Relations. *The Mutual Security Act of 1952: Report of the Committee on Foreign Relations on S.3086.* 82nd Cong., 2nd sess., 1952. S. Rep. 1490. Serial 11567.

———. Senate. Committee on Foreign Relations. *Studies on Review of United Nations Charter.* 83rd Cong., 2nd sess., 1954. S. Doc. 164. Serial 11760.

———. Senate. Committee on Foreign Relations. *The Hidden Gulag: Putting Human Rights on the North Korea Policy Agenda—Hearings before the Subcommittee on East Asian Affairs.* 108th Cong., 1st sess., November 4, 2003.

———. Senate. Committee on Government Operations. *The Status of World Health in Outline Text and Chart.* 86th Cong., 1st sess., 1959. S. Rep. 161. Serial 12149.

———. Senate. Committee on the Judiciary. *U.S.S.R. Labor Camps: Hearings before the Subcommittee to Investigate the Administration of the Internal Security Act and Other Internal Security Laws.* 93rd Cong., 1st sess., February 1, 1973.

U.S. Delegation to the United Nations Regional Cartographic Conference. *Official Report of the United States Delegation to the United Nations Regional Cartographic Conference for Africa, Nairobi, Kenya, July 1–13, 1963.* Prepared by H. Arnold Karo. Washington, D.C.: Government Printing Office, 1963.

———. *Report of the United States Delegation to the Fifth United Nations Regional Cartographic Conference for Asia and the Far East, Canberra Australia, March 8–22, 1967.* Prepared by G. Etzel Pearcy. Washington, D.C.: Government Printing Office, 1967.

U.S. Department of Defense. *Soviet Military Power.* Washington, D.C.: Government Printing Office, 1981.

———. *Soviet Military Power.* Rev. ed. Washington, D.C.: Government Printing Office, 1983.

U.S. Department of State. *Energy Resources of the World.* Washington, D.C.: Government Printing Office, 1949.

———. *Geographic Bulletin*, 1965–83. Records of the Geographer. Cartographic & Architectural Records. National Archives II, College Park, Md.

———. *Geographic Notes*, 1964–88. Records of the Geographer. Cartographic & Architectural Records. National Archives II, College Park, Md.

———. "NSC-68: A Report to the President Pursuant to the President's Directive of January 31, 1950." *Foreign Relations of the United States: 1950.* 1:234–92. Washington, D.C.: Government Printing Office, 1950.

———. "Security Council Rejects Soviet Complaint against U.S. in RB-47 Incident; U.S.S.R. Casts 88th and 89th Vetoes." *Department of State Bulletin* 43 (1960): 235–44.

U.S. Department of the Army. *U.S.S.R.: Analytical Survey of Literature 1976 Edition.* Washington, D.C.: Government Printing Office, 1976.

BOOKS, BOOK CHAPTERS, JOURNAL ARTICLES, FILMS, AND WEBSITES

Adler, Les K., and Thomas G. Paterson. "Red Fascism: The Merger of Nazi Germany and Soviet Russia in the American Image of Totalitarianism, 1930's–1950's." *American Historical Review* 75 (1970): 1046–64.

Ager, John. "Maps and Propaganda." *Bulletin for the Society of University Cartographers* 11 (1979): 1–15.

Agnew, John. *Geopolitics: Re-envisioning World Politics*. 2nd ed. New York: Routledge, 2003.

Agnew, John, Katharyne Mitchell, and Gearóid Ó Tuathail, eds. *A Companion to Political Geography*. Malden, Mass.: Blackwell, 2003.

Alexander, Lewis. "Samuel Whittemore Boggs: An Appreciation." *Annals of the Association of American Geographers* 48 (1958): 237–43.

American Congress on Surveying and Mapping. "Obituaries: Samuel Whittemore Boggs." *Surveying and Mapping* 14 (1954): 517.

American Federation of Labor. *Slave Labor in Russia: The Case Presented by the American Federation of Labor to the United Nations*. Washington, D.C.: American Federation of Labor, 1949.

———. *Slave Labor in the Soviet World*. New York: Free Trade Union Committee, 1951.

Amishai-Maisels, Ziva. *Depiction and Interpretation: The Influence of the Holocaust on the Visual Arts*. Oxford: Pergamon Press, 1993.

Anderson, Benedict. *Imagined Communities: Reflections on the Origins and Spread of Nationalism*. Rev. ed. London: Verso, 1991.

Anderson, James. "Ideology in Geography: An Introduction." *Antipode* 5 (1973): 1–6.

Arendt, Hannah. *The Human Condition*. Garden City, N.Y.: Doubleday, 1959.

Ashley, Richard K. "The Geopolitics of Geopolitical Space: Toward a Critical Social Theory of International Politics." *Alternatives* 12 (1987): 403–34.

———. "The Poverty of Neorealism." *International Organization* 38 (1984): 225–86.

Ashley, Richard K., and R. B. J. Walker. "Speaking the Language of Exile: Dissident Thought in International Studies." *International Studies Quarterly* 34 (1990): 259–68.

Atkinson, Nathan S. "Newsreels as Domestic Propaganda: Visual Rhetoric at the Dawn of the Cold War." *Rhetoric & Public Affairs* 14 (2011): 69–100.

Ayers, Edward L. "Mapping Time." In *GeoHumanities: Art, History, Text at the Edge of Place*, edited by Michael Dear, Jim Ketchum, Sarah Luria, and Douglas Richardson, 215–25. London: Routledge, 2011.

Baar, Edward J. "The Manipulation of Projections for World Maps." *Geographical Review* 37 (1947): 112–13.

Bach, Jonathan, and Susanne Peters. "The New Spirit of German Geopolitics." *Geopolitics* 7 (Winter 2002): 1–18.

Baker, Anne. *Heartless Immensity: Literature, Culture, and Geography in Antebellum America*. Ann Arbor: University of Michigan Press, 2006.

Bakhtin, M. M. *The Dialogic Imagination: Four Essays*. Translated by Caryl Emerson and Michael Holquist. Austin: University of Texas Press, 1981.

Barnes, Trevor J. "Geographical Intelligence: American Geographers and Research and Analysis in the Office of Strategic Service, 1941–1945." *Journal of Historical Geography* 32 (2006): 149–68.

———. "Geography's Underworld: The Military-Industrial Complex, Mathematical Modeling and the Quantitative Revolution." *Geoforum* 39 (2008): 3–16.

———. "Obituaries, War, 'Corporeal Remains,' and Life: History and Philosophy of Geography, 2007–2008." *Progress in Human Geography* 33 (2009): 693–701.

Barnes, Trevor J., and James S. Duncan, eds. *Writing Worlds: Discourse, Text & Metaphor in the Representation of Landscape.* London: Routledge, 1992.

Barnes, Trevor J., and Matthew Farish. "Between Regions: Science, Militarism, and American Geography from World War to Cold War." *Annals of the Association of American Geographers* 96 (2006): 807–26.

Barnes, Trevor J., and Derek Gregory, eds. *Reading Human Geography: The Poetics and Politics of Inquiry.* London: Arnold, 1997.

Barnes, Trevor J., and Claudio Minca. "Nazi Spatial Theory: The Dark Geographies of Carl Schmitt and Walter Christaller." *Annals of the Association of American Geographers* 103 (2013): 669–87.

Barnett, Thomas P. M. *Globlogization* (blog). http://thomaspmbarnett.com/weblog/.

———. *The Pentagon's New Map.* New York: G. P. Putnam's Sons, 2004.

Barney, Timothy. "Power Lines: The Rhetoric of Maps as Social Change in the Post-Cold War Landscape." *Quarterly Journal of Speech* 95 (2009): 412–34.

Bartley, Russell H. "The Piper Played to Us All: Orchestrating the Cultural Cold War in the USA, Europe, and Latin America." *International Journal of Politics, Culture, and Society* 14 (2001): 571–619.

Barton, Ben F., and Marthalee S. Barton. "Ideology and the Map: Toward a Postmodern Visual Design Practice." In *Professional Communication: The Social Perspective*, edited by Nancy Roundy Blyler and Charlotte Thralls, 49–78. Newbury Park, Calif.: Sage, 1993.

Baughman, James L. *Henry R. Luce and the Rise of the American News Media.* Boston: Twayne, 1987.

Beer, Francis A., and Robert Hariman. "Realism and Rhetoric in International Relations." In *Post-Realism: The Rhetorical Turn in International Relations*, edited by Francis A. Beer and Robert Hariman, 1–30. East Lansing: Michigan State University Press, 1996.

———. "Strategic Intelligence and Discursive Realities." In *Post-Realism: The Rhetorical Turn in International Relations*, edited by Francis A. Beer and Robert Hariman, 387–414. East Lansing: Michigan State University Press, 1996.

Beloff, Max. "The Third World and the Conflict of Ideologies." In *The Third World: Premises of U.S. Policy*, edited by W. Scott Thompson, 11–23. San Francisco: Institute for Contemporary Studies, 1978.

Berger, John. *Ways of Seeing.* London: Penguin, 1972.

Berger, Mark T. "The End of the 'Third World'?" *Third World Quarterly* 15 (1994): 257–75.

Bhabha, Homi. "The Other Question." In *Contemporary Postcolonial Theory*, edited by Padmini Mongia, 37–54. London: Arnold, 1996.

Biggs, Michael. "Putting the State on the Map: Cartography, Territory, and European State Formation." *Comparative Studies in Society and History* 41 (1999): 374–405.

Black, Jeremy. "Historical Atlases." *Historical Journal* 37 (1994): 643–67.

———. *Maps and Politics.* Chicago: University of Chicago Press, 1997.

Bocking, Stephen. "A Disciplined Geography: Aviation, Science, and the Cold War in Northern Canada, 1945–1960." *Technology & Culture* 50 (2009): 265–90.

Boggs, S. W. "An Atlas of Ignorance: A Needed Stimulus to Honest Thinking and Hard Work." *Proceedings of the American Philosophical Society* 93 (1949): 253–58.

———. "Geographic and Other Scientific Techniques for Political Science." *American Political Science Review* 42 (1948): 223–28.

———. *International Boundaries—A Study of Boundary Functions and Problems*. New York: Columbia University Press, 1940.

———. "A New Equal-Area Projection for World Maps." *Geographical Journal* 73 (1929): 241–45.

———. "Mapping the Changing World: Suggested Developments in Maps." *Annals of the Association of American Geographers* 31 (1941): 119–28.

———. "National Claims in Adjacent Seas." *Geographical Review* 41 (1951): 185–209.

———. "This Hemisphere." *Journal of Geography* 44 (1945): 345–55.

Borges, Jorge Luis. *A Universal History of Infamy*. Translated by Norman Thomas di Giovanni. New York: E. P. Dutton, 1972.

Boria, Edoardo. "Geopolitical Maps: A Sketch History of a Neglected Trend in Cartography." *Geopolitics* 13 (2008): 278–308.

Bostdorff, Denise. *Proclaiming the Truman Doctrine*. College Station: Texas A&M University Press, 2008.

Bowman, Isaiah. "The Geographical Situation of the United States in Relation to World Policies." *Geographical Journal* 112 (1948): 129–42.

———. "Geography vs. Geopolitics." *Geographical Review* 32 (1942): 646–58.

Brandt Commission. *Common Crisis: North-South, Co-operation for World Recovery*. Cambridge, Mass.: MIT Press, 1983.

Brannon, Monica M. "Standardized Spaces: Satellite Imagery in the Age of Big Data." *Configurations* 21 (2013): 271–99.

Bratton, Benjamin H. "Introduction: Logistics of Habitable Circulation." In *Speed and Politics*, by Paul Virilio, 7–25. Los Angeles: Semiotext(e), 2006.

Briesemeister, William. "A New Oblique Equal-Area Projection." *Geographical Review* 43 (1953): 260–61.

———. "A World Equal-Area Projection for the Future: The Selection of the Most Suitable Equal-Area Projection for the Purposes of Plotting World Wide Statistics in This Present Day of Super Speed, Jet Planes and Intercontinental Missiles." *Nachrichten aus dem Karten-und Vermessungswesen*, ser. 2 (1959): 60–63.

British Pathé. "U.S. Declares Reds Pushed RB-47 Off Course." New York: News of the Day, 1960. Newsreel, 2 min. http://www.britishpathe.com/record.php?id=67796.

Brown, Tim, and Graham Moon. "From Siam to New York: Jacques May and the 'Foundation' of Medical Geography." *Journal of Historical Geography* 30 (2004): 747–63.

Bruckner, Martin, ed. *Early American Cartographies*. Chapel Hill: University of North Carolina Press, 2010.

———. *The Geographic Revolution in Early America: Maps, Literacy, & National Identity*. Chapel Hill: University of North Carolina Press, 2006.

Bruckner, Martin, and Hsuan L. Hsu, eds. *American Literary Geographies: Spatial Practice and Cultural Production 1500-1900*. Newark: University of Delaware Press, 2007.

Brugioni, Dino A. *Eyes in the Sky: Eisenhower, the CIA, and Cold War Aerial Espionage*. Annapolis, Md.: Naval Institute Press, 2010.

Brummett, Barry. "Perfection and the Bomb: Nuclear Weapons, Teleology, and Motives." *Journal of Communication* 39 (1989): 85–95.

Brunn, Stanley D. "Geopolitics in a Shrinking World: A Political Geography of the Twenty-First Century." In *Political Studies from a Spatial Perspective*, edited by A. D. Burnett and P. J. Taylor, 131–56. Chichester: John Wiley & Sons, 1981.

Bryan, G. S. Review of *Look at the World: The* Fortune *Atlas for World Strategy*, by Richard Edes Harrison. *Scientific Monthly* 59 (1944): 475–76.

Brzezinski, Zbigniew. *In Quest of National Security*. Edited by Marin Strmecki. Boulder, Colo.: Westview Press, 1988.

Buchanan, Keith. "Profiles of the Third World." *Pacific Viewpoint* 5 (1964): 97–126.

Bunge, William. "Classics in Human Geography Revisited—Author's Response: Geography the Innocent Science." *Progress in Human Geography* 25 (2001): 75–76.

———. "Comment in Reply to Donald W. Fryer." *Annals of the Association of American Geographers* 64 (1974): 482–84.

———. "Epilogue: Our Planet Is Big Enough for Peace but Too Small for War." In *A World in Crisis? Geographical Perspectives*, edited by R. J. Johnston and P. J. Taylor, 289–91. Oxford: Blackwell, 1986.

———. "The First Years of the Detroit Geographical Expedition: A Personal Report." In *Radical Geography: Alternative Viewpoints on Contemporary Social Issues*, edited by Richard Peet, 31–39. Chicago: Maaroufa Press, 1977.

———. *Fitzgerald: Geography of a Revolution*. Cambridge, Mass.: Schenkman Publishing, 1971.

———. "Fred K. Schaefer and the Science of Geography." *Annals of the Association of American Geographers* 69 (1979): 128–32.

———. "The Geography." *Professional Geographer* 25 (1973): 331–37.

———. "Geography Is a Field Subject." *Area* 15 (1983): 208–10.

———. "The Geography of Human Survival." *Annals of the Association of American Geographers* 63 (1973): 275–95.

———. "Less Free? Letter to the Editor." *American Association of University Professors Bulletin* 49 (1963): 382.

———. *Nuclear War Atlas*. New York: Blackwell, 1988.

———. *Theoretical Geography*. Lund Studies in Geography, Series C General and Mathematical Geography no. 1. Lund: C. W. K Gleerup Publishers, 1966.

Burnett, Alan. "Propaganda Cartography." In *The Geography of Peace and War*, edited by David Pepper and Alan Jenkins, 60–89. New York: Blackwell, 1985.

Burnett, D. Graham. *Masters of All They Surveyed: Exploration, Geography, and a British El Dorado*. Chicago: University of Chicago Press, 2000.

Campbell, David. *Writing Security: United States Foreign Policy and the Politics of Identity*. Minneapolis: University of Minnesota Press, 1992.

Caputi, Jane. "Nuclear Visions." *American Quarterly* 47 (1995): 165–75.

Cardwell, Curt. *NSC-68 and the Political Economy of the Early Cold War*. New York: Cambridge University Press, 2011.

Carruthers, Susan. *Cold War Captives: Imprisonment, Escape, and Brainwashing*. Berkeley: University of California Press, 2009.

Casey, Edward S. *Getting Back into Place: Toward a Renewed Understanding of the Place-World*. 2nd ed. Bloomington: Indiana University Press, 2009.

Chaliand, Gerard, and Jean-Pierre Rageau. *A Strategic Atlas: Comparative Geopolitics of the World's Powers*. Translated by Tony Berrett. 2nd ed. New York: Harper & Row, 1985.

Chambers, Whittaker. *Witness*. Washington, D.C.: Regnery Gateway, 1952.

Chapman, Sydney. *IGY: Year of Discovery*. Ann Arbor: University of Michigan Press, 1959.

Chaturvedi, Sanjay. *The Polar Regions: A Political Geography*. Chichester: John Wiley & Sons, 1996.

Chernus, Ira. *Apocalypse Management: Eisenhower and the Discourse of National Insecurity*. Stanford, Calif.: Stanford University Press, 2008.

———. *Eisenhower's Atoms for Peace*. College Station: Texas A&M University Press, 2002.

Chilton, Paul A. "The Meaning of *Security*." In *Post-Realism: The Rhetorical Turn in International Relations*, edited by Francis A. Beer and Robert Hariman, 193–216. East Lansing: Michigan State University Press, 1996.

Chovitz, Bernard, and Irene Fischer. "A New Determination of the Figure of the Earth from Arcs." *Transactions of the American Geophysical Union* 37 (1956): 534–45.

Christaller, Walter. *Central Places in Southern Germany*. Translated by Carlisle W. Baskin. Englewood Cliffs, N.J.: Prentice Hall, 1966.

Clark, Gordon L., and Michael Dear. *The Future of Radical Geography*. Urban Planning Policy Analysis and Administration, Department of City and Regional Planning, Discussion Paper D78-11. Cambridge, Mass.: Harvard University, 1978.

Clarke, Keith, and John G. Cloud. "On the Origins of Analytical Cartography." *Geographic Information Science* 27 (2000): 195–204.

Cloud, John. "American Cartographic Transformations during the Cold War." *Cartography and Geographic Information Science* 29 (2002): 261–82.

———. "The Case of the Missing Overlays: A Strategy for the History of the Digital Transition in Cartography." AutoCarto Proceedings of the annual convention of the Cartography and Geographic Information Society, 2005. http://www.cartogis.org/publications/proceedings.php?year=2005.

———. "Crossing the Olentangy River: The Figure of the Earth and the Military-Industrial-Academic-Complex, 1947–1972." *Studies in the History and Philosophy of Modern Physics* 31 (2000): 371–404.

———. "Hidden in Plain Sight: CORONA and the Clandestine Geography of the Cold War." PhD diss., University of California, Santa Barbara, 1999.

———. "Hidden in Plain Sight: The CORONA Reconnaissance Satellite Programme and Clandestine Cold War Science." *Annals of Science* 58 (2001): 203–9.

———. "Imaging the World in a Barrel: CORONA and the Clandestine Convergence of the Earth Sciences." *Social Studies of Science* 31 (2001): 231–51.

Cohen, Saul B. *Geography and Politics in a World Divided*. 2nd ed. New York: Oxford University Press, 1973.

———. "Geopolitical Change in Post-Cold War Era." *Annals of the Association of American Geographers* 81 (1991): 551–80.

———. "A New Map of Global Geopolitical Equilibrium: A Developmental Approach." *Political Geography Quarterly* 1 (1982): 223–41.

Cohn, Carol. "Wars, Wimps, and Women: Talking Gender and Thinking War." In *Gendering War Talk*, edited by Miriam Cooke and Angela Woollacott, 227–46. Princeton, N.J.: Princeton University Press, 1993.

Collier, Peter. "The Impact on Topographic Mapping of Developments in Land and Air Survey, 1900–1939." *Cartography and Geographic Information Science* 29 (2002): 155–74.

Collis, Christy, and Klaus Dodds. "Assault on the Unknown: The Historical and Political Geographies of the International Geophysical Year (1957–58)." *Journal of Historical Geography* 34 (2008): 555–73.

Committee of Soviet Scientists for Peace against the Nuclear Threat. *Space-Strike Arms and International Security: Report of the Committee of Soviet Scientists for Peace, against the Nuclear Threat.* Moscow: Novosti Press Agency Publishing, 1985.

Connery, Christopher L. "Pacific Rim Discourse: The U.S. Global Imaginary in the Late Cold War Years." *Boundary 2* 21 (1994): 30–56.

Consolidated Vultee Aircraft Corporation. *Maps . . . And How to Understand Them.* 3rd ed. New York: Consolidated Vultee Aircraft Corporation, 1943.

Cook, Karen Severud. "The Historical Role of Photomechanical Techniques in Map Production." *Cartography and Geographic Information Science* 29 (2002): 137–54.

Cooper, John C. *The Right to Fly.* New York: Henry Holt, 1947.

Cosgrove, Denis E. *Apollo's Eye: A Cartographic Genealogy of the Earth in the Western Imagination.* Baltimore: Johns Hopkins University Press, 2001.

———. "Book Review Essay: Epistemology, Geography, and Cartography: Matthew Edney on Brian Harley's Cartographic Theories." *Annals of the Association of American Geographers* 97 (2007): 202–9.

———. "Contested Global Visions: One-World, Whole-Earth, and the Apollo Space Photographs." *Annals of the Association of American Geographers* 84 (1994): 270–94.

———. *Geography and Vision: Seeing, Imagining and Representing the World.* New York: Palgrave Macmillan, 2008.

Cosgrove, Denis E., and Veronica della Dora. "Mapping Global War: Los Angeles, the Pacific, and Charles Owens's Pictorial Cartography." *Annals of the Association of American Geographers* 95 (2005): 373–90.

Costigliola, Frank. " 'Unceasing Pressure for Penetration': Gender, Pathology, and Emotion in George Kennan's Formulation of the Cold War." *Journal of American History* 83 (1997): 1309–39.

Cox, Kevin R. "Classics in Human Geography Revisited—Commentary 1." *Progress in Human Geography* 25 (2001): 71–73.

Crampton, Jeremy W. "Cartography's Defining Moment: The Peters Projection Controversy, 1974–1990." *Cartographica* 31 (1994): 16–32.

———. *Mapping: A Critical Introduction to Cartography and GIS.* Malden, Mass.: Wiley-Blackwell, 2010.

———. "Maps as Social Constructions: Power, Communication and Visualization." *Progress in Human Geography* 25 (2001): 235–52.

———. "Reflections on Arno Peters (1916–2002)." *Cartographic Journal* 40 (2003): 55–56.Crampton, Jeremy W., and Stuart Elden, eds. *Space, Knowledge, and Power: Foucault and Geography*. London: Ashgate, 2007.

Crampton, Jeremy W., and John Krygier. "An Introduction to Critical Cartography." *ACME: An International E-Journal for Critical Geographies* 4 (2006): 11–33.

Crittenberger, Lt. Gen. Willis D. "The Relationship of Mapping and Charting to the Defense and Development of the Americas." *Surveying and Mapping* 10 (1950): 5–8.

Crone, G. R. "The Future of the International Million Map of the World." *Geographical Journal* 128 (1962): 36–38.

Cull, Nicholas J. *The Cold War and the United States Information Agency—American Propaganda and Public Diplomacy, 1945–1989*. Cambridge: Cambridge University Press, 2008.

Cullather, Nick. "'The Target Is the People': Representations of the Village in Modernization and U.S. National Security Doctrine." *Cultural Politics* 2 (2006): 29–48.

Curry, Michael. "Beyond Nuclear Winter: On the Limitations of Science in Political Debate," *Antipode* 18 (1986): 244–67.

Cutter, Susan L. "Geographers and Nuclear War: Why We Lack Influence on Public Policy." *Annals of the Association of American Geographers* 78 (1988): 132–43.

Dahl, Edward H., ed. "Commentary: Reader's Responses to J. B. Harley's 'Deconstructing the Map.'" Featuring Robert Baldwin, Michael Blakemore, Matthew H. Edney, Anne Godlewska, Richard Helgerson, Christian Jacob, Walter D. Mignolo, Wolfgang Natter and John Paul Jones III, D. R. F. Taylor, Denis Wood, and Kees Zandlivet. *Cartographica* 26 (1989): 89–127.

Dahl, Roald. *The BFG*. New York: Farrar, Straus and Giroux, 1982.

Dalby, Simon. *Creating the Second Cold War: The Discourse of Politics*. London: Pinter Publishers, 1990.

———. "Geopolitical Discourse: The Soviet Union as Other." *Alternatives* 13 (1988): 415–42.

———. "Imperialism, Domination, Culture: The Continued Relevance of Critical Geopolitics." *Geopolitics* 13 (2008): 413–36.

———. "The Pentagon's New Imperial Cartography." In *Violent Geographies: Fear, Terror, and Political Violence*, edited by Derek Gregory and Allan Pred, 295–308. New York: Routledge, 2007.

Daley, Patrick J. "Mapping the Environment: Contested Physical and Cultural Terrain in the 'Far North.'" *Journalism and Communication Monographs* 1 (2000): 263–300.

Dallin, David J., and Boris I. Nicolaevsky. *Forced Labor in Soviet Russia*. New York: Octagon, 1974.

Davies, William. "Interpretive Cartography." *Surveying and Mapping* 11 (1951): 121–22.

Davisson, Amber. "Beyond the Borders of Red and Blue States: Google Maps as a Site of Rhetorical Invention in the 2008 Election." *Rhetoric & Public Affairs* 14 (2011): 101–23.

Day, Dwayne A., John M. Logsdon, and Brian Latell, eds. *Eye in the Sky: The Story of the Corona Spy Satellites*. Washington, D.C.: Smithsonian Institution Press, 1998.

Dear, Michael, Jim Ketchum, Sarah Luria, and Doug Richardson, eds. *GeoHumanities: Art, History, Text at the Edge of Place*. London: Routledge, 2011.

DeBres, Karen. "Political Geographers of the Past IV: George Renner and the Great Map Scandal of 1942." *Political Geography Quarterly* 5 (1986): 385–94.

De Certeau, Michel. *The Practice of Everyday Life*. Translated by Steven Rendall. Berkeley: University of California Press, 1984.

Deleuze, Gilles, and Felix Guattari. *A Thousand Plateaus: Capitalism and Schizophrenia*. Translated by Brian Massumi. Minneapolis: University of Minnesota Press, 1987.

Demko, George J. "Geography beyond the Ivory Tower." *Annals of the Association of American Geographers* 78 (1988): 575–79.

———. "On Geography, Geographers and Things Nuclear." *Annals of the Association of American Geographers* 78 (1988): 715.

Demko, George J., and William B. Wood, eds. *Reordering the World: Geopolitical Perspectives on the 21st Century*. Boulder, Colo.: Westview Press, 1994.

Der Derian, James. "A Reinterpretation of Realism: Genealogy, Semiology, Dromology." In *Post-Realism: The Rhetorical Turn in International Relations*, edited by Francis A. Beer and Robert Hariman, 277–304. East Lansing: Michigan State University Press, 1996.

———. "The (S)pace of International Relations: Simulation, Surveillance, and Speed." *International Relations Quarterly* 34 (1990): 295–310.

Derrida, Jacques. "No Apocalypse, Not Now (Full Speed Ahead, Seven Missiles, Seven Missives)." *Diacritics* 14 (Summer 1984): 20–31.

De Seversky, Alexander P. *Air Power: Key to Survival*. London: Herbert Jenkins, 1952.

———. *Victory through Air Power*. New York: Simon & Schuster, 1942.

Dickinson, Greg, Carole Blair, and Brian L. Ott, eds. *Places of Public Memory: The Rhetoric of Museums and Memorials*. Tuscaloosa: University of Alabama Press, 2010.

Diercks, Colonel Frederick O. "The Role of the Topographic Map in the Missile Age." *Surveying and Mapping* 19 (1959): 349–54.

Dirlik, Arif. "Spectres of the Third World: Global Modernity and the End of the Three Worlds." *Third World Quarterly* 25 (2004): 131–48.

Disney, Walt. *Victory through Air Power*. Walt Disney Pictures, 1943. YouTube video, 70 min. (10 parts). http://www.youtube.com/watch?v=paY6y87rrpE.

Dodds, Klaus. "Cold War Geopolitics." In *A Companion to Political Geography*, edited by John Agnew, Katharyne Mitchell, and Gearóid Ó Tuathail, 204–18. Malden, Mass.: Blackwell, 2003.

———. "Geopolitics and Foreign Policy: Recent Developments in Anglo-American Political Geography and International Relations." *Progress in Human Geography* 18 (1994): 186–208.

———. "Political Geography III: Critical Geopolitics after All These Years." *Progress in Human Geography* 25 (2001): 469–84.

———. "Taking the Cold War to the Third World." In *The American Century: Consensus and Coercion in the Projection of American Power*, edited by David Slater and Peter J. Taylor, 166–80. Oxford: Blackwell, 1999.

Dodds, Klaus, and James Derrick Sidaway. "Locating Critical Geopolitics." *Environment and Planning D: Society and Space* 12 (1994): 515–24.

Doel, Ronald E. "Constituting the Postwar Earth Sciences: The Military's Influence on the Environmental Sciences in the USA after 1945." *Social Studies of Science* 33 (2003): 635–66.

Doel, Ronald E., Tanya J. Levin, and Mason K. Marker. "Extending Modern Cartography to the Ocean Depths: Military Patronage, Cold War Priorities, and the Heezen-Tharp Mapping Project, 1952–1959." *Journal of Historical Geography* 32 (2006): 605–26.

Dorn, Michael L. "(In)temperate Zones: Daniel Drake's Medico-Moral Geographies of Urban Life in the Trans-Appalachian American West." *Journal of the History of Medicine and Allied Science* 55 (2000): 256–91.

Doty, Roxanne Lynn. *Imperial Encounters: The Politics of Representation in North-South Relations*. Minneapolis: University of Minnesota Press, 1996.

Dragga, Sam, and Dan Voss. "Cruel Pies: The Inhumanity of Technical Illustrations." *Technical Communication* 48 (2001): 265–74.

Driver, Felix. *Geography Militant: Cultures of Exploration and Empire*. Oxford: Blackwell, 2001.

Dudziak, Mary L. *Cold War Civil Rights: Race and the Image of American Democracy*. Princeton, N.J.: Princeton University Press, 2000.

Edsall, Robert M. "Iconic Maps in American Political Discourse." *Cartographica* 42 (2007): 335–47.

Edney, Matthew. *Mapping an Empire: The Geographical Construction of British India, 1765–1843*. Chicago: University of Chicago Press, 1997.

———. "The Origins and Development of J. B. Harley's Cartographic Theories." *Cartographica* 40 (2005): 1–115.

Edwards, Paul N. *The Closed World: Computers and the Politics of Discourse in Cold War America*. Cambridge, Mass.: MIT Press, 1996.

Escobar, Arturo. "Culture, Economics, and Politics in Latin American Social Movements Theory and Research." In *The Making of Social Movements in Latin America: Identity, Strategy, and Democracy*, edited by Arturo Escobar and Sonia E. Alvarez, 62–85. Boulder, Colo.: Westview Press, 1992.

Farish, Matthew. "Archiving Areas: The Ethnogeographic Board and the Second World War." *Annals of the Association of American Geographers* 95 (2005): 663–79.

———. *The Contours of America's Cold War*. Minneapolis: University of Minnesota Press, 2010.

———. "Disaster and Decentralization: American Cities and the Cold War." *Cultural Geographies* 10 (2003): 125–48.

———. Review of *Mandarins of the Future: Modernization Theory in Cold War America*, by Nils Gilman. *Journal of Historical Geography* 31 (2005): 809–11.

Farish, Matthew, and P. Whitney Lackenbauer. "High Modernism in the Arctic: Planning Frobisher Bay and Inuvik." *Journal of Historical Geography* 35 (2009): 517–44.

Felt, Hali. *Soundings: The Story of the Remarkable Woman Who Mapped the Ocean Floor*. New York: Henry Holt, 2012.

Ferguson, Kennan. "Unmapping and Remapping the World: Foreign Policy as Aesthetic Practice." In *Challenging Boundaries*, edited by Michael J. Shapiro and Hayward R. Alker, 165–91. Minneapolis: University of Minnesota Press, 1996.

Finnegan, Cara. *Picturing Poverty: Print Culture and FSA Photographs*. Washington, D.C.: Smithsonian Books, 2003.

———. "Studying Visual Modes of Public Address: Lewis Hine's Progressive-Era Child Labor Rhetoric." In *The Handbook of Rhetoric and Public Address*, edited by Shawn J. Parry-Giles and J. Michael Hogan, 250–70. Malden, Mass.: Wiley-Blackwell, 2010.

Fischoff, Baruch, Nick Pidgeon, and Susan T. Fiske. "Social Science and the Politics of the Arms Race." *Journal of Social Issues* 39 (1983): 161–80.

Foresman, Timothy W., ed. *The History of Geographic Information Systems: Perspectives from the Pioneers*. Upper Saddle River, N.J.: Prentice Hall, 1998.

Foss, Karen A., and Stephen W. Littlejohn. "*The Day After*: Rhetorical Vision in an Ironic Frame." *Critical Studies in Mass Communication* 3 (1986): 317–36.

Foucault, Michel. "Questions on Geography." In *Power/Knowledge: Selected Interviews and Other Writings*, translated and edited by Colin Gordon, 63–77. New York: Pantheon, 1980.

Foxall, Andrew. "A 'New Cold War': Redrawing the MAP/map of Europe." *Political Geography* 28 (2009): 329–31.

Freedman, Lawrence. *Atlas of Global Strategy*. New York: Facts on File, 1985.

Fryer, Donald W. "A Geographer's Inhumanity to Man." *Annals of the Association of American Geographers* 64 (1974): 479–82.

Fulbright. J. William. "The War and Its Effects: The Military-Industrial-Academic Complex." In *Super-State: Readings in the Military-Industrial Complex*, edited by Herbert I. Schiller and Joseph D. Phillips, 171–78. Urbana: University of Illinois Press, 1970.

Fure-Slocum, Eric. "Housing, Race, and the Cold War in a Labor City." In *Labor's Cold War: Local Politics in a Global Context*, edited by Shelton Stromquist, 163–203. Urbana: University of Illinois Press, 2008.

Gaddis, John Lewis. "On Moral Equivalency and Cold War History." *Ethics & International Affairs* 10 (1996): 131–48.

———. *Strategies of Containment: A Critical Appraisal of Postwar American National Security Policy*. New York: Oxford University Press, 1982.

Gaddis, John Lewis, and Paul Nitze. "NSC-68 and the Soviet Threat Reconsidered." *International Security* 4 (1980): 164–76.

Gall, James. "Use of Cylindrical Projections for Geographical, Astronomical, and Scientific Purposes." *Scottish Geographical Magazine* 1 (1885): 119–23.

Gardiner, Richard A. "A Re-appraisal of the International Map of the World (I.M.W.) on the Millionth Scale." *International Yearbook on Cartography* 1 (1961): 31–47.

Garrison, William L. *Studies of Highway Development and Geographic Change*. Seattle: University of Washington Press, 1959.

Garthoff, Raymond L. "Foreign Intelligence and the Historiography of the Cold War." *Journal of Cold War Studies* 6 (2004): 21–56.

Gauhar, Altaf. "Willy Brandt." *Third World Quarterly* 1 (1979): 7–19.

George, Jim. "Understanding International Relations after the Cold War: Probing beyond the Realist Legacy." In *Challenging Boundaries*, edited by Michael J. Shapiro and Hayward R. Alker, 33–79. Minneapolis: University of Minnesota Press, 1996.

German Cartographical Society. "The So-Called Peters Projection." *Cartographic Journal* 22 (1985): 108–10.

Gilmartin, Patricia. "The Design of Journalistic Maps/Purposes, Parameters and Prospects." *Cartographica* 22 (1985): 1–18.

Ginsburg, Norton. *Atlas of Economic Development*. Chicago: University of Chicago Press, 1961.

Glassman, Jim. "On the Borders of Southeast Asia: Cold War Geography and the Construction of the Other." *Political Geography* 24 (2005): 784–807.

Glennon, Michael J. *Constitutional Diplomacy*. Princeton, N.J.: Princeton University Press, 1990.

Godlewska, Anne, and Neil Smith, eds. *Geography and Empire*. Oxford: Blackwell, 1994.

Goodchild, Michael F. "Stepping over the Line: Technological Constraints and the New Cartography." *American Cartographer* 15 (1988): 311–19.

———. "Theoretical Geography (1962): William Bunge." In *Key Texts in Human Geography*, edited by Phil Hubbard, Rob Kitchin, and Gill Valentine, 9–16. London: Sage, 2008.

Goodnight, G. Thomas. "The Personal, Technical, and Public Spheres of Argument." *Journal of the American Forensics Association* 18 (1992): 214–27.

———. "Ronald Reagan's Re-formulation of the Rhetoric of War: Analysis of the 'Zero Option,' 'Evil Empire,' and 'Star Wars' Addresses." *Quarterly Journal of Speech* 72 (1986): 390–414.

Gottmann, Jean. "Spatial Partitioning and the Politician's Wisdom." *International Political Science Review* 1 (1980): 432–55.

Graebner, Norman A. "Myth and Reality: America's Rhetorical Cold War." In *Critical Reflections on the Cold War*, edited by Martin J. Medhurst and H. W. Brands, 20–37. College Station: Texas A&M University Press, 2000.

Gramling, Oliver. *AP: The Story of News*. New York: Farrar and Rinehart, 1940.

Greene, Owen, Barry Rubin, Neil Turok, Philip Webber, and Graeme Wilkinson. *London after the Bomb: What a Nuclear Attack Really Means*. Oxford: Oxford University Press, 1982.

Gregory, Derek. *Geographical Imaginations*. Cambridge, Mass.: Blackwell, 1994.

Gusterson, Hugh. "Nuclear Weapons and the Other in the Western Imagination." *Cultural Anthropology* 14 (1999): 111–43.

Hagan, Susan M. "Visual/Verbal Collaboration in Print: Complementary Differences, Necessary Ties, and an Untapped Rhetorical Opportunity." *Written Communication* 24 (2007): 49–83.

Hagen, J. "Redrawing the Imagined Map of Europe: The Rise and Fall of the 'Center.'" *Political Geography* 22 (2003): 489–517.

Hall, Derek R. "A Geographical Approach to Propaganda." In *Political Studies from Spatial Perspectives*, edited by A. D. Burnett and P. J. Taylor, 313–30. Chichester: John Wiley & Sons, 1981.

Hall, H. Duncan. "Zones of the International Frontier." *Geographical Review* 38 (1948): 615–25.

Hall, R. Cargill. "The Eisenhower Administration and the Cold War: Framing American Astronautics to Serve National Security." *Prologue: Quarterly of the National Archives* (Spring 1995): 59–69.

———. "From Concept to National Policy: Strategic Reconnaissance in the Cold War." *Prologue: Quarterly of the National Archives* (Summer 1996): 107–25.

———. "SAMOS to the Moon: The Clandestine Transfer of Reconnaissance Technology between Federal Agencies." Report, Office of the Historian, National Reconnaissance Office. Chantilly, Va.: National Reconnaissance Office, 2001. http://www.nro.gov/foia/docs/foia-samos.pdf.

Halliday, Fred. *The Making of the Second Cold War.* London: Verso, 1983.

Hankins, Grace Croyle. *Our Global World: A Brief Geography for the Air Age.* New York: Gregg, 1944.

Hariman, Robert. "Political Parody and Public Culture." *Quarterly Journal of Speech* 94 (2008): 247–72.

Harley, J. B. "Cartography, Ethics and Social Theory." *Cartographica* 27 (1990): 1–23.

———. "Deconstructing the Map." *Cartographica* 26 (1989): 1–19.

———. "Deconstructing the Map." In *Writing Worlds: Discourse, Text & Metaphor in the Representation of Landscape*, edited by Trevor J. Barnes and James S. Duncan, 231–47. London: Routledge, 1992.

———. "The New History of Cartography." *UNESCO Courier* 44 (1991): 10–15.

———. *The New Nature of Maps: Essays in the History of Cartography.* Edited by Paul Laxton. Baltimore: Johns Hopkins University Press, 2001.

———. "Silences and Secrecy: The Hidden Agenda of Cartography in Early Modern Europe." *Imago Mundi* 40 (1988): 57–76.

Harmon, Katherine. *You Are Here: Personal Geographies and Other Maps of the Imagination.* New York: Princeton Architectural Press, 2004.

Harris, Trevor, and Daniel Weiner. "Empowerment, Marginalization, and 'Community-Integrated' GIS." *Cartography and Geographic Information Systems* 25 (1998): 67–76.

Harrison, Richard Edes. "Annals Map Supplement Number Two: The Floor of the World Ocean." *Annals of the Association of American Geographers* 51 (1961): 343.

———. "Art and Common Sense in Cartography." *Surveying and Mapping* 19 (1959): 27–28.

———. *Look at the World: The Fortune Atlas for World Strategy.* New York: Alfred A. Knopf, 1944.

———. "The Nomograph as an Instrument in Map Making." *Geographical Review* 33 (1943): 655–57.

Harrison, Richard Edes, and Robert Strausz-Hupe. "Maps, Strategy, and World Politics." In *Foundations of National Power*, edited by Harold Sprout and Margaret Sprout, 64–68. Princeton, N.J.: Princeton University Press, 1945.

Hart, Roderick P., and Kathleen E. Kendall. "Lyndon Johnson and the Problem of Politics: A Study in Conversation." In *Beyond the Rhetorical Presidency*, edited by Martin J. Medhurst, 77–103. College Station: Texas A&M University Press, 1996.

Hartnett, Stephen. "Michel de Certeau's Critical Historiography and the Rhetoric of Maps." *Philosophy and Rhetoric* 31 (1998): 283–302.

Hartshorne, Richard. "The Functional Approach in Political Geography." *Annals of the Association of American Geographers* 40 (1950): 95–130.

———. *The Nature of Geography: A Critical Survey of Current Thought in the Light of the Past*. Lancaster, Pa.: Association of American Geographers, 1949.

Hartung, William D. *The Economic Consequences of a Nuclear Freeze*. New York: Council on Economic Priorities, 1984.

Harvey, David. "Cosmopolitanism and the Banality of Geographical Evils." *Public Culture* 12 (2000): 529–64.

———. *Social Justice and the City*. Baltimore: Johns Hopkins University Press, 1973.

Hawk, David. *The Hidden Gulag: The Lives and Voices of "Those Who Are Sent to the Mountains."* 2nd ed. Washington, D.C.: Committee for Human Rights in North Korea, 2012. http://www.hrnk.org/uploads/pdfs/HRNK_HiddenGulag2_Web_5-18.pdf.

Heffernan, Michael. "The Politics of the Map in the Early Twentieth Century." *Cartography and Geographic Information Science* 29 (2002): 207–26.

Heininen, Lassi, and Heather N. Nicol. "The Importance of Northern Dimension Foreign Policies in the Geopolitics of the Circumpolar North." *Geopolitics* 12 (2007): 133–65.

Hendershot, Cyndy, and Antony Oldknow. "Virtual Slide Set #1: Cold War Popular Magazine Cartography." Hermon Dunlap Smith Center for the History of Cartography, 2002.

Henrikson, Alan K. "All the World's a Map." *Wilson Quarterly* 3 (1979): 164–77.

———. "America's Changing Place in the World: From 'Periphery' to 'Centre'?" In *Centre and Periphery: Spatial Variation in Politics*, edited by Jean Gottmann, 73–100. London: Sage, 1980.

———. "The Geographical 'Mental Maps' of American Foreign Policy Makers." *International Political Science Review* 1 (1980): 495–530.

———. "The Map as an 'Idea': The Role of Cartographic Imagery during the Second World War." *American Cartographer* 2 (1975): 19–53.

———. "Maps, Globes, and the 'Cold War.'" *Special Libraries* 65 (1974): 445–54.

———. "The Power and Politics of Maps." In *Reordering the World: Geopolitical Perspectives on the 21st Century*, edited by George J. Demko and William B. Wood, 94–116. Boulder, Colo.: Westview Press, 1994.

Herb, Guntram H., Jouni Häkli, Mark W. Corson, Nicole Mellow, Sebastian Cobarrubias, and Maribel Casas-Cortes. "Intervention: Mapping Is Critical!" *Political Geography* 28 (2009): 332–42.

Herzstein, Robert E. *Henry R. Luce, Time, and the American Crusade in Asia*. Cambridge: Cambridge University Press, 2005.

Hewitt, Kenneth. "Place Annihilation: Area Bombing and the Fate of Urban Places." *Annals of the Association of American Geographers* 73 (1983): 257–84.

Heyman, Rich. "'Who's Going to Man the Factories and Be the Sexual Slaves if We All Get PhDs?' Democratizing Knowledge Production, Pedagogy, and the Detroit Geographical Expedition and Institute." *Antipode* 39 (2007): 99–120.

Heynen, Nik, and Trevor J. Barnes. "Foreword to the 2011 Edition: Fitzgerald Then and Now." In *Fitzgerald*, by William Bunge, vii–xiii. Athens: University of Georgia Press, 2011.

Hill, Herbert. "The CIA in National and International Labor Movements." *International Journal of Politics, Culture, and Society* 6 (1993): 405–7.

Hinks, Arthur R. "Some New Effects in Map Projection: Review." *Geographical Journal* 104 (1944): 123–27.

Hogan, J. Michael. "Apocalyptic Pornography and the Nuclear Freeze: A Defense of the Public." *Argument and Critical Practices: Proceedings of the Fifth SCA/AFA Conference on Argumentation*, edited by Joseph W. Wenzel, 541–48. Annandale, Va.: Speech Communication Association, 1987.

———. *The Nuclear Freeze Campaign: Rhetoric and Foreign Policy in the Telepolitical Age*. East Lansing: Michigan State University Press, 1994.

Holleran, Michael. "America's Place in the World." *Reviews in American History* 30 (2002): 419–24.

Holloway, Rachel L. "The Strategic Defense Initiative and the Technological Sublime: Fear, Science, and the Cold War." In *Critical Reflections on the Cold War*, edited by Martin J. Medhurst and H. W. Brands, 209–32. College Station: Texas A&M University Press, 2000.

Horvath, Ronald J. "Machine Space." *Geographical Review* 64 (1974): 167–88.

Howitt, Richard. "Scale." In *A Companion to Political Geography*, edited by John Agnew, Katharyne Mitchell, and Gearóid Ó Tuathail, 138–57. Malden, Mass.: Blackwell, 2003.

Huggan, Graham. "Decolonizing the Map: Post-Colonialism, Post-Structuralism and the Cartographic Connection." *Ariel* 20 (1989): 115–31.

Hughes, Thomas L. "Scholars and Foreign Policy: Varieties of Research Experience." *Background* 9 (1965): 199–214.

Hutcheon, Linda. *A Theory of Parody: The Teachings of Twentieth-Century Art Forms*. Urbana: University of Illinois Press, 2000.

Independent Commission on International Development Issues. *North-South: A Program for Survival; The Report of the Independent Commission on International Development Issues under the Chairmanship of Willy Brandt*. Cambridge, Mass.: MIT Press, 1980.

International Confederation of Free Trade Unions. *Stalin's Slave Camps: An Indictment of Modern Slavery*. Brussels: ICFTU, 1951.

Iriye, Akira. *Global Community: The Role of International Organizations in the Making of the Contemporary World*. Berkeley: University of California Press, 2002.

Ishay, Micheline. "Promoting Human Rights in the Era of Globalization and Interventions: The Changing Spaces of Struggle." *Globalizations* 1 (2004): 181–93.

Ivie, Robert L. "Cold War Motives and the Rhetorical Metaphor: A Framework of Criticism." In *Cold War Rhetoric: Strategy, Metaphor, and Ideology*, edited by Martin J. Medhurst, Robert L. Ivie, Philip Wander, and Robert L. Scott, 71–79. New York: Greenwood, 1990.

———. "The Prospects of Cold War Criticism." In *Cold War Rhetoric: Strategy, Metaphor, and Ideology*, edited by Martin J. Medhurst, Robert L. Ivie, Philip Wander, and Robert L. Scott, 203–7. New York: Greenwood, 1990.

Jacob, Christian. *The Sovereign Map: Theoretical Approaches in Cartography throughout History*. Translated by Tom Conley. Chicago: University of Chicago Press, 2006.

———. "Toward a Cultural History of Cartography." *Imago Mundi* 48 (1996): 191–98.

Johnston, R. J., and P. J. Taylor. *A World in Crisis? Geographical Perspectives*. Oxford: Blackwell, 1986.

Johnston, R. J., Peter J. Taylor, and Michael J. Watts, eds. *Geographies of Global Change: Remapping the World in the Late Twentieth Century*. Cambridge, Mass.: Blackwell, 1995.

Jonsson, Christer, Sven Tagil, and Gunnar Torqvist. *Organizing European Space*. London: Sage, 2000.

Joyner, Christopher C., and Scott A. Lawson. "The United States and UNESCO: Rethinking the Decision to Withdraw." *International Journal* 41 (1985–86): 37–71.

Kadmon, Naftali. "Toponymy and Geopolitics: The Political Use—and Misuse—of Geographical Names." *Cartographic Journal* 41 (2004): 85–87.

Kahin, George McTurnan. *The Asian-African Conference, Bandung Indonesia, April 1955*. Port Washington, N.Y.: Kennikat Press, 1956.

Kaiser, Ward L. *A New View of the World: A Handbook to The World Map: Peters Projection*. New York: Friendship Press, 1987.

Kaiser, Ward L., and Denis Wood. "Arno Peters—The Man, the Map, the Message." *Cartographic Journal* 40 (2003): 53–54.

———. *Seeing through Maps: The Power of Images to Shape Our World View*. Amherst, Mass.: ODT, 2001.

Kane, Thomas. "Foreign Policy Suppositions and Commanding Ideas." *Argumentation and Advocacy* 28 (1991): 80–91.

Kaplan, Caren. "Precision Targets: GPS and the Militarization of U.S. Consumer Identity." *American Quarterly* 58 (2006): 693–714.

Katz, Arthur M. *Life after Nuclear War: The Economic and Social Impacts of Nuclear Attacks on the United States*. Cambridge, Mass.: Ballinger, 1982.

Kennan, George F. *Realities of American Foreign Policy*. Princeton, N.J.: Princeton University Press, 1954.

Kennan, George F. (X). "The Sources of Soviet Conduct." *Foreign Affairs* 25 (1947): 566–82.

Kidron, Michael, and Ronald Segal. *The State of the World Atlas*. New York: Simon & Schuster, 1981.

Kidron, Michael, and Dan Smith. *The War Atlas: Armed Conflict—Armed Peace*. New York: Simon & Schuster, 1983.

Kimball, Miles. "London through Rose-Colored Graphics: Visual Rhetoric and Information Graphic Design in Charles Booth's Maps of London Poverty." *Journal of Technical Writing and Communication* 36 (2006): 353–81.

Kimble, George H. T. "The Role of Surveying and Mapping in Developing the Economy of Nations." *Surveying and Mapping* 11 (1951): 104–8.

King, Geoff. *Mapping Reality: An Exploration of Cultural Geographies.* New York: St. Martin's Press, 1996.

Kingsbury, Paul, and John Paul Jones III. "Walter Benjamin's Dionysian Adventures on Google Earth." *Geoforum* 40 (2009): 502–13.

Kirby, Andrew. "What Did You Do in the War, Daddy?" In *Geography and Empire,* edited by Anne Godlewska and Neil Smith, 300–15. Oxford: Blackwell, 1994.

Kirsch, Scott. "Peaceful Nuclear Explosions and the Geography of Scientific Authority." *Professional Geographer* 52 (2000): 179–92.

———. *Proving Grounds: Project Plowshare and the Unrealized Dream of Nuclear Earthmoving.* New Brunswick, N.J.: Rutgers University Press, 2005.

Kitchin, Rob, and Martin Dodge. "Rethinking Maps." *Progress in Human Geography* 31 (2007): 331–44.

Klinghoffer, Arthur Jay. *The Power of Projections: How Maps Reflect Global Politics and History.* Westport, Conn.: Praeger, 2006.

Koch, Tom. *Cartographies of Disease: Maps, Mapping, & Medicine.* Redlands, Calif.: ESRI Press, 2005.

Kolacny, Antonin. "Cartographic Information—A Fundamental Concept and Term in Modern Cartography." *Cartographic Journal* 6 (1969): 47–49.

———. "The Importance of Cartographic Information for the Comprehending of Messages Spread by the Mass Communication Media." *International Yearbook of Cartography* 11 (1971): 216–22.

Kraig, Robert Alexander. "The Tragic Science: The Uses of Jimmy Carter in Foreign Policy Realism." *Rhetoric & Public Affairs* 5 (2002): 1–30.

Kramer, Sidney A. Review of *Look at the World,* by Richard Edes Harrison. *Far Eastern Survey* 16 (1947): 96.

Kress, Gunther, and Theo van Leeuwen. "Colour as a Semiotic Mode: Notes for a Grammar of Color." *Visual Communication* 1 (2002): 343–68.

———. *Reading Images: The Grammar of Visual Design.* New York: Routledge, 1996.

Kruszewksi, Charles. "The Pivot of History." *Foreign Affairs* 32 (1954): 388–401.

Kumar, Sangeet. "Google Earth and the Nation State: Sovereignty in the Age of New Media." *Global Media and Communication* 6 (2010): 154–76.

Kurian, George. *Atlas of the Third World.* London: Mansell Publishing, 1983.

LaFeber, Walter. *America, Russia, and the Cold War, 1945–1996.* 8th ed. New York: McGraw-Hill, 1997.

Lacoste, Yves. "Geography and Foreign Policy." *SAIS Review* 4 (1984): 213–27.

———. "An Illustration of Geographical Warfare: Bombing of the Dikes on the Red River, North Vietnam." *Antipode* 5 (1973): 1–13.

Laitinen, Kari. "Post-Cold War Security Borders: A Conceptual Approach." In *Routing Borders between Territories, Discourses, and Practices,* edited by Eiki Berg and Henk Van Houtum, 13–33. Burlington, Vt.: Ashgate, 2003.

Larabee, Ann E. "Ground Zero: The City, the Bomb and the End of History." *Canadian Review of American Studies* 22 (1991): 263–80.

Latham, Michael E. *Modernization as Ideology: American Social Science and Nation-Building in the Kennedy Era.* Chapel Hill: University of North Carolina Press, 2000.

Latour, Bruno. "Drawing Things Together." In *Representation in Scientific Practice*, edited by Michael Lynch and Steve Woolgar, 19–68. Cambridge, Mass.: MIT Press, 1990.

Lefebvre, Henri. *The Production of Space.* Translated by Donald Nicholson-Smith. Malden, Mass.: Blackwell, 1991.

———. "Reflections on the Politics of Space." *Antipode* 8 (1976): 30–37.

Leffler, Melvyn P. "The American Conception of National Security and the Beginnings of the Cold War, 1945–48." *American Historical Review* 89 (1984): 346–81.

Lentricchia, Frank. *Criticism and Social Change.* Chicago: University of Chicago Press, 1983.

Leslie, Stuart W. *The Cold War and American Science: The Military-Industrial-Academic Complex at MIT and Stanford.* New York: Columbia University Press, 1993.

Levander, Caroline Field, and Robert S. Levine, eds. *Hemispheric American Studies.* New Brunswick, N.J.: Rutgers University Press, 2008.

Levine, Isaac Don. *Eyewitness to History: Memoirs and Reflections of a Foreign Correspondent for Half a Century.* New York: Hawthorn Books, 1973.

———, ed. *Plain Talk: An Anthology from the Leading Anti-Communist Magazine of the 40s.* New Rochelle, N.Y.: Arlington House Publishers, 1976.

Lewis, Martin W., and Karen E. Wigen. *The Myth of Continents: A Critique of Metageography.* Berkeley: University of California Press, 1997.

Lieber, Albert C. "International Cooperation in Mapping." *Surveying and Mapping* 14 (1954): 71–74.

Lippmann, Walter. *The Cold War: A Study in U.S. Foreign Policy.* New York: Harper, 1947.

———. *Public Opinion.* New York: Free Press, 1965.

———. *U.S. Foreign Policy: Shield of the Republic.* Boston: Little, Brown, 1943.

Livingstone, David N. *The Geographical Tradition.* Oxford: Blackwell, 1992.

Locke, Arthur S. *Guidance: Principles of Guided Missile Design.* Princeton, N.J.: Van Nostrand, 1955.

Loper, Herbert B. "The Role of Surveying and Mapping in National Defense." *Surveying and Mapping* 11 (1951): 363–65.

Loxton, John. "The Peters Phenomenon." *Cartographic Journal* 22 (1985): 106–8.

Luce, Henry R. "The American Century." *Life*, February 17, 1941, 61–65. Reprinted in *Diplomatic History* 23 (1999): 159–71.

Lynch, Michael. "Pictures of Nothing? Visual Construals in Social Theory." *Sociological Theory* 9 (1991): 1–21.

MacDonald, Fraser. "Geopolitics and 'the Vision Thing': Regarding Britain and America's First Nuclear Missile." *Transactions of the Institute of British Geographers* 31 (2006): 53–71.

———. "Space and the Atom: On the Popular Geopolitics of Cold War Rocketry." *Geopolitics* 13 (2008): 611–34.

MacDougall, Robert. "Red, Brown and Yellow Perils: Images of the American Enemy in the 1940s and 1950s." *Journal of Popular Culture* 32 (1999): 59–75.

MacEachren, Alan M. *How Maps Work: Representation, Visualization, and Design.* New York: Guilford, 1995.

Mackinder, Halford. *Democratic Ideals and Reality: A Study in the Politics of Reconstruction.* NDU Press Classic Edition. Washington, D.C.: National Defense University Press, 1996.

———. "The Round World and the Winning of the Peace." *Foreign Affairs* 21 (1943): 595–605.

MacLeish, Archibald. "The Image of Victory." In *Compass of the World: A Symposium on Political Geography*, edited by Hans W. Weigert and Vilhjalmur Stefansson, 1–11. New York: Macmillan, 1944.

Macmillan, Bill. "Classics in Human Geography Revisited—Commentary 2: Geography as Geometry." *Progress in Human Geography* 25 (2001): 73–75.

Makagon, Daniel. "Mapping the City through Sound." Paper presented at the annual convention of the National Communication Association, San Francisco, November 2010.

Malin, James C. "Space and History: Reflections on the Closed-Space Doctrines of Turner and Mackinder and the Challenge of Those Ideas by the Air Age, Part 2." *Agricultural History* 18 (1944): 107–26.

Maling, Derek. "A Minor Modification to the Cylindrical Equal-Area Projection." *Geographical Journal* 140 (1974): 509–10.

Manzione, Joseph. "'Amusing and Amazing and Practical and Military': The Legacy of Scientific Internationalism in American Foreign Policy, 1945–1963." *Diplomatic History* 24 (2000): 21–55.

Marcuse, Peter, and Ronald van Kempen, eds. *Globalizing Cities: A New Spatial Order?* Malden, Mass.: Blackwell, 2000.

Marshall, General George. *General Marshall's Report: The Winning of the War in Europe and the Pacific (Biennial Report of the Chief of Staff of the United States Army July 1, 1943 to June 30, 1945 to the Secretary of War).* New York: Simon & Schuster, 1945.

Marti-Ibanez, Felix. "Foreword: Medical Geography and History." In *The Ecology of Human Disease*, by Jacques M. May, ix–xxi. New York: MD Publication, 1958.

Massey, Doreen B. *For Space.* Thousand Oaks, Calif.: Sage, 2005.

———. *Space, Place, and Gender.* Minneapolis: University of Minnesota Press, 1994.

Mathieson, R. S. "Nuclear Power in the Soviet Bloc." *Annals of the Association of American Geographers* 70 (1980): 271–79.

Matless, David, Jonathan Oldfield, and Adam Swain. "Encountering Soviet Geography: Oral Histories of British Geographical Studies of the USSR and Eastern Europe 1945–1991." *Social & Cultural Geography* 8 (2007): 353–72.

———. "Geographically Touring the Eastern Bloc: British Geography, Travel Cultures, and the Cold War." *Transactions of the Institute of British Geographers* 33 (2008): 354–75.

May, Jacques M. *Ecology of Human Disease.* New York: MD Publications, 1958.

———. *The Ecology of Malnutrition in Central and Southeastern Europe: Austria, Hungary, Rumania, Bulgaria, Czechoslovakia.* New York: Hafner, 1966.

———. "Map of the World Distribution of Cholera," and "Distribution of Cholera, 1816–1950—Atlas of Distribution of Diseases, Plate 2." *Geographical Review* 41 (1951): 272–73.

———. "Map of the World Distribution of Malaria Vectors," and "Distribution of Malaria Vectors—Atlas of Distribution of Diseases, Plate 3." *Geographical Review* 41 (1951): 638–39.

———. "Map of the World Distribution of Poliomyelitis, 1900–50," and "Distribution of Poliomyelitis, 1900–50—Atlas of Distribution of Diseases, Plate 1." *Geographical Review* 40 (1950): 646–48.

———. "Medical Geography: Its Methods and Objectives." *Geographical Review* 40 (1950): 9–41.

———. *Siam Doctor.* Garden City, N.Y.: Doubleday, 1949.

May, Jacques M., with Irma S. Jarcho. *The Ecology of Malnutrition in the Far and Near East: Food Resources, Habits, and Deficiencies.* New York: Hafner, 1961.

May, Jacques M., and Donna L. McLellan. *The Ecology of Malnutrition in the Caribbean; The Bahamas, Cuba, Jamaica, Hispaniola, Puerto Rico, the Lesser Antilles, and Trinidad and Tobago.* New York: Hafner, 1973.

———. *The Ecology of Malnutrition in Eastern Africa and Four Countries of Western Africa; Equatorial Guinea, the Gambia, Liberia, Sierra Leone, Malawi, Rhodesia, Zambia, Kenya, Tanzania, Uganda, Ethiopia, the French Territory of the Afars and Issas, the Somali Republic, and Sudan.* New York: Hafner, 1963.

———. *The Ecology of Malnutrition in Mexico and Central America: Mexico, Guatemala, British Honduras, Honduras, El Salvador, Nicaragua, Costa Rica and Panama.* New York: Hafner, 1972.

May, Jacques M., and Donna L. McLellan. *The Ecology of Malnutrition in Western South America: Colombia, Ecuador, Peru, Bolivia, and Chile.* New York: Hafner, 1974.

McAlister, Joan Faber. "Going Off the Map: The Racial (Re)Ordering of South African Townships." Paper presented at the annual convention of the National Communication Association, San Francisco, November 2010.

McClure, Kevin R., and Lisa Laidlaw McClure. "Postmodern Parody: *Zelig* and the Rhetorical Subversion of Documentary Form." *Qualitative Research Reports in Communication* 2 (2001): 81–88.

McHaffie, Patrick H. "Manufacturing Metaphors: Public Cartography, the Market, and Democracy." In *Ground Truth: The Social Implications of Geographic Information Systems,* edited by John Pickles, 113–29. New York: Guilford Press, 1995.

———. "Towards the Automated Map Factory: Early Automation at the U.S. Geological Survey." *Cartography and Information Science* 29 (2002): 193–206.

McKerrow, Raymie E. "Space and Time in the Postmodern Polity." *Western Journal of Communication* 63 (1999): 271–90.

McMahon, Robert J. "'By Helping Others, We Help Ourselves': The Cold War Rhetoric of American Foreign Policy." In *Critical Reflections on the Cold War,* edited by Martin J. Medhurst and H. W. Brands, 233–46. College Station: Texas A&M University Press, 2000.

McMaster, Robert, and Susanna McMaster. "A History of Twentieth-Century American Academic Cartography." *Cartography and Geographic Information Science* 29 (2002): 305–21.

McMaster, Robert B., and Norman J. W. Thrower. "The Early Years of American Academic Cartography: 1920–45." *Cartography and Geographic Information Systems* 18 (1991): 151–55.

McOmber, James B. "Requiem for the 'Rhetoric of Doom.'" *Peace and Conflict: Journal of Peace Psychology* 2 (1996): 89–91.

Meade, Melinda S., and Robert J. Erickson. *Medical Geography*. New York: Guilford, 2000.

Mechling, Elizabeth Walker, and Jay Mechling. "The Campaign for Civil Defense and the Struggle to Naturalize the Bomb." *Western Journal of Speech Communication* 55 (1991): 105–33.

———. "Hot Pacifism and Cold War: The American Friends Service Committee's Witness for Peace in 1950s America." *Quarterly Journal of Speech* 78 (1992): 173–96.

Medhurst, Martin J., ed. *Beyond the Rhetorical Presidency*. College Station: Texas A&M University Press, 1996.

———. "Rhetoric and Cold War: A Strategic Approach." In *Cold War Rhetoric: Strategy, Metaphor, and Ideology*, edited by Martin J. Medhurst, Robert L. Ivie, Philip Wander, and Robert L. Scott, 19–27. New York: Greenwood, 1990.

Medhurst, Martin J., and H. W. Brands, eds. *Critical Reflections on the Cold War: Linking Rhetoric and History*. College Station: Texas A&M University Press, 2000.

Medhurst, Martin J., Robert L. Ivie, Philip Wander, and Robert L. Scott. *Cold War Rhetoric: Strategy, Metaphor, and Ideology*. New York: Greenwood, 1990.

Meinig, Donald W. "Culture Blocs and Political Blocs: Emergent Patterns in World Affairs." *Western Humanities Review* 10 (1956): 203–22.

———. "Geography as an Art." *Transactions of the Institute of British Geographers* 8 (1983): 314–28.

———. *The Shaping of America: Global America, 1915–2000*. New Haven, Conn.: Yale University Press, 2004.

Merret, Christopher. "Spatial Representation: The Map, Its Use and Abuse." *S.A. Archives Journal* 32 (1990): 38–54.

Meyer, Stephen. *Stalin over Wisconsin: The Making and Unmaking of Militant Unionism, 1900–1950*. New Brunswick, N.J.: Rutgers University Press, 1992.

Methvin, Eugene H. "Isaac Don Levine: Herald of Free Russia." *Modern Age* (1995): 241–49.

Michie, Helena, and Ronald R. Thomas, eds. *Nineteenth-Century Geographies: The Transformation of Space from the Victorian Age to the American Century*. New Brunswick, N.J.: Rutgers University Press, 2003.

Mignolo, Walter. "The Many Faces of Cosmo-polis: Border Thinking and Critical Cosmopolitanism." *Public Culture* 12 (2000): 721–48.

Miller Center. "Video: Address to the Nation on the Situation in Southeast Asia (April 30, 1970), Richard Milhous Nixon." University of Virginia, 2013. Video, 22 min. http://millercenter.org/scripps/archive/speeches/detail/3890.

Miller, Christopher C. "A Beast in the Field: The Google Maps Mashup as GIS/2." *Cartographica* 41 (2006): 187–99.

Miller, O. M. "Notes on Cylindrical World Map Projections." *Geographical Review* 32 (1942): 424–30.

Mirowski, Philip. *Machine Dreams: Economics Becomes a Cyborg Science.* Cambridge: Cambridge University Press, 2002.

Mitchell, Gordon R. "Japan-U.S. Missile Defense Collaboration: Rhetorically Delicious, Deceptively Dangerous." *Fletcher Forum of World Affairs* 25 (2001): 85–108.

Mitchell, Peta. "'The Stratified Record upon Which We Set Our Feet': The Spatial Turn and the Multilayering of History, Geography, and Geology." In *GeoHumanities: Art, History, Text at the Edge of Place*, edited by Michael Dear, Jim Ketchum, Sarah Luria, and Douglas Richardson, 71–81. London: Routledge, 2011.

Mittman, Asa. "Inverting the Panopticon: Google Earth, Wonder and Earthly Delights." *Literature Compass* 9 (2012): 938–54.

Monmonier, Mark. *How to Lie with Maps.* 2nd ed. Chicago: University of Chicago Press, 1996.

——. *Mapping It Out: Expository Cartography for the Humanities and Social Sciences.* Chicago: University of Chicago Press, 1993.

——. *Maps with the News: The Development of American Journalistic Cartography.* Chicago: University of Chicago Press, 1989.

——. *Rhumb Lines and Map Wars: A Social History of the Mercator Projection.* Chicago: University of Chicago Press, 2004.

Monmonier, Mark, and David Woodward. "The Exploratory Essays Initiative: Background and Overview." *Cartography and Information Science* 29 (2002): 133–35.

Mora, Silvestro, and Pietro Zwierniak. *Giustizia Sovietica.* Rome: Magi-Spinetti, 1945.

Moran, Dominique. "Soviet Cartography Set in Stone: The 'Map of Industrialization.'" *Environment and Planning D: Society and Space* 24 (2006): 671–89.

Morgan, Ted. *A Covert Life: Jay Lovestone—Communist, Anti-Communist, and Spymaster.* New York: Random House, 1999.

Morrison, Joel L. "The Science of Cartography and Its Essential Processes." *International Yearbook of Cartography* 16 (1976): 84–97.

Murphy, Alexander B. "Historical Justifications for Territorial Claims." *Annals of the Association of American Geographers* 80 (1990): 531–48.

Newman, Robert P. "NSC (National Insecurity) 68: Nitze's Second Hallucination." In *Critical Reflections on the Cold War: Linking Rhetoric and History*, edited by Martin Medhurst and H. W. Brands, 56–90. College Station: Texas A&M University Press, 2000.

Nijman, Jan. "The Limits of Superpower: The United States and the Soviet Union since World War II." *Annals of the Association of American Geographers* 82 (1992): 681–96.

Ninkovich, Frank. *Modernity and Power: A History of the Domino Theory in the Twentieth Century.* Chicago: University of Chicago Press, 1994.

North Atlantic Treaty Organization. *NATO and the Warsaw Pact: Force Comparisons.* Brussels: NATO Information Service, 1984.

Novick, Peter. *The Holocaust in American Life.* Boston: Houghton Mifflin, 1999.

Nystuen, John D., ed. *The Philosophy of Maps.* Michigan Inter-University Community of Mathematical Geographers Discussion Paper #12. Detroit: Wayne State University, 1968.

O'Donovan, Diarmuid. *The State of Health Atlas: Mapping the Challenges and Causes of Disease.* Berkeley: University of California Press, 2008.

O'Gorman, Ned. "Eisenhower and the American Sublime." *Quarterly Journal of Speech* 94 (2008): 44–72.

———. *Spirits of the Cold War: Contesting Worldviews in the Classical Age of American Security Strategy.* East Lansing: Michigan State University Press, 2012.

———. "'The One Word the Kremlin Fears': C. D. Jackson, Cold War 'Liberation,' and American Political-Economic Adventurism." *Rhetoric & Public Affairs* 12 (2009): 389–428.

O'Loughlin, John. "Ordering the 'Crush Zone': Geopolitical Games in Post–Cold War Eastern Europe." In *Geopolitics at the End of the Twentieth Century*, edited by Nurit Kliot and David Newman, 34–56. New York: Routledge, 2000.

Olson, Lester C., Cara A. Finnegan, and Diane S. Hope, eds. *Visual Rhetoric: A Reader in Communication and American Culture.* Los Angeles: Sage, 2008.

Olsson, Gunnar. "Lines of Power." In *Writing Worlds: Discourse, Text & Metaphor in the Representation of Landscape*, edited by Trevor J. Barnes and James S. Duncan, 86–96. London: Routledge, 1992.

———. *Lines of Power/Limits of Language.* Minneapolis: University of Minnesota Press, 1991.

Openshaw, Stan, and Philip Steadman. "The Geography of Two Hypothetical Nuclear Attacks on Britain." *Area* 15 (1983): 193–201.

Openshaw, Stan, Philip Steadman, and Owen Greene. *Doomsday: Britain after Nuclear Attack.* Oxford: Blackwell, 1983.

Osborne, Milton E. *Strategic Hamlets in South Viet-Nam: A Survey and Comparison.* Ithaca, N.Y.: Cornell University Press, 1965.

Osgood, Kenneth. *Total Cold War: Eisenhower's Secret Propaganda Battle at Home and Abroad.* Lawrence: University Press of Kansas, 2006.

Oshinsky, David M. *Senator Joseph McCarthy and the American Labor Movement.* Columbia: University of Missouri Press, 1976.

Ó Tuathail, Gearóid. *Critical Geopolitics: The Politics of Writing Global Space.* Borderlines. Vol. 6. Minneapolis: University of Minnesota Press, 1996.

———. "The Critical Reading/Writing of Geopolitics: Re-reading/Writing Wittfogel, Bowman and Lacoste." *Progress in Human Geography* 18 (1994): 313–32.

———. "(Dis)placing Geopolitics: Writing on the Maps of Global Politics." *Environment and Planning D: Society and Space* 12 (1994): 525–46.

Ó Tuathail, Gearóid, and John Agnew. "Geopolitics and Discourse: Practical Geopolitical Reasoning in American Foreign Policy." *Political Geography* 11 (1992): 190–204.

Ó Tuathail, Gearóid, and Simon Dalby, eds. *Rethinking Geopolitics*. London: Routledge, 1998.

Ó Tuathail, Gearóid, and Timothy W. Luke. "Present at the (Dis)Integration: Deterritorialization and Reterritorialization in the New Wor(1)d Order." *Annals of the Association of American Geographers* 84 (1994): 381–98.

Overseas Development Institute. *EEC and the Third World*. New York: Holmes & Meier, 1981.

Packard, Leonard O., Bruce Overton, and Benjamin De Kalbe Wood. *Our Air-Age World: A Textbook in Global Geography*. New York: Macmillan, 1944.

Painter, David S. "Explaining U.S. Relations with the Third World." *Diplomatic History* 19 (1995): 525–48.

Parker, Jason C. "Small Victory, Missed Chance: The Eisenhower Administration, the Bandung Conference, and the Turning of the Cold War." In *The Eisenhower Administration, the Third World, and the Globalization of the Cold War*, edited by Kathryn C. Statler and Andrew L. Johns, 153–74. Lanham, Md.: Rowman & Littlefield, 2006.

Parry-Giles, Shawn J. "Rhetorical Experimentation and the Cold War, 1947–1953: The Development of an Internationalist Approach to Propaganda." *Quarterly Journal of Speech* 80 (1994): 448–67.

———. *The Rhetorical Presidency, Propaganda, and the Cold War, 1945–1955*. Westport, Conn.: Praeger, 2002.

Pearce, Kimber Charles. "Narrative Reason and Cold War Economic Diplomacy in W. W. Rostow's *Stages of Economic Growth*." *Rhetoric & Public Affairs* 2 (1999): 395–414.

———. *Rostow, Kennedy, and the Rhetoric of Foreign Aid*. East Lansing: Michigan State University Press, 2001.

Pearcy, G. Etzel. "The Air Age: Fact or Fantasy? An Evaluation of the Global Air Transportation Pattern." *Journal of Geography* 46 (1947): 304–12.

Pearson, Alastair, D. R. Fraser Taylor, Karen D. Kline, and Michael Heffernan. "Cartographic Ideals and Geopolitical Realities: International Maps of the World from the 1890s to the Present." *Canadian Geographer* 50 (2006): 149–76.

Peebles, Curtis. *The Corona Project: America's First Spy Satellites*. Annapolis, Md.: Naval Institute Press, 1997.

Peet, Richard. "The Development of Radical Geography in the United States." In *Radical Geography: Alternative Viewpoints on Contemporary Social Issues*, edited by Richard Peet, 1–30. Chicago: Maaroufa Press, 1977.

———. *Modern Geographical Thought*. Malden, Mass.: Blackwell, 1998.

———, ed. *Radical Geography: Alternative Viewpoints on Contemporary Social Issues*. Chicago: Maaroufa Press, 1977.

Pepper, David, and Alan Jenkins, eds. *The Geography of Peace and War*. New York: Blackwell, 1985.

———. "No Special Place for Geographers—No 'Places' At All." *Annals of the Association of American Geographers* 78 (1988): 716–17.

———. "Reversing the Nuclear Arms Race: Geopolitical Bases for Pessimism." *Professional Geographer* 36 (1984): 419–27.

Perkins, Chris. "Cartography—Cultures of Mapping: Power in Practice." *Progress in Human Geography* 28 (2004): 381–91.

———. "Cartography—Mapping Theory." *Progress in Human Geography* 27 (2003): 341–51.

Perry, Joanne M. "Harrison's *Fortune* Maps, 1933–1938: An Annotated Cartobibliography." *SLA G&M Bulletin*, no. 157 (September 1989): 46–56.

———. "Harrison's *Fortune* Maps, 1939–1945: An Annotated Cartobibliography." *SLA G&M Bulletin*, no. 148 (June 1987): 13–20.

Peters, Arno. *Der europa-zentrische Charakter unseres geographischen Weltblides und seine Uberwindung.* Dortmund: W. Grosschen-Verlag, 1976.

———. *Die Neue Kartographie/The New Cartography.* Translated by Ward Kaiser, D. G. Smith, and Heinz Wohlers. New York: Friendship Press, 1983.

———. *Peters Atlas of the World.* New York: Harper & Row, 1990.

Pickles, John, ed. *Ground Truth: The Social Implications of Geographic Information Systems.* New York: Guilford, 1995.

———. *A History of Spaces: Cartographic Reason, Mapping and the Geo-Coded World.* London: Routledge, 2004.

———. "Review Article: Social and Cultural Cartographies and the Spatial Turn in Social Theory." *Journal of Historical Geography* 25 (1999): 93–98.

———. "Text, Hermeneutics and Propaganda Maps." In *Writing Worlds: Discourse, Text & Metaphor in the Representation of Landscape,* edited by Trevor J. Barnes and James S. Duncan, 193–230. London: Routledge, 1992.

Pletsch, Carl E. "The Three Worlds, or the Division of Social Scientific Labor, Circa 1950–1975." *Comparative Studies in Society and History* 23 (1981): 565–90.

Polelle, Mark. *Raising Cartographic Consciousness: The Social and Foreign Policy Vision of Geopolitics in the Twentieth Century.* Lanham, Md.: Lexington, 1999.

Porter, Phil, and Phil Voxland. "Distortion in Maps: The Peters Projection and Other Devilments." *Focus* (1986): 22–30.

Postnikov, Alexey V. "Maps for Ordinary Consumers versus Maps for the Military: Double Standards of Map Accuracy in Soviet Cartography, 1917–1991." *Cartography and Geographic Information Science* 29 (2002): 243–60.

Powell, Colin L., with Joseph E. Persico. *My American Journey.* New York: Random House, 2003.

Powell, Louis H. "New Uses for Globes and Spherical Maps." *Geographical Review* 35 (1945): 49–58.

Power, Marcus. *Rethinking Development Geographies.* London: Routledge, 2003.

Pratt, Mary Louise. *Imperial Eyes: Travel Writing and Transculturation.* New York: Routledge, 2008.

Prelli, Lawrence J., ed. *Rhetorics of Display.* Columbia: University of South Carolina Press, 2006.

———. "Visualizing a Bounded Sea: A Case Study in Rhetorical Taxis." In *Rhetorics of Display,* edited by Lawrence J. Prelli, 90–120. Columbia: University of South Carolina Press, 2006.

Prescott, Victor. "Contributions of the United Nations to Solving Boundary and Territorial Disputes, 1945–1995." *Political Geography* 15 (1996): 287–318.

Quam, Louis O. "The Use of Maps in Propaganda." *Journal of Geography* 42 (1943): 21–32.

Raffestin, Claude. "From Text to Image." *Geopolitics* 5 (2000): 7–35.

Randall, Vicky. "Using and Abusing the Concept of the Third World: Geopolitics and the Comparative Political Study of Development and Underdevelopment." *Third World Quarterly* 25 (2004): 41–53.

Randviir, Anti. "Spatialization of Knowledge: Cartographic Roots of Globalization." *Semiotica* 150 (2004): 227–56.

Ranelagh, John. *The Agency: The Rise and Decline of the CIA*. London: Weidenfield and Nicolson, 1986.

Rice, Jeff. *Digital Detroit: Rhetoric and Space in the Age of the Network*. Carbondale: Southern Illinois University Press, 2012.

Ristow, Walter W. "Air Age Geography: A Critical Appraisal and Bibliography." *Journal of Geography* 43 (1944): 331–43.

———. "Journalistic Cartography." *Surveying and Mapping* 17 (1957): 369–90.

Roberts, Susan, Anna Secor, and Matthew Sparke. "Neoliberal Geopolitics." *Antipode* 35 (2003): 886–97.

Robinson, Arthur H. "Arno Peters and His New Cartography." *American Cartographer* 12 (1985): 103–11.

———. "The Future of the International Map." *Cartographic Journal* 2 (1965): 23–26.

———. "Rectangular World Maps—No!" *Professional Geographer* 42 (1990): 101–4.

Robinson, Arthur H., Joel L. Morrison, and Phillip C. Muehrcke. "Cartography, 1950–2000." *Transactions of the Institute of British Geographers* 2 (1977): 3–18.

Robinson, Arthur H., and Barbara Bartz Petchenik. *The Nature of Maps*. Chicago: University of Chicago Press, 1976.

Roosevelt, Franklin Delano. "Fighting Defeatism: February 23, 1942." In *FDR's Fireside Chats*, edited by Russell D. Buhite and David W. Levy, 206–18. Norman: University of Oklahoma Press, 1992.

Rostow, W. W. *Open Skies: Eisenhower's Proposal of July 21, 1955*. Austin: University of Texas Press, 1982.

———. *The Stages of Economic Growth: A Non-Communist Manifesto*. Cambridge: Cambridge University Press, 1960.

Rowe, Aimee Carrillo. "'Whose America?' The Politics of Rhetoric and Space in the Formation of U.S. Nationalism." *Radical History Review* 89 (2004): 115–34.

Royal Geographic Society. "Dr W Bunge." *Area* 19 (1987): 254.

Said, Edward. "Orientalism." In *The Edward Said Reader*, edited by Moustafa Bayoumi and Andrew Rubin, 63–114. New York: Vintage, 2000.

———. *Orientalism*. New York: Pantheon, 1978.

Samuels, Marwyn. "To Rescue Place." *Progress in Human Geography* 16 (1992): 597–604.

Saull, Richard. "Locating the Global South in the Theorisation of the Cold War: Capitalist Development, Social Revolution and Geopolitical Conflict." *Third World Quarterly* 26 (2005): 253–80.

Saunders, Frances Stonor. *Who Paid the Piper? The CIA and the Cultural Cold War*. London: Granta, 1999.

Schiappa, Edward. "The Rhetoric of Nukespeak." *Communication Monographs* 56 (1989): 253–72.

Schulten, Susan. *The Geographical Imagination in America, 1880–1950.* Chicago: University of Chicago Press, 2001.

———. *Mapping the Nation: History and Cartography in Nineteenth-Century America.* Chicago: University of Chicago Press, 2012.

———. "Richard Edes Harrison and the Challenge to American Cartography." *Imago Mundi* 50 (1998): 174–88.

Schwartz, Joan M., and James R. Ryan, eds. *Picturing Place: Photography and the Geographical Imagination.* New York: I. B. Tauris, 2003.

Scott, James C. *Seeing Like a State: How Certain Schemes to Improve the Human Condition Have Failed.* New Haven, Conn.: Yale University Press, 1998.

Scott, Robert L. "Cold War and Rhetoric: Conceptually and Critically." In *Cold War Rhetoric: Strategy, Metaphor, and Ideology,* edited by Martin J. Medhurst, Robert L. Ivie, Philip Wander, and Robert L. Scott, 1–16. New York: Greenwood, 1990.

Sempa, Francis P. *Geopolitics: From the Cold War to the 21st Century.* New Brunswick, N.J.: Transaction Publishers, 2002.

Shapiro, Michael J. *The Politics of Representation.* Madison: University of Wisconsin Press, 1988.

———. *Violent Cartographies: Mapping Cultures of War.* Minneapolis: University of Minnesota Press, 1997.

Shapiro, Michael J., and Hayward R. Alker, eds. *Challenging Boundaries: Global Flows, Territorial Identities.* Minneapolis: University of Minnesota Press, 1996.

Sharp, Joanne P. *Condensing the Cold War: Reader's Digest and American Identity.* Minneapolis: University of Minnesota Press, 2000.

Sidaway, James. "Overwriting Geography: Mackinder's Presences, a Dialogue with David Hooson." *Geopolitics* 14 (2009): 163–70.

Sidorov, Dmitri. "Visualizing the Former Cold War Other: Images of Eastern Europe in World Regional Textbooks in the United States." *Journal of Education, Media, Memory, and Society* 1 (2009): 39–58.

Skop, Jacob. "The Effects of User Requirements on Map Design." *Surveying and Mapping* 18 (1958): 315–18.

Slater, David. "Geopolitical Imaginations across the North-South Divide: Issues of Difference, Development and Power." *Political Geography* 16 (1997): 631–53.

Slater, David, and Peter J. Taylor, eds. *The American Century: Consensus and Coercion in the Projection of American Power.* Oxford: Blackwell, 1999.

Sloan, G. R. *Geopolitics in United States Strategic Policy, 1890–1987.* New York: St. Martin's Press, 1988.

Smith, David M. "New Directions in Human Geography in the USSR." *Area* 15 (1983): 21.

———. "Radical Geography: The Next Revolution?" *Area* 3 (1971): 153–57.

Smith, Jonathan M. "Geographical Rhetoric: Modes and Tropes of Appeal." *Annals of the Association of American Geographers* 86 (1996): 1–20.

Smith, Neil. *American Empire: Roosevelt's Geographer and the Prelude to Globalization.* Berkeley: University of California Press, 2003.

————. "The Lost Geography of the American Century." *Scottish Geographic Journal* 115 (2001): 1–18.

Smith, Paul A. "Aviation Development and Its Mapping Needs." *Surveying and Mapping* 14 (1954): 64–70.

Snyder, John P. *Flattening the Earth: Two Thousand Years of Map Projections.* Chicago: University of Chicago Press, 1993.

————. "Social Consciousness and World Maps." *Christian Century* (February 24, 1988): 190–92.

Soffner, Heinz. "War on the Visual Front." *American Scholar* 11 (1942): 465–76.

Soja, Edward W. *The Political Organization of Space.* Commission on College Geography Resource Paper no. 8. Washington, D.C.: Association of American Geographers, 1971.

————. *Postmodern Geographies: The Reassertion of Space in Critical Social Theory.* London: Verso, 1989.

————. "The Socio-spatial Dialectic (1989)." In *Reading Human Geography*, edited by Trevor J. Barnes and Derek Gregory, 244–56. London: Arnold, 1997.

Solzhenitzyn, Aleksandr. *Gulag Archipelago, 1918–1956: An Experiment in Literary Investigation.* Translated by Thomas P. Whitney. New York: Harper & Row, 1974.

————. *Warning to the West.* New York: Farrar, Straus and Giroux, 1976.

Sparke, Matthew. "A Map that Roared and an Original Atlas: Canada, Cartography, and the Narration of Nation." *Annals of the Association of American Geographers* 88 (1998): 463–95.

————. *In the Space of Theory: Postfoundational Geographies of the Nation State.* Minneapolis: University of Minnesota Press, 2005.

Speier, Hans. "Magic Geography." *Social Research* 8 (1941): 310–30.

Spykman, Nicholas. *America's Strategy in World Politics: The United States and the Balance of Power.* New York: Harcourt, Brace and Company, 1942.

————. "Frontiers, Security, and International Organization." *Geographical Review* 32 (1942): 436–47.

Sriskandarajah, Dhananjayan. "Long Underwear on a Line? The Peters Projection and Thirty Years of Carto-Controversy." *Geography* 88 (2003): 236–44.

Stalker, Peter. "Map Wars." *New Internationalist*, March 1989. http://www.newint .org/features/1989/03/05/wars/.

Statler, Kathryn C., and Andrew L. Johns, eds. *The Eisenhower Administration, the Third World, and the Globalization of the Cold War.* Lanham, Md.: Rowman & Littlefield, 2006.

Stoler, Ann Laura. *Haunted By Empire: Geographies of Intimacy in North American History.* Durham, N.C.: Duke University Press, 2006.

Stoler, Mark. *Allies and Adversaries: The Joint Chiefs of Staff, the Grand Alliance, and U.S. Strategy in World War II.* Chapel Hill: University of North Carolina Press, 2000.

Stone, Kirk H. "World Air Photo Coverage." *Professional Geographer* 11 (1959): 2–7.

Stuckey, Mary. "Competing Foreign Policy Visions: Rhetorical Hybrids after the Cold War." *Western Journal of Communication* 59 (1995): 214–27.

Suri, Jeremi. "The Cold War, Decolonization, and Global Social Awakenings: Historical Intersections." *Cold War History* 6 (2006): 353–63.

Swanberg, W. A. *Luce and His Empire.* New York: Scribner, 1972.

Swift, John. *Palgrave Concise Historical Atlas of the Cold War.* New York: Palgrave
Macmillan, 2003.

Tan, Seng, and Amitav Acharya, eds. *Bandung Revisited: The Legacy of the 1955
Asian-African Conference for International Order.* Singapore: NUS Press, 2008.

Taylor, Bryan C. "The Bodies of August: Photographic Realism and Controversy
at the National Air and Space Museum." *Rhetoric & Public Affairs* 1 (1998):
331–61.

———. "'A Hedge against the Future': The Post-Cold War Rhetoric of Nuclear Weapons Modernization." *Quarterly Journal of Speech* 96 (2010): 1–24.

———. "Nuclear Pictures and Metapictures." *American Literary History* 9 (1997): 567–97.

———. "Nuclear Weapons and Communication Studies: A Review Essay." *Western
Journal of Communication* 62 (1998): 300–15.

———. "'Our Bruised Arms Hung Up as Monuments': Nuclear Iconography in Post-
Cold War Culture." *Critical Studies in Media Communication* 20 (2003): 1–34.

Taylor, Bryan C., and Stephen Hartnett. "'National Security, and All That It
Implies . . .': Communication and (Post-) Cold War Culture." *Quarterly Journal
of Speech* 86 (2000): 465–87.

Thomas, Alan, and Ben Crow. *Third World Atlas.* 2nd ed. Washington, D.C.: Taylor &
Francis, 1994.

Thompson, Dorothy, ed. *Over Our Dead Bodies: Women against the Bomb.* London:
Virago, 1983.

Thompson, E. P. *The Heavy Dancers.* New York: Pantheon, 1985.

Tietge, David J. *Flash Effect: Science and the Rhetorical Origins of Cold War America.*
Athens: Ohio University Press, 2002.

Tobler, Waldo R. "Analytical Cartography." *American Cartographer* 3 (1976): 21–31.

———. "Automation and Cartography." *Geographical Review* 49 (1959): 526–34.

Tomlinson, B. R. "What Was the Third World?" *Journal of Contemporary History* 38
(2003): 307–21.

Tosevic, Dimitri J. *The World Crisis in Maps.* New York: Wilfred Funk, 1954.

Triumph of the Will, special ed. DVD. Directed by Leni Riefenstahl. 1934; Eureka,
Calif.: Synapse Films, 2001.

Troy, Thomas M., Jr. Review of *The Cultural Cold War: The CIA and the World of
Arts and Letters*, by Frances Stonor Saunders. *Studies in Intelligence* 46 (2002).
https://www.cia.gov/library/center-for-the-study-of-intelligence/csi-publications/
csi-studies/studies/vol46no1/article08.html.

Tuan, Yi-Fu. "Humanistic Geography." *Annals of the Association of American
Geographers* 66 (1976): 266–76.

———. *Space and Place: The Perspective of Experience.* Minneapolis: University of
Minnesota Press, 1977.

Turnock, David. "American Geographers and the Geography of East Central Europe."
GeoJournal 59 (2004): 77–89.

Tyner, Judith A. "Persuasive Cartography." *Journal of Geography* 81 (1982): 141–44.

United Nations Department of Social Affairs. *Modern Cartography: Base Maps for World Needs.* Lake Success, N.Y.: United Nations, 1949.

——. *World Cartography.* Vols. 1–5. New York: United Nations, 1951–55.

United Nations Department of Public Information. *United Nations Yearbook Collection, 1946–2002.* New York: United Nations, 2002. CD-ROM.

United Nations Regional Cartographic Conference for Asia and the Far East. *Official Report on United Nations Regional Cartographic Conference for Asia and the Far East, Mussoorie, India, February 15–28, 1955.* New York: United Nations, 1955.

U.S.S.R. Academy of Sciences, National Committee of Soviet Geographers. *Soviet Geographical Studies.* Moscow: "Social Sciences Today" Editorial Board, 1976.

U.S.S.R. Ministry of Defense. *Disarmament: Who's Against?* Moscow: Military Publishing House, 1983.

——. *Whence the Threat to Peace.* Moscow: Military Publishing House, 1982.

——. *Whence the Threat to Peace.* New ed. Moscow: Military Publishing House, 1984.

Van der Woude, Joanne. "Why Maps Matter: New Geographies of American Culture." *American Quarterly* 60 (2008): 1073–87.

Vasiliev, Irina Re. "Mapping Time." *Cartographica* 34 (1997): 1–50.

Verdery, Katherine. "Whither 'Nation' and 'Nationalism'?" In *Mapping the Nation*, edited by Gopal Balakrishnan, 226–34. London: Verso, 1996.

Virilio, Paul. *Speed and Politics.* Translated by Marc Polizzotti. 1977; Los Angeles: Semiotext(e), 2006.

——. *War and Cinema: The Logistics of Perception.* Translated by Patrick Camiller. London: Verso, 1984.

Virilio, Paul, and Sylvere Lotringer. *Pure War: Twenty Five Years Later.* Translated by Mark Polizzotti. 1983; Los Angeles: Semiotext(e), 2008.

Vujakovic, Peter. "Arno Peters' Cult of the 'New Cartography': From Concept to World Atlas." *Bulletin for the Society of University Cartographers* 22 (1988): 1–6.

——. "Arno Peters: The Man and His Map." *Cartographic Journal* 40 (2003): 51–52.

——. "Damn or Be Damned: Arno Peters and the Struggle for the New Cartography." *Cartographic Journal* 40 (2003): 61–67.

——. "Editorial: 'Between a Rock and a Hard Place'—Mapping Places in a Volatile World." *Cartographic Journal* 40 (2003): 217–18.

——. "The Extent of Adoption of the Peters Projection by 'Third World' Organizations in the UK." *Bulletin of the Society of University Cartographers* 21 (1987): 11–16.

——. "Mapping the War Zone: Cartography, Geopolitics and Security Discourse in the UK Press." *Journalism Studies* 3 (2002): 187–202.

——. "'A New Map Is Unrolling before Us': Cartography in News Media Representations of Post-Cold War Europe." *Cartographic Journal* 36 (1999): 43–57.

——. "Whatever Happened to the 'New Cartography': The World Map and Development Mis-education." *Journal of Geography in Higher Education* 26 (2002): 369–80.

Walker, Martin. "Variable Geography: America's Mental Maps of a Greater Europe." *International Affairs* 76 (2000): 459–74.

Wallerstein, Immanuel. "The Unintended Consequences of Cold War Area Studies." In *The Cold War & The University: Toward an Intellectual History of the Postwar Years*, edited by Noam Chomsky, 195–31. New York: W. W. Norton, 1997.

Wander, Philip. "The Rhetoric of American Foreign Policy." *Quarterly Journal of Speech* 70 (1984): 339–52. Reprinted, with revisions, in *Cold War Rhetoric: Strategy, Metaphor, and Ideology*, edited by Martin J. Medhurst, Robert L. Ivie, Philip Wander, and Robert L. Scott, 153–83. New York: Greenwood, 1990.

Warner, Deborah Jean. "From Tallahassee to Timbuktu: Cold War Efforts to Measure Intercontinental Distances." *Historical Studies in the Physical and Biological Sciences* 30 (2000): 393–415.

———. "Political Geodesy: The Army, the Air Force, and the World Geodetic System of 1960." *Annals of Science* 59 (2002): 363–89.

Warner, Michael. "Origins of the Congress for Cultural Freedom, 1949–50." *Studies in Intelligence* 38 (1995). https://www.cia.gov/library/center-for-the-study-of-intelligence/csi-publications/csi-studies/studies/95unclass/Warner.html.

Weart, Spencer R. *Nuclear Fear: A History of Images*. Cambridge, Mass.: Harvard University Press, 1988.

Weigert, Hans W. "Maps Are Weapons." *Survey Graphic* 30 (1941): 528–30.

Weigert, Hans W., and Vilhjalmur Stefansson, eds. *Compass of the World—A Symposium on Political Geography*. New York: Macmillan, 1944.

Weigert, Hans W., Vilhjalmur Stefansson, and Richard Edes Harrison, eds. *New Compass of the World—A Symposium on Political Geography*. New York: Macmillan, 1949.

Weinberger, Caspar W. *Fighting for Peace: Seven Critical Years in the Pentagon*. New York: Warner Books, 1990.

———. *In the Arena: A Memoir of the 20th Century*. Washington, D.C.: Regnery, 2001.

Westad, Odd Arne. *The Global Cold War: Third World Interventions and the Making of Our Times*. Cambridge: Cambridge University Press, 2006.

White, Donald A. "History and American Internationalism: The Formulation from the Past after World War II." *Pacific Historical Review* 58 (1989): 145–72.

White, Gilbert F. "The Changing Dimensions of the World Community." *Journal of Geography* 59 (1960): 165–70.

———. "Geographers in a Perilously Changing World." *Annals of the Association of American Geographers* 75 (1985): 10–16.

White, Richard. "The Geography of American Empire." *Raritan* 23 (2004): 1–19.

Whitelegg, John. "William Bunge: The Nuclear War Atlas Video." *Area* 17 (1985): 266.

Whittlesey, Derwent. "The Horizon of Geography." *Annals of the Association of American Geographers* 35 (1945): 1–36.

Why We Fight. DVD. Directed by Frank Capra. 1944; Washington, D.C.: National Archives of the United States, 2013.

Wilford, John Noble. *The Mapmakers: The Story of the Great Pioneers in Cartography from Antiquity to the Space Age*. New York: Vintage, 1982.

Willkie, Wendell. *One World*. New York: Simon and Schuster, 1943.

Wilkinson, H. R. *Maps and Politics: A Review of Ethnographic Cartography of Macedonia*. Liverpool: University Press of Liverpool, 1951.

William F. Eisner Museum of Advertising & Design. "Boris Artzybasheff." Grassi Collection. www.theeisner.com (website under construction).

Williams, Frank E. "Lawrence Martin, 1880–1955." *Annals of the Association of American Geographers* 46 (1956): 357–64.

Williams, Gavin. "The Brandt Report: A Critical Introduction." *Review of African Political Economy* 19 (1980): 77–86.

Wilson, Leonard S. "Geographic Training for the Postwar World: A Proposal." *Geographical Review* 38 (1948): 575–89.

———. "Lessons from the Experience of the Map Information Section, OSS." *Geographical Review* 39 (1949): 298–310.

Winichakul, Thongchai. *Siam Mapped: A History of the Geo-Body of a Nation.* Honolulu: University of Hawai'i Press, 1994.

Wittfogel, Karl A. "Geopolitics, Geographical Materialism and Marxism." *Antipode* 17 (1985): 21–72.

Wolf-Phillips, Leslie. "Why Third World?" *Third World Quarterly* 1 (1979): 105–15.

Wood, Denis. *The Power of Maps.* New York: Guilford, 1992.

Wood, Denis, and John Fels. "Designs on Signs/Myth and Meaning in Maps." *Cartographica* 23 (1986): 54–103.

———. "The Natures of Maps: Cartographic Constructions of the Natural World." *Cartographica* 43 (2008): 189–202.

———. *The Natures of Maps: Cartographic Constructions of the Natural World.* Chicago: University of Chicago Press, 2008.

Wood, M. "Visual Perception and Map Design." *Cartographic Journal* 5 (1968): 54–64.

Woods, Matthew. "Inventing Proliferation: The Creation and Preservation of the Inevitable Spread of Nuclear Weapons." *Review of International Affairs* 3 (2004): 416–42.

Woodward, David. "The Study of the History of Cartography: A Suggested Framework." *American Cartographer* 1 (1974): 101–15.

Woodward, David, with J. Brian Harley. *The History of Cartography.* 3 vols. Chicago: University of Chicago Press, 1987–2007.

World Bank. *World Bank Atlas, 1975.* Washington, D.C.: World Bank, 1975.

Woytinsky, Wladimir S., and Emma S. Woytinsky. *World Population and Production: Trends and Outlook.* New York: Twentieth Century Fund, 1953.

Wray, Thomas. "Contrary View: The Peters Map Is a Myth." *Canadian Geographic* 97 (1978): 28–29.

Wright, John K. *Geography in the Making: The American Geographical Society, 1851–1951.* New York: American Geographical Society, 1952.

———. "Map Makers Are Human: Comments on the Subjective in Maps." *Geographical Review* 32 (1942): 527–44.

———. "Terrae Incognitae: The Place of the Imagination in Geography." *Annals of the Association of American Geographers* 37 (1947): 1–15.

———. "The World in Maps: The American Geographical Society's Exhibition." *Geographical Review* 30 (1940): 1–18.

Wright, Richard. *The Color Curtain: A Report on the Bandung Conference.* New York: World Publishing, 1956.

Young, William R. "Gulag—Slavery, Inc.: The Use of an Illustrated Map in Printed Propaganda." In *Psychological Warfare Casebook*, edited by William E. Daugherty, 597–601. Baltimore: Johns Hopkins University Press, 1958.

Zeigler, Donald J. "Post-Communist Eastern Europe and the Cartography of Independence." *Political Geography* 21 (2002): 671–86.

Zeigler, Donald J., James H. Johnson Jr., and Stanley D. Brunn. *Technological Hazards*. Washington, D.C.: American Association of Geographers, 1983.

Zelinsky, Wilbur. "In Memoriam: Richard Edes Harrison, 1901–1994." *Annals of the Association of American Geographers* 85 (1995): 187–91.

Zelizer, Barbie. *Remembering to Forget: Holocaust Memory through the Camera's Eye*. Chicago: University of Chicago Press, 1998.

Žižek, Slavoj. *Welcome to the Desert of the Real!* New York: Verso, 2002.

Zoppo, Ciro E., and Charles Zorgbibe, eds. *On Geopolitics: Classical and Nuclear*. Dordrecht: Martinus Nijhoff Publishers, 1985.

Index

Bowman, Isaiah, 5, 36, 65, 73
Brandt, Willy, 167
Bratton, Benjamin, 191
Braunsdorf, G. W., 102
Briesemeister equal-area projection, 153, 157
Brown, Desloge, 77
Brummett, Barry, 212
Bunge, William, 13, 14, 58, 220, 226; and *Nuclear War Atlas*, 23, 176, 200–213; and rise of radical geography, 192–200, 221
Bush, George H. W., 2, 3, 23, 183, 215

Cambodia, 165, 166
Campaign for Nuclear Disarmament (CND), 199
Campbell, David, 158
Canada, 49, 97, 100, 196, 199, 200, 206
Can America Be Bombed?, 25
Capital, 34, 58; role in Cold War, 10, 64, 141, 146, 168; as depicted in maps, 17, 54, 85, 106, 110, 155
Cardwell, Curt, 145
Carruthers, Susan, 120, 125
Carter, Jimmy, 183
Cartogram, 85
"Cartohypnosis," 46, 72, 85, 92, 93, 227
Central America, 145, 201
Central Intelligence Agency (CIA), 2, 3, 62, 89, 109, 137, 164, 183, 204; and "'Gulag'—Slavery, Inc.," 120, 124, 134, 220
Central Place Theory, 197, 198
Chambers, Whittaker, 121
Chapin, Robert M., 104, 105, 106
Chaturvedi, Sanjay, 133
Chernus, Ira, 175
Chicago Tribune, 123
Chile, 123, 131
China, 96, 132, 149, 203
Cholera, 152, 153
Christaller, Walter, 197, 198
Christian Science Monitor, 129
Churchill, Winston, 44

Circulation of maps: and rhetorical implications, 14–16, 116, 129, 218, 221–22, 224; and function in Cold War, 78, 94, 100, 116, 219, 221–22; and "'Gulag'—Slavery, Inc.," 120, 123, 129, 130
Citizen cartographers, 225, 226
Citizenship and maps, 33, 96, 99, 130, 133
Civic Education Inc., 77
Civilization, cartographic depiction of, 147, 148, 154, 155, 162
Civil War, U.S., 99, 149
"Clearing & Colder," 106
"Closest Neighbours Ever," 200
Cloud, John, 7, 19, 58, 62, 70, 165, 179
Coastal Survey, U.S., 163
Collier's, 82
Colonialism, 141, 154, 166, 167
Color and maps, 48, 99, 104, 105, 152–53, 157, 165, 206, 208
Columbia University, 73, 82, 159
Committee on Present Danger (CPD), 183
Communication and cartographic advancements, 34, 45, 47, 53, 64, 85, 93
Communism, 10, 80, 121, 122; and maps, 17, 99, 105, 106, 111, 130, 131, 206, 221, 227; and Third World development, 143, 146, 154
"The Communist Fastness," 56, 57 (ill.)
"Concept of Operations of US Strategic Offensive Forces on the Basis of Major Military Exercises," 188
Conference on Psychological Strategy in the Cold War, 120
Congress, 25, 30, 87, 117, 132; and global health and development, 17, 146, 156, 222; and congressional reports and maps, 22, 109–11, 157, 217, 220
Containment: as depicted on maps, 4, 110, 111, 116, 129, 219, 224; Cold War ideology of, 10, 28, 64, 157, 217; policy debates around, 116, 120, 140, 175, 200
Cooper, John Cobb, 31

CORONA, 19, 70, 165
Cosgrove, Denis, 44, 81, 218
Costigliola, Frank, 111
"Cost per Soldier," 110
Council on Foreign Relations, 148, 154
Cuban Missile Crisis, 180, 181
Cull, Nicholas, 130
Curry, Michael, 198, 199, 213
Cutter, Susan, 210
Czechoslovakia, 39, 215

Dahl, Roald, 1, 2, 3, 23, 214, 227
Dalby, Simon, 146, 183, 223
Dallin, David, 121, 122
Data: global scope of in Cold War, 5, 10, 70, 137, 142, 147–48, 149, 157, 158, 159, 167–68; geographic, 7, 17, 85, 92, 116, 133, 155, 184; maps as managers of, 14, 61–62, 65, 138, 140, 152–53, 179, 189–90; and new technologies, 19, 69, 74, 162–63, 180–82; and quantitative revolution, 45, 194–95, 198; critiques of use of, 165, 166, 212
Debate at Oxford, 170, 171, 172, 175, 212, 213
Decolonization, 16, 17, 20, 137, 138; increasing role for maps and, 10, 136, 140, 161; and U.S. development projects, 12, 54, 141, 143, 163, 164; challenges to Cold War superpowers and, 142, 166, 167, 168
Defense, 6, 17, 70; and applications of new mapping technologies, 26, 68, 155–56; on Cold War maps, 110, 166. See also Department of Defense; Militarization
Defense Planning Group, 215, 216, 223
Demko, George, 94
Democratization, 10, 22, 144, 212
Department of Defense, 12, 164, 194; cartographic challenges to, 13, 198, 200, 212; and Weinberger propaganda, 19, 22, 170, 171, 172–73, 177, 183–85, 187, 190–91; and militarization of Cold War, 65, 169,

178, 180, 181, 186, 219, 220; and post–Cold War concerns, 215, 216, 223
Department of State, 8, 31, 32, 46, 109, 170, 225; and use of cartography in Cold War foreign policy, 7, 60, 62, 63, 66, 67, 94, 220, 222; and collaborations with other Cold War institutions, 7, 68, 70, 165; and approach to Third World development, 13, 136–37, 139, 144, 145; and sponsorship of " 'Gulag'— Slavery, Inc.," 16, 120, 121, 124, 131, 132, 133; and Office of Geographer, 21, 71–77, 79, 85, 87, 91, 92; use of artists in, 56, 81, 82, 83, 84
Der Derian, James, 176, 186, 190
De Seversky, Alexander, 30, 32, 35
Détente, 173, 184
Deterrence, 168, 173, 178, 183, 190
Development, 4, 20, 22, 135, 177, 223, 225; and maps of global health, 17, 147, 148, 152, 154, 156; as Cold War ideology, 54, 140–43, 154, 164; as plank in U.S. foreign policy, 76, 86, 88, 144–46; and cartographic investment in developing countries, 158–63, 222; critiques of, 166, 167
Development of the Soviet Ballistic Missile Threat (1960), 182
DEW Line (Distant Early Warning System), 178
Dickinson, Greg, 9
Die Nation, 131
Digitization, 19, 221, 225–26; and effect on cartography, 7, 175, 176, 178–79, 214, 219; and quantitative revolution, 13, 194–95; and nuclear deterrence, 22, 168, 176, 178–79, 180–84, 190–91; and decolonization, 138–39, 143, 162; critiques of, 198, 208, 212
Diplomacy. See Foreign policy
Dirksen, Everett, 122
Disarmament, 23, 170–72, 176, 192–93, 196–204, 212–13

Hartshorne, Richard, 65
Haushofer, Karl, 36, 46, 67, 92
Havel, Vaclav, 215–17
Health, mapping of, 7, 16, 22, 144–48,
    149, 152, 156, 158. See also *Atlas of
    Disease*
Heffernan, Michael, 6, 86
Hemispheres, 5, 49, 87, 201; shifts in
    American concept of, 2, 27, 31–32,
    103; S. W. Boggs on, 71, 75–76, 78–80
Henrikson, Alan K., 2, 6, 27, 66
Hewitt, Kenneth, 199
Heyman, Rich, 196
Heynen, Nik, 192
Hippocrates, 148–49
Hiroshima, bombing of, 177, 201
Hiss, Alger, 121
Hitler, Adolf, 36, 44, 67, 122
Hogan, J. Michael, 207
Holloway, Rachel, 190
Holocaust, 16, 122, 128
Hope, Diane, 4, 58
Horvath, Ronald, 200
Hough, Floyd, 61, 62, 65, 68, 95
House Foreign Affairs Committee, 77
House Un-American Activities
    Committee (HUAC), 22, 111
"How Communists Menace Vital
    Materials," 111, 114 (ill.)
"How Could Soviet Attack Come?" 107
"How Strategic Material Circulates," 106,
    107 (ill.)
Huggan, Graham, 143
Hughes, Thomas L., 136
Hull, Cordell, 79
"Human Head on Geographical Globe,"
    83, 84 (ill.)
"Human Head on Seven Well-Known
    Map Projections," 83, 84 (ill.)
Humanism and cartography, 81, 83, 195,
    197, 205, 209
Human rights, 7, 132, 168, 225, 226
Humor in maps, 126, 208, 209, 210
Humphrey, Hubert, 156, 157, 221
Hutcheon, Linda, 209

Hydrogen bomb, 166, 196, 203
Hyperinternationalism, 176, 188, 213, 219

Icons, 110–11, 116, 145, 167, 185, 188;
    on journalistic maps, 102–4, 108; in
    "'Gulag'—Slavery, Inc.," 117, 126; in
    Nuclear War Atlas, 201–2, 205–7, 209
Idealism, 11, 198, 211; tensions with
    realism, 28, 64, 66, 91, 93, 164; and
    U.S. global power, 28, 68, 94, 97,
    160; and S. W. Boggs, 68, 84–85, 86,
    88–89, 91, 93, 94
Ideology, 20, 72, 215; as shaped by maps,
    3, 4, 15, 23, 38, 120, 134, 140, 213, 217,
    226; and American history, 5–6, 65,
    224; tensions with strategy, 11–14, 29,
    47, 117, 166, 221–22; and U.S. portrayal
    of Soviet Union, 21, 94, 97, 99, 105,
    111, 123, 126, 128, 130; and three
    worlds concept, 22, 54, 139, 140–41,
    147, 166; and shift to internationalism,
    27–28, 35, 54, 56, 70, 101, 220; and
    science, 86, 167, 178, 208–9, 211
Image, 63, 94, 218; role in maps,
    1–2, 6, 19, 33, 168, 209; and
    internationalism, 8, 27, 35, 48, 59,
    168, 219; and circulation, 15, 19, 120,
    140; of commitment, 18, 21, 100–101,
    109, 116–17, 124, 140
Immutable mobiles, maps as, 14, 18, 137,
    217–18
Imperialism, 5, 12, 67, 80, 86, 92, 154,
    171, 188
Independent Commission on
    International Development Issues, 167
India, 12, 157, 161
Intelligence, 61, 225; and Cold War
    maps, 3, 92, 124; shifts in role of, 7,
    62, 71, 73, 74–75, 179; and geographic
    data, 21, 70, 86, 87–88, 91, 163
Inter-American Geodetic Survey, 158, 159
Interface, maps as, 214, 225; and Cold
    War digitization, 7, 162, 169, 179,
    181–82, 212; and policy makers, 138,
    140, 148, 158, 162, 176

International Geophysical Year, 1957–58, 159
Internationalism, 169, 222; as U.S. ideology, 2, 4, 27, 29, 34, 38, 93; and role of images, 8, 48, 55, 101, 189, 213, 218–20; and government policy, 27, 59–60, 63, 66–67, 68, 85, 90, 109, 160; in popular cartography, 29, 47–48, 52–53, 54, 85; debates over, 82, 87–88, 90
International Map of the World (IMW), 86, 87, 88, 90, 222
Interventionism, 140, 146, 148, 156, 164, 166
Iran, 105, 125, 157
Iraq, 105, 223
Iron curtain, 16, 58, 90, 99, 104, 106, 122, 130, 159
Irony in maps, 208, 209
Isolationism, 26, 35, 49, 53, 87
Italy, 35, 39, 48

Japan, 42, 48, 214
Johnson, Douglas, 73
Johnson, Lyndon Baines, 86, 199
Joint Chiefs of Staff, 42
Journalistic cartography, 8, 16, 18, 45, 121; and air-age globalism, 20–21, 26, 27, 29, 36; and popular magazines, 22, 39, 100–109, 120; and portrayal of Cold War, 22, 58, 100–109, 120, 128–29, 188; and government cartography, 74, 86, 93, 110, 116, 134–35; and newspapers, 100–104
Journal of Geography, 79

Karo, H. Arnold, 163
Kendall, Kathleen E., 8
Kennan, George, 18, 28, 59, 66, 108, 111, 116, 200
Kennedy, John F., 70, 86, 180
Kent State University shooting, 165–66
Khrushchev, Nikita, 58, 70
Kimble, George, 67, 68
Kirkpatrick, Jeane, 183

Kitchin, Rob, 18
Knowledge production, 89, 226; and cartographic expertise, 68–70, 92, 97, 160–61, 164, 166; against Soviet Union, 116, 120, 125, 127, 130; and development, 136, 137, 142, 146, 160–61, 164; and global health, 144, 152, 156–58
Korea, 17, 96, 99, 106, 110, 155, 196
"Korea's Waistland," 106
Kotschnig, Walter, 90, 91
Kremlin, 59, 171, 178
Krivitsky, Walter, 121

Labor, 16, 220; and international Cold War, 122–25, 129–30; and domestic Cold War, 124, 129–30, 133
Lacoste, Yves, 166
Lapham, Lewis, 216, 217
Latin America, 32, 131, 158, 159, 162
Latour, Bruno, 14, 137, 218
Lefebvre, Henri, 63
Lenin, V. I., 121
Levine, Isaac Don, 121, 122, 123, 125, 127, 221
Lewis, Martin W., 144
Liberalism, 27, 146. *See also* Internationalism; Modernism
Liberation, 10, 28, 86, 141
Library of Congress, 26, 73, 109, 110
Lieber, Albert, 64, 159
Life, 22, 37, 39, 56, 61–62, 104, 106–8, 120, 135, 159
Light, Richard, 149
"Lineup for Two Worlds," 103, 103 (ill.)
Lippmann, Walter, 42, 81
Lodge, Henry Cabot, 115, 116, 179, 222
"Long Telegram," 28, 111
Look at the World: The Fortune Atlas for World Strategy, 29, 40, 43, 45, 46, 47, 82
Loper, Herbert, 68
Lovestone, Jay, 124
Luce, Clare Boothe, 30
Luce, Henry, 34, 35, 45, 81, 104

MacDonald, Fraser, 192
Machine space, 200
Mackinder, Halford, 40, 42, 92, 93, 188, 224
MacLeish, Archibald, 35
Magazines, maps in, 29, 39, 104–9, 120. *See also* Harrison, Richard Edes
Malin, James C., 34
Malta, 2–3, 23
Manichaeism, 204
Manifest destiny, 5, 35, 52, 56, 57, 85, 224
"The Map Doctor," 149
Map evaluation studies at Department of State, 92
Maps: as representations, 1, 14, 18, 63, 66, 72; silences in, 3; as worldviews, 3, 13; and materiality, 15, 17, 23–24, 217; as discourse, 29, 32, 37, 55; as weapons, 33, 62, 94; as mental maps, 66; and pictorial style, 103–5; as logos, 126
Map Series 1301, Army Map Service, 88
Marginalia in cartography, 127, 128
Marshall, George, 56, 71, 110, 144, 221
Marshall Plan, 110, 144
Martin, Lawrence, 73
Massey, Doreen, 189
"Massive Retaliatory Power," 108
May, Jacques, 149, 152, 153, 154, 155, 156, 157, 222
McCarthyism, 124
McCormack, Alfred, 91
McHaffie, Patrick, 180
McNamara, Robert, 165
McNulty, William, 224
Medhurst, Martin, 11
Medical geography, 140–41, 147, 148–56, 157–58
Mediterranean, 32, 44, 56
Meinig, D. W. (Donald W.), 142, 166
Mercator projection, 71, 75, 83, 102, 110, 157, 188; challenges to during air age, 20, 32, 39, 46, 77–78, 93

Metaphors on maps, 99, 104, 106, 111, 116
Middle East, 44, 145
Mignolo, Walter, 168
Militarization, 20, 132, 224; and Cold War policy, 7, 13, 28, 70, 108, 128–29; and portrayal on maps, 94, 101, 104–6, 108, 110–11, 120, 128–29, 226; critiques of, 163–66, 212
Military cartography: collaborations with academic and government cartography, 63, 97, 100, 159, 193; and global security in Cold War, 148, 149, 154–55, 159, 165, 166; and defense propaganda, 177–82, 183–92
Military-government-academic complex, 6, 72, 178, 181, 183, 193, 204
Miller cylindrical projection, 71, 77, 78, 83, 89, 90, 137
Minca, Claudio, 197
Minneapolis Star Tribune, 129
Mirowski, Philip, 178
Missiles. *See* Nuclear weapons
Mitchell, Gordon, 212
Mitchell, Peta, 226
Mobility and maps, 33, 34, 40
Models and nuclear cartography, 194, 195, 197, 198, 199
Modernism, 8, 12, 65, 66, 146, 197, 211
Modernization, 9, 142, 219, 225; and Cold War policy, 10–11, 144, 146, 156; and controversies, 11, 164, 167; and cartography as medium for, 17, 22, 135, 140, 147, 162
Molotov, Vyacheslav, 104
Monmonier, Mark, 38, 40, 102
Monroe Doctrine, 32, 79
Morality, 28; and activist mapping, 13, 192, 197–98, 200–201, 211; geographic debates over, 59, 65, 76, 191, 197–98, 212–13
"Moscington," 204
Moscow, 40, 80, 99, 111, 185, 204
Mullen, Roy, 165
Mutual Security Act, 17, 22, 109, 110, 156